Praise for *Three Days at the Brink*

"In his monumental new book about one of history's most epic events, Bret Baier has outdone himself yet again. I could not put this extraordinary book down. *Three Days at the Brink* is a masterpiece: elegantly written, brilliantly conceived, and impeccably researched. This book not only sparkles but is destined to be a classic!"   —Jay Winik, *New York Times* bestselling author of *1944* and *April 1865*

"Bret Baier's *Three Days at the Brink* is a riveting reevaluation of how the Big Three leaders—FDR, Churchill, and Stalin—collaborated to win World War II for the Allies and then created a Cold War superpower global order. With characteristic intellectual verve and brilliant analysis, Baier allows readers to freshly understand how the Tehran Conference shaped world history. Essential reading by a first-rate storyteller!"
    —Douglas Brinkley, professor of history at Rice University and author of *American Moonshot* and *Rightful Heritage: Franklin D. Roosevelt and the Land of America*

"In this brisk, readable, and compelling book, Bret Baier takes us into a crucial period of World War II and calls our attention to an important hinge of world history."
    —Michael Beschloss, *New York Times* bestselling author of *Presidents of War*

"In the past three years, Bret Baier, perhaps America's top newscaster, has become one of America's best historians as well. In *Three Days at the Brink*, Baier completes a trilogy of books on the beginning, middle, and end of the Cold War. For a third time, Bret Baier has identified and examined a pivotal event—lasting roughly three days—that enables him to combine political and diplomatic analysis with political biography. *Three Days* is a fascinating narrative that doubles as a political portrait of FDR and a history of the momentous

P9-DME-000

Tehran conference at which FDR reached agreement with Churchill and Stalin on grand strategy against Germany. For it is FDR the visionary and leader who guides America through depression and victory in World War II. And the decisions finalized in FDR's culminating meetings with Churchill and Stalin at Tehran, while assuring the defeat of Nazi Germany, could not resolve Soviet-Allied tensions, inexorably leading the three powers toward Cold War. *Three Days at the Brink*, in sum, examines victory over Germany in light of the ensuing Cold War, as well as the human element and the complexities inherent in the conduct of international affairs in the world we inhabit. *Three Days at the Brink*—along with Baier's books on Eisenhower and Reagan—will be widely read and discussed, and prove to be must-reading for everyone interested in political biography, history, World War II, postwar history, and public affairs today."

—David Eisenhower, director, the University of Pennsylvania's Institute for Public Service, and author of *Eisenhower: At War*, a finalist for the Pulitzer Prize in History

"Bret Baier's *Three Days at the Brink* gives us an exciting, moment-by-moment account of the Tehran Conference and its aftermath. Much of this well-researched and highly readable book is devoted to FDR and his leadership role in the three-day historic meeting, where he persuaded Stalin and a reluctant Churchill to agree to the daring strategy he advocated—i.e., the cross-Channel invasion of Europe that ultimately defeated Hitler and won World War II."

—Selwa "Lucky" Roosevelt, former Chief of Protocol for the Reagan Administration

"*Three Days at the Brink* is a compelling account of FDR's political life and career. It is especially fascinating and intriguing when discussing the intimate details surrounding the final days of negotiations among FDR, Churchill, and Stalin (and their surrogates) on the organization and future of

Europe after World War II. This book, along with Bret Baier's two prior works, distinguishes him as not only a renowned journalist but a superb storyteller and historian. Americans can learn much from Bret Baier and his latest gem."

—Mark R. Levin, #1 *New York Times*
bestselling author of *Unfreedom of the Press*

"Recount[s] the larger story of WWII and the three world leaders (FDR, Churchill, Stalin) who met in Tehran to determine the war's endgame. It's a fascinating story, dramatically written. . . . Baier re-creates [the Tehran Conference] vividly. He is especially strong in detailing what he calls FDR's delicate gamble at Tehran, seeming to favor Stalin over the sensitive Churchill so as to serve the larger aim of defeating Hitler." —*Booklist*

"Highly readable. . . . Dramatic. . . . Compelling."
—*Publishers Weekly*

"Important. . . . [Baier has] the writer's gift of narrative, and the reporter's attention to factual detail. . . . A well-told, highly readable, and accurate account of the involvement of our nation in one of those crucial moments that determine the course of world history." —*Washington Times*

"A fascinating look at diplomacy at its most urgent and its most unusual at a time when the fate of the free world was at stake."
—*Toronto Times*

"Baier weaves an intriguing tale focused mostly on Roosevelt but also featuring compelling profiles of Churchill and Stalin."
—*Valdosta Daily Times*

ALSO BY BRET BAIER

Special Heart

Three Days in January

Three Days in Moscow

THREE
DAYS AT
THE BRINK

FDR'S DARING GAMBLE
TO WIN WORLD WAR II

BRET BAIER

WITH CATHERINE WHITNEY

wm

WILLIAM MORROW
An Imprint of HarperCollinsPublishers

*To the veterans of World War II and D-Day who
died on the beaches of Normandy and to those
who are still living today. Thank you for your
service, your sacrifice, and for saving the world.*

HarperCollins books may be purchased for educational, business,
or sales promotional use. For information, please email the Special
Markets Department at SPsales@harpercollins.com.

A hardcover edition of this book was published in 2019 by William
Morrow, an imprint of HarperCollins Publishers.

FIRST WILLIAM MORROW PAPERBACK EDITION PUBLISHED 2020.

Library of Congress Cataloging-in-Publication Data has been applied for.

ISBN 978-0-06-290569-7

20 21 22 23 24 LSC 10 9 8 7 6 5 4 3 2 1

CONTENTS

INTRODUCTION

FINDING FDR

June 6, 2019

Dressed in a navy-blue suit and electric-blue tie, President Donald J. Trump spoke slowly, opening a historic speech touching on service, sacrifice, and how the US military alongside Allied forces saved the world. For all the bitter partisan fighting back in the US hovering over almost every aspect of the Trump presidency, this speech seemed to wholly transcend it. Marking the seventy-fifth anniversary of the D-Day invasion at the American cemetery in Colleville-sur-Mer, Normandy, President Trump directly addressed the more than 170 surviving veterans of the June 6, 1944, invasion who were in the crowd.

"To more than one hundred and seventy veterans of the Second World War who join us today, you are among the very greatest Americans who will ever live," the president said. "You are the pride of our nation. You are the glory of our republic. And we thank you from the bottom of our hearts." As the president turned around to look at the veterans behind him, a long-sustained applause led to a standing ovation and a few tears in the eyes of those veterans.

The past is ever-present. The nation and the world paused to commemorate the seventy-fifth anniversary of D-Day as I was completing my work on this book. At a time of great conflict and division—when once again we are struggling to define who we are as nations and allies—the leaders of the free world stood on the cliffs above the Normandy beaches where we were once united in common cause.

"We are gathered here on freedom's altar," President Trump said in his remarks, and his words resonated. Normandy was the altar where nearly 10,000 Allied soldiers lost their lives, and their sacrifice was not in vain.

It was my desire to try to capture that moment of time that led me to write this book, which focuses on FDR and the three critical days of the Tehran Conference where the decision was made to launch Operation Overlord, the decisive battle of the war that came to be known as D-Day. World War II still has an influence on our lives, although it is growing more distant. According to the Department of Veterans Affairs, those who served in that war are dying at a rate of 372 veterans per day. Sixteen million of them fought; only 600,000 remain. How do we preserve the experience of that time and explain its meaning for future generations? I always tell my two sons, Paul, twelve, and Daniel, nine, that history is a living thing, and I've found that to be true for myself. I was born twenty-six years after D-Day, but growing up it felt as if it was part of my story, too. Respecting and revering the veterans who came to be known as the "Greatest Generation" was standard practice. Today, as the remaining veterans of D-Day live out their final years, their resolute faces and words bring us back to our greatest legacy as a people.

Writing about history is an immersive experience. As I found with my other books, on Dwight Eisenhower and Ronald Reagan, nothing helps with the experience more than a trip to a presidential library—this time, a trip to the Franklin D.

Roosevelt Presidential Library and Museum in Hyde Park, New York. About forty miles north of West Point, above the Hudson River, the vistas are breathtaking in all seasons. Touring the grounds can put you back in FDR's time. The stately family home, now showing the wear of age, is just a few yards from the museum, and walking the long driveway it's easy to picture Roosevelt, his legs shrunken by polio and encased in steel braces, struggling for hours at a time, trying to walk again. He never succeeded, but he also never stopped trying.

Driving the backroads of the property, one can imagine FDR doing the same in his 1936 Ford Phaeton Convertible with special hand controls. Mounted on the steering column is a device that produced lit cigarettes at the push of a button—a one-of-a-kind feature. He loved that car and often drove along the side roads and hills of Hyde Park, taking the curves at breakneck speed.

On a hill at the easternmost corner of the property is Top Cottage, which FDR built as a private retreat. The long, flat porch of the modest cottage was the setting of a picnic the Roosevelts hosted for King George VI and Queen Elizabeth of England in 1939. (FDR drove them there from the main house himself, and after that ride the queen vowed to never get back in a car with him again.)

But the true work takes place in the reading room of the library, with its aged books lining the walls. There are over 17 million documents in the FDR archives, and almost one million of them are available digitally. But there is something special about being there and holding the documents in your hands. Unlike at the Eisenhower Library, gloves are not required. The archivists thought gloves would make it hard to turn pages, which is true. Here are the drafts of speeches, always of special interest to me, with edits scribbled in Roosevelt's hand; the ur-

gent cables at critical moments of the war; the correspondence
between the president and Winston Churchill and Joseph Stalin, some of the letters in longhand. Collected in large bound
books are the records of the Tehran Conference with Winston
Churchill and Joseph Stalin, the centerpiece of this book. The
firsthand accounts of observers and translators bring one into
the room as they fiercely debated the wisdom of a cross-Channel
invasion on western Europe. Trying to put the reader in the
room is what the Three Days series is all about.

In Tehran, the complex relationship of the three men was
on full display. Churchill, a man of great passion and conviction, had been in this war longer than the others, and felt his
unique position gave additional legitimacy to his voice. After all, Britain had stood firm against Hitler while the United
States was trying to avoid the war and the Soviet Union was
signing a non-aggression pact with Germany. Stalin, a dictator whose hidden depths masked his true agenda, could be
an uncomfortable partner, given his history. However, the
sacrifices endured by his countrymen, with millions of lives
lost to Nazi aggression, gave his proposals special standing.
FDR as the mediator, and in the eyes of the others the final
word, had an agenda complicated by the drain on American
lives and treasure of the Pacific War and the knowledge that
any invasion of western Europe would occur on the backs
of American soldiers. Their frank, often brutal, conversations
are a revelation. The sheer human drama of this meeting, at
the conference table and behind the scenes, is a time capsule
that when broken open, foretells the next three quarters of a
century.

Much has been written about this period. A staff member at the FDR Library told me he thought Roosevelt was
the most written about person in American history, and I can

understand why he'd think that. Many great historians have explored aspects of his life and contribution. I don't aspire to match the genius of historians, but intend to put my personal journalist's spin on the great events of Roosevelt's day, culminating with the Tehran Conference and the decision to launch Operation Overlord. That meeting may have won the war, but it also set the stage for the beginning of the Cold War. I am not a historian. I am a reporter of history. And this book, like the other two in the series, hopefully sheds light on a crucial moment in time and one of America's most consequential leaders.

It is the small human details that intrigue me, the desire to pull back the curtain, see them as they were, and ask what that means for us. Roosevelt, Churchill, and Stalin were men of their time, but in a sense, they are men of *our* time, too. The leader of this daring trio, FDR stands apart as a man truly formed by crisis and loss, a person of great gifts and also great personal flaws, who chose to rise above the traumatic events of his time and take a chance on the unknown future.

As the third book in my presidential series, *Three Days at the Brink: FDR's Daring Gamble to Win World War II* rounds out the story of twentieth-century leadership, and is a dramatic prelude to my other books—Eisenhower at the early, most dangerous days of the Cold War, with Stalin breaking all the promises he'd made to Roosevelt; and Reagan, bringing an end to the Cold War with a dramatic diplomatic strategy alongside his Soviet counterpart Mikhail Gorbachev. Like Eisenhower and Reagan, Roosevelt was a leader who transcended his political party to fulfill a higher purpose in the presidency. Looking at it today, with fresh ripples forming in the global power structure, it can feel as if in one way or another we're still immersed in the same debates—still focused on a world-view from seventy-five years ago. In the living history of our times, the leaders from our past call upon us to help them fulfill their dreams.

—Bret Baier
October 2019

THE "BIG THREE" DINNER PARTY

November 28, 1943

In the heavily armed and gated Soviet Embassy compound in Tehran, Iran, President Franklin D. Roosevelt was hosting a steak-and-baked-potato dinner for his indispensable wartime counterparts, Prime Minister Winston Churchill and Marshal Joseph Stalin. The meal was being prepared by Roosevelt's cherished Filipino mess crew, who knew exactly how he liked his steaks grilled. The cooks had arrived that afternoon to find that, inexplicably, someone had removed the stove, and they'd scrambled to create a makeshift kitchen from scratch, installing a range and kitchen equipment in an empty room at the embassy.

The circumstance that placed the president of the United States in Tehran for a meeting with Churchill and Stalin was a crisis point in the Second World War. After more than four years of fighting, the free world was at the brink. Adolf Hitler's armies had surged across western Europe and into the Soviet Union and the Mediterranean. The Allies had fought hard, and in the last year they had scored important victories at the edges of Axis-controlled territory: a successful campaign in North Africa; inroads into southern Italy, where Benito Mussolini's government had collapsed; and a brutal victory in Stalingrad. In the Pacific theater, Allied victories at Midway and Guadalcanal had created positive momentum. But the successes felt piecemeal in the larger scheme of things. It might have seemed as though the Germans and Japanese were finally on the defensive, but overconfidence would have been a mistake. The Axis Powers still dominated Europe and Asia. Nazi Germany's systematic extermination of Jews, forever after known as the Holocaust, proceeded unchecked throughout its territory. Moreover, the price of the Allies' precious few victories had been astonishingly high—the Soviets had lost a million men at Stalingrad—underscoring the grave challenge that lay ahead. The Allies could not afford to miscalculate against an enemy so undaunted by defeat, so relentless in the face of overwhelming odds. They needed the kind of decisive win that would put the Nazis on their heels.

This was the critical issue that confronted the Big Three in Tehran. Each came with his own vision of the future. Stalin was adamant that a second front be opened in Europe as soon as possible. Churchill was unpersuaded, believing that the Mediterranean would be a more fruitful arena. FDR was in the middle, leaning toward Stalin's view but hesitant on the question of timing. One thing was clear: the next great battle was on the horizon, and those three days in Tehran would determine its course. Hitler could still win the war. What were they willing to do to stop him?

Theirs was at times an uneasy alliance. Churchill, the most passionate of the three, felt he deserved accommodation since Great Britain had held off the Nazis virtually alone in the early years of the war. Stalin countered that more than the other na-

tions, the USSR had suffered a true invasion of its land, cost-
ing millions of lives. He believed he was owed a rallying Allied
endeavor—a second front in Europe that would relieve pressure on the embattled eastern front by forcing Hitler to move
troops to the new theater. And he wasn't shy about saying that
if the United States and Great Britain were unwilling, they were
cowards.

FDR, who was meeting Stalin for the first time, was determined to show the Soviet leader a full measure of respect, even
if his attentiveness wounded the feelings of Churchill, who had
been his closest confidant during the war. For Roosevelt, the
Tehran meeting was a victory of sorts. He had been trying for
more than a year to get Stalin into the same room, and he was
eager to make the most of it. Among other issues, he was intent on enlisting Stalin in the war with Japan, which the United
States was fighting mostly alone, with limited help from Great
Britain. The urgency could not be overstated. If the Big Three
did not come to common terms during that meeting, the Allied
effort could falter. They needed a united policy at a time when
the Soviets were fighting for their lives and Hitler's domination
of western Europe had remained largely unchallenged.

Roosevelt's stay at the Soviet compound, after Stalin had
turned over a building for his use, was an unexpected development and one that peeved Churchill. Originally, Roosevelt
had planned to headquarter at the US Embassy and to hold
meetings there, although it was not a large facility. Churchill
had offered the British Embassy compound as an alternative. At
that point, Stalin had swept in with an invitation of his own,
cleverly orchestrating Roosevelt's acceptance by presenting a
vague but plausible rumor that agents of Hitler had parachuted
in nearby and were plotting an assassination attempt on the Big
Three. Soviet agents had learned of the plot in time to arrest

some of the instigators, but they did not know if any of the agents had escaped into the hills and were planning to go ahead with an attack. Tehran, wrote Bill Yenne in his book about the plot, "was a hub of international intrigue with an underworld of double and even triple agents." Even if Roosevelt were safe in the US Embassy, the same could not be said for Stalin and Churchill and their staffs, who would be forced to make daily mile-long journeys through treacherous streets to meetings at the US Embassy.

The prospect of the leaders of what Churchill called "the greatest concentration of power the world had ever seen" being eliminated was chilling. After twenty years in power, Stalin had no natural heir, and the messy political aftermaths of Churchill's and Roosevelt's deaths would impede the momentum of the war. (For one thing, Roosevelt's vice president, Henry Wallace, was an outspoken isolationist.)

The Soviets argued that the president would be safest in the fortresslike Soviet Embassy, and it was spacious enough for the meetings. Churchill argued that the same could be said for the British Embassy, which was right next door to the Soviets', but Roosevelt accepted Stalin's offer—the first of a series of what felt like rebuffs to his old friend Churchill. In truth, Roosevelt might have viewed it as a strategic opportunity to be close to Stalin.

"I am placing a very great importance on the personal and intimate conversations which you and Churchill and I will have, for on them the hope of the future world will greatly depend," Roosevelt wrote to Stalin a month before the conference. However, the conference was extremely difficult to set up, and it almost didn't happen. The barrier, in Roosevelt's opinion, was Stalin's insistence that it be held in Tehran. Stalin argued that he needed to be close to home because of his duties there. Roosevelt countered that he could not be so far away from the United States and out of touch with Congress during that critical time, since the rough, mountainous terrain made it difficult for cables to be sent and received. In one letter to Stalin, he pointedly added, "I am not in any way considering the fact that from the United States territory I would have to travel six thousand miles and you would only have to travel six hundred miles from Russian territory." But he added, "I would gladly go ten times the distance to meet you were it not for the fact that I must carry on a constitutional government more than one hundred and fifty years old."

Stalin held firm. Eventually, when it became clear that he would not attend a conference if it were not in Tehran, Roosevelt folded, graciously writing Stalin that he had cleared up his constitutional barriers. ". . . I have decided to go to Tehran, and this makes me especially happy."

After Roosevelt accepted Stalin's invitation to stay at the Soviet Embassy, the Secret Service sprang into action. It created a huge motorcade from the US Embassy, with a stand-in posing as Roosevelt in the presidential car. The president sneaked out in a separate car and traveled anonymously via back roads.

Once Roosevelt and his staff were settled in at the embassy, there was some awkwardness. It was lavish in its facade and accommodations but not very comfortable. The Americans knew that their rooms were bugged, and Roosevelt took special care to avoid saying anything he wouldn't want overheard. His staff was a bit rattled by the way Stalin himself kept popping into the president's office to see that all was well, like an obsequious but not entirely trustworthy hotel manager. Members of Roosevelt's entourage also noticed that the maids, waiters, and bellmen all had bulges at their hips that appeared to be firearms and suspected that they were not in fact servants but members of the NKVD, Stalin's secret police.

The old calculations of which nations constituted friend or foe were very much on everyone's minds. The Soviets might have been necessary allies, but they could be sneaky. For one thing, the story of a potential assassination attempt by Nazi infiltrators might have been a ruse—an invention by Stalin to persuade Roosevelt to stay with him.

While the mess crew was hard at work in the kitchen, in another part of the compound an introductory meeting of the Big Three was taking place. It was the first time that Roosevelt, Churchill, and Stalin were in the same room together.

Introduced earlier that afternoon, Roosevelt and Stalin had sized each other up in a private meeting. Stalin had brought his interpreter, but Roosevelt, wanting to demonstrate trust, did not have his own interpreter in the room. Stalin was impressed by Roosevelt's powerful personality and intellect, and he felt chastened when he saw the extent of his infirmity. He suddenly realized how difficult it must have been for the wheelchair-bound president to make the journey of thousands of miles by sea and air. He graciously promised Roosevelt that their next meeting would be in a more convenient setting for the president—a promise he broke when he demanded Yalta, on the Black Sea, even farther from the United States, as the location of their second summit.

For his part, Roosevelt was surprised to see that Stalin was short—only five feet, six inches tall—but stocky, with broad shoulders and an expansive waist. His camel-hair coat over a dark blue uniform gave him an aura of elegance and a stature beyond his size. Stalin was pleasant, even witty, but his eyes were inscrutable, his mouth masked behind his thick mustache. Roosevelt would later describe the Soviet leader as "a man hewn out of granite." At the same time, he believed he could chip away at that granite—that Stalin would give in if it suited his own needs. Courting the Soviet leader was high on Roosevelt's list of priorities. He needed him, even if their closeness hurt Churchill's pride.

At the dinner hour, as was his custom, Roosevelt arrived in the dining room before the others, to avoid being wheeled in as they watched. He was seated in his armless wheelchair at the drinks table, where he was mixing his signature martini cocktail: two parts gin, one part dry vermouth, shaken with ice and garnished with an olive. When the others entered, he handed them their drinks. Stalin sipped his doubtfully, and Roosevelt asked him how he liked it. Stalin politely replied that it was all right but "cold on the stomach."

Stalin preferred vodka and wine to gin, but he was no slouch in the drinking department. It was said that as an infant he'd been given a vodka-soaked rag to suck on while he was teething, and he currently made sure that his soldiers received a daily ration of vodka. He enjoyed the procession of toasts at public events—it was typical at Russian dinners for there to be as many as forty toasts. The US ambassador to the Soviet Union, Averell Harriman, observed that Stalin enjoyed watching others get drunk, perhaps because it gave him the upper hand, but he took care to avoid inebriation himself, often sneaking water into his vodka glass.

Despite the alcohol-fueled bonhomie at the table, there was a degree of tension. Churchill, well lubricated but unbowed, felt aggrieved, like a shunned spouse, as he watched Roosevelt turn on the charm for Stalin, even calling him "Uncle Joe." He knew that Roosevelt had met privately with Stalin that day, and he had been hurt when the president had denied him a similar meeting. Churchill could not resist counting up slights, real or imagined. He would be the first to admit that weakness, once having said, "No lover ever studied the whims of his mistress as

I did those of President Roosevelt." Yet he saw that they were more than whims on FDR's part. Rationally, he understood Roosevelt's strategy to bring Stalin into alignment. But he bristled that it was often at his expense.

Near the end of the meal, an attack of severe indigestion sent Roosevelt to bed early, leaving Churchill and Stalin to snipe at each other without a mediator. Clamping his teeth down on his smoldering cigar, Churchill glowered at Stalin, who chain-smoked cigarettes and made his case with a chilly smugness. Yet they talked. It was a striking sight. In other circumstances, they would have been natural-born enemies. Circumstances required them to engage in the painful exercise of reaching agreement, with Roosevelt serving as the leader who would help them envision and cement a partnership that would win the war.

That first dinner foreshadowed the dynamic that would continue over the next three days, when the greatest questions of the war would be debated. The central issue: What was to be the next big front? Would they finally dare a cross-Channel landing in France—and would they do it soon, as Stalin was urging? Did they have the troops and the air and sea power to make the push? The English Channel had blocked German advances during World War I, and even Hitler, at his boldest in 1940, had not crossed the Channel to invade Great Britain. If they went ahead, which US general had the skill to serve as supreme commander of that mission? Could they summon the nerve and the resources for an operation whose success could win the war but whose failure could mean defeat?

Beneath the strategizing there were the underlying questions: Could they afford to trust one another? Could they afford *not* to? Though they were allies, each of the Big Three had pursued war policy mostly from his own platform, which reflected their national priorities. In order to launch the next great mission, they would need to act as one. Stalin would have to quell his biases toward the West and allow a level of partnership that had not been realized before. Churchill would have to overcome his deep misgivings about Stalin's true allegiance. Roosevelt would have to rise above the quarreling by both sides and help them achieve unity.

The story of that vital conference provides an inside view of the intimate interactions of great powers at a perilous time in history, showing both gifted leadership and human flaws. The principals' debates would range from the profound to the petty, from the emotional to the calculated, as they sought common ground. Practiced in manipulation, each of the leaders carried his own wish list and used his persuasive power to shift the dialogue in his favor. All felt the weight of history, but only history would tell how deeply their decisions would impact the shape of the world, for both good and ill.

Through it all, Roosevelt was, by consent of the others, the lead strategist for the future and the one man who could, in effect, allow or deny the others their place in history. In the silence of his private quarters, he worried about his master strategy and the pragmatic concerns that made an alliance with a man like Stalin necessary. Stalin's ruthless grip on power, his bloody regime that exiled or murdered his personal and political enemies, his dictatorial control over his people, were of great concern. Clearly Stalin was a transactional leader; he sought relations with the Western powers because he needed them to defeat Hitler. But could he be a reliable partner? Roosevelt longed to give Stalin the benefit of the doubt, to see him as a collaborator in building a free and equal world. If he was haunted by doubts, he didn't allow them to show. Instead, he placed a great deal of trust in his adviser Harry Hopkins, who assured him that Stalin wanted only safety and prosperity for his people, as any leader might.

In the stifling quarters of the Soviet Embassy, Roosevelt could contemplate his ideals for the future, in the same way an architect sketches the framework of a building. But the mysteries loomed large. He was meeting Stalin for the first time, and it would require all his skill to reel him in to his side, without giving him too much room to grow stronger. Of all the moments of his life, when the weight of the future seemed to press down on his crippled frame, this, he saw, was perhaps the most significant challenge he would face—how to embrace a man who could become his enemy while he still had the space to make him a partner.

He knew that. They could not leave Tehran without a plan. In that watershed moment of the war, it was time to make a daring gamble.

It was a challenge he had been preparing for all his life.

PART ONE

THE MAKING OF FDR

CHAPTER 1

TO WHOM MUCH IS GIVEN

Franklin Delano Roosevelt's mother, Sara, once denied that her aspirations for her son had reached as high as the White House or the world stage. "Did I ever think when he was little that Franklin might be president?" she wrote. "Never, oh never! That was the last thing I should ever have imagined for him, or that he should be in public life of any sort . . . What was my ambition for him? Very simple—it might even be thought not very ambitious . . . to grow to be like his father, straight and honorable, just and kind, an upstanding American." Given the intensity of her devotion to her only son and the firm grip she held on his development, Sara Delano Roosevelt's modest vision seems disingenuous. He was in every way her golden boy, groomed for an impact far greater than that of a Hyde Park, New York, country gentleman.

Sara Roosevelt would live to see her son elected president of the United States three times before her death. (He would be elected to a fourth term after she died.) Indeed, he reached such heights that he can sometimes seem like an imposing blank canvas onto which generations have projected their hopes and dreams. We magnify the stature of certain leaders, and history further cements the impressions. Reality—the deeper truths, the human failings, the paradoxes—is far more interesting and instructive.

One of those paradoxes, as Roosevelt biographer Jean Smith posed it: "How this Hudson River aristocrat . . . became the champion of the common man." It's an intriguing question. Often Americans look to popular leaders to mirror their essence, particularly their humble roots; to listen for them to say, "I understand your plight because I am like you." That was clearly the case for Dwight D. Eisenhower, born in the hardscrabble arena of late-nineteenth-century Kansas; or Ronald Reagan, whose family suffered from the joint demons of poverty and alcoholism. But it's not always the case. The wealth of FDR's parental families, the Roosevelts and the Delanos, ensured that he would never want for anything material, and it would also give him the benefit of world travel, the best schools, and immersion in a circle of influence not available to most people. But the jolting counterbalance to a smooth destiny was polio. Just as his political life was gaining momentum, FDR was felled and crippled, suffering permanent paralysis and a years-long battle to bring himself back to his life's work, while facing the bitter truth that he would never walk again. The crucible of his devastating illness and its paralyzing effects seemed to enlarge him as a man and gave him a depth and purpose that had not been noticeable before. The historian and Roosevelt biographer Doris Kearns Goodwin wrote in *Leadership: In Turbulent Times*, "Franklin Roosevelt's ordeal provides the most clear-cut paradigm of how a devastating crucible experience can, against all expectation and logic, lead to significant growth, intensified ambition, and enlarged gifts for leadership." And as the political commentator George Will put it, "Just as the irons were clamped on his legs, the steel entered his soul."

But those are only pieces of the story. While the question of his privileged status is interesting and the daunting challenge of his disability dramatic, it must also be said that Roosevelt was endowed with a number of natural talents and characteristics that served his mission in life well: an optimistic personality, a sincere charm and enjoyment of people, an unwavering self-confidence, a deeply felt sense of fairness, an instinct for risk taking, a thirst for learning, a strong will—and perhaps above all, the ability to communicate, to reach out and touch Americans with the deep timbre of his voice and the power of his words. The iconic image of Roosevelt is the one that stays with us—the jaunty pose with a cigarette holder, the wide grin, the energy vibrating off him in waves.

He also had his share of flaws. He could be remote, treacherous, self-indulgent, and careless with those who loved him most. He was raised with the impression of being the sun around whom all the planets circled, and that elevated self-regard was often manifested in unattractive ways. But at the time he entered the presidency, what mattered most to people was the picture of sheer buoyancy. Stunned by the Great Depression, floundering in a sea of debt and despair, Americans found in Roosevelt a man who seemed able to ride the waves. He gave them a reason to hope.

Roosevelt did not live to write a memoir. Nor did he keep a diary of his thoughts and reflections, as many presidents have. His interior life was largely hidden, recalled only by those who were close to him. Even they acknowledged that his true feelings were beyond their reach. In his long hours of solitary poring over his stamp collection, his thoughts were in shadow. In his closest relationships, even with his wife and children, he was pleasant and patient, yet struggled with true intimacy. But in historical memory he has become one of the rare presidents to transcend party politics, joining George Washington and Abraham Lincoln in that distinction. This complex picture, the measure of a man of both great strengths and personal short-comings, is Roosevelt's full legacy.

FRANKLIN ROOSEVELT WAS BORN on January 30, 1882, at the family estate in Hyde Park, New York, to James Roosevelt and Sara Delano Roosevelt. Sara's difficult labor lasted more than twenty-four hours and almost came to disaster when she was given too much chloroform for the pain. She was unconscious when her son was delivered, blue and still; she didn't witness the desperate effort to breathe life into his tiny mouth. By the time she awoke, she was happily handed a squalling infant. James wrote in Sara's diary, "At quarter to nine, my Sallie had a splendid large baby boy. He weighed 10 lbs., without clothes." The danger was momentarily forgotten, although Sara never bore another child.

James and Sara had wed two years earlier—he a widower of fifty-two, she a self-proclaimed spinster of twenty-six. Before she met James, Sara had abandoned all idea of marriage, and her family money provided her the freedom to travel the world and do as she pleased. James, less wealthy than the Delanos but still well off, had graduated from Harvard Law School, only to discover he despised the practice of law. He preferred business pursuits, investments of varying success, and the genteel life of a landowner and country gentleman, dabbling in local affairs while enjoying his boating and horse stables. He lived happily with his first wife—his second cousin Rebecca Brien Howland—and their son, James Roosevelt Roosevelt (the double last name used instead of "Jr."), known as Rosy. For years, Rebecca had suffered from ill health, and she died of a massive heart attack while on a day trip aboard their yacht. She was forty-five.

James's world was shattered, and he thought he'd never

marry again. But four years after Rebecca's death, at a dinner party hosted by Mrs. Theodore Roosevelt, Sr., his attention was drawn to the beautiful daughter of his friend Warren Delano, Jr., and hers to him. Their attraction to each other grew, despite the age difference, which worried Sara's father. After all, she was the same age as Rosy. But their love prevailed, and they were married within six months.

They embarked on a ten-month European honeymoon, and by the time they returned, Sara was five months pregnant. Refusing the confinement that was typical for pregnant women then, she remained active until the day she went into labor.

James and Sara named their son Franklin after Sara's favorite uncle and settled into their family life at the estate at Hyde Park, known as Springwood (a name mostly dropped in favor of simply Hyde Park). It was a beautiful setting, high above the Hudson River, a retreat from the world where Sara could nurture her son, who became the great love and chief occupation of her life.

As was the case with so many other presidents, Franklin Roosevelt's mother was the wind beneath his expansive wings. The image of Franklin as a pampered little prince might seem inescapable, especially in light of the girlish ringlets and Little Lord Fauntleroy outfits his mother favored when he was small—until he demanded a haircut. That characterization sells Sara short, however. More than his appearance, she was deeply interested in her son's intellectual, emotional, and character development, and she was often unconventional in her parenting approach. Once, when Franklin was five, she noticed that he seemed sad and asked him if he was unhappy. He replied solemnly, "Yes, I am unhappy." She asked him why, and he clasped his hands together with urgency and cried, "Oh, for freedom!"

Concerned, Sara discussed the matter with James, and they

worried together about whether they were too controlling. (Although Franklin was only *five*!) So Sara devised a plan. The next day she told her son he could do whatever he pleased for the entire day, and she would step back and not interfere. He raced off to play, happy to be ignored by his mother. When he returned at the end of the day, sated with freedom and looking the worse for wear, Sara concluded he had learned that freedom wasn't all it was cracked up to be. Life resumed as normal.

Sara had an unusual perspective on parenting. She believed that children were essentially miniature adults. "I've always believed that children had pretty much the same thoughts as adults," she said. In her mind, all they were lacking was the vocabulary to express these thoughts. That capacity was best cultivated through reading. Encouraged by his mother to choose his own reading material, Franklin became obsessed with history, especially naval history. His love of the sea was a theme that would last his lifetime.

With no siblings (except for his adult half brother Rosy) and homeschooled by governesses and tutors until the age of fourteen, Franklin learned to enjoy the company of adults and also to feel content being on his own. He developed a life of the mind that could often seem beyond his years and adopted passions that would stay with him for life, such as his beloved stamp collecting, which would later soothe him during the most trying times of his presidency.

Sara realized that Franklin was somewhat sheltered, but she never thought he was lonely. Endlessly curious, he had a gift for making an adventure out of any situation. "I do not believe I have ever seen a little boy who seemed always to be so consistently enjoying himself," she wrote. That quality seemed to follow him through life—his White House secretary Grace Tully later noted that he was "never boring or bored."

Even though he spent much time alone, Franklin was a sociable boy, and when other children were present, he loved their company, falling naturally into the role of leader when they played games. *Too* naturally, his mother thought. When she observed Franklin's habit of ordering his playmates around while organizing a sport or building a fort, she mildly suggested that he give others a turn at command. "Mummie," he replied, "if I didn't give the orders, nothing would happen."

His father, whom he adored, gladly became his companion in adventures of boyhood and exposed him to the joys of outdoor living: sailing the glorious Hudson River, horseback riding, and shooting. They spent a great deal of time together, so Franklin was blessed with the best of both his parents. James and Sara were also intent on exposing their son to life beyond the cosseted world of their Hyde Park estate, and they traveled widely as a family. In his first fourteen years, Franklin accompanied them on eight trips to Europe—lengthy journeys by sea.

By the time Franklin was fourteen, his parents decided he needed more formal schooling, and they enrolled him at Groton School, the elite Massachusetts boarding academy founded by Endicott Peabody, a college friend of Theodore Roosevelt, who had begun a prestigious career in finance before quitting to become an Episcopal priest. His philosophy of education was centered around spartan living, religious observance, physical exercise, and devotion to the public good. That life-shaping environment would make a tremendous impact on Franklin, who would say, "As long as I live, the influence of Dr. and Mrs. Peabody means and will mean more to me than that of any other people next to my father and mother." In the beginning, though, he had to overcome two barriers. The first was his size; he was small and thin then, although that impediment would eventually resolve itself. The second was that he was joining a class that had already been together since the boys were twelve, so he had to endure being the new kid. That, too, was eventually overcome thanks to Franklin's determination to get along and become one of the boys. If he was lonely at first, or dismayed by the strict environment or rough treatment, he never let on in his twice-weekly letters home. That took great self-control and served the purpose of easing his mother's fears. "It was no time at all, I am told, after he was thrown with boys of his own age that his timidity went out like ice in a spring flood," Sara wrote with satisfaction. "Almost overnight he became sociable and gregarious and entered with the frankest enjoyment into every kind of school activity."

It wasn't quite as easy as that. Franklin loved sports but failed to make the football or baseball team and was relegated to the role of baseball manager, a tedious behind-the-scenes job that involved organizing equipment and being at the beck and call of the players. He did the job cheerfully, without complaint, and his lack of self-pity endeared him to his classmates.

Decades later, when Franklin was president, Charles R. Nutter, one of his instructors, wrote a positive but less-than-glowing evaluation of the boy he had known at Groton:

> The fact is—from my remembrance—Franklin was colorless; a nice, pleasant boy who did not get into trouble and did do as he should. But remained submerged. I have been asked about his school days by those who know I was at Groton at the time, and I always say that if I had been told there was a potential President in his form he would have footed the possibilities. . . . I remarked that he was colorless. This condition might be of comfort and inspiration to others who are colorless.

James and Sara kept their distance as they had been told to do, though it was difficult for Sara, who found her son's brief letters home maddeningly unrevealing. Only once did she break protocol, when Franklin came down with scarlet fever and was quarantined in the school infirmary. Prevented from being at his bedside, she devised a plan to be close to him. She wrote, "Several times each day I would climb a tall, rickety ladder, and, by seating myself on the top, manage to see into the room and talk with our small, convalescing scapegrace."

James Roosevelt had always impressed upon his son that it was the responsibility of Christians to help those who were less fortunate, and that message was reinforced at Groton. Franklin joined the Groton Missionary Society to do charitable works. He was assigned to help an eighty-four-year-old black woman, the widow of a Civil War drummer—plowing her driveway when it snowed, feeding her chickens, and stocking her coal bin. He also spent two two-week stints at the Missionary Society's New Hampshire summer camp for poor children.

Summer holidays were spent at Campobello, a small Canadian island off the coast of Maine, where the family had a cottage. Franklin loved the remote place and found it a welcome escape. He'd continue to vacation at Campobello throughout his life. It was on vacation there as a teenager that he adopted a new passion: golf. His mother was dismissive of the sport, calling it a "newfangled game," but Franklin fell in love with it. He built a golf course on the island and instituted an annual tournament. The island's other residents didn't entirely see the point of sectioning off the pristine grassland, so often the golfers' swings had to dodge grazing sheep. He would continue to be an avid golfer well into adulthood, and those who played with him said he had a powerful swing and an ability to hit long drives. (If not for polio, he'd certainly have ranked as a top presidential golfer.)

After graduating from Groton, Franklin went to Harvard College in 1900. He immediately immersed himself in the life there, including many extracurricular activities. He sang with the glee club and became involved in politics. Although his side of the Roosevelt family, including his father, was Democrat, and Franklin thought of himself as a Democrat, he was an enthusiastic supporter of his Republican cousin Theodore Roosevelt, Jr., who had been nominated for vice president on William McKinley's ticket. Franklin stepped out of his partisan bubble to join the Republican Club, and when the McKinley-Roosevelt ticket won, he accompanied his classmates on a torchlight victory parade into Boston.

But the excitement of victory was soon marred by terrible news from home. His mother sent word to Boston that his father, who was seventy-two, had suffered a heart attack. She assured Franklin that he was recuperating in New York City. But as the weeks went on, Franklin grew frustrated by the slow course of his father's recovery. Agonizing, he wrote to his parents, "I am too distressed about Papa and cannot understand why he does not improve more quickly." James did not improve. Finally, in early December, a telegram arrived from Sara: the situation was dire; Franklin must come to New York. He was by his father's side when he died on December 8, 1900.

In 1902 and 1903, Sara would rent a house in Boston so she could be close to him, and he was glad to have her nearby. They were all each other had.

During his freshman year, Franklin pursued an activity that would become his passion for his entire career at Harvard: working for the prestigious *Harvard Crimson*. It was not easy to gain acceptance to that elite publication, and he failed at his first attempt. But a bit of daring and family connection delivered him a major scoop that secured his position. In April 1901, he learned through the family grapevine of a secret visit to Harvard being planned by his cousin Theodore, now vice president. He was to speak to the constitutional government class of his friend Professor Abbott Lawrence Lowell. Franklin, knowing that the vice president was with Lowell at his home, broke all protocol to visit him there. He then wrote about the secret appearance on campus the next day, and a huge crowd of two thousand students showed up outside Lowell's classroom. Lowell wasn't pleased, but for Franklin it was considered a major journalistic coup.

When summer came, Sara announced that she could not bear to go to Campobello, their usual vacation spot. Seeking escape from situations that would remind her of her husband, she took Franklin on a sea voyage to Europe. As they were returning, they learned that President McKinley had been assassinated. At only forty-three, Cousin Teddy was now the twenty-sixth president of the United States. That was big news for the sprawling Roosevelt clan, one branch in Oyster Bay, Long Island (Teddy's family), and one in Hyde Park. If Franklin looked at his distant cousin, for whom he had such great admiration, and thought, "Maybe me someday," he never said it. But he loved adventure, and it seemed that as president his cousin Teddy was having a fine one.

From the outside Theodore Roosevelt's life could look magical and monumental. He seemed larger than life, although he was only five feet, ten inches tall. His forceful presence was manifested by his burly weight, bushy walrus mustache, wide, toothy grin, and tremendous energy. He was physically fearless in a manner that could take a young boy's breath away, yet warm and genuine in his enjoyment of people—especially children. He was a loving, engaged father to his large brood of six—one by his first wife, Alice, and five more by his second wife, Edith. He was infinitely likable because people were captivated by his sincerity and by the sheer joy he took in his endeavors. He was mesmerizing on the stump, pounding his fist in the air and issuing declarations in sharp, clipped sentences, his powerful body bent forward persistently. Franklin respected him, for although they were of different parties they shared so many of the same beliefs that the term "Roosevelt Republican" was later coined to describe a common progressive mentality. Above all, Theodore Roosevelt appeared to be the avatar of a new century, with lofty goals of economic equity, conservation, military strength, and globalization. At heart he was a reformer, determined to make a strong imprint on the nation he loved.

At Harvard, Franklin looked on with admiration, seeking ways he could emulate his cousin. As Meredith Hindley describes it in "The Roosevelt Bond," he began to wear pince-nez instead of glasses and was heard to mimic the president's expressions, such as "de-e-e-lighted!"

SARA FELT SECURE IN the belief that she knew everything there was to know about her son, but he kept one side of his life hidden from her. She was under the impression that Franklin was indifferent to the charms and persuasions of women. Actually, he dated many young women in college and worked diligently to keep his exploits from his mother. At least one young lady, the Boston heiress Alice Sohier Shaw, whom he courted fervently, recalled his ardor as bordering on inappropriate, and she rejected his talk of marriage. She was also put off by his declaration that he wanted at least six children, saying that she "did not wish to be a cow."

Soon Franklin became interested in another young woman, his fifth cousin once removed, Anna Eleanor Roosevelt, who was a niece of President Roosevelt. They had seen each other on occasion at family functions since they had been small children but didn't know each other well. Then in the summer of 1902, as Sara and Franklin rode the train from New York City to Hyde Park, Franklin was walking through the cars when he came upon Eleanor, her head bent over a book. He stopped to talk. He was so interested in their conversation that he stayed for an hour and then invited Eleanor to come and pay her respects to his mother, her aunt Sallie.

Months later, Franklin saw Eleanor again at a family event, and he began to ask her out for tea and coffee. At a White House dinner, they sat side by side. Franklin was undoubtedly dazzled by Eleanor's proximity to the president he admired so deeply, but he was also drawn to her personality. He saw beneath her shy manner a warmth that touched him and also an open-minded interest in the world. She had depth.

Eleanor's difficult upbringing was also intriguing to a man who had been so protected. She had been born to privilege as the daughter of Theodore Roosevelt's younger brother Elliott and Anna Rebecca Hall, a leading socialite of the era. Theirs was a combustible match, due to Anna's high expectations and Elliott's chronic drinking. Anna, unprepared to deal with her erratic husband, became increasingly withdrawn, including in her relationship with Eleanor. She spent long periods at her mother's house in Tivoli, New York, feeling ill and incapable of shaking herself out of her doldrums. She mourned her lost youth, the gaiety of her life, and the happy girl she once had been. Although she bore two more children with Elliott—Elliott, Jr., and Gracie Hall (a boy, known as Hall)—their relationship remained poor. Elliott's siblings looked on in horror as their brother deteriorated further into alcoholism, but he refused to accept help or counsel from them. Eleanor clung to her father, taking his side against her mother, who was often critical of Eleanor's plain looks and shyness. In Eleanor's eyes, only her father understood her and loved her unconditionally. She loved him so much that she found ways to forgive him his alcohol-fueled outbursts.

Tragically, Anna succumbed to diphtheria when Eleanor was eight, while her father was in a sanatorium in Europe. Elliott, Jr., soon died of scarlet fever and diphtheria. Two years later, Elliott died when he jumped from a sanatorium window in a fit of delirium. Orphans, Eleanor and Hall went to live with Anna's mother, a strict and unaffectionate woman. Eleanor's life was cloistered and lonely. Her one respite was summer visits to the Roosevelt compound at Oyster Bay, Long Island, where she vacationed with the lively clan, which often included her uncle Ted. He was loving toward her and also challenged her to be bolder—he being the best model for that. When he saw that she could not swim and was afraid of the water, he told her to be brave and jump off the dock. She did, though it didn't go well. She floundered, flailing and gasping for air. Never mind, Uncle Ted said, pulling her out of the water. As with his own children he was trying to teach his shy niece that if you acted fearlessly, you would become fearless. It was a theme he often preached—that you could train yourself to be unafraid—and his words made an impact on Eleanor; she would have many opportunities to practice that philosophy in her future.

At fifteen, Eleanor escaped her grim living environment when she was sent to Allenswood, a finishing school in London. There her life opened up in a new way. For the first time in her life she had friends and people who appreciated her for herself. She reveled in the experience of being popular, and she cherished the guidance of the headmistress, Mlle. Souvestre, who took a special interest in her and opened her eyes to the world. She even took Eleanor with her on trips across Europe and taught her to appreciate the customs of people who were very different from herself. She encouraged the shy girl to speak up for herself, and in that way Eleanor blossomed and became more self-assured.

Eleanor was not a pretty woman. Her aunt Edith, Uncle Ted's wife, once sniped about Eleanor's prominent overbite, saying "Her mouth and teeth seem to have no future." But she was striking—tall (five feet eleven) and slender, with waist-length hair and clear blue eyes.

Franklin and Eleanor engaged in an elaborate subterfuge throughout 1903 to keep their budding relationship secret from Sara. They had to be careful not to be seen together in public, but sometimes their meetings were right in front of Sara, under the guise of family gatherings. Once Franklin arranged to have Eleanor invited for a few days to Campobello, which she found a bit tedious since she couldn't swim and wasn't interested in learning to play golf. But once out sailing with Franklin, she had him to herself again.

Reflecting on that time, Eleanor later wrote in her memoir, "As I try to sum up my own development in the autumn of 1903 I think I was a curious mixture of extreme innocence and un-worldliness with a great deal of knowledge of some of the less agreeable sides of life—which, however, did not seem to make me any more sophisticated or less innocent."

She was also keenly aware of the restrictions imposed by her gender. Young women at the turn of the twentieth century were required to be shy and unassuming around men. You could not approach a man unless he approached you first, could not write or receive a letter from a man until you knew him quite well, could not receive gifts, especially jewelry, for fear of being labeled a "loose" woman, could not kiss a man until you were engaged or even married. So although Eleanor might have been naturally shy in those days, she was not allowed to be anything else.

Franklin proposed to Eleanor on November 21, 1903, referring obliquely to the moment in his diary—"After lunch I have a never to be forgotten walk with my darling." Eleanor accepted. Now to tell Mother, which Franklin dreaded. He was so reluctant that he suggested to Eleanor that they keep their relationship hidden. She saw no point to that; it would only prolong the difficult revelation. He had to agree.

Franklin knew it would be the hardest conversation he'd ever had with his mother. First, there would be the exposure of his deception, which would hurt Sara, who thought she had the most intimate knowledge of his life. Then there would be the fact of the engagement; bringing a new woman into his life was a matter that would have to be handled delicately.

Following the family Thanksgiving in 1903, Franklin took his mother aside and delivered the news that he was in love with Cousin Eleanor and wanted to marry her. As expected, Sara was stunned. She wasn't the first mother to find a child's choice of spouse wanting. Handsome, with an endearing charm and a sparkling charisma, Roosevelt was a popular young man, while Eleanor was awkward, the pitiable orphan girl. Sara never said it out loud, but she wondered how her gregarious, outgoing son could love such a woman.

But love her he did. It was precisely her distinctive nature that had attracted Roosevelt, who'd known many frivolous girls. Sara hardly knew how to respond, except to say that at twenty-one and in the midst of school, Franklin was not ready to be married. She urged him to take more time to consider. She gave that advice still believing that her son could hardly know what he was doing, being inexperienced with women. "It probably surprised us only because he had never been in any sense a ladies' man," she wrote of Franklin's announcement. "I don't believe I remember ever hearing him talk about girls or even a girl . . ." It didn't occur to her that Franklin might have a side to his life of which she knew nothing.

Later, back in Boston, Franklin wrote to Sara, hoping to ease her mind:

Dearest Mama,

I know what pain I must have caused you and you know I wouldn't do it if I could only have helped it—*mais tu sais, me voilà* [but you know, here I am]. That's all that could be said—I know my mind, have known it for a long time, and know that I could never think otherwise. Result: I am the happiest man just now in the world; likewise the luckiest—And for you, dear Mummy, you know that nothing can ever change what we have always been & always will be to each other—only now you have two children to love & to love you—and Eleanor as you know will always be a daughter to you in every true way—

Eleanor gave it a try as well:

Dear Cousin Sally,

I know how you feel & how hard it must be, but I do so want you to learn to love me a little. You must know that I will always try to do what you wish for I have grown to love you very dearly during the past summer. It is impossible for me to tell you how I feel toward Franklin. I

can only say that my one great wish is to always prove
worthy of him.

Sara still exerted substantial power over the purse strings,
and Franklin was reluctant to upset his mother, to whom he
was devoted. Though she did not reject the marriage outright,
she pressured Franklin to wait. She finally secured his agreement to wait a year to make an announcement, and if at that
time he still wanted to marry Eleanor, she would give the marriage her full blessing.

It was a difficult year. Sara kept a firm hand on their secret relationship, providing Eleanor a glimpse of the control she
would continue to hold over their marriage. Eleanor distracted
herself by pursuing an independent and worthwhile direction,
working at the University Settlement House in New York, helping young immigrant women. She relished her role, boldly taking
the streetcar to work and immersing herself in the lives of those
less fortunate than she. Franklin was kept busy with school and
reluctantly agreed to take a world trip with his mother near the
end of the year of waiting. To Sara's disappointment, the distance from Eleanor did not dampen his ardor.

On October 11, 1904, Franklin gave Eleanor a diamond
ring from Tiffany for her birthday, and the engagement was
officially announced on December 1.

Eleanor's uncle President Roosevelt wrote to Franklin, giving his blessing. "We are greatly rejoiced over the good news.
I am as fond of Eleanor as if she were my daughter," he wrote,
"and I like you, and trust you, and believe in you. No other
success in life—not the Presidency, or anything else—begins to
compare with the joy and happiness that come in and from the
love of the true man and the true woman."

The wedding was scheduled for March 17, 1905, in New
York City. The couple was delighted when the president, who

planned to be in town for the St. Patrick's Day Parade, agreed to attend and give Eleanor away. Two weeks before the wedding, on March 4, Franklin and Eleanor attended Roosevelt's inauguration in Washington. Teddy had won reelection in 1904 with the largest majority ever recorded. First thrown into office by brutal fate, he had now achieved it on his own terms. His inaugural address was a bold claim on the future, emphasizing the United States' generosity of spirit and responsibilities in a world that was already shrinking:

> Much has been given us, and much will rightfully be expected from us. We have duties to others and duties to ourselves; and we can shirk neither. We have become a great nation, forced by the fact of its greatness into relations with the other nations of the earth, and we must behave as beseems a people with such responsibilities. Toward all other nations, large and small, our attitude must be one of cordial and sincere friendship. We must show not only in our words, but in our deeds, that we are earnestly desirous of securing their good will by acting toward them in a spirit of just and generous recognition of all their rights . . . we must show, not merely in great crises, but in the everyday affairs of life, the qualities of practical intelligence, of courage, of hardihood, and endurance, and above all the power of devotion to a lofty ideal, which made great the men who founded this Republic in the days of Washington, which made great the men who preserved this Republic in the days of Abraham Lincoln.

Eleanor, her mind consumed with her upcoming wedding, later admitted, "I have no recollection of what he said!" Afterward, there were lunch at the White House and the inaugural parade, which was the largest of its kind, with thousands participating, including six Indian chiefs, mounted on horses and wearing elaborate headdresses.

On March 17, family and friends gathered in the spacious parlor of cousin Susie Parish's house on East 76th Street in New York City for the wedding. It was an event of some note, not the least because of the presence of the president. Eleanor looked luminous in her gown, described in the society pages as a "white satin princess robe, flounced and draped with old point lace, and with a white satin train. The bride's point lace veil was caught with orange blossoms and a diamond crescent." The article also mentioned that Eleanor wore a pearl collar, which was a gift from Sara.

Crowds gathered on the street outside, hoping to catch a glimpse of the president. His presence overwhelmed the event, and as the couple was exchanging vows, the solemnity of the ceremony was interrupted by the loud sounds of the parade down Fifth Avenue, the mob singing "The Wearing of the Green." Reverend Endicott Peabody presided, and the president handed over his niece with a wide grin. After the ceremony, he kissed Eleanor and beamed at Franklin. "Well, Franklin," he said, "there's nothing like keeping the name in the family."

The president stole the show at the wedding, which was expected. As his irreverent daughter Alice once accurately described it, "My father always has to be the bride at every wedding, the corpse at every funeral, and the baby at every christening."

Franklin and Eleanor got a taste of that at their reception. As they took their places at the head of the receiving line, they were surprised to find themselves alone. Their guests were in the next room, crowding around the president and hanging on his every word. Decades later, Franklin would joke about it in a presidential radio address, speaking of his wedding day. "On that occasion, New York had two great attractions," he said, "the St. Patrick's Day Parade, and President Theodore Roosevelt, who had come from Washington to give the bride away. . . . I might add that it was wholly natural and logical that in the spotlight of these two simultaneous attractions, the bride and bridegroom were almost entirely overlooked . . ." An afterthought at their own wedding, in time they would have their moment in the spotlight.

Finally, the reception over, they headed for Grand Central Station and took the train to Hyde Park. Sara had given them free use of the house for the first week of their honeymoon. As their life together spread out before them, they had little premonition of the course their future would take, with full measures of opportunity, disappointment, tragedy, and power.

Their marriage was truly a meeting of the minds on the larger issues of the day, but it never achieved the intimacy that Eleanor longed for and Franklin was unable to give. Eleanor suffered from his lack of attention in the early years, as she entered a decade of constant pregnancy, delivering six children in all, under the controlling direction of her mother-in-law. Franklin had little patience for her complaints, which he regarded as women's business. Eleanor despaired over her inadequacies as a wife and mother, while Franklin launched a political career that would be his true passion. Their children, raised mostly by Sara, would suffer from that lack of attention and later have trouble in their own lives and marriages. Yet although neither Franklin nor Eleanor came naturally to the role of spouse or parent, they would find ways to become indispensable to each other through the great and compelling forces of the era in which they lived.

CHAPTER 2

INTO THE ARENA

Watching her husband on the political stump for the first time, Eleanor Roosevelt saw him as a high-strung, nervous speaker, given to long pauses that left her breathless with worry that there wouldn't be a next word. Time would smooth out his rough edges, but in any case, the voters in upstate New York were willing to give him some leeway. He was, after all, a *Roosevelt*.

Roosevelt's decision to run for the state senate in 1910 had come after three years' suffering in the practice of law with the New York City firm of Carter, Ledyard & Milburn. Like his father, James, before him, Franklin hated the legal grind. And increasingly, he felt the call of public service. He had been inspired by the forceful presidency of his cousin, whose second term had ended in 1909. And perhaps he'd listened to Theodore's powerful words in 1910, when he had spoken to an audience in Paris about the demands of citizenship:

> The credit belongs to the man who is actually in the arena, whose face is marred by dust and sweat and blood; who strives valiantly; who errs, who comes short again and again, because there is no effort without error and shortcoming; but who does actually strive to do the

deeds; who knows great enthusiasms, the great devotions; who spends himself in a worthy cause; who at the best knows in the end the triumph of high achievement, and who at the worst, if he fails, at least fails while daring greatly, so that his place shall never be with those cold and timid souls who neither know victory nor defeat.

Theodore Roosevelt's charge—"daring greatly"—resonated then and has continued to inspire generations even to this day. In 1910, Franklin Roosevelt thrilled to the challenge, and in his heart he felt an obligation to do so. When John Mack, the Dutchess County district attorney, asked him to run for the Poughkeepsie state assembly seat being vacated by a sitting Democrat, Franklin thought it was the perfect place to start a political career. However, the assemblyman decided not to retire, and Roosevelt was faced with a more difficult challenge. The state senate seat representing three counties—Dutchess, Putnam, and Columbia, stacked along the Hudson River—was also open, but it had always been a Republican stronghold. Any Democratic candidate would probably be a sacrificial lamb, with little hope of victory. Roosevelt stepped in, but to the dismay of party leaders, he wasn't the slavish loyalist they had been looking for. At the nominating convention, he made his stance clear: "I accept this nomination with absolute independence," he proclaimed. "I am pledged to no man; I am influenced by no special interests, and so I shall remain."

At twenty-eight, Roosevelt lacked Teddy's fire and his unrestrained passion, and he had yet to find his voice (either literally or figuratively), but he had a charm of his own. Despite their party differences, the refrains of their campaigns sounded very similar. TR and FDR, as their names were abbreviated, spoke the same language on many issues they cared about. TR was delighted that his cousin was entering politics and never spoke a word against him. FDR would make the centerpiece of his first campaign and his early political life an issue TR had also cared about: the threat of special interests and "bossism" to electoral integrity. In FDR's case, the enemy was Tammany Hall, the Democratic political machine. Named after the long-standing fraternal organization the Tammany Society of New York City, its influence had spread throughout the state, strengthening the control of party bosses and creating a swamp of electoral corruption.

With only a month to make his case, FDR campaigned tirelessly, driving through the farmlands in an open-topped red Maxwell touring car, a nod to his wealth that normally might have turned off the farmers but instead had the opposite effect. Here was a young, modern man, tall, slender, and handsome. And although he could be an awkward campaigner, he won people over with his self-deprecating humor. "I'm not Teddy," he told his audiences. "A little shaver [chap] said to me the other day that he knew I wasn't Teddy. I asked him why and he replied, 'Because you don't show your teeth.'"

That first campaign experience sparked something new in FDR. Touring the back roads through the villages and farmlands of upstate New York, places he'd rarely noticed and never before visited, he stopped to speak whenever he spotted a gathering of even a few people. He was so energized by the campaign that his enthusiasm could get the better of him. On one occasion, he accidentally spent a few hours campaigning across the state line in Connecticut, only later realizing that he'd been speaking to people who couldn't vote for him.

Dismissing his opponent, Senator John F. Schlosser of Fishkill Landing, a well-known lawyer and staunch Republican, he told his audiences, "I do not know who Senator Schlosser represents, . . . But I do know that he has not represented me, and I do know that he has not represented hundreds of Republicans & Independents throughout the District."

He continued to press the issue of corruption in politics. "What the voters have got to do is to clean their house this year," he said in an October 21 speech. "They are going to discharge the unfaithful servant, and they are going to put in a new servant who stands for cleanliness, honesty and economy, and the people of the state are going to get a clean house, a house of which they will be proud."

As FDR returned to Hyde Park the night before the election, his thoughts turned to his father. He hoped he'd make him proud. Speaking to a crowd that was gathered there, he said emotionally, "You have known what my father stood for before me, you have known how close he was to the life of this town, and I do not need to tell you that it is my desire always to follow in his footsteps."

To the shock of the establishment, FDR won his previously Republican district and was elected with a relatively comfortable margin: 15,708 to 14,568. He benefited from a Democratic midterm wave across the nation and in New York State. But the chief credit for his victory was his own relentless campaign; he might not have shaken *every* constituent's hand, but he had certainly tried. Especially notable was his success in the Republican rural areas.

Once elected, Roosevelt moved his family to Albany, the state capital, an unusual thing to do because the legislature met for less than three months a year. They rented a large furnished house that cost three times his annual salary of $1,500. With an instinct for the grand gesture, he wanted his constituents to see him hard at work for them every day of the year. And with his mother's financial support, he could afford to do it.

For Eleanor, the move freed her from her cloistered life in a house controlled mostly by Sara. The early years of her marriage had been consumed by childbirth—Anna in 1906, James in 1907, Franklin, Jr., in 1909, and Elliott, born weeks before the election in 1910. Furthermore, there had been a great loss the previous year, when Franklin, Jr., had died in infancy, a tragedy Eleanor blamed on herself. "I felt . . . in some way I must be to blame," she wrote. "I even felt that I had not cared enough about him." Through it all she was very much in the shadow of her mother-in-law, whose take-charge mastery of her family's life left her feeling inadequate and unheard.

Now, for the first time, she would have a home of her own and, better than that, a purpose. Although she dutifully wrote to Sara every day, she was feeling a new self-awareness. "I wanted to be independent," she wrote in her memoir about that period. "I was beginning to realize that something within me craved to be an individual."

In the senate, FDR didn't waste any time making his mark. He was generally viewed with suspicion and disdain by the old guard. *The Roosevelts*, people groused, were a family of elitist troublemakers. They couldn't be contained. The Republicans in Albany had battled Teddy's assault on the party elders. Now the Democrats had Franklin to contend with. Those who'd hoped he'd sit quietly until he learned the ropes were disappointed. The first controversy involved the appointment of a US senator. In those days, senators were elected by state legislatures, and since the Democrats had control in Albany, they could choose a Democrat. (The system would change in 1913, when the Seventeenth Amendment, calling for the popular election of US senators, was enshrined in the Constitution.) The party's choice was William F. Sheehan, known as "Blue-Eyed Billy," a politician of solid connections and suspect wealth who was comfortably in the pocket of Tammany Hall. A group of insurgent Democrats objected, and FDR joined their midst. He felt it was his duty, as a representative of upstate New York, to reject the influence of New York City and Tammany Hall. It was a brutal battle, but FDR cheerfully told a *New York Times* reporter, "There is nothing I love as much as a good fight. I never had as much fun in my life as I am having right now." The insurgency won. When the senate pulled Sheehan out of the running and chose a different candidate, FDR claimed a moral victory, even though the replacement was equally tied to special interests.

The party struck back. Democrats complained that FDR was an elitist, a snob, an interloper. Pundits wondered if the young Roosevelt had shot himself in the foot with the party. With less than two years until the next election, he'd better watch his back.

Enter the man determined to be FDR's kingmaker.

Newspaperman Louis McHenry Howe was at first sight a very odd character. He was a wispy little man with a rough exterior, a high, gnomelike forehead, and protruding teeth that led some critics to call him "ghoulish." A careless chain smoker, with cigarette ash cascading in grimy waves onto his clothing, he presented an unappetizing picture. But having freelanced for the *New York Herald* for many years, he knew politics, and he latched on to the young senator early on. Born about a decade before FDR to a wealthy Indianapolis family, Howe was drawn to FDR from the start. In a private interview with the senator, he listened with great interest as FDR talked enthusiastically about the problem of "bossism" in the political system.

Howe later said of that interview, "I was so impressed with Franklin Roosevelt . . . almost at that very first meeting. I made up my mind that he was Presidential timber and that nothing but an accident could keep him from becoming President of the United States."

Howe thought that FDR had potential but was green. From then on he insinuated himself into FDR's circle, teaching him the finer points of political action, showing him how to stand his ground while using caution. In the coming years, he would be by FDR's side as his fixer, whisperer, and strategist. At that early point, though, FDR was naive, unformed. His chief ideas were borrowed from his cousin. He had yet to establish a firm set of ideals, except the general sense that he wanted to be a fair representative to his constituents. He was meeting regular, unprivileged people for the first time in his life, and if he had a gift it was that he was a good listener. He was sincerely interested in hearing what they had to say. He wanted to learn. His constituents sensed his sincerity and responded to his high-spirited enjoyment of the process.

FDR loved the political whirlwind, the heated debates, and the exchange of ideas. He often brought colleagues and political friends home, where they spent long evenings in the library among billowing clouds of cigar and cigarette smoke, which rose up through the ceiling. At times the smoke grew so thick that Eleanor was forced to move her sleeping children to a higher floor so they would not breathe the noxious fumes.

He was finding his path, thinking about issues in a new way, and becoming progressive, even as Eleanor held back. Her reticence to embrace prowomen issues of the day would be a shock to those who later viewed her as a feminist icon. Neither she nor Sara believed that women had a right to vote, but when FDR announced his support for the suffrage movement, Eleanor went along. "I realized that if my husband was a suffragist, I probably must be, too," she wrote.

FDR ran for reelection in 1912, which was also a presiden-

tial election year. TR, itching to get back into the game, decided
to run for the Republican nomination against the sitting president, William Howard Taft. TR had all but ushered Taft into
office, but now he was disillusioned by Taft's failure to advance
a reform agenda. TR did well in the primaries, and the night
before the convention he delivered a fiery speech. "With unflinching hearts and undimmed eyes, we stand at Armageddon
and we battle for the Lord," he cried. He earned wild cheers
from the crowd, but he lost the nomination.

With the race set between Taft and Democrat Woodrow
Wilson, the scholarly and restrained governor of New Jersey
and former president of Princeton University, TR decided he
could not let it stand. He launched an independent candidacy.
"I'm as strong as a bull moose," he had once declared about
himself, and his Progressive Party became known as the Bull
Moose Party.

In Albany, there was dissent in the Roosevelt household
about the election. FDR had openly joined Wilson's campaign,
while Eleanor privately wished that circumstances would allow
him to get behind Uncle Ted. That could not be, of course. It was
the first time two Roosevelts were positioned against each other
in an important election. Despite Eleanor's hand-wringing, neither man begrudged the other his necessary loyalty.

TR continued his quixotic mission. Drama followed him.
Campaigning in Milwaukee near the end of the election season,
he was shot in the chest in an assassination attempt by John
Flammang Schrank, a New York City saloon keeper. Schrank
wrote that he had seen a vision of the assassinated President
William McKinley in a dream—the dead president rising from
the grave to point a damning finger at TR. The bullet struck
TR's glasses case and a wad of speech papers in his vest before
entering his body. TR paused in his remarks. He did not col-

lapse to the ground or summon medical help. Instead, ever the showman, he softened his voice and told the shocked crowd:

> Friends, I shall ask you to be as quiet as possible. I don't know whether you fully understand that I have just been shot—but it takes more than that to kill a Bull Moose. But fortunately, I had my manuscript, so you see I was going to make a long speech, and there is a bullet [pointing to his chest]—there is where the bullet went through—and it probably saved me from it going into my heart. The bullet is in me now, so that I cannot make a very long speech, but I will try my best.

He continued to speak for ninety minutes before agreeing to be treated. He recovered from his injury, but Schrank's bullet would remain lodged in his chest for the rest of his life. It was a striking, heroic moment, but would it help his candidacy?

In New York, FDR also confronted a terrible election dilemma when he and Eleanor contracted typhoid six weeks before the election. Unable to leave his bed, FDR called on Howe, who was currently unemployed, to take over. Howe made the rounds in FDR's red Maxwell and also relied on mass mailings to targeted groups and bold newspaper ads, which were effective. Howe had never run a political campaign before, but he used his instincts. As he later wrote, "It was in what many campaign managers dismiss carelessly as 'the sticks' that I concentrated my efforts. I stayed out of such centres as Poughkeepsie and Beacon, where the opposition was strongly entrenched. But I worked the rural districts night and day." His effort succeeded. FDR easily won reelection.

The news from Oyster Bay wasn't so good. TR's brave handling of the assassination attempt won him praise, but his campaign never gained traction. Americans rarely go backward to recapture the past, and TR's reign was clearly over. It was a new era, and the populace favored the cautious, seemingly morally upright Wilson, who would not give them constant heart palpitations. TR's third-party candidacy split the Republican vote, ensuring Wilson's election. Many Republicans were angry at TR, calling him a spoiler. Rather than winning their love and gratitude, he had earned their contempt. Stunned by his loss and the anger of his fellow Republicans, he sunk into despair and remained secluded at Oyster Bay. It took time for him to regain his optimism and stamina, but when he did, he chose a dramatic return—outside the realm of politics. In late 1913, he embarked upon an expedition to the Amazon rain forest that fell just short of a suicidal mission. He nearly died of malaria and a severe infection and barely made it home alive. But when he returned, looking frail and sickly, he flashed his familiar toothy grin and the crowds in New York responded with love.

When it came to selecting his cabinet, Wilson made two particularly notable choices. The first, for secretary of state, was William Jennings Bryan, a die-hard pacifist whose views about US neutrality in the world matched Wilson's. The second, for secretary of the navy, was Josephus Daniels, a newspaper editor and campaign supporter, who had little knowledge of the navy or the sea. That was the arena that FDR soon joined. When he and Eleanor attended Wilson's inauguration in Washington, Daniels pulled FDR aside. "Would you like to come to Washington as assistant secretary?" Daniels asked him.

"I'd like it bully well," FDR replied with a grin.

FDR LOVED HIS NEW role—the pomp and ceremony, the camaraderie, and most of all, the big ships and the bracing wind of the sea air. "I now find my vocation combined with my avocation," he wrote to a friend. He also relished having a role that was truly important. With 65,000 men, both navy and civilian, under his direction, and a budget of $150 million, he thought he could make a difference in ensuring the United States' military strength. From Oyster Bay, TR praised him: "I was very pleased to hear you were appointed assistant secretary of the navy. It is interesting to see that you are at another place which I myself once held. I know you will enjoy yourself to the full as assistant secretary and you will do capital work."

But it was a steep learning curve, as FDR had never been in the military. "I am baptized, confirmed, sworn in, vaccinated—and somewhat at sea," he confessed to Sara. He had brought Howe along as his assistant to aid that effort, but Howe, too, knew nothing about the navy. They were a team of amateurs.

In Washington, where the family was renting TR's sister Bamie's house, Eleanor found herself swept into the wives' circle of social obligation. Her life revolved around a daily series of house calls: Mondays, the wives of Supreme Court justices; Tuesdays, the wives of congressmen; Wednesdays, at home receiving visitors; Thursdays, the wives of senators; and Friday, the wives of diplomats. Her son James, who was sometimes asked to accompany her, recalled how her "painful shyness weighed heavily on her in those days," and the visits were very difficult. "How well I remember the ritual, for, as I grew older, Mother would make me dress in my blue suit and long black stockings and go along to deposit her calling cards at the homes where she didn't have to pay a formal visit," he wrote. "I was as reluctant as Mother about knocking on those strange doors but I could not talk her out of pressing me into service as her footman. I felt greatly imposed upon!"

It didn't come naturally to her, but Eleanor grew in the role, to the point where she didn't slow down when she found herself pregnant for the fifth time. Instead, she hired a secretary, a lovely, soft-spoken, well-educated young woman named Lucy Mercer.

Eleanor was not enamored of grand ships the way her husband was. She was a reluctant visitor to battleships and cruisers—afraid she would embarrass her husband by getting seasick—but the children loved the excursions, and FDR was bursting with pride and delight to show off his domain. Once he made a particularly dramatic gesture when he was concerned about his children's vulnerability to a polio epidemic. He convinced Daniels to let him take a destroyer to Campobello to bring them home to Washington.

With that job, FDR was more often at home with his family in Washington, and the children adored him. They especially cherished the times they were at play with him, and perhaps he had occasion to recall during those years the wonderful romps he'd engaged in with his own father. He was gentle with his "chicks," a lousy disciplinarian and a total failure at punishments. That task was consigned to Mother, who didn't like being a disciplinarian, either, but was forced into the role. James recounted one occasion when the rebellious little Elliott did something so egregious that it warranted his father's attention. Elliott, full of fear, was taken by his mother to FDR's study. FDR sat him on his knee, put his arm around him, and proceeded to chat gently with him about a variety of things, never mentioning his transgression.

"In half an hour Mother came back and said, 'Is everything settled?'

"Father replied, 'Everything is settled.'"

Sunday mornings would usually find FDR on the golf course, while Eleanor took the children to church. He had become obsessed with the sport and was known to play as many as thirty-six and even fifty-four holes of golf at once, perfecting his powerful long drive. Eleanor had once tried to learn the game on vacation at Campobello, thinking it would be nice to play with her husband. As she hacked at the grass, FDR had suggested she might prefer another sport.

Life seemed satisfying and filled with opportunity during that period—especially if you were privileged enough to have access to travel and other luxuries, as the Roosevelts were. FDR's job with the navy was serious business, of course, but he wasn't burdened by the conflicts afflicting Europe and the Far East.

The situation was tumultuous. Rapid expansion of imperial nations had created a mammoth stalemate and a growing unrest among their colonial possessions. To further strengthen their hand, these empires had created alliances, pledging to support one another in the event of war. The alliances included France and Russia; Russia and Serbia; Germany, Italy, and Austria-Hungary; Great Britain, France, and Belgium; Great Britain, France, and Russia; and Great Britain and Japan. The United States was not involved in those imperial power structures, and most people dismissed them as Old World disputes that had little to do with the United States.

The power equation was unsustainable without conflict erupting. War was "structurally unavoidable," former secretary of state Henry Kissinger said in a Reuters panel discussion on the causes of World War I, "because these countries were tied together with a system of alliances and their war plans depended on mobilization schedules . . . any trivial event, as long as it could trigger an alliance, was likely to produce a general war." And that's what happened.

The spark that lit a global war was the result of Serbian

dissent over the colonial rule of Austria-Hungary and the Ottoman Empire. On June 28, 1914, Archduke Franz Ferdinand of Austria was assassinated in Sarajevo while inspecting territories in Bosnia and Herzegovina. That led Austria to declare war on Serbia, with the support of Germany. Russia countered in defense of Serbia, and the war was on.

Within a month, the alliances were in force, with Germany declaring war on France and Belgium; Austria on Russia and Belgium; France and Great Britain on Austria; and Japan on Germany. Ultimately the war was configured into two forces: the Central Powers, which included Germany, Austria-Hungary, the Ottoman Empire, and Bulgaria; and the Allied Powers, which included France, the British Empire, Italy, Russia, and Japan.

FDR was among those who believed the United States should add its might to the fight against Germany and the Central Powers, but Wilson was disinclined to act. "The United States must be neutral in fact as well as in name during these days that are to try men's souls," he declared.

FDR was dismayed by the government's decision to stay neutral. He began to question his role, wondering if he could have any effect on the nation's course. There was an open seat for the US Senate in New York, and he decided to make a run—while not resigning from his position as assistant secretary of the navy. He was wise to keep his day job, for he was swiftly defeated in the primary.

As the war went on, with the Allied Powers suffering significant defeats, FDR was eager to improve the United States' naval readiness. He was a voice in the wilderness, his concerns largely dismissed by Wilson and Bryan, who thought the military should shrink, and by Daniels, who followed Wilson's lead without dissent. FDR was distraught to see the United States sitting on the sidelines during the Great War.

The folly of that stand became clear in 1915, when the Germans announced restrictions in the seas around Great Britain, stating that any ship caught in those waters would be torpedoed, even if it was a passenger or commercial ship from the neutral United States. Several small commercial transports were attacked, but the Wilson administration refused to take any action. Bryan said that if US companies wanted to take the risk, it was up to them to suffer the consequences. But the severity of the situation hit home on May 7. A British Cunard ocean liner, the RMS *Lusitania*, the largest ship in the world, was traveling from New York to Liverpool with 1,959 passengers and crew when it was torpedoed near the coast of Ireland. It took only twenty minutes for the ship to sink, killing 1,198 people, including 128 American citizens. The Germans claimed that the ocean liner had been secretly carrying munitions under the veil of being a passenger ship. Americans were appalled, and calls for the United States to enter the war grew louder.

Bryan was not persuaded. Instead, he blamed the British for an incendiary action that had resulted in American deaths and reached out to the Germans to settle the matter diplomatically. Wilson strongly disagreed with that position and overruled Bryan, calling on the Germans to cease military actions against commercial ships on the high seas. Bryan was so distraught about Wilson's message, which he thought broke his pledge of neutrality, that he resigned as secretary of state.

After the sinking of the *Lusitania*, American public opinion began to lean toward joining the war, and FDR was hopeful that Wilson was paying heed. He felt demoralized when Wilson campaigned for reelection with the slogan "He kept us out of war." From Oyster Bay, TR decried "the lily-livered skunk" in the White House.

Wilson won reelection by a narrow margin, but as he took

office for a second term, war was in the air. Two weeks after the inauguration, the Germans torpedoed three US merchant ships, and it finally seemed to be enough. "My God, why doesn't he do something?" howled TR from the sidelines, referring to Wilson. "If he does not go to war with Germany I shall skin him alive!"

On April 2, Wilson called together a joint session of Congress to make his declaration of war. FDR sat in a front row to hear it, and even Eleanor attended, watching from the gallery. Wilson's speech to Congress was workmanlike; he had written it in a day's time without the help of a speechwriter. He had come at last to a solemn conclusion:

> Armed neutrality is ineffectual enough at best; in such circumstances and in the face of such pretensions it is worse than ineffectual; it is likely only to produce what it was meant to prevent; it is practically certain to draw us into the war without either the rights or the effectiveness of belligerents. There is one choice we cannot make, we are incapable of making: we will not choose the path of submission and suffer the most sacred rights of our nation and our people to be ignored or violated. The wrongs against which we now array ourselves are no common wrongs; they cut to the very roots of human life.

FDR wanted to enlist in the service and go to the front, and TR, whose sons were all joining up, was egging him on. In TR's view, the definition of service was to join the war as a fighter. But it was not to be. FDR was told that his service with the navy was too important to the war effort.

After war was declared, TR went to Washington, DC, to

speak with the president. At fifty-nine, he was intent on impressing upon everyone that he was fit and vigorous. His proposal was rash: he had organized a group of experienced officers who were willing to serve under him at the front, a plan reminiscent of the "Rough Riders" regiment he had led in Cuba during the Spanish-American War. Neither the White House nor the War Department had much use for TR's scheme, which they viewed as not only ludicrous but a relic of a different era. This was a world war, with all the organizational complexity and military discipline that demanded.

When FDR and Eleanor visited TR after his White House meeting, they found him boiling about his reception and itching to serve. They sympathized and were gentle with him, and FDR promised to put in a good word for him, but FDR, who was responsible for the vast bureaucracy of a navy now at war, recognized that his cousin's days of physical service were over. He could not help noticing that his cousin was beset by the physical afflictions of a hard-lived life. He was blind in one eye and partly deaf, and he lacked the physical stamina of his youth.

FDR's primary job during the war was to oversee tens of thousands of civilian employees, including the difficult task of dealing with entrenched labor unions. He and Eleanor found their lives increasingly running on separate tracks. Eleanor, too, felt the call to service, and she now thought she had the freedom to engage. Her fifth child, also named Franklin, Jr., after his deceased brother, had been born in 1914, and her sixth and final child, John, in 1916. "For ten years I was always just getting over having a baby or about to have one," she said, "and so my occupations were considerably restricted . . ." Now she had an opportunity to do more. She became a volunteer for the Red Cross, working long days into the night with Lucy Mercer by her side, organizing canteens that would serve free hot meals to soldiers on their way to the front, and visiting the war wounded, whose terrible injuries and haunted eyes had a profound effect on her.

FDR, whose all-consuming duties lacked glamour and proximity to the war, gazed across the pond with some admiration for Daniels's British counterpart, a man named Winston Churchill, who was first lord of the Admiralty, with responsibility for the British navy. Though the two men met in passing, Churchill took little notice of FDR, who would one day be his closest ally and friend during a second great war.

Eager to see the action firsthand, FDR visited the front lines in France during the summer of 1918. He sailed aboard the destroyer USS *Dyer* and on the way started a diary, which he filled with eloquent prose:

> The good old ocean is so absolutely normal just as it always has been, sometimes tumbling about and throwing spray . . . sometimes gently lolling about . . . But now though the Ocean looks much unchanged the doubled number of lookouts shows that even here the hand of the Hun False God is reaching out to defy nature; that ten miles ahead of this floating City of Souls a torpedo may be waiting to start on its quick run . . .

While FDR was at sea, TR's youngest son, Quentin, serving with the army air service's 95th Aero Squadron, was shot down over France. The Germans, who were shocked to learn they'd killed President Theodore Roosevelt's son, buried him with military honors and erected a cross inscribed "Lieutenant Roosevelt, Buried by the Germans." Two of TR's other sons, Archibald and Theodore, Jr., were in France recovering from war wounds. FDR was frustrated that he was not in uniform while those brave Roosevelts were so courageously going into battle.

In France, FDR had an opportunity to visit the front lines. He toured the battlefields at Château-Thierry, Belleau Wood, and Verdun, where brutal battles had occurred, with many casualties. FDR captured his experience in a log he kept during the trip, writing of "discarded overcoats, rain-stained love letters ... and many little mounds, some wholly unmarked, some with a rifle stuck, bayonet down, in the earth, some with a helmet, and some too with a whittled cross with a tag of wood or wrapping paper hung over it and in a pencil scrawl an American name."

The devastation made a deep impression on him. Decades later, in 1936, while campaigning for his second term as president, he recalled his visit to the fields of conflict while vowing to keep the United States out of another European war. He had not *seen* war, but he had seen its aftermath:

> I have seen war. I have seen war on land and sea. I have seen blood running from the wounded. I have seen men coughing out their gassed lungs. I have seen the dead in the mud. I have seen cities destroyed. I have seen two hundred limping, exhausted men come out of line— the survivors of a regiment of one thousand that went forward forty-eight hours before. I have seen children starving. I have seen the agony of mothers and wives. I hate war.

Returning by sea from his grueling trip, FDR fell ill with double pneumonia, his chronically weak constitution getting the better of him. When he arrived, he had to be carried off the ship on a stretcher. Eleanor took him home and tucked him into bed while she began unpacking his luggage. There she found a bundle of love letters from Lucy Mercer, her assistant. Eleanor was crushed. She would later tell a friend that the bottom had dropped out of her world. It was the greatest shock and blow she had experienced in her marriage. She had never suspected the affair, although it wasn't a total secret to others. TR's daughter Alice Roosevelt Longworth, for one, had seen the couple out in Washington and had even invited them to dine when Eleanor was at Campobello with the children.

"So what *did* take place on those summer evenings in that open car, under the silvery moon, on the back roads of Virginia?" their biographer Hazel Rowley asked in *Franklin and Eleanor: An Extraordinary Marriage.* In other words, did FDR and Lucy Mercer have a full-fledged sexual affair? The final truth went with them to their graves.

Eleanor was aware that her handsome husband was flirtatious and adored by women around town. In truth, she had always harbored a fear in her heart that she was no match for her husband and was soothed only by his vow of fidelity, which she had trusted in spite of her insecurities. Now that he had broken that vow, how could their marriage continue? Stoically, she offered to divorce FDR. She also confided in Sara, who was disgusted with her son and outraged on Eleanor's behalf.

It is unknown whether FDR seriously considered the idea of divorce, but in the end, it was a nonstarter. Sara threatened to cut him off from funds, and Howe warned him that a divorce would end his political career. Besides, FDR loved his family, in spite of straying from his marriage. He did not want to leave them. Was there love between him and Eleanor? Although Eleanor addressed her letters to him "Dearest Honey," and he affectionately called her "Babs," and while away would write, "I long so to be with you," their relationship was not particularly romantic at that point. It was, however, devoted. He might have fallen in love with Lucy Mercer, but his love for his wife existed on a different plane. He could not see himself living without her. So he made amends as best he could and vowed never to see Lucy again—a promise he didn't fully keep.

Eleanor would never get over it. There was no mention of the affair in her memoirs, but she confided her deep misery to those closest to her. Her sense of betrayal was high, and she never accepted even the smallest responsibility for the conditions that had led her husband to stray.

As FDR recovered from his illness and he and Eleanor struggled to recover from the damage to their marriage, they were uplifted by the declaration of armistice on November 11. By early October, acknowledging defeat, Germany had asked the Allies to begin armistice talks. In the end, Germany was forced to accept harsh conditions, including giving up its arsenal and some territories and paying $37 billion in reparations. Those humiliating and devastating conditions fueled a burning rage among the German people that would grow into a movement to restore German greatness—the origins of Nazism.

Trying his best to restore his relationship with Eleanor and recapture their closeness, FDR invited her to join him on a voyage to Europe, where he had postwar naval business. FDR and Eleanor set sail for Europe aboard the USS *George Washington*. On their way, they received word that Theodore Roosevelt had died suddenly in his sleep at Oyster Bay. The cause was a blood clot, a silent thief in the night that had stolen his life. He was sixty years old.

The *New York Times* reported that five airplanes from Quentin Roosevelt Field, a Long Island airport named in tribute to TR's dead son, had flown in a V formation over the Roosevelt home, dropping wreaths of laurel in the yard around the house.

One could say that TR had achieved everything in his life a man could hope for. He was the very model of what he called "the strenuous life," the great ideal he practiced and preached—the choice to be in the arena, the understanding that "our country calls not for the life of ease but for the life of strenuous endeavor." That was TR's lasting legacy: he fully embraced the great adventure of the American dream.

"OH! DEAR, I WISH I could see you or at least hear from you. I hate politics!" In June 1920, when she wrote that, Eleanor was at Campobello with the children while FDR was far away and out of touch in San Francisco, where he was attending the Democratic National Convention. If she had been hoping that their lives might be headed in a calmer direction, she was mistaken. Unbeknown to her, FDR's name had been placed in nomination for vice president on the ticket of James M. Cox, the governor of Ohio.

The Democratic platform was one FDR could get behind, progressive and international, approving Wilson's signature idea of the League of Nations and also supporting women's suffrage. Earlier that month, the Nineteenth Amendment, giving women the right to vote, had been passed by Congress, and it would go on to be ratified on August 18. In the November election, eight million women would cast votes.

FDR's nomination wasn't accidental or surprising. He'd been quietly campaigning for months, building support in the party. But his impressive performance at the convention sealed the deal. The delegates responded to the self-assured young man who rose to give a speech seconding the nomination of New York governor Al Smith. Cox noticed as well, and when he finally secured the nomination on the forty-fourth ballot, he told his advisers that his choice for vice president was Franklin Roosevelt. "His name is good, he's right geographically, and he's anti-Tammany." There were seven other contenders, but they quickly fell into line behind Cox's choice. FDR was elated to be on the ticket, and he resigned his job with the navy to embark on a presidential campaign.

FDR's boss, Josephus Daniels, wrote him after the nomination, "I always counted on your zeal, your enthusiasm, your devoted patriotism and efficient and able service, and always found you equal to the big job in hand. My thought and feeling has been that of an older brother . . . and I shall always rejoice in your successes and victories . . ."

In Chicago, Republican delegates nominated Ohio senator Warren Harding, who vowed to campaign against Wilson's League of Nations and for a return to normalcy. Likable and experienced in government, he argued that the nation was weary of progressives such as TR and Wilson and needed a chance to recover from twenty years of upheaval. His vice presidential nominee, Massachusetts governor Calvin Coolidge, echoed the message. Theirs would be a calm campaign, which Harding would wage largely from his front porch in Marion, Ohio. But he had a not-so-secret weapon—the services of a prominent adman, Albert Lasker, who developed the first real advertising-based presidential campaign. The slogans poured out in searing, persuasive prose, declaring "America first" and "Independence means independence, now as in 1776." They appealed to a war-weary populace with the seductive notion that the United States didn't have to be a leader on the global stage to be a great nation.

One ad referred to Cox as "wiggle and wobble," a label that brought cheers and laughs. On the stump, FDR tried to joke about the advertising campaigns, citing huge and costly billboards with the slogan on full display. He declared that the "wiggle and wobble moniker" could well apply to Harding himself. But it was a half-hearted comeback.

Reluctant but dutiful, Eleanor was enlisted in the campaign under the tutelage of Howe. On a four-week train trip west, she was the only woman on board, and she had to contend with the rowdy newspapermen. She'd never had much to do with the press, and she was wary of them, fearing they'd push her to say the wrong thing. But on that arduous trip, full of long rides and multiple speeches each day, her resistance fell away and they became companionable. She described how the newsmen would stand at the back of the hall while FDR gave the same speech for the umpteenth time, making faces at her to try to break her feigned attentiveness.

Many people were put off by FDR's self-satisfied performance on the stump. He seemed to think too much of himself, and he misread the public mood as he sang the praises of the outgoing Wilson and spoke glowingly of the promise of international collaboration. Indeed, the president was missing in action during the campaign. In the fall of 1919, Wilson had suffered a massive stroke that had left him bedridden, partially paralyzed, and mentally confused. His wife, Edith, kept him shut up in the White House and carefully monitored his contact with aides. As word reached Capitol Hill that the president might be too incapacitated to serve, there was discussion about what action to take. Vice President Thomas R. Marshall was unwilling to make a move, fearing it would look opportunistic, and there was little Congress could do, absent Wilson's resignation. That was almost fifty years before the Twenty-fifth Amendment was ratified, establishing a constitutional process for transferring power if a president is unable to serve.

Unknown at the time, Edith essentially assumed the presidency for the remainder of her husband's term. It was a massive deception. She called it "stewardship," but it was more than that. Under the radar, she had become the first woman president, as her husband clung to power. Here was another presidential leader, like TR, who simply could not let go of his place in the sun, even when he had ceased to shine. (Notably, when Dwight Eisenhower suffered a heart attack and a small stroke during his presidency, he ordered his press secretary to tell the American people the truth about his condition, not wanting to repeat Wilson's shameful charade.)

On election day, Harding won the White House with the largest popular-vote margin ever recorded. Back home in Hyde Park, FDR was left to contemplate what the defeat meant for his political future. He felt adrift—on the one hand, determined to stand as the loyal opposition; on the other, not certain what his role could be. He was as committed as ever to building a new and stronger Democratic Party—but how?

By his side was an unusual cadre of men who had supported him during the campaign. They included Louis Howe; the journalist Stephen Early, who had met FDR during his 1912 campaign; Marvin McIntyre and Renah F. Camalier, who had served with him when he was assistant secretary of the navy; Charles H. McCarthy, his New York campaign manager; Thomas Lynch, a Poughkeepsie politician and friend; and reporters Kirke L. Simpson and Stanley Prenosil. After the defeat, he gathered them together and presented each of them with a set of cuff links, one with FDR's initials and one with the person's initials. From then on, they became known as the Cuff Links Gang and would meet yearly for elaborate themed parties around the time of Roosevelt's birthday. Some of them would also play significant roles in his future administrations.

FDR's political life thus far had been seamless as he checked the boxes: election to state government, serving in the administration, a place on a national ticket. There was a sense of inevitability to his rise, but it lacked substance. It had height but not depth. Everyone talked about his family connections, his attractive personal qualities, his hard work, but few could identify his compelling reason for being in the arena. He was thoughtful but not driven, political but not particularly idealistic—always running to catch the next wave of public opinion. To that point there had never been a moment in his life when he'd felt true jeopardy or personal crisis. His mother had built him a pedestal at birth, and he'd stood atop it for thirty-nine years, tall and confident, beating back every challenge.

Then, in an instant, he toppled. FDR was a man accustomed to asserting a cool control over his life and ambitions, and what happened was one thing he could not govern: the crippling, irreversible invasion of poliomyelitis.

CHAPTER 3

THE CRUCIBLE

Franklin Roosevelt was exhausted. He had been working hard in the months since the election. On hiatus from politics, he took a prestigious job as vice president of the New York office of the Fidelity and Deposit Company of Maryland, while working part-time practicing law. He also immersed himself in public works, such as the Boy Scouts and other philanthropic endeavors. He was laboring in the wings, preparing for his next political opportunity, which Howe, among others, thought might come in the 1922 election for US senator from New York.

During the summer of 1921, he'd been busy, including a special appearance at a Boy Scout gathering at Bear Mountain in upstate New York. By the time he joined his family at Campobello in August, he felt drained of energy and ready for a break. He assumed that a vigorous immersion in the outdoor life he loved was just the antidote he needed.

On August 10, he went sailing with Eleanor and his older children in the Bay of Fundy, aboard the little sailboat *Vireo*, which he had bought to teach his children to sail. As he was preparing tackle for fishing, he slipped overboard. The water was so cold "it seemed paralyzing," he would recall. It was a brief submersion, and he pulled himself back into the boat and continued on.

Later, he joined other volunteers to put out a small forest fire and went swimming with the kids. Afterward, they jogged back the two miles from the pond to the house. Normally, he loved those jogs from the swimming pond, but that day, something was off. He didn't feel "the glow I'd expected." When he reached the house the mail was in with several newspapers and he sat reading for a while, "too tired even to dress. I'd never felt quite that way before." Soon he announced that he was too tired to eat dinner and went straight to bed. He thought he might be coming down with a cold.

The next morning he woke with a high fever of 102 degrees Fahrenheit and an excruciating pain in the back of his legs. Eleanor called the local doctor, who examined him and said he had a bad summer cold. That was a credible explanation for Eleanor, who had often seen her husband plagued by colds. But his pain kept getting worse, and by the next day he was paralyzed from the waist down.

A second doctor was called in—a surgeon vacationing nearby who had once operated on President Grover Cleveland. He determined the problem to be a blood clot on FDR's lower spine, which he predicted would dissolve on its own in the coming months. He prescribed vigorous massage to help dissolve the clot.

Howe, who had come to Campobello when he heard of FDR's distress, did not entirely trust the doctor's judgment because he was a surgeon, not a diagnostician. Howe thought that FDR needed a proper diagnosis, and he reached out to FDR's uncle Franklin Delano, who consulted with a doctor in Washington. Based on a description of the symptoms alone, the doctor suggested poliomyelitis, an infectious disease attacking the central nervous system, that affected primarily children and was commonly known as infantile paralysis, though it could sometimes attack adults. He recommended that Delano speak with specialists at the Peter Bent Brigham Hospital in Boston. Doctors there recommended a spinal tap, and after some resistance on the part of the patient, the test was agreed to. Dr. Robert Lovett, a medical director of the Brigham Infantile Paralysis Clinic, came to Campobello to examine FDR. His observation and the results of the spinal tap confirmed the diagnosis of poliomyelitis.

The historian Geoffrey C. Ward, who himself was afflicted with polio at the age of nine and wears leg braces, provided an emotional reflection for the Ken Burns documentary *The Roosevelts* on what FDR might have been experiencing when he found himself paralyzed: "It produces terror, unreasoning terror. You just can't believe that the legs that you depended on simply do not work. . . . He was a great dancer, he was a great golfer, he loved to run. None of that would ever happen again."

But at first FDR didn't know that. Even with the devastating diagnosis, there was optimism. Dr. Lovett thought he didn't have the severest form of the disease, and there was every reason to believe that the paralysis was temporary. FDR wrote optimistically to Daniels, "I am sure you will be glad to learn that the doctors are most encouraging."

Sara was vacationing in Europe and wasn't notified of FDR's condition. When she returned, she did not find her son at the dock to greet her, as was customary. Instead she found Rosy, carrying a note from Eleanor: "Franklin has been quite ill and so can't go down to meet you on Tuesday to his great regret."

Eleanor defended her decision to keep the news from Sara until she returned, saying she hadn't wanted to cause her anxiety when she was too far away to do anything about it. But it's not hard to imagine that Eleanor was also determined to seize control while she still could.

Devastated by the news, Sara rushed to her son's side. She found him bedridden but hopeful that the trial would pass. The optimistic scenario never came to be. Although FDR regained the full use of his upper body, his legs remained paralyzed. Still he fought on. He believed he would walk again, and that single-minded goal had the effect of keeping his mind and spirit alert and focused on the future. That's not to say he didn't have times of depression and even despair, but he repeatedly rose above dark thoughts. "His reaction to any great event was always to be calm," Eleanor observed. "If it was something that was bad, he just became almost like an iceberg."

In September, the family returned to New York City, residing in the house on East 65th Street, where Roosevelt could be close to doctors. They could no longer keep the news private, and newspaper headlines about FDR's polio welcomed them home. Less than a year earlier, he had been a candidate for vice president. Now, though the press wasn't yet writing his political obituary, speculation ran high about whether the promising young man was at the end of his career.

While the nation at large was focused on what FDR's paralysis meant politically, at home there was a more fundamental reality to struggle with. In the early period, the terrified children were mostly kept away from their father, due to concerns that they might contract polio from him. They were told very little. At one point, fifteen-year-old Anna, the eldest, hid in a closet to overhear conversations between her parents and the doctor.

James, thirteen, was consumed with dread. "Just the month before he came to Campobello . . . this big, wonderful father of mine had taken me to see the Dempsey-Carpentier world's heavyweight championship fight in Jersey City," he recalled glumly, "and on the way out I got pulled away from him in the crowd and was scared to death until he found me. Would he ever, I wondered, take me anywhere again?"

When the danger of infection had passed, FDR was determined to ease his children's fears, to show them they had not lost their father. Whenever they entered his room, he made a supreme effort to laugh and joke with them, and he demanded that they tell him every detail of their lives.

That first autumn, James went off to Groton, dreading the further deterioration that would occur in his absence. When he went home for Christmas, he was expecting to see a wasted, bedridden cripple, a shadow of his father's former self. He entered his father's room and later wrote about what happened next:

> Pa read me like a book, and he worked a small miracle for me. He was propped up on pillows, and those trapezes and rings over his bed on which he already was exercising his upper body upset me a bit. Pa instantly made me forget it. His chin still stuck out and he was grinning and he stretched out his arms to me. "Come here, old man!" he said.

James rushed into his father's arms and discovered that the familiar powerful arms had not been wasted by the disease. He cried a little, but then within moments they were chatting merrily about Groton.

All the children received the same treatment, which included wrestling on the floor and general roughhousing. At the same time, FDR eased their worries by talking matter-of-factly about his condition and letting them see his legs.

At first Anna was shy with her father and obsessed with worry about his pain. But his genial nature and openness about his plight eased her fears.

. . . his own spirit was transmitted to all of us. He apparently knew it would be a shock for us to realize that the useless muscles in his legs would cause atrophy. . . . So Father removed the sadness by showing us his legs. He gave us the names of each of the muscles in them, then told us which ones he was working hardest on at that moment. He would shout with glee over a little movement of a muscle that had been dormant. So, gradually, I almost forgot that he had once had well-developed muscles. The battle Father was making became a spirited game.

Howe had planned to retire from politics and government and take a job with an oil company that would give him some financial security. But now he realized that he had a higher mission. He stayed with FDR at Campobello, telling Eleanor, "This is my job—helping Franklin." He was nearby when the family moved to New York City, where FDR could be near his doctor. That became a problem for Anna when Howe was given her bedroom.

Nudged on by her grandmother, who despised Howe, Anna sulked at the injustice of it. "Granny, with a good insight into my adolescent nature, started telling me that it was inexcusable that I, the only daughter of the family, should have a tiny bedroom in the back of the house, while Louis enjoyed a large, sunny front bedroom with his own private bath." Anna blamed her mother, who she thought ignored her and didn't listen to her, and Eleanor later agreed that there was some truth to that. Her primary focus was on her husband.

Howe and Eleanor were aligned on one point: they realized that the motivation to heal and even thrive had to come from FDR's sense that he could follow his ambitions. They knew him well. He needed to be in the fray, to live a vital life.

Sara disagreed. She thought her son should accept a pastoral retirement at Hyde Park. To that end, she began to consider Howe the enemy, the man who would drag her fragile son back into the public squall of politics. Privately, she referred to him as that "dirty, ugly little man." Howe was just as distasteful in his habits as ever—an abominable houseguest who left a trail of ash wherever he went. But his devotion to FDR was unwavering, as was his determination to restore him to public life.

Eleanor also held firm. This she knew above all: sentencing her husband to a useless life would be like pounding a nail into his coffin. She fought for him, and in doing so she fought for herself, too—for the first time in her life. As James put it, "The day of the timid, fluttering, inept housewife, subservient to the whims of her husband and her mother-in-law, was over."

Sara thought she knew her son better than anyone else, including Eleanor. But, like many doting mothers, she couldn't quite see her son as a man in his own right with a wife capable of articulating his best interests. She did not take well to Eleanor's new confidence. She saw her grip slipping away, but in time she came to accept her son's determination to remain active in society, whatever the cost.

"I hoped he would devote himself to his restoration of health and to the writing perhaps of the books he had always longed to get on paper," she wrote in her memoir about FDR. "But Franklin had no intention of conforming to my quiet ideas for his future existence. He was determined to ignore his disability and carry on from where he had left off."

Further undermining Sara's desires, FDR's political friends from the Cuff Links Gang rushed to his side. Steve Early, who was back with the Associated Press, was profoundly shaken to hear of his friend's illness, recalling his strength and vitality of the previous years. On September 16, Early wrote to FDR:

My Dear Boss,

Is there a mite for me to give or do? I feel there is not, but I cannot refrain from extending the offer. Please know our love goes out to you and yours in distress and nothing would give me greater joy than to be used, if use for me can be found. It's unnecessary to say, I hope and pray for your rapid and complete recovery.

Affectionately,
Stephen

Months later, in January, Early joined members of the Cuff Links Gang in New York City to celebrate FDR's birthday, as they had pledged to do every year. Apart from Howe, who had stayed by FDR's side, the other members had not seen FDR since he had become ill. None of them knew what to expect, but Early dreaded the idea that the "happy-hearted" man they loved would be greatly diminished. Instead, as Early recounted, they were stunned:

We found him, as high of heart, as gay in humor, and more overwhelmingly interested in politics—national, state, international—than he had ever been. It was dumbfounding. Men of courage are no rarity, but a man who could face such a cruel stroke of fortune so blithely with so utterly an unchanged demeanor, with an outlook on the world, and its affairs, so unaffected with such utter absence of repining—this was beyond anything I had ever known. I think we were all a bit dazed.

It had seemed unthinkable, but the men left FDR's side that day imagining a political future for him. He was glad to comply. He worked tirelessly on his recovery. Advice poured in from other polio sufferers, including the suggestion to swim in warm water as therapy. When he tried that, in addition to the potentially therapeutic effects of the water, he found that being in a pool restored him to his upright self, the buoyancy lifting him onto his feet. He became a believer. He was interested when he heard about a spa near Bullochville, Georgia, south of Atlanta, which was named for the family of TR's mother, Martha Bulloch Roosevelt, who had settled in Georgia before the Civil War. Bullochville was down on its luck but featured restorative warm springs heavily laced with healing minerals. He arranged to visit the area and spent six weeks there. In spite of the town's shoddy appearance, he fell in love with the waters and could spend long hours in the pool without growing tired.

Seeing that her husband was in good hands, Eleanor was able to leave his side and return to New York. His secretary, Marguerite "Missy" LeHand, stayed behind by FDR's side. LeHand had first entered the orbit during FDR's vice presidential campaign, and after the election Eleanor had invited her to Hyde Park to help with correspondence and secretarial duties. Tall and attractive with a fine temperament and flawless skills, she soon caught FDR's eye, and he had asked her to be his full-time secretary. She became his indispensable aide when he was stricken with polio.

From then on, Warm Springs, as the spa's area was renamed, became like a second home to FDR. He felt at ease with his fellow "polios." In that setting, he didn't have to be ashamed of his shriveled legs or pretend to abilities he didn't have. He relished his role as teacher and leader. He was the main event at Warm Springs. Others came because of him, and he was exhilarated by the unique leadership challenge of inspiring and teaching the young children and adults around him. He spent so much time teaching and leading others in exercises that he was nicknamed "Dr. Roosevelt," which delighted him.

"He had always loved people," the historian Doris Kearns Goodwin observed. "He had always connected with them. But now he needed them."

When he was back home in Hyde Park, FDR continued his rehabilitation, determined to walk again. With his legs in heavy steel braces, leaning on crutches, he practiced maneuvering along the long driveway, never actually standing on his feet but swiveling from one leg to the next and propelling himself forward by the force of his upper-body strength. It was a grueling ordeal, drenching him in sweat, and he repeated the process over and over again but without achieving the use of his legs. Two years after he was afflicted, a thorough examination of his muscles showed no real progress. His physician described his walking maneuver as "flail legs."

Physically, FDR never conquered the crippling ailment. But mentally, he rose above it, and it strengthened him, as if he had been waiting all his life for a challenge large enough for his ambitions. Some might regard FDR's paralysis as the great tragedy of his life, but in a deeper sense it made him a better man. In the long years of battle, he left behind the glib politician, the callow youth, the self-satisfied child of privilege. He developed qualities he'd never had before: patience, deliberation, reliance on others, and empathy. Those were necessary adaptations, as important to him as his physical labors.

His previously slender, erect upper body filled out with the musculature of a body builder whose arms could lift his entire weight when necessary. His face, once thin, also filled out, becoming heavier and livelier. His lower body was inert, his legs sometimes encased in the steel braces that would allow him to inch along if he could hold on to something or someone for support. He could even give the appearance of walking, but he never actually walked again.

He had to reshape his view of the world and of his ability, and when all was said and done he chose not to be crippled. That wasn't denial as much as intention.

As Sara wrote, "He steadfastly refused to concede even to himself that he was functioning under a handicap and to this day I don't believe any one has ever heard him make any reference to his illness. I know I never have."

Optimism, everyone agreed, was the hallmark of FDR's years in rehabilitation. If he ever truly felt hopeless, he didn't share it. He believed he had a responsibility to keep everyone else's spirits up, not only for their sake but for his own. In addition to his naturally upbeat personality, his approach to his illness was an extension of the stoicism bred into him from childhood. He'd been taught never to complain or admit defeat. But he was aided in the pursuit of optimism by the notes and letters that came to him from across the nation. He was especially touched and heartened to hear from fellow polio sufferers. This is a typical exchange of letters:

Mr. F. D. Roosevelt
Fellow Sufferer,

Through the enclosed clipping, I have just learned the pretty and truthful name of that from which I have suffered for eleven years, compelled to walk with a cane, though a young girl, only 87½ years old. Except for that, though so young, I should clip around like a young girl, as are others of my age.

Hoping your trouble will not stay as long as mine has.

Yours very respectfully,
Elizabeth Carleton

My dear Miss Carleton,

I appreciated your little note very much and enjoyed reading the poetry.

If I could feel assured that time could treat me so lightly as to leave me at eighty-seven and a half years with all my vigor, powers and only a cane required, I would consider that my future was very bright indeed. There are not many people who can equal that record, even though they have been fortunate enough not to have been fellow-sufferers, with you and me, of infantile paralysis.

Very sincerely yours,
Franklin D. Roosevelt

FDR HAD STAYED CLOSE to Al Smith, who was reelected governor of New York in 1922, after two years out of office. "Frank" and "Al," as they referred to each other, had always been an odd couple. Smith, an Irish Catholic from the Lower East Side of New York City, a son of Tammany Hall, was an unlikely partner of the aristocratic, Tammany Hall–loathing Roosevelt. But a funny thing happened on the way to political influence: FDR softened his attitude toward Tammany Hall politics, his abhorrence overcome by the progressive, urbanized policies of men such as Smith. Perhaps, he thought, there could not be one without the other. Now Smith had a higher aspiration: the presidency. Behind the scenes, Howe had been talking to Smith, and he made a bold suggestion: Why not ask FDR to give his nominating speech at the Democratic National Convention, which would be held at Madison Square Garden in New York City on June 24, 1924?

At first it seemed like the antithesis of a strong voice of support; it was hard to imagine a crippled man on the stage, who might fall or collapse in a heap. But Smith took the chance, and FDR was happy to oblige.

He refused to be pushed onstage in a wheelchair. "Jimmy," he said to his son, "would you care to come along and lend me your arm?"

James was elated. FDR had developed a system for moving in an upright position relying on a strong crutch under one arm and an even stronger human prop on the other side holding him up. His legs were locked into braces to hold them steady, and with the strength of his powerful arms he propelled himself forward.

FDR and James practiced the fifteen-foot walk to the podium many times, and although James was a strong young man, his father's iron grip on his arm caused him some pain. On the day of the nominating speech, they made their way slowly across the stage, FDR beaming as if he didn't have a care in the world and James grimacing—"His fingers dug into my arm like pincers."

At last they reached the podium, where they executed a slow pivot that left FDR leaning forward and gripping the rostrum as fifteen thousand conventioneers erupted in a roaring ovation. He was so afraid of falling that he didn't dare lift his arms. Eventually the cheering crowd fell silent with a sense of awe. Here was the man they had always known, standing tall, his beautiful smile radiating from a face that was older but entirely recognizable. And when he began to speak, his powerful voice rumbled across the hall, as commanding as ever. His speech was down to earth, portraying Smith as a beloved figure, "the Happy Warrior of the political battlefield":

> If you would know what the hearts of the masses hold for him, ask anyone; when you leave this session ask the woman who serves you in the shop; the banker who cashes your check; the man who runs your elevator; the clerk in your hotel . . . and you will be told with a convincing unanimity that first in the affections of the people of this state, first far above all others and the power of all others to attain, is the man who has been twice honored with election to the governorship of the State of New York.

Smith did not prevail, losing the nomination to former ambassador to the United Kingdom John W. Davis, on the 103rd ballot. Roosevelt stood for him then, too, being the one to announce to the delegates that "for the good of the party," Smith was withdrawing. Davis was nominated and then went on to lose decisively to the sitting president, Calvin Coolidge, who had stepped into office when Harding had died the previous year.

Despite the fate of Al Smith and eventually Davis, a victor did emerge from the convention: FDR himself. The delegates thrilled at seeing FDR, and the clamor for him was heartfelt and wildly enthusiastic. The *New York Evening World* called him the real hero of the convention: "Adversity has lifted him above the bickering, the religious bigotry, conflicting personal ambitions and petty sectional prejudices. . . . Roosevelt might be a pathetic, tragic figure but for the fine courage that flashes in his smile. It holds observers enchained."

As for the gentle deception—that he could stand, that he could walk—it served to strengthen his own frame of mind and was an expression of a vitality that was utterly authentic. The bias against those who were crippled was a reality, and in FDR's mind the worst of it was the pity, the paternalism, the dismissiveness. If he could find a way to help people see him for who he really was on the inside by manipulating their view of the outside, so be it. In that he largely succeeded.

He told James that the convention appearance was an hour or so stolen from his sickness, but in fact it was more than that; it was the beginning of a comeback to the public stage.

Howe never stopped believing in FDR's potential.

"Do you really believe that Franklin has a political future?" Eleanor asked him once, feeling doubtful.

"I believe someday Franklin will be president," he said.

And in working to ensure FDR a vital future, Howe inadvertently opened the door for Eleanor as well. He thought that the best thing for FDR would be to keep his name and ideas in the public arena. To that end, he encouraged Eleanor to get out in public and make contacts of her own. Slowly, Eleanor began to engage in the political scene. When Nancy Cook, the assistant to Harriet May Mills, the director of the new women's division of the Democratic State Committee, invited her to speak, she reluctantly agreed and then found she enjoyed the involvement. That activity would become her launching pad for activism and independence, and Cook would become one of her dearest friends, along with Cook's partner, Marion Dickerman. The three women began to spend more and more time together, which was not a problem for FDR because at that point the Roosevelts had begun to live separate-but-together lives—separate in their daily involvements and often locations; together in their ideas about the world, government, and FDR's political future.

Their devotion never ended, but time and circumstances had allowed them to outgrow the marital conventions and subterfuge that had made Eleanor so unhappy and unfulfilled.

Eleanor, Cook, and Dickerman often spent time at Hyde Park, but when Sara closed the big house for the winter, they were left adrift. When Eleanor mentioned to FDR how disappointed she was by that, he suggested they build a cottage on the large property, distant from the house on the lovely Val-Kill stream. It was a generous gift to his wife and her friends, an acknowledgment of Eleanor's independence, and perhaps also a form of payback for her years of dedication and hardship. FDR immediately wrote to a contractor friend, enlisting him to build the cottage on the stream and dig out a swimming pool as well. When it was completed, Cook and Dickerman lived there, and Eleanor visited whenever she liked. FDR called it the Honeymoon Cottage, and it must have felt that way to Eleanor. For the first time, she had her own plans and was setting up house with her own things. Despite later conjectures about an affair, it was more likely that Eleanor was reveling in a sense of liberation and strong platonic love. From then on, Eleanor rarely stayed at the Hyde Park house. In time the women set up a small furniture factory at Val-Kill to encourage local artisans.

During that time, Eleanor also began earning her own income, giving lectures, writing magazine articles, and even appearing on radio broadcasts. Not only symbolically but practically, that increased her independence, something Sara abhorred—"When I began to earn money it was a real grief to her," Eleanor observed.

LeHand stepped in to fill many of Eleanor's roles, and this time Eleanor did not object to having a woman close to her husband. It is unknown whether the relationship ever turned sexual (most people doubt it), but LeHand did achieve an intimacy of close companionship that continued until a stroke in 1941 forced her into retirement and out of FDR's orbit. As one aide observed, "There was no doubt that Missy was as close to being a wife as he ever had or could have."

Also frequently present in those days and for the rest of his life was FDR's distant cousin Margaret "Daisy" Suckley. She had started going to Hyde Park to keep him company when he was first recuperating from polio, at the request of Sara, who thought her son was lonely. It was an easy jaunt for Suckley, who lived with her mother at nearby Wilderstein, her family home. She had never married, and she and Roosevelt soon became close. He found that he could tell Suckley anything, and he came to trust her with the innermost thoughts he wouldn't dare admit to others, even (especially) his wife. Their regular correspondence, captured in Geoffrey Ward's 1995 book, *Closest Companion: The Unknown Story of the Intimate Friendship Between Franklin Roosevelt and Margaret Suckley*, showed the ease of their relationship, which could dwell on everything from home gossip to politics to war strategy.

The unconventional nature of the Roosevelt marriage would have raised eyebrows in any era, but it seemed to be a necessity born of colliding needs and personalities. Eleanor's impatience with what she experienced as the dreariness of domesticity, her disdain for sexual intimacy (she once told her daughter, Anna, that it was something to be endured), her revulsion for the dirty business of politics, her inability to be happy, playful, or at ease in social situations were in direct opposition to her husband's passions. FDR's self-centeredness, his exuberant sexuality, his playfulness, his grandiose visions, his longing for love and acceptance (which was gladly provided by the women in his close circle—Lucy Mercer, Missy LeHand, and Daisy Suckley—as well as his male acolytes, particularly Howe) were anathema to

Eleanor. At the same time, Eleanor's devotion to him and willingness to bear his standard despite her feelings, her unceasing care for him, her discretion about his flaws, and her pride in his achievements gave their marriage a solid if unconventional standing. During FDR's years of rehabilitation, they achieved what amounted to a loving truce that gave both of them the freedom to be more of themselves.

In 1927, FDR decided to purchase the resort at Warm Springs and turn it into a rehabilitation facility. Almost nobody in his inner circle thought it was a good idea, including Eleanor, who was concerned about the high cost of putting their brood through school. But he was determined, and the Georgia Warm Springs Foundation for Infantile Paralysis was created. FDR always called it his greatest legacy.

AL SMITH HAD HIS eye on the presidency once again. In 1928, he was planning to run, and he was looking to FDR to be his handpicked successor as governor of New York. Once again, FDR nominated Smith at the Democratic National Convention in Houston, but he had not yet decided whether to run for governor. He felt he needed more time for rehabilitation before he ran for office. By the time of the state nominating convention, he had still not decided but was leaning against the idea and was far away from New York in Warm Springs. He figured that the nomination couldn't touch him when he was not present.

For days FDR ducked Governor Smith's urgent calls—he knew their purpose—but he finally answered, and when Smith entreated him, once again, to run, he said no.

"If the convention nominates you anyway, will you decline to run?" Smith asked craftily.

There was a momentary silence. The anticipated no did not

come, and Smith chose to take that as a yes. He began to work the phones, telling people to expect a Roosevelt candidacy.

Anna, who had married in 1926 and was home nursing an infant, sent a telegram to her father at Warm Springs. Her youthful marriage had admittedly been a means of escape from the chaos of her family's life, but now she was looking at her father with new eyes. She wired her father her approval of a candidacy, while knowing her mother would not be happy about it.

The next day, the convention nominated FDR by acclamation. Surprisingly, Louis Howe was distressed by the turn of events. As the self-appointed architect of FDR's political comeback, his master plan was for FDR to reenter politics in 1932, first as governor of New York and then as a candidate for president in 1936. He thought 1928 was too soon—FDR wasn't ready.

But FDR accepted the nomination. Eleanor agreed with Howe that the timing was wrong, but she supported her husband's decision—albeit desultorily—wiring him:

REGRET THAT YOU HAD TO ACCEPT, BUT KNOW THAT
YOU FELT IT OBLIGATORY

Smith was delighted, and he dismissed worries about Roosevelt's physical abilities. "A governor does not have to be an acrobat," he said in arguing FDR's case. "We do not elect him for his ability to do a double back flip or a handspring." At the same time, FDR was very intent on projecting the right image of authority. He asked the press not to show images or film of him being carried from his car, and the press complied. From then on, the press avoided filming him being carried and often captured images of him standing. He adopted a casual slouch when leaning against a lectern, making it look like an afterthought. In time he grew strong enough to use his arms, waving or pounding the air in a manner reminiscent of Cousin Teddy.

It turned out there was no cause for concern about FDR's fitness to run. He campaigned with the same fierce energy with which he had won the campaigns of his youth, visiting every one of New York's sixty-two counties. In fact, he credited the campaign with improving his health. "If I could campaign another six months," he joked at the end, "I believe I could throw away my crutches."

Once he was running, FDR needed to get up to date on New York politics quickly. For that he enlisted Samuel Rosenman, a young man who had served in the legislature and was attuned to New York politics. Rosenman would become one of FDR's closest aides and his primary speechwriter.

Rosenman did not know FDR, but he'd heard plenty about him during the years before polio. "I had heard stories of his being something of a playboy and idler, of his weakness and ineffectiveness," he wrote. "That was the kind of man I had expected to meet. But the broad jaw and upthrust chin, the piercing, flashing eyes, the firm hands—they did not fit the description."

Rosenman's start as a speechwriter came inauspiciously after a busy day of campaigning. He'd compiled some documents for FDR as the basis of an upcoming speech, but the candidate handed them back to him. "Sam," he said, "I've got to run now and meet some of the local political brethren. I'm afraid I'll be busy most of the evening. Suppose you knock out a draft of what you think I ought to say tomorrow night, and let me have it in the morning. We'll go over it together tomorrow."

Rosenman was struck dumb. That wasn't a role he had expected to play or one he had any confidence in. However, he realized that resistance was futile. As FDR was being wheeled out, he grinned at his chagrined aide. "Don't stay up all night—do the best you can," he said.

When Rosenman presented his draft the next morning, FDR deemed it competent but dull, and they worked on it together. FDR dictated new paragraphs and textual changes, adding force and spirit to Rosenman's dry words, and Rosenman had the feeling that he was learning from a master. That night, as Rosenman listened to the speech being delivered, he felt as inspired as if he were hearing the words for the first time, even though he'd spent most of the day working on the draft. For the rest of the campaign, he would be by FDR's side, discovering that writing speeches was not about arranging words on a page but a living exercise, growing organically out of the experience on the trail. FDR had mastered the art of the speech as a conversation with his audience.

FDR had long been doubtful that the Democrats could prevail in the presidential election in 1928, given the nation's state of prosperity. Nor did it help that Smith was a practicing Catholic. At the time, there was a strong bias against Catholics in office, and a Catholic had never been elected president. It was feared that a Catholic would be required by his religion to take orders from the pope. (Those fears made a reappearance in 1960 when John F. Kennedy ran for president, but they gained little purchase, especially after he gave a forceful speech on the separation of church and state.)

Herbert Hoover, the Republican avatar of the Roaring Twenties economy, soundly defeated Smith, and it looked as if the defeat of other Democrats would follow. The night of the election, watching the returns at the Biltmore Hotel in New York City, FDR was convinced that he had lost his race. Even New York State went for Hoover. But when he woke the next morning, he learned he'd squeaked by with a narrow victory of

25,000 votes out of 4 million. Now he was stepping into yet another job Cousin Teddy had held: governor of New York State. He was back in the arena.

Smith was devastated by his loss. His biographer Terry Golway described him as "a broken man, a lost soul" after the defeat. But Smith thought there was one ray of hope: he could return to New York, where he'd hold court in the back room of the governor's mansion and in effect be a shadow governor. Despite his glowing support for FDR, he didn't expect him to be much of a chief executive; he figured he'd spend much of his time at Warm Springs. No problem—Smith had already filled the key roles in the governor's office with his handpicked supporters. But to his dismay, FDR immediately replaced Smith's people with his own and strongly took the reins, pledging to be his own man. His relationship with Smith deteriorated, and they were never close again. "Do you know, by God," Smith was heard to complain bitterly, "that he has never consulted me about a damn thing since he has been governor?"

After the election, FDR called Rosenman aside. "Sam, I shall want you to act as the counsel to the governor," he said, adding enthusiastically, "We will have a fine, stimulating time together."

Rosenman hadn't expected that, and he asked for a week to think about it. FDR agreed.

Shortly after, local newspapers headlined his appointment. Shocked, Rosenman called Roosevelt and asked him if he'd made the announcement.

Roosevelt laughed. "Yes, I made up your mind for you."

Rosenman ended up being glad he had. He loved the job, in the process becoming intimately familiar with the way FDR thought and how he formed his thoughts into words. He admired the way his boss constantly checked in with both advisers and ordinary constituents. Rosenman watched him "squeeze every bit of information he wanted from a visitor." Not only that, he had a talent for making each visitor feel as though the governor's legislative success depended on input from that person.

"Tell me," he'd say, "what would you recommend if you were governor?" It was an irresistible overture.

Rosenman observed that the quality that helped FDR through difficult times was his positive outlook. He was not a worrier. He didn't second-guess himself. And he didn't dwell on his impediments. "The first physical thing that struck you on meeting Roosevelt was that huge, powerful body without the use of legs," Rosenman wrote. "As you got to know Roosevelt, it was also the first thing you forgot." Without a hint of irony or chagrin, FDR would say things such as "I've got to run now" when it was time to end a meeting.

As governor, faced with a Republican legislature and critical newspaper coverage, FDR decided to take his case directly to the people. In 1929, that was no easy feat, but radio was beginning to make an entrance, and by that time millions of Americans had radios in their homes. FDR began addressing his constituents in "fireside chats" over the radio, a form of outreach he would continue to great effect during his presidency.

In his 1929 fireside chat giving an annual report, he reached out in a bipartisan appeal: "I am very mindful of the fact that I am the governor, not just of the Democrats, but of Republicans and all other citizens of the state. That is why this talk . . . will be just as much as I can make [it] nonpartisan in character. I want merely to state facts and leave the people of the state to draw their own conclusions."

FDR revealed himself to be a canny politician. "Never let your opponent pick the battleground on which you fight," he said during his 1930 reelection campaign. "If he picks one, stay out of it and let him fight all by himself." Although he had barely squeaked by in his first election for governor, he won the second by a huge margin of 725,000 votes, including comfortably winning the Republican counties of upstate New York.

For a man molded by crisis, the times presented another one.

THE STOCK MARKET CRASH of October 24, 1929—Black Thursday—obliterated the prosperity of the 1920s and sent the nation reeling. It was an overnight calamity, but the crisis had been building for years. The heady expansion of the stock market during the 1920s had masked an underlying decline on Main Street. Rising unemployment, falling wages, and losses in the manufacturing and agricultural sectors had led to sharp devaluations in the worth of stocks and an investor panic that finally brought the stock market down.

The beginning of a worldwide depression that would continue for a decade was a rolling disaster. In the early days after the crash, President Hoover, aided by the press, was determined to paint a hopeful picture, promising that the strong economy could shoulder the blow. He urged reporters to resist writing gloom-and-doom pieces that would alarm their readers.

In his first public address on the crisis on November 25, President Hoover urged the country to rise above despair, blaming a "purely psychological" response to the decline in purchasing and production. He told the nation that the problem existed only in the stock market and not in the economy, as if the two were not intimately intertwined.

Within the year, the full impact of the depression had spread to nearly every household. Unemployment had risen from

3.14 percent to 8.67 percent. It would reach nearly 25 percent by 1932. As Hamilton Cravens expressed it in his compilation on the Great Depression, "the country was sent into a painful tailspin as a mysterious illness infected and spread to its every organ." The illness struck the most vulnerable first, as any crisis does, paralyzing the farm communities and the working poor. But it soon spread to the middle class, dealing a crushing economic and emotional blow. The 1920s had been all about delivering prosperity to hardworking Americans, and now they were faced with the humiliation of being unable to pay their bills or feed their families. Even those who managed to hold on to their jobs found their paychecks cut to poverty wages. Others did anything they could to raise cash or find food. Unemployed workers sold apples on the street in New York. Thousands of dispossessed and desperate farmers, further assaulted by drought, packed the roads heading west, where they hoped against hope to find sustenance and opportunity. Thousands more stood in bread lines organized by charitable organizations. The faces of the men and women in bread lines and at soup kitchens, captured in stunning photographs, showed the shock of their crushed dreams. The suicide rate rose to 17 per 100,000 Americans.

As the alarm grew, Hoover resisted calls for federal aid, urging states to step in and help their people. In New York, Governor Roosevelt aggressively took on the challenge of lifting his state out of economic ruin. Looking back from his activist presidency, one can see many of the seeds of his later initiatives. In a sense the New Deal was crafted in the cities and back roads of New York, where he saw how much people were suffering.

FDR was increasingly critical of Hoover's insistence that the federal government should not provide unemployment relief but rather leave the job to charitable organizations, volunteers, and local governments. Roosevelt responded in Albany by asking the legislature to examine the issue of unemployment insurance and other means of supporting the unemployed. He recommended that $20 million in new taxes be raised to start a works program. In his August 28, 1931, message to the legislature, he called on its members to do their duty:

> Our government is not the master but the creature of the people. The duty of the State toward the citizens is the duty of the servant to its master. The people have created it; the people, by common consent, permit its continued existence. One of these duties of the State is that of caring for those of its citizens who find themselves the victims of such adverse circumstances as makes them unable to obtain even the necessities for mere existence without the aid of others.

Herbert Hoover became a convenient scapegoat for the ills of the Great Depression. In some respects, he'd landed in the White House as the unluckiest politician alive—the recipient of a downturn not of his making. But he never got his arms around it, and that doomed him.

In office, battling the calamity, Hoover was far from the "do-nothing" president he has been accused of being. But his proposals, which might have been sound economic policy during ordinary times, were ineffective in stanching the impact of the terrible global crisis. Instead of federal aid, he preached a combination of volunteerism and local government aid. It was a weak response. The public mood, even among Republicans, was vastly altered by the sheer horrors of the Great Depression—much as a person who suffers devastation in a hurricane might seek help he had never considered necessary before. The Great Depression was like a hurricane whose gale-force winds lasted years, not days.

As the historian William Leuchtenburg observed, Hoover's call for volunteers and local governments to help suffering communities would have been a pragmatic and even uplifting appeal in any other time. "But how could a city like Toledo, where 80 percent of the working force was unemployed, possibly meet the needs of the jobless through its own resources?"

As the economy grew worse, Hoover bore the brunt of the public ire.

By 1931, unemployment was nearly 25 percent, and banks were failing at a rapid rate. Still he could not find a fix. To make matters worse, he did not have the right demeanor for the times. Instead of empathy and leadership, he was defensive, his statistics-laden speeches attempting to show that things weren't so bad, when clearly they were. "No one is actually starving," he said, also stating that "the hoboes are better fed than they've ever been." It was a demoralizing message for the hopeless nation.

The Republican Party was loath to challenge Hoover in 1932, regardless of his flaws. But the Democrats were galvanized, and many heads turned in FDR's direction.

"I want to step on any talk of that kind with both feet," said FDR at first, no doubt enjoying the turn of phrase. But his demurrals were unconvincing. As the activist governor of New York State, he had positioned himself to be the voice of the nation. He was the most talked about prospect for 1932, and in the early days, no other Democrat even came close. FDR would soon find out, however, that the worshipful coverage had its limits. He would not be able to skate into office on public admiration alone. The knives were out among other contenders, with Al Smith leading the pack. FDR was about to embark upon the toughest campaign of his career.

CHAPTER 4

IN THE FOOTSTEPS OF COUSIN TEDDY

In early 1887, when he was five years old, Franklin Roosevelt had accompanied his father, James, to the White House for a farewell meeting with President Grover Cleveland, a friend of the family, who was completing his second term in office. The president bent down to address the boy. "My little man," he said, "I am making a strange wish for you. It is that you may never be President of the United States." Everyone smiled at the charming joke. But in some corner of his consciousness, FDR had never abandoned the thought, and later, after his cousin Teddy became president, it was common speculation that the handsome and likable Franklin might someday follow in his footsteps. That speculation paused but did not end when polio struck, and FDR emerged from a decade of physical struggle with a new gravitas. In his second term as governor of New York, he was far more emotionally and intellectually suited for the office than he had been before he became ill.

On January 22, 1932, as his fiftieth birthday approached, FDR announced that he would be a candidate for president of the United States. It's fair to say that most politicians contemplating a run for the White House begin the journey by conferring with their family. FDR did not do that. He never shared his plans with Eleanor, although she knew full well that he was likely to run. Their awkward arrangement continued, for though he assumed her support, he was unwilling to seek it. Eleanor was unhappy with her husband's decision to run for president, but she wouldn't have dreamed of saying so—although her occasionally sullen manner could betray her true sentiments. She was guilty about her feelings, thinking them selfish, yet she never gave expression to her doubts.

Rosenman believed that Roosevelt suited the mood of a nation seeking change. "The dictum of Macaulay, 'Reform if you would preserve,' was one of Roosevelt's maxims, which he quoted frequently and observed always. That is why he was always so receptive to new ideas; that is why in administering affairs of state he believed so strongly in 'bold, persistent experimentation.' "

Perhaps the most important addition to FDR's team was James A. Farley, the secretary of the New York State Democratic Committee, who had worked in local and state politics his entire life as if he'd been born into them. He was a great addition to FDR's team: likable, energetic, and diplomatic enough to share the leadership with the prickly Howe. "Big Jim," as his old friends called him, was tall and burly, with a shiny bald head and a beaming, good-natured personality. In many ways, he was the antithesis of the seedy, bad-humored Howe.

Farley had an instinct for politics and how to wrangle support for his candidate. He noted that "grand opera never has had and never will have as many prima donnas as politics." So, in introducing Roosevelt, he had to be careful to consider the egos and sensitivities of many other politicians, particularly during the perilous primary season. Farley would become FDR's delegate-whisperer, traveling the country to talk to delegates and win support for FDR in a crowded field that included nine candidates, two of them imposing contenders: Al Smith, making another run; and Speaker of the House John Nance Garner, a florid, cigar-chomping Texan who had the advantage of being the favorite of the newspaper powerhouse William Randolph Hearst.

Early on, Rosenman suggested that they gather together a group to talk about issues—which came to be known as Roosevelt's Brain Trust. Rather than the usual bankers and industrialists, who had failed to come up with solutions during the tortured years of the Great Depression, Rosenman said they should look to the universities, to the nimble minds of scholars. Their first pick was a professor of government and public law at Columbia University named Raymond Moley. Moley, in turn, brought in two of his colleagues, the economist Rexford Tugwell and a law professor, Adolf Berle, with Moley remaining the first among equals. He was close to FDR and was also a fine writer, penning dramatic prose early in FDR's candidacy that was an ode to the "forgotten man." It came about when the radio program *Lucky Strike Hour* offered candidates ten minutes to speak. Roosevelt took full advantage of the offer, and the speech became one of his most popular:

> It is said that Napoleon lost the battle of Waterloo because he forgot his infantry—he staked too much upon the more spectacular but less substantial cavalry. The present administration in Washington provides a close parallel. It has either forgotten or it does not want to remember the infantry of our economic army.
>
> These unhappy times call for the building of plans that rest upon the forgotten, the unorganized but the indispensable units of economic power, for plans like

those of 1917 that build from the bottom up and not from the top down, that put their faith once more in the forgotten man at the bottom of the economic pyramid.

Al Smith was outraged by the "forgotten man" speech, perhaps because it struck such a chord with the public. In a thinly veiled response, he railed, "I will take off my coat and fight to the end against any candidate who persists in any demagogic appeal to the masses of working people in this country to destroy themselves by setting class against class and rich against poor." As he was a long-standing populist street fighter, his cry made little sense, but he let his emotions get the better of him.

Publicly, Hoover dismissed FDR's candidacy and expressed confidence that he would easily win reelection. He said he expected the Depression to be as good as over by election day. But it's evident that he worried more about Roosevelt than he let on. In April, he invited the nation's governors to dinner at the White House. FDR attended with Eleanor, and as at all public occasions, he went through the grueling and painful process of "walking" upright, gripping the arms of aides. When they arrived at the hall, he was exhausted by the exertion and looked forward to sitting down. But Hoover was not yet in the room, and it was protocol for everyone to remain standing until the president was seated. Roosevelt was sweating, and a White House aide asked if he'd like to take a seat. He refused the offer, gritting his teeth and remaining upright for thirty long minutes until Hoover arrived. Of course, Roosevelt's aides and Eleanor thought Hoover had deliberately been late to make FDR look weak. If so, the tactic didn't work.

Rosenman had become indispensable to FDR, but he had another ambition. When a state supreme court position became available, Rosenman admitted that he would like to serve on the bench. FDR didn't like the idea. He needed Rosenman, and he expected him to come to Washington with him if he was elected. But he reluctantly agreed and nominated Rosenman for the court. He was scheduled to begin his new duties in New York City on April 15. But in the end, Roosevelt couldn't quite let go, and Rosenman would frequently be called on to do double duty. Often, he made the long train ride to Albany to help with strategy and speeches, catching the midnight train home so he could be in court the following morning. Before the Democratic National Convention in June, FDR invited Rosenman and his wife to come to Albany for the duration. "Better bring a lot of pencils along," he said. "We have to whip the acceptance speech into fine form."

Chicago was the favored convention location of both parties in 1932, thanks in large part to the salesmanship of Chicago's mayor, Anton Cermak, who presented his city as a shining exemplar of the modern era. He offered the site, Chicago Stadium on Madison Street, which had opened in 1929 and was the world's largest indoor arena. Normally a sports stadium, it was repurposed by Cermak as an ideal setting for the nation's favorite political sport. And although the stadium was located in Chicago's Skid Row and the streets around it were choked with soup lines and the homeless, Cermak convinced the party that Chicago was a city of the future, with the dazzling fairgrounds for the 1933 World's Fair nearly completed.

The Republican National Convention, held from June 14 to 16, was a fast two-day rubber stamp for Hoover, the delegates eager to get out of town without lingering on the crumbling economy and the devastation in the streets. A telegram was sent to Hoover, informing him of his overwhelming victory. "I am deeply grateful for the highest honor that the party can confer," he wrote back. "It marks your approval and your confidence." Not quite. The mood at the convention was more like resignation, lifted only by the distraction of a rousing platform fight over Prohibition. The end result was a half-hearted call for states to examine whether Prohibition—a ban on the production and sale of liquor—should be repealed. (The Democrats would offer a more full-throated endorsement for the end of Prohibition at their convention, acknowledging the unpopularity of liquor laws that many people did not follow. FDR, who had previously been a politically correct "dry," although he liked a drink, changed to the popular prorepeal posture in campaigning for president, though not too enthusiastically. As Farley observed, he was wet but not "dripping wet.")

The Democratic National Convention two weeks later, from June 27 to July 2, was longer and messier. Although FDR had been a standout in the previous two conventions, he stayed more than eight hundred miles away in Albany during this one. His powerful speeches in favor of Al Smith were distant memories as the two men faced each other for the nomination. John Nance Garner was back home in Washington, but he was ably represented by a seasoned Texas congressman named Sam Rayburn. Al Smith made a point to be at the convention, hoping his presence would hold the others at bay. He'd always been good at personal persuasion, and he hoped he could win the delegates to his side if he could speak to them face-to-face.

At the convention, Howe and Farley worked the floor, setting up phone calls with FDR back in Albany so he could make personal appeals to delegates. James was also at the convention. His father had enlisted him to ride herd on the Massachusetts delegation—not an easy task, as it was solidly in Smith's corner.

At the time, only one-third of delegates were secured in primaries; the rest were chosen by party leaders or at state conventions. There were 1,154 delegates at stake, with a two-thirds majority needed to win. FDR was ahead at the start, with more than six hundred votes secured. A delegate arrangement between other contenders, especially Smith and Garner, or the emergence of a compromise candidate, could have destroyed FDR's chances.

Delegates endured long hours of speeches in blistering heat. Farley had the foresight to bring a supply of fans bearing FDR's image. The hall got so hot that even delegates supporting other candidates gratefully used them.

In another clever ploy, Farley created a large multicolored map of the country, with different colors designating the chosen candidate of each state. It gave the impression that Roosevelt was the overwhelming favorite, since there was no weighting for delegate numbers. Farley installed the map in a central location at the Congress Hotel, where it would be seen by all the delegates. According to some delegates interviewed later, Farley's map had the desired effect of making Roosevelt's opponents look weak.

Finally, the balloting began in the early-morning hours of July 1. The first ballot yielded a slight increase for FDR but still not enough. The second ballot inched his lead further along, but he was still short of the necessary two-thirds. Smith held his position at second place, with Garner in third.

Back in the Albany war room, Roosevelt sat with his family, aides, and advisers, the radio tuned to the convention proceedings. As the night went on, some fell asleep, but Roosevelt, Eleanor, Sara, and his closest aides were alert and focused. As Rosenman described the scene:

> We presented a strange picture along about three o'clock in the morning there in the small sitting room of the Executive Mansion. The Governor, his wife, his mother

and I sat listening to the radio. He was in his shirt sleeves, silent, puffing on one cigarette after another. The phone was at his side, and he used it frequently. He seemed deeply interested in the convention oratory, nodding approval of some parts, shaking his head in disapproval of others, laughing aloud when the eloquence became a little too "spread-eagle" in tone.

To distract himself from the stressful ups and downs of the convention voting, Rosenman pulled out his notes for the acceptance speech, which had been mostly written by Moley but still lacked a soaring ending. Rosenman decided to tackle the ending, eventually scribbling a line on a scrap of paper: "I pledge you, I pledge myself, to a *new deal* for the American people."

When he handed the scrap to Roosevelt, he glanced at the words and nodded. He thought it was "all right," he said before returning his attention to the radio.

Meanwhile, in Chicago, Farley was trying to work a backroom deal with Garner that would prove decisive. Farley proposed that in exchange for a place on the ticket, Garner would back FDR, which would mean delivering his substantial block of votes from Texas and California.

FDR and Garner were not natural allies. Garner was a fiscal conservative with a public antipathy to "Yankees," and he often sided with Hoover on economic matters. It was unclear whether Garner would even want to trade his powerful speakership for the number two slot. Further complicating matters was Hearst, Garner's influential backer, who was no fan of Roosevelt but who disliked Smith even more. Would Hearst agree to the arrangement?

In the early-morning hours, Hearst gave his approval, and Garner called Rayburn in Chicago. It was a deal. Rayburn headed to the floor to confer with the pro-Garner delegations. A reporter, following a rumor, skeptically asked Rayburn if it was really true that he was backing FDR. "I'm a little older than you are, son," Rayburn replied, "and politics is funny." He might have added, "And revenge is sweet." As the *New York Times* put it, the move "furnished revenge on Alfred E. Smith for William Randolph Hearst." (For the record, Farley later wrote that Hearst had had nothing to do with the decision; others disagree.)

As the conventioneers gathered for the fourth ballot, William McAdoo, the head of the California delegation, rose and addressed them: "California came here to nominate the President of the United States. She did not come here to deadlock the convention. California—44 votes for Roosevelt."

Listening to the radio in Albany, FDR grinned. "Good old McAdoo," he said.

The room around him erupted, everyone suddenly wide awake. Eleanor and LeHand embraced, the Roosevelt children danced around, Rosenman beamed. They knew this was it. In Chicago, the groundswell was under way, as delegates began changing their votes. Smith might have seen the end coming, but he refused to release his delegates.

Normally, the nominee did not accept the nomination at the convention but held a ceremony weeks later. Now Roosevelt announced that he was going to do something bold: he was going to go to Chicago that day and accept the nomination in person. He felt that would convey a sense of urgency and also show the nation that he was strong and prepared, not a weak, fading cripple. He knew that Smith, who had once preached the irrelevancy of Roosevelt's disability, had been putting out the word that he was as good as a dead man. He'd prove otherwise. And he wasn't going by train. He was going to fly!

Through stormy skies, it was a risky, gut-slamming voyage in a private plane, requiring stops in Buffalo and Cleveland for refueling. When the plane finally landed in Chicago, a huge crowd met them, including the highly agitated Louis Howe. He'd read the speech FDR was preparing to give, and he thought it was terrible. He handed FDR a replacement speech he had written.

FDR began to decline. "But Louis, you know I can't deliver a speech that I've never done any work on myself, and that I've never even read. It will sound stupid, and it's silly to think that I can."

Howe continued to argue with him, and FDR grumbled, "Dammit, Louie, *I'm* the nominee." But he agreed to read Howe's version. He was sensitive to Howe's feelings, his agonies about being replaced after all he'd given. Ultimately, he saw that he could replace the first page of the speech with Howe's version. The rest he kept as Moley had written it. The last paragraphs brought the conventioneers to their feet:

Out of every crisis, every tribulation, every disaster, mankind rises with some share of greater knowledge, of higher decency, of purer purpose. Today we shall have come through a period of loose thinking and descending morals, an era of selfishness of individual men and women and of whole nations. Blame not governments alone for this. Blame ourselves in equal share. Let us be frank in acknowledgment of the truth that many amongst us have made obeisance to Mammon, that the profits of speculation, the easy road without toil have lured us from the old verities. To return to higher standards we must abandon the false prophets and seek new leaders of our own choosing. . . .

I pledge you, I pledge myself to a new deal for the American people. Let us all here assembled constitute ourselves prophets of a new order of competence and of courage. This is more than a political campaign. It is a call to arms.

Give me your help, not to win votes alone—but to win in this crusade to return America to its own people.

"Happy Days Are Here Again" played as delegates danced in the aisles and FDR grinned and waved. Al Smith left Chicago without a word to Roosevelt, stung by the rejection of his party.

The "new deal" was headlined in major newspapers the next day. By election day, it was capitalized: the New Deal.

HERBERT HOOVER HAD NO sooner accepted his party's nomination for a second term in office than thousands of angry war veterans stormed down Pennsylvania Avenue. Scarred, jobless, hungry, and psychologically burned, the men had begun to arrive in Washington in May, seeking relief. In the European war, they had endured the rat-infested foxholes, the mind-destroying mustard gas, and the constant barrages of artillery fire, and they had been lauded as heroes when they returned home. The nation had expressed its gratitude. In 1924, Congress had passed legislation granting them special compensation bonuses for their service: $1 a day for service at home, up to $500; and $1.25 a day for service overseas, up to $625. Certificates were granted to 3.5 million servicemen, scheduled to mature in 1945. But the Depression had created an urgency; they needed their bonuses now. So the self-proclaimed Bonus Expeditionary Force, also known as the Bonus Army, gathered in Washington to plead with Congress for an advance on their compensation.

They vowed to stay until they were given the relief they deserved and set up tent cities around the Washington area. The largest, housing some ten thousand veterans and their families, was at Anacostia Flats, across the Potomac from the Capitol.

Sympathetic to their plight, the House had passed legislation to pay bonus money, but on June 17, the measure was defeated in the Senate by a vote of 62 to 17. There would be no bonus payments. The shaken veterans flooded the area, continuing their aggrieved march for more than a month. Their presence was a drumbeat: *Let the nation know our suffering! Let the president, comfortable in his White House, know our suffering!*

The Hoover administration was silent, unmoved. But it was a sense of futility rather than a cold heart that motivated the president. Truly, any president, faced with a massive mob of protest, is in a tough spot: do nothing, and the city is overwhelmed; take decisive action, and the optics look terrible. Hoover had another choice, of course—to try to negotiate at least some payment for the veterans—but that was unlikely. His closest advisers were urging him to hold firm against making a payment.

By the end of July, Hoover decided that the display must end. His attorney general ordered the veterans to leave and their camps to be disbanded. But when police tried to enforce the action, they were met with resistance, and two of the marchers were killed. Hoover ordered the army to clear the camps. Six hundred armed soldiers marched into the streets. Five tanks rolled along at their rear, with Army Chief of Staff Douglas MacArthur in command. The acclaimed military leader was now prepared to fire on men who had served under him in war. "You will use such force as is necessary to accomplish your mission," he told the troops. (Dwight Eisenhower, then serving as

MacArthur's chief military aide, had tried to talk his boss out of it, thinking it was inappropriate for the chief of staff to serve as the riot police. But MacArthur rebuffed him and ordered him to go along.)

As crowds swarmed in alarm and fear, MacArthur's forces drove the Bonus Army out of the city and then set fire to its camps. It was over, but the episode came to symbolize a federal government that had lost its moorings and, many thought, its moral purpose. Hoover would later try to defend his action, suggesting that the veterans had been plants organized by the Communists. But nobody believed it because by the late summer of 1932, the sense of desperation expressed by the veterans was shared across the United States. FDR observed that Hoover's action might have lost him the election, though his words were somewhat hypocritical as FDR had not supported paying the Bonus Army and might have made the same choice had he been in office.

Meanwhile, reconciliation, or at least its appearance, was in the air in the Roosevelt-Smith relationship. At the New York State Democratic Convention to choose a gubernatorial candidate, the newly nominated Roosevelt took the stage. Looking down, he saw Smith below as a delegate and motioned him to the stage.

"Hello, Frank, I'm glad to see you," Smith said.

"Hello, Al, I'm glad to see you too—and that's from the heart."

The crowd erupted in wild cheering, with the joy that comes from seeing two warring siblings make amends. Roosevelt and Smith would never be exactly friendly, but they could at least show unity in a common cause.

With a realistic promise of victory, party advisers, nervous about FDR's health, told him that his best bet would be to run a cautious campaign, giving some radio speeches but avoiding a grueling national tour. They wanted to play it safe, urging a "front porch" strategy, but FDR was in no mood for that. He loved campaigning, and he was itching to get out on the road. He launched a nine-thousand-mile cross-country trip aboard a specially outfitted campaign train. As Farley marveled, "There is nothing in politics—or out of it—that has the lure and fascination of a presidential candidate's special train."

Often, FDR was accompanied by family members, especially James. James recalled "the little family act" they put on over and over again during a whistle-stop tour of the country. FDR would come out to the rear platform on James's arm. They had perfected their moves to the point that FDR's reliance on James's steadying bulk was hardly noticeable. "This is my little boy, Jimmy," FDR would begin his remarks. "I have more hair than he has!" James found the joke as thin as his hair, but the crowds loved it.

For the most part, FDR didn't suffer any embarrassing physical mishaps on the road. However, on one occasion, when he was standing and gripping a podium at a rally in Georgia, the podium fell over, toppling Roosevelt into the orchestra pit below. Without missing a beat, his aides dragged him back onto the stage, and he continued speaking. No mention was made of the fall, but when he finished, he got a standing ovation from the crowd. Notably, the incident was missing from press reports of the speech.

Moley, who went along on many of the trips, called FDR a "troubadour" on the trail. "Campaigning for him was unadulterated joy," he wrote, describing the experience in sweeping prose. "It was broad rivers, green forests, waving corn, and undulating wheat; it was crowds of friends, from the half dozen who, seated on a baggage truck, waved to the cheery face at the speeding window . . . it was hands extended in welcome, voices warm with greeting, faces reflecting his smile along the interminable wayside." Sometimes, when traveling in an open car, FDR was mobbed by fans. In San Francisco, there was a close call when an overly enthusiastic supporter grabbed his hand while the car was moving and nearly yanked off his arm.

Busily working over speeches, Moley discovered the special challenge of discarding the comfortable New Yorker prose and speaking to each part of the nation in its own terms. He was sensitive to the need to calibrate speeches so they would appeal to different regional audiences—as he said of one speech, "It won the Midwest without waking up the dogs of the East."

There was also an acknowledgment of the unique communication challenges of the era. Speeches were aired on the radio, but outside the closed confines of a studio, the technology was rudimentary. Once, when FDR was scheduled to speak out in the open with a broadcast transmitted over the radio, a veteran senator took Moley aside. "Now, before we get talking about the substance of this thing, remember this," he said. "Our man is going to be talking in an open field. His speech is going to be broadcast, but there won't be auxiliary microphones spread around to pick up applause. There'll have to be a helluva lot of cheering—and *loud* cheering—if the speech isn't going to sound like a dud to people listening at home." He suggested that Moley construct the speech so that there were clear applause lines every four hundred to six hundred words, so the radio audience could hear the enthusiasm.

In contrast to Roosevelt's tour across the country, President Hoover preferred a "Rose Garden" campaign strategy, staying close to home to take care of the nation's business and delivering only a handful of speeches. He felt trapped by circumstances, failing to realize that his case might have looked stronger if people could have seen and touched him. His was a heavy burden that felt ill defined by political slogans, and his unpopularity was clear. Sometimes, as a respite, he'd travel to his retreat on the Rapidan River in the Blue Ridge Mountains of Virginia. He'd bought the property after taking office in 1929. Rapidan had many bucolic features, but Hoover treasured it most for the opportunity to go fly-fishing—his greatest passion. He wisely realized that the president, with the stresses of the nation and the world on his shoulders, should have a place to ease the pressure. Rapidan was the precursor of Roosevelt's Shangri-La, later renamed Camp David.

The obligations of the Great Depression were so great that they followed Hoover to Rapidan. By the time of the 1932 campaign, he used the camp mostly for high-level meetings. Unfortunately, that didn't stop the press from writing about Hoover "going fishing" while the nation crumbled.

It was unfair, but Hoover was a victim of the political reality that once a narrative takes hold, it is rarely possible to shake loose from it. He could not escape the constant messages about his failures.

The night before the election, with most of his family decamped to New York City, FDR stayed at Hyde Park with Moley. They sat before the fire and talked quietly about the campaign. The next morning, Eleanor arrived to vote, and then they all went to the city to wait for the election returns. By evening, there was growing confidence in the Roosevelt camp that FDR would win, but no one knew for sure; Gallup didn't start producing polls until 1936. Family and friends gathered for a buffet dinner at the Roosevelts' East 65th Street house before heading over to Democratic National Committee headquarters at the Biltmore Hotel. FDR sat at a large table, with a radio and telephones, and kept score as the night went on. Rosenman was there with his wife, and at one point in the evening he noticed two men, strangers, enter the room and stand next to FDR. He learned that they were Secret Service, at the ready if Roosevelt prevailed.

As the returns came in, the news kept getting better, and the mood was celebratory. The only person missing from the celebration was Howe, who'd remained closeted in his office blocks away, poring over returns and mumbling pessimistically about the tallies—refusing to take "yes" for an answer.

Late in the evening, when it was undeniable that FDR would prevail, Farley and Eleanor went to see Howe and urge him to join them at headquarters. Howe, pouring a glass from a dusty bottle of Madeira, smiled and took a sip, but he refused to budge until Hoover conceded, which he did at 2:00 A.M.

It was a landslide. FDR carried forty-two states, with 472 electoral votes to Hoover's six states and 59 electoral votes. The popular vote margin was vast: 22.8 million to 15.7 million votes.

Eleanor was happy for her husband, thinking that the victory "would make up for the blow that fate had dealt him when he was stricken with infantile paralysis." But in her own heart she felt turmoil. She'd enjoyed her newfound independence. The White House was the antithesis of freedom; she would belong to the nation now and would have to fight for every small measure of privacy.

At the end of the long night, after Hoover had conceded, James took his father home and helped him into bed. They sat talking for a long time. Finally James rose to leave, kissing the president-elect good night. FDR looked up at his son. "You know, Jimmy," he said softly, "all my life I have been afraid of only one thing—fire. Tonight I think I'm afraid of something else."

James leaned in. "Afraid of what, Pa?" he asked.

"I'm just afraid that I may not have the strength to do this job," FDR replied in a rare moment of self-doubt that he would share only with a most trusted person. James might have tried to object, but his father went on, "After you leave me tonight, Jimmy, I am going to pray. I am going to pray that God will help me, that he will give me the strength and guidance to do this job and to do it right. I hope you will pray for me, too, Jimmy."

Gazing down at his father's earnest face, James realized that he was embarking on the loneliest journey of all, one that no human companion could ease. He left FDR to his prayers, and when he reached his own room, he began to pray, as his father had asked.

THEODORE ROOSEVELT ONCE DIVIDED presidents into two camps—James Buchanan types, who remained inactive in the midst of national crises; and Abraham Lincoln types, who boldly used their power to act decisively. According to Grace Tully, who had begun working as an assistant to Missy LeHand and would follow FDR to the White House as his personal secretary, FDR viewed Hoover as a Buchanan type, who abdicated his sworn duty and his constitutional power to lift the United States out of the Depression. Nevertheless, he was prepared to bury his personal feelings about the president in order to ensure a smooth transition. That, however, was not to be. Hoover wanted something much more from FDR than a typical transitional role.

Within days of his victory, FDR received a telegram from Hoover, inviting him to the White House on November 22 to discuss foreign war debts. That, right away, was a red flag. FDR was open to engaging in transition meetings, but he certainly didn't want to get embroiled in the debt question before assuming office in March. Hoover had placed a moratorium on repayments in June 1931 that was scheduled to be lifted on December 15. The British and French were lobbying for a delay, and Hoover had to make a decision.

Moley noted that "there was nothing ambiguous about the suggestion that Roosevelt should share with him the responsibilities for action on the December 15 problem." Roosevelt thought it inappropriate to engage in policy making before taking office, and he was concerned about Hoover's intention. He responded, agreeing to a meeting but emphasizing that it would be "wholly informal and personal." He worried that Hoover might try to corral him into a joint plan, and he was concerned when he learned that Secretary of the Treasury Ogden Mills would be joining the discussion. He decided to take Moley along as a witness and adviser.

FDR sympathized with Hoover's dilemma, but he worried about a collaboration that would give the false impression that he agreed with the president's policy platform. FDR planned to focus on domestic issues early in his presidency, and he didn't want to take on a complicated foreign negotiation right out of the gate.

Roosevelt and Moley entered the White House and were ushered into the Red Room, where Hoover was waiting, his face a mask, with Mills at his side. After they greeted each other, Hoover took a seat on a red divan, with Roosevelt next to him on an upright chair. Moley and Mills sat across from them. Hoover puffed on a cigar as the other three lit cigarettes.

Meetings between victor and defeated are never easy, but it was in Roosevelt's nature to be warm and personable, to break down resistance through friendly conversation. He began his meeting with Hoover with light chatter. But his manner and attempts at conversation did nothing to melt the frozen demeanor of the man he had defeated for office. Mills was similarly chilly. Moley wrote that "it was clear that you could have scoured the country without finding two people who distrusted Roosevelt—as a human being and as a President-elect—more than that pair."

Hoover launched into a lengthy lecture on the debt question and then said he wanted to restart the Debt Commission; he invited Roosevelt to participate in naming members. Roosevelt declined. Until he was president, he didn't want to put a personal stamp on any efforts.

The meeting failed to meet Hoover's objective of bringing FDR into his policy fold, and it did little to further the transition process. But one can empathize with Hoover's plight. At the time, the lame-duck period between the election and inauguration was lengthy—almost four months. That was especially problematic given the dire state of the nation. With the economy on the precipice of collapse, Hoover felt an obligation to use every tool at his disposal to address the crisis, even if it meant drawing FDR into an unusual collaboration. FDR could not know the awful burden of that responsibility; he was still in the glow of victory, feeling that the hard work of governing could wait. Hoover wanted nothing of FDR's sunny platitudes. He needed his help. FDR believed that Hoover was well meaning, but he recognized the president's plea for the minefield it was: if he allowed himself to be enlisted in the service of Hoover's policy, it would leave him hamstrung when he took office. Thus the impasse.

After the meeting, FDR asked Moley to join him at Warm Springs, where he would work on the architecture of his administration. While there, he explained that he was going to appoint Howe to the position of chief secretary—a role that predated chief of staff, which didn't exist then. He wanted Moley by his side as well.

Moley balked, telling FDR that he was completely unsuited to the restrictive organizational environment and wanted to continue as a professor. Roosevelt said he understood, but he'd found just the right title that would give Moley both prestige and the freedom to continue working with FDR as he always had: assistant secretary of state. In that position, Moley could help translate policy into action. FDR needed him.

"I have no Cabinet yet," he said. "I can't call in many people for advice and help without inviting speculation about whether I'm going to appoint them. That will embarrass them and me." Moley *knew* him, he argued. He knew how he thought. He understood the issues. Roosevelt was unwilling to take no for an answer. Moley said he'd think about it, but he was doubtful. "I was no professional daredevil, spoiling to pitch camp in a mound of dynamite sticks," he wrote of his reluctance to join the administration. However, FDR got what he wanted, and Moley came on board, for a while at least.

Another visitor to Warm Springs was the newsman Stephen Early, an original member of the Cuff Links Gang, who now had a job at Paramount, overseeing the newsreel business. Roosevelt told him he wanted him to join his administration as press secretary. For Early, it was a call he could not refuse, but he told Roosevelt that he could come for only two years. Roosevelt smiled and said that would be fine. (Early would end up staying for twelve years.)

The appointment deeply disappointed Howe, who had cast himself in the role. As James Roosevelt observed, "Smoking, coughing, sloppy cut Howe wanted desperately to be father's first press secretary, but father felt him unfit for this public position."

Early's experience in the ways of the working press would prove invaluable, although he knew it would be a treacherous arena. He said that accepting FDR's offer was "like sticking one's hand into the lion's mouth."

The effort to put together a full cabinet consumed much of FDR's attention in the months between the election and the inauguration. It was a chaotic process because he wasn't interested in filling the jobs with cronies and he didn't really have a script for the kind of people he was looking for. He wanted to check a few boxes—especially geographical distribution and the first appointment ever of a woman secretary. He hoped, especially in the two main positions, secretary of state and secretary of the Treasury, to find men who supported his views. However, the full picture of the New Deal was still coming into view, and at that point it existed mostly as an oratorical vision. Given the mess the country was in, few people were rushing to join Roosevelt's White House. It was a little like setting sail on a ship full of leaks; much better to wait until the worst of the leaks had been plugged before boarding the ship.

Tennessee senator Cordell Hull quickly emerged as a leading candidate for secretary of state. Hull was a Howe favorite, a southerner who'd helped swing the South to FDR early in the campaign. Although he'd served eleven terms in Congress before his election to the Senate, Hull, understated and notoriously inarticulate, might have seemed an unlikely choice for the nation's top diplomat. Several Democratic senators thought so, appealing to Moley to ask his boss to reconsider. They didn't think that Hull had either the international experience or the personal skills for the role. Perhaps he'd be better off at the Treasury, they suggested. FDR held firm, and although Hull took more than a month to say yes, he eventually agreed. He would remain in the post until the end of Roosevelt's third term, when he stepped down for health reasons.

Since neither FDR nor Hull had much international experience, it promised to be a steep learning curve, but Hull had very definite opinions. A longtime free trader, he was set to go up against hardened anti-internationalist, protariff forces, including his new assistant secretary, Moley. The two would soon be engaged in a public fight that would end with Moley leaving the administration within a year. FDR, who wanted to focus on national recovery, realized that some of his major initiatives had global implications, as the domestic situation was tied to the global economic depression. Hull was there to set the course. "In many ways," Hull's biographer Michael A. Butler wrote, "this Tennessee politician would prove a transitional figure between the old democracy and the New Deal and between the pre–World War I era and the contemporary world."

Clearly, Roosevelt expected to be the face of his own economic policy, but he also wanted a strong Treasury secretary who was aligned with his policies. The name that kept coming up was that of Virginia senator Carter Glass, who had served for two years as Wilson's Treasury secretary, had been a senator since 1920, and before that had been a congressman for many years. Glass immediately let it be known he had one big problem with FDR's program: his plan to abandon the gold standard. The gold standard was the linkage of the value of currency to that of gold. By ending the gold standard, more currency would be available in the economy, but Glass, among others, feared that the result could be an overabundance that would cause inflation. He turned down FDR's offer, citing his wife's poor health.

Quickly, FDR picked William Woodin, a Republican industrialist and director of the Federal Reserve Bank of New York. He felt comfortable with Woodin, whom he knew through the Warm Springs Foundation, where Woodin was a trustee. But just as he was getting ready to announce Woodin, Glass re-emerged, possibly changing his mind about the appointment. Howe and Moley wanted Woodin and quickly sent a coded wire to FDR at Warm Springs:

PREFER A WOODEN ROOF TO A GLASS ROOF OVER SWIMMING POOL.

FDR laughed loudly when he read the message, and he took it to heart. It would turn out not to be the best choice. Although the sixty-four-year-old Woodin was engaged in the early days of the administration, he fell gravely ill and resigned in December 1933. He died the following May. Woodin was replaced by Henry Morgenthau, Jr., who would remain Treasury secretary until the end of Roosevelt's presidency.

FDR liked and respected his old friend and Dutchess County neighbor, although Morgenthau could be overly sensitive and was known for the frequency of his resignation letters, which he then took back. He was more conservative than the president and would often spar with FDR as the New Deal plans were outlined, but he would truly come into his own as the nation faced war. A Jew of German origin, Morgenthau was an early influence in helping FDR come around on the fight against Hitler. He would later be intimately involved in the creation of a postwar plan.

For secretary of the interior, a vital role in the economic recovery, FDR chose Harold Ickes, a progressive Republican who had campaigned for Teddy Roosevelt's ill-fated third party in 1912 and who had joined Republicans for FDR in 1932. After meeting with Ickes once, FDR told Howe and Moley, "I liked the cut of his jib." What he meant by that is not entirely clear, as Ickes was a notoriously ill-tempered and personally unsavory character—he would title his memoir *The Autobiography of a Curmudgeon.* But he did turn out to be an able administrator of the Public Works Administration, one of the signature programs of the New Deal, and would remain in his position throughout FDR's terms in office.

Like interior, the role of secretary of agriculture would be critical to the nation's revival. FDR's choice was Henry A. Wallace, whose father had served in that role for Harding and Coolidge. Wallace came from a long-standing Iowa farming family and was also the editor of a family farm journal. He was a political newcomer but made an immediate good impression for his dedication to the plight of rural farm communities, which he believed had been disproportionately harmed by the economic crisis. He would soon become a regular presence on the road, giving powerful speeches in the manner of a holy warrior. He often quoted the Bible and spoke about New Deal programs, such as the Agricultural Adjustment Act, which had reduced surpluses and increased agricultural prices, as Christian obligations.

FDR and Wallace were very different people, but FDR no doubt appreciated a man who compared his cause to a moral crusade. He would reward Wallace by choosing him as his running mate for his third term.

Frances Perkins, whom FDR had appointed commissioner of the Department of Labor in New York State when he was governor, was his choice for secretary of labor, the first woman to serve as a cabinet secretary. Perkins had been a devoted and effective champion of labor issues for more than twenty years, ever since she had personally witnessed the devastating fire at the Triangle Shirtwaist Company in 1911. She watched as forty-seven women jumped to their deaths from high floors, and she afterward became an advocate for safe working conditions. She would later say that the fire had been "the day the

New Deal was born." She would remain with Roosevelt's administration until the end, making a large contribution, including drafting the Social Security Act.

Montana senator Thomas J. Walsh was FDR's choice for attorney general. A savvy politician and Democratic Party leader, he would never take office. On the train coming to Washington for the inauguration, he suffered a fatal heart attack. Roosevelt quickly named Homer Cummings, who had been an effective delegate wrangler for Roosevelt at the 1932 convention. Cummings had been slated for a job as governor general of the Philippines, but he changed course. Cummings would be a party to FDR's highly controversial and ultimately failed effort to pack the Supreme Court with judges who favored FDR's initiatives. He might rather have been in the Philippines.

THE ECONOMY WAITED FOR no man. The Depression worsened as Inauguration Day approached. On February 14, 1933, the Michigan governor announced an eight-day bank moratorium in the state, trying to halt the run on banks that had swept the nation. The following day, FDR was in Miami to deliver an address to an American Legion gathering. Twenty thousand people crowded into Bayfront Park to listen to Roosevelt, who was accompanied by Chicago mayor Anton Cermak. Roosevelt's car pulled up to a platform where a microphone had been installed, and he lifted himself onto the back of his seat and delivered a short, rousing speech to the crowd. Then he sat back down. At that moment, five shots rang out, striking Cermak, who was standing on the running board, and four bystanders. FDR, who was the intended target, was spared, probably due to the quick action of a woman in the crowd. Lillian Cross had been standing next to the shooter as he lifted his gun, and she swung her purse and hit him in the arm, shifting his aim just enough to miss Roosevelt.

The Secret Service rushed Roosevelt away from the scene, but he stopped them when he saw Cermak lying on the ground. He ordered him placed in his car, and he cradled Cermak all the way to the hospital. There he comforted the injured and waited to hear about Cermak's condition. Cermak had barely survived the shooting and was fighting for his life. He finally succumbed on March 6. The others recovered.

The shooter was an unemployed bricklayer named Giuseppe Zangara, who told police he hated everyone who was rich and that he had intended to kill Roosevelt. After Cermak's death, the assassin was tried for first-degree murder and received the death penalty. Mrs. Cross, whose quick action had saved the president-elect, was invited to FDR's inauguration and attended the inaugural ball.

After the incident, Moley, who had been in a car following FDR, stood by, waiting for the shock to hit Roosevelt. It never happened. "There was nothing—not so much as the twitching of a muscle," Moley recalled. "He just went on as usual."

Three days after the assassination attempt, FDR received a telegram from Hoover on the worsening bank crisis, imploring FDR to join him in making a joint public statement agreeing to a series of measures to restore public confidence. Roosevelt's secretary, Grace Tully, wrote that Roosevelt considered the request "cheeky." She explained, "By implication, it asked Roosevelt to abandon his own program and accept that of a discredited administration . . . to commit himself in advance to a policy which was becoming increasingly untenable."

Hoover kept trying. Shortly before the inauguration, he attempted again to enlist FDR in making a joint proclamation calling for a bank holiday. "Like hell I will," FDR replied. "If you haven't the guts to do it yourself, I'll wait until I'm president to do it."

Hoover was furious. He felt that Roosevelt was playing politics with the life of the nation, and in a sense, he was right. FDR did not want Hoover's name affixed to any successful effort. In a move that no doubt angered Hoover, Roosevelt announced a bank holiday two days after taking office.

PART TWO

SEEKING GREATNESS

CHAPTER 5

THE MIGHTY PEN

February 27, 1933

At Hyde Park, FDR seated himself before a small card table in the glow of an evening fire, prepared to tackle the inauguration address, which he would deliver on March 4. The previous day, Moley had presented a typed draft of the speech for his review, and FDR had spent the day going over it line by line. Now, he told Moley, by way of an editing process, he wanted to copy the draft in longhand, making edits as he went along.

He carefully copied the draft on a legal pad, rewriting sentences and discussing each phrase with Moley. It was a laborious process that went on late into the night—somewhat baffling to Moley, but he didn't object. Once the fully recopied and edited draft was completed, Moley rose and tossed his typewritten version into the fire. "This is your speech now," he declared.

Indeed, FDR's handwritten copy became the official version. To this day, it remains at the FDR Library in Hyde Park, with a note from Roosevelt attached: "The Inaugural Address as written at Hyde Park on Monday, February 27, 1933. I started it about 9:00 P.M. and ended at 1:30 A.M. A number of minor changes were made in subsequent drafts but the final draft is substantially the same as this original." (Decades later,

JFK was said to have used a similar technique of copying his speechwriter's draft of his inauguration address in longhand so it would appear to be entirely his own. Perhaps he got the idea from FDR!)

Moley, who would grow disillusioned with the Roosevelt administration early on, later defended his authorship of the original, which he'd set alight. He resented the omission of his role in its creation so much that he wrote a second memoir in 1966 to set the record straight. "Some historians accept the note as an indication that on the night of February 27 Roosevelt sat down all alone in his library at Hyde Park and dashed off the draft," he wrote. ". . . The omission of the fact that I was present with him that night, that I had put before him a draft that I had prepared after much consideration and many conferences with him seems strange . . ."

But although it might have been poor form for FDR to create a public record that was not exactly truthful, it was equally poor form for Moley to claim authorship. As Dwight Eisenhower's speechwriter Malcolm Moos would later note, "Presidential speechwriters know that presidents have ownership of their speeches by virtue of the fact that they deliver the words and are held to account for them." He was describing the collaborative process employed by many presidents and one that FDR employed—never a lone man's work and the drafts laden with the principal's pencil marks, until no one could say for sure who made which contribution.

Notably, the original handwritten version did not have the speech's most famous words, "The only thing we have to fear is fear itself," in the first paragraph. Instead, it read:

I am certain that my fellow Americans expect that on my induction into the Presidency I will address them

with a candor and a decision which the present situation
of our Nation impels. This is no occasion of soft speaking or the raising of false hopes.

FDR continued to work on the speech for the rest of the
week, and when the final version was typed, it contained a re-
vised first paragraph:

> I am certain that my fellow Americans expect that on
> my induction into the Presidency I will address them
> with a candor and a decision which the present situation
> of our nation impels.
>
> This is preëminently the time to speak the truth, the
> whole truth, frankly and boldly. Nor need we shrink
> from honestly facing conditions in our country today.
> This great nation will endure as it has endured, will re-
> vive and will prosper.
>
> So first of all let me assert my firm belief that the
> only thing we have to fear is fear itself—nameless, un-
> reasoning, unjustified terror which paralyzes needed ef-
> forts to convert retreat into advance.
>
> In every dark hour of our national life a leadership
> of frankness and vigor has met with that understanding
> and support of the people themselves which is essential
> to victory. I am convinced that you will again give that
> support to leadership in these critical days.

It has never been entirely clear where the new first paragraph came from. Rosenman investigated the matter and finally
decided that the words were FDR's own, although Moley insists
the paragraph was written by Howe. Whatever their origin,
they had the desired impact. To this day, we can listen to the

scratchy audio of FDR's voice coming over the wireless, the timbre breaking through. Millions of Americans heard the speech on their radios, and the line about fear stayed with them. Many decades later, people still consider it a rallying cry for the era.

Was the phrase a bit of magical thinking? The nation was in the height of a catastrophic economic depression. Surely, there was plenty to fear: poverty, hunger, violence, the collapse of the social fabric. FDR's words were not a denial of the brutal realities but a call to transcend them. He'd experienced in his own life the emotionally paralyzing effects of fear when he had first discovered he could not use his legs. He was calling on the nation's citizens to be fearless, to rise above their circumstances.

Roosevelt loved speech writing, speech making, and simply speaking, as he did in his fireside chats. His emotionally loaded words were calls to action, to courage, and to renewal. He gave hundreds of speeches, many of them memorable, during his twelve-plus years in office. Yet he would not have an official speech-writing force in the White House, as later presidents did. Rather, he relied on a collection of trusted aides and former supporters—people who knew his thinking and could capture his intention. Chief among them early on were Rosenman and Moley.

The two men didn't always get along, as they had very different styles and approaches. Rosenman thought that Moley could be smug and was overly deferential to people of importance. But each served FDR in his own way, with the ever-gloomy Howe wringing his hands in the background.

Once in the White House, Roosevelt would prioritize the speech-writing shop. At least several evenings a month, he would call in various aides and advisers, including Rosenman, mix them drinks, order up a tray of sandwiches, and settle in for a speech-writing session. He insisted on being closely involved in the process, and when he finally took his leave, the others would remain behind, sometimes long into the night, perfecting the text and submitting draft after draft to the stenographer's pool to type.

FDR was an inveterate editor, constantly rereading and reshaping his speeches, adding words and changing the order of paragraphs. The process helped him memorize the speeches so he could speak more intimately to his audiences.

Rosenman described Roosevelt's speeches as tools of invention. Most of his big ideas were without precedent, as were his greatest challenges. He was writing the script for the hard task at hand, but when he spoke plain words they sometimes sounded like poetry.

FDR was extremely sensitive to the perception that his speeches were not of his own making. He set the record straight in his official papers:

In preparing a speech I usually take the various drafts and suggestions which have been submitted to me and also the material which has been accumulated in the speech file on various subjects, read them carefully, lay them aside, and then dictate my own draft, usually to Miss Tully. Naturally, the final speech will contain some of the thoughts and even some of the sentences which appeared in some of the drafts or suggestions submitted.

I suppose it is human that two or three of the many persons with whom I have consulted in the preparation of speeches should seek to give the impression that they have been responsible for the writing of the speeches, and that one or two of them should claim authorship or should state that some other individual was the author. Such assertions, however, are not accurate.

Fully appreciating that the reading copies of FDR's speeches and fireside chats were historical documents, Tully made sure they were returned to her for safekeeping after FDR delivered each speech or broadcast.

MARCH 3, 1933, THE day before the inauguration, the Roosevelts and their son James visited the White House for a traditional social call. As they entered, FDR was greeted enthusiastically by an usher who had been there since TR's days. Ushered into the Green Room on the first floor, they were made to wait. Mrs. Hoover entered after a few minutes, but there was no sign of the president for half an hour—the second time he'd kept FDR waiting for a noticeably long time. When Hoover finally arrived, FDR was surprised to see that he was accompanied by Ogden Mills. Clearly Hoover once again intended to turn their social call into a policy meeting.

James recalled the tense moment. "I sat there fascinated as Father gave me one of my earliest lessons in how to avoid political booby traps." When Hoover said he'd invited Mills, thinking he might be helpful to their discussion, FDR swiftly replied that he would not presume to bring up any serious discussion on a purely social occasion, and in any case, he'd want his own advisers present for such a meeting. His response stopped Hoover, but the conversation after that was barely civil.

Finally the visit came to an end. "Mr. President," Roosevelt said in an attempt to be gracious, "as you know, it is rather difficult for me to move in a hurry. It takes me a little while to get up, and I know how busy you must be, sir, so please don't wait for me."

Hoover rose and gave Roosevelt a cold look. "Mr. Roosevelt, after you have been president for a while, you will learn that the President of the United States waits for no one." He walked out without another word, leaving his embarrassed wife behind to say her flustered good-byes. James was enraged by the rudeness, but his father shrugged it off. He understood Hoover. He knew what it felt like to lose an election. He also accepted that the president was angry at him for not collaborating with him during the transition.

The next morning, Saturday, March 4, the skies were overcast but the temperature was mild as FDR and his family attended services at St. John's Episcopal Church across from the White House, beginning a tradition other presidents-elect would follow. The now-elderly Reverend Endicott Peabody, Roosevelt's former schoolmaster, led the service. Afterward, the president-elect returned to his hotel before emerging again for the short trip to the White House's north entrance. He did not go inside but waited for Hoover in the car, which would be followed by one carrying First Lady Lou Hoover and Eleanor.

During what must have seemed an interminable thirty-minute ride to the Capitol, Hoover and FDR sat mostly in silence. FDR tried a couple of times to make conversation and received no response.

Large crowds lined the roadway, cheering loudly. Roosevelt glanced at Hoover, who was staring straight ahead, his hands in his lap. He felt the crowds deserved acknowledgment—a smile and a wave—but he did not want to overstep if the president made no move. Hoover knew the cheers were not for him, and he refused to do anything. Finally, FDR threw caution to the wind, removed his top hat, and began to wave it in the air, to the delight of the crowds.

Observing Hoover's pinched face and drooping shoulders, Eleanor felt some sympathy for the defeated president, calling him a victim of circumstances and of his own belief system.

"He had served the country well during World War I, and there is no question but that during his term of office he wanted to do what was best for the country," she wrote.

When it was time to take the oath (Vice President Garner having done so privately in the Senate chamber), FDR rose. Before a crowd of 150,000 people, as the Marine Band played "Hail to the Chief," he gripped James's reliable arm and made his way the 146-foot distance to the podium on the East Portico of the Capitol building. Chief Justice Charles Evans Hughes stood to deliver the oath of office. FDR laid his hand on the heirloom family Dutch Bible, which was opened to First Corinthians 13:13: "And now abideth faith, hope and charity, these three, but the greatest of these is charity." He repeated the oath, then swiveled at the podium to face the crowd as a twenty-one-gun salute rang out. Then he began to speak, forcefully delivering his well-worked opening and then going on for another twelve minutes, with both bracing prose and hard truths, knowing that millions of Americans were tuned in to their radios, breathlessly seeking some modicum of hope. His manner was certain, his demeanor almost cheerful, his words decisive:

> If I read the temper of our people correctly, we now realize as we have never realized before our interdependence on each other; that we cannot merely take but we must give as well; that if we are to go forward, we must move as a trained and loyal army willing to sacrifice for the good of a common discipline, because without such discipline no progress is made, no leadership becomes effective. We are, I know, ready and willing to submit our lives and property to such discipline, because it makes possible a leadership which aims at a larger good. This

I propose to offer, pledging that the larger purposes will bind upon us all as a sacred obligation with a unity of duty hitherto evoked only in time of armed strife.

With this pledge taken, I assume unhesitatingly the leadership of this great army of our people dedicated to a disciplined attack upon our common problems. . . .

The people of the United States have not failed. In their need they have registered a mandate that they want direct, vigorous action. They have asked for discipline and direction under leadership. They have made me the present instrument of their wishes. In the spirit of the gift I take it.

In this dedication of a Nation we humbly ask the blessing of God. May He protect each and every one of us. May He guide me in the days to come.

As the crowd roared, the new president grabbed his son's arm and slowly made his way off the stage. Hoover rose and quickly exited. Like every president being replaced, he knew he was no longer the story of the day. "Democracy is not a kind employer," he wrote of his ouster. "The only way out of elective office is to get sick or die or get kicked out." Even so, in the coming days he would begin to feel a tremendous sense of relief, no longer waking to the fearful circumstances that were his to resolve. Now the fate of the nation was in another man's hands.

Roosevelt had always loved parades, and the inauguration parade was a marvel, with forty marching bands and representatives from all the states. General MacArthur was the grand marshal. FDR stayed to watch until the end, and when he entered the White House for the first time as president, he found a mobbed reception of two thousand people, organized by his wife, under way. He slipped past the crowds and went upstairs to the Lincoln Study for a mass swearing in of his cabinet. They'd all been rapidly confirmed that day, without objection, as a rare nod to the urgency of the times.

After dinner with a large gathering of the Roosevelt clan, including the Oyster Bay contingent, which had not often supported him (and many of whom had likely voted for Hoover), Eleanor left with family members for the inaugural ball, while Roosevelt retired to the Lincoln Study with Howe. They sat and talked late into the evening. For twenty-two years they'd been a team, Howe believing in FDR even when he could not summon the faith to believe in himself. Unsentimental, irascible, and single-minded, Howe was as responsible as anyone for putting FDR into the White House, which is why the president was so forgiving of his churlish, sulking behavior, his fractious relationships with everyone around him, and his sense of entitlement. Howe would continue to call the president "Franklin," a proof of intimacy that no one could take away.

CHAPTER 6

GOVERNING IN CRISIS

Stephen Early, the new press secretary, was certain of one thing: he didn't want the president's relationship with the press to have any of the lingering stuffiness and distancing of the Hoover years—what the *New York Times* had called "a citadel of aloofness." Windows and doors must be opened. Transparency must be a rule, not an exception. Correspondents and the president must engage in frank exchanges. It was a heady goal and not exactly practical. Many presidents had promised new eras of openness and transparency before taking office, but the doors had soon been closed.

Still, Early thought they could do better. He advised FDR to avoid playing favorites with certain newsmen as Hoover had done; it only inspired resentment and rebellion among the rest of the reporters. He also thought that the process of asking and answering questions should be spontaneous. In the previous administration, reporters had been required to submit their questions in writing, and then the president would decide which ones to answer. So few questions were ever answered that many of the press had given up on submitting them.

And the press conferences should be frequent and on a schedule when possible; Early suggested Wednesday mornings at 10:00, to meet the deadlines of the afternoon papers, and Friday afternoons at 4:00, for the weekend and Sunday papers.

On March 8, at 10:10 A.M., 125 reporters were summoned into the Oval Office for the first press conference with President Roosevelt. They were packed tightly in the 546-square-foot room. Seated behind his desk, the president greeted each of them with a word and a handshake. His opening statement took them all by surprise. "I am told that what I am about to do will become impossible, but I am going to try it," he said. "We are not going to have any more written questions and of course while I cannot answer seventy-five or a hundred questions because I simply haven't got the physical time, I see no reason why I should not talk to you ladies and gentlemen off the record just the way I have been doing in Albany and the way I used to do it in the Navy Department down here."

It was great news for reporters, but there was a catch. For one thing, he told them he would not respond to speculation or answer any "if" questions. Follow-up questions—FDR called them "cross-examination"—would not be permitted. In addition—and this was more meaningful—he would reserve the right to speak off the record and on background during his press conferences.

At first the reporters felt confused and blindsided by this rule, as FDR constantly prevaricated—"off the record . . . on background."

"Mr. President," a reporter asked, "how did you like your first week in the White House?"

"Off the record, I haven't had enough sleep, otherwise fine," the president replied to laughter.

Still, most reporters found the genial, freewheeling sessions valuable as inside views of the president's thinking and demeanor. He didn't hold back, even if his comments were not supposed to be quoted directly. The sessions were fun, and they had an intimate feeling—until a reporter tried to file a story. As the noted international journalist John Gunther put it, "Mr. Roosevelt's features expressed amazement, curiosity, sympathy, decision, playfulness, dignity and surpassing charm. Yet he said almost nothing. Questions were deflected, diverted, diluted. Answers—when they did come—were concise and clear. But I never met anyone who showed greater capacity for avoiding a direct answer while giving the questioner a feeling that his question had been answered."

Early was pulling strings in the background, telling reporters when they were allowed to quote something directly. Those lines he mimeographed and handed out, in an effort to control the press. In general, however, reporters were pleased with the signals they were getting from Early, who, as one of their own, understood them and tried to accommodate them.

Roosevelt's strict rules didn't last long. The newspaper editors weren't having it. However, whatever the content, the access was prized, and FDR enjoyed talking about his programs and sparring with the press. In his first term alone, he held 337 press conferences.

One thing missing from the press conferences was diversity. No African American reporters were admitted, on the pretext that only daily newspapers could be represented and most black papers were weeklies. Neither were women reporters invited, despite FDR's addressing the gathering as "ladies and gentlemen."

Eleanor was concerned about the exclusion of women. She rightly judged that if a female reporter was excluded from the source of news, she would be less competitive and might even lose her job. Urged on by her friend Associated Press reporter Lorena Hickok, Eleanor began a practice of women-only news conferences. Thirty-five female journalists attended the first one, held in the Red Room on March 6. Eleanor announced that they would cover issues of importance to the women of the nation and not encroach on her husband's turf—policy. That was a half measure, and it didn't last long. Within a short time, Eleanor was dealing with national issues and even breaking news—as when she announced that beer would be served in the White House when Prohibition was repealed. The women's press conferences provided positive coverage for Eleanor and gave her a public profile she had not had before.

Much has been made of FDR's strong legislative response to the Great Depression during his first year in office. But it wasn't just the programs that mattered. In his private moments, he imagined what the people were feeling and experiencing and wondered how he could reach out to them, as both a teacher and a truth teller. He understood that the government's role was more than just giving aid; it was bringing the people along to be the architects of their own destiny. To accomplish that, he reinstituted the practice of fireside chats he had used while governor, as a way of having a conversation with Americans in the intimacy of their living rooms. His first chat on Sunday, March 12, was held on CBS and introduced by Robert Trout: "The president wants to come into your house and sit at your fireside for a little fireside chat." Although they summoned up the cozy image of the president sitting before the fire speaking personally to Americans, the "chats" actually took place as he sat behind a desk crowded with microphones, a reading light, a glass of water, cigarettes, and a transcript. About thirty folding chairs were set up for an invited audience.

The performance itself was conversational and warm, instructive and a dose of straight talk that gave listeners a sense of being part of the program. "I want to talk for a few minutes with the people of the United States about banking," he opened his first chat on March 12.

He began it as a tutorial:

First of all let me state the simple fact that when you deposit money in a bank the bank does not put the money into a safe deposit vault. It invests your money in many different forms of credit—bonds, commercial paper, mortgages and many other kinds of loans. In other words, the bank puts your money to work to keep the wheels of industry and of agriculture turning around. A comparatively small part of the money you put into the bank is kept in currency—an amount which in normal times is wholly sufficient to cover the cash needs of the average citizen. In other words the total amount of all the currency in the country is only a small fraction of the total deposits in all of the banks.

Then he shifted to the crisis:

What, then, happened during the last few days of February and the first few days of March? Because of undermined confidence on the part of the public, there was a general rush by a large portion of our population to turn bank deposits into currency or gold. A rush so great that the soundest banks could not get enough currency to meet the demand. The reason for this was that on the spur of the moment it was, of course, impossible to sell perfectly sound assets of a bank and convert them into cash except at panic prices far below their real value.

By the afternoon of March 3 scarcely a bank in the country was open to do business. Proclamations temporarily closing them in whole or in part had been issued by the Governors in almost all the states.

It was then that I issued the proclamation providing for the nation-wide bank holiday, and this was the first step in the Government's reconstruction of our financial and economic fabric.

Americans listened, and they responded. Roosevelt's declaration of a bank holiday on March 6 and his instructive fireside chat had the effect of instantly ending a run by people trying to withdraw their money from the failing banks. He'd also called Congress into an emergency session, giving it a proposal allowing the government some control over banks, choosing which of them could be saved and reorganizing others. Those that could not be helped would be allowed to fail. The result was the Emergency Banking Relief Act. The dramatic stopgap and FDR's confident message to the nation had the desired effect. In the coming weeks, Americans began to redeposit almost $1 billion into their banks.

And so the New Deal was under way. FDR kept Congress in session for three months as he issued a rapid-fire alphabet soup of legislative initiatives, including the Federal Emergency Relief Act (FERA), which provided assistance to the unemployed through the states; the Agricultural Adjustment Act (AAA), which limited surpluses and raised farm prices; the Public Works Administration (PWA), which created jobs through ambitious projects, such as building plants, bridges, and hospitals; the United States Banking Act, also known as the Glass-Steagall Act, which created the FDIC, giving the federal government the supervision of banks; the Securities Exchange Act, which created the Securities and Exchange Commission (SEC), to help regulate the stock market and prevent another crash; the Civilian Conservation Corps (CCC), which put young, unemployed men, including unemployed World War I veterans, to work planting trees, restoring forests, and building campgrounds; the National Industrial Recovery Act (NIRA), which regulated wages and prices in industry; and the Civil Works Administration (CWA), which also harnessed the working power of the unemployed to build a national infrastructure. Thanks to Eleanor, those jobs would also be open to women.

In the beginning, FDR managed to get just about everything he asked for. As the social commentator and humorist Will Rogers joked about the overwhelmingly positive public response, "If he burned down the capitol we would cheer and say 'well, we at least got a fire started anyhow.'"

THE ROOSEVELT WHITE HOUSE was noisy, messy, chaotic, and entirely different from anything seen before. Grandchildren ran about, having free run of the house and gardens. Once the Roosevelts' son John dropped off his infant at the White House without notice, and FDR had to personally call up and order diapers. It could seem like bedlam, but FDR and Eleanor were at ease in the chaos.

The Roosevelts wanted the White House to serve as a people's house, which was impractical, but they gave it a go in the early days. FDR told the staff that any person who called the White House in trouble—about putting food on the table or paying the mortgage—must be spoken with and helped, if possible. Everyone, from the highest-ranked individuals to the secretaries, pitched in to answer those calls.

Never before or since had so many stragglers, guests, and workers been invited to live on the premises, either temporarily or permanently. Eleanor thought nothing of inviting guests to stay over on the thinnest pretense. Missy LeHand had a suite of rooms on the third floor. Eleanor's close friend Lorena Hickok moved in as well. Henrietta Nesbitt and her husband, down-and-out neighbors from Hyde Park, were installed at Eleanor's direction. Nesbitt was given charge of the kitchen, despite having no experience and, by all accounts, little talent. She would be a thorn in FDR's side for the entire course of his presidency. The meals prepared at her direction were atrocious: tasteless, dreary menus that featured such unappetizing items as gelatin-filled salads, bread-and-butter sandwiches, deviled eggs with tomato sauce, and prune whip. State dinners became an embarrassment, private meals a misery. Eleanor, who cared little about cuisine and believed that the White House meals should reflect the frugal entrées of the nation's Depression-era dinner tables, ignored her husband's entreaties. Eleanor's biographer Blanche Wiesen Cook even suggested a more nefarious reason for Eleanor's refusal to give her husband the food he liked. Cook speculated that it "was one expression of her passive-aggressive behavior in a marriage of remarkable and labyrinthine complexity."

The only arena Nesbitt couldn't touch was FDR's daily cocktail hour—the Children's Hour, as he called it. There he would mix his strong martinis and LeHand would arrange more appetizing tidbits, fortifying the president for the grim dinner ahead.

Sara, who was approaching eighty when FDR took office, spent most of her time at Hyde Park, although she still took her European vacations in the summer and was a regular guest at the White House, where she reigned supreme in the "queen's suite" and happily filled Eleanor's place when she was absent. Sara's devotion to her son was unwavering. "You are my life," she told him, and that was certainly true. Sara loved to gossip about her daughter-in-law and to express her disapproval for the way she brought riffraff into the White House—left-leaning activists, women who dressed like men, poor people looking for a handout.

During one of her early visits, Sara voiced dismay that the

domestic staff was made up of so many African Americans. She thought they should be replaced by whites, and she made such a big deal of it that Eleanor dropped her normal deference to her mother-in-law and replied sharply, "I have never told you this before, but I must tell you now. You run your house, and I'll run mine."

Sara was proud of her son and never stopped being his biggest fan, but she was something of a snob who dressed and acted in an imperious manner, borrowed from another era. She considered politics a very unappetizing business. In time, she had come to accept the less-than-presentable Howe, but she could not hide her horror at some of the politicians and favor seekers who trooped through Hyde Park and now the White House.

Eleanor became an activist first lady who set her own pace and went where she wanted, including inner-city neighborhoods and farm and mining communities. FDR took his wife's wanderings in stride. One day she'd scheduled a prison visit in Baltimore but left that morning without telling the president. Later, FDR called her secretary, Malvina "Tommy" Thompson, looking for her.

"She's in prison, Mr. President," Thompson told him.

"I'm not surprised," FDR said. "But what for?"

In her travels, Eleanor insisted on driving her own car, often alone, and chafed at the security restrictions demanded by her position. She disliked having the Secret Service around. After fruitless efforts to corral the wandering first lady, the Secret Service finally took action. As Eleanor recalled in her autobiography, "After the head of the Secret Service found I was not going to allow an agent to accompany me everywhere, he went one day to Louis Howe, plunked a revolver down on the table and said, 'Well, all right, if Mrs. Roosevelt is going to drive around the country alone, at least ask her to carry this in the car.' " Eleanor agreed, and their bodyguard Earl Miller stepped in to give the first lady shooting lessons. From then on, she carried a gun. She acknowledged that she was not an expert shot, although "if inheritance has anything to do with it, I ought to be, for my father could hold his own even in the west in those early days when my uncle, Theodore Roosevelt, had a ranch in the Dakotas. These things do not however go by inheritance, and my opportunities for shooting have been few and far between, but if the necessity arose, I do know how to use a pistol." Her children loved to tease her about the gun, calling her "Dead-Eye Nell" and "Annie Oakley Roosevelt."

Sara had never approved of Eleanor's independence, and now she got in her barbs, when she could, about the first lady's extensive travels out into the country. After Eleanor made a well-publicized visit to a mine, Sara added a postscript to a letter to FDR: "I hope Eleanor is with you this morning. . . . I see she has emerged from the mine . . . that is something to be thankful for."

Surrounding Roosevelt inside the White House was a coterie of aides, a mixed bag in terms of their styles and contributions. Tully colorfully described them as having "histrionic talent" and wrote, "Most of them sensed and demonstrated an intellectual compatibility with the Boss; most of them were sincere, able and thoroughly loyal to the President. A few were misfits whose intellectual insincerity or frustrated selfishness resulted in their being dropped from the 'big time' cast. As far as I know none of either category were Rasputins with evil designs . . ."

Even so, as in any administration, there were spats and sometimes all-out brawls among aides and cabinet members, and FDR often had to be the mediator. He didn't mind when disputes were aired at the weekly cabinet meetings, but he hated it when they spilled outside—especially when there were leaks to the press. He disliked rancor and as a leader always tried to put a positive spin on events. It was both a gift and a weakness, for it sometimes meant protecting those who didn't deserve it and ignoring those who could cause his administration real harm. However, most of the cabinet would have considered the benefit greater than the downside. "I and everyone else came away from an interview with the President feeling better," Frances Perkins observed. "It was not that he had solved my problem or given me a clear direction which I could follow blindly, but that he had made me more cheerful, stronger, more determined to do what, while I talked with him, I had clearly seen was my job and not his. It wasn't so much what he said as the spirit he conveyed."

The resounding midterm victory of Democrats in 1934 gave FDR renewed confidence that the nation was on his side, but 1935 would finally break the spell and begin a period of conflict. Both Democrats and Republicans balked at FDR's plan for a social security bill calling for taxes to be withheld throughout workers' lives, with a form of pension issued after retirement. Democrats criticized the idea of taking any money from workers' paychecks, while Republicans argued that it would create a budget-busting welfare state. Though the Social Security Act ultimately passed and was signed into law, it was clear that Congress was becoming less malleable. So were the courts. Suddenly FDR seemed less like a savior and more like an embattled chief executive.

Then the Supreme Court stepped in to deliver two major blows. The first was a unanimous ruling that the National Industrial Recovery Act, which had set wage and price controls, was an unconstitutional move to centralize executive powers. Jeff Shesol, the author of *Supreme Power: Franklin Roosevelt and the Supreme Court*, wrote that FDR was stunned by the decision, especially the defection of the liberals, such as Justice Louis Brandeis, who had always been reliable "yes" votes. But more bad news was in store. Throughout the year, the Court chipped away at elements of the New Deal, culminating in a December ruling against one of FDR's favorite projects, the Agricultural Adjustment Act. FDR was furious, and although the AAA was up for renewal in Congress and looked likely to fail there, he railed against the Court for acting as a "super-legislature." Roosevelt was not the first nor the last president to attack the Supreme Court for overreaching, but many thought he was the one who had overstepped his executive authority. It had been easy at the height of the Depression to justify emergency efforts, even when they seemed to stretch constitutional powers. But times were changing.

By 1936, as Roosevelt faced an election year, his popular support seemed to be waning, and he was getting battered by the press. Democrats in Congress wanted to scale back on New Deal initiatives, and with the nation more solvent, they urged him to rein in his proposals. Even his own aides were doubting him. When Roosevelt enlisted Moley to draft a convention speech, he was appalled at the conservative tone of Moley's prose. He tossed the draft and called in others, including Rosenman, to write a new speech behind Moley's back.

For the first time in his political career, FDR wouldn't have Howe by his side to badger him and bring the party faithful into line. Howe's health had been failing for some time. Finally, in September 1935, he was admitted to the hospital, and he never left. He died on April 18, 1936.

Roosevelt insisted on holding the funeral at the White House, but he remained silent about Howe, offering no words to express his grief or eulogies to praise Howe's life. Eleanor spoke to the press on the family's behalf while her husband was closeted in his office, speaking to no one. Only at the interment in Fall River, Massachusetts, did the president show his grief. As Howe's coffin was lowered into the ground, FDR gave a faint sob and his eyes filled with tears. His irreplaceable friend, the first person who had believed he could be president, was gone.

Once again, FDR went on the road during the campaign. His opponent was Alf Landon, the Republican governor of Kansas, whose campaign slogan was "I will not promise the moon." He was affable, somewhat liberal, and probably not as political as he needed to be. At one point during the campaign, FDR was in Topeka and Landon invited him to the governor's mansion. There, the two men set aside their political competition to meet as president and governor.

Landon lost in a landslide that was even greater than in FDR's 1932 victory. Cheerful and self-deprecating in defeat, he once called himself "an oilman who never made a million, a lawyer who never had a case and a politician who carried only Maine and Vermont." Active in business for the remainder of his career, he remained a Republican Party stalwart. His daughter, Nancy Landon Kassebaum, would represent Kansas in the Senate for twenty years.

Shortly before Landon's one hundredth birthday in 1987, he received a personal visit from President and Mrs. Reagan. "In a hundred years, Alf Landon chased many dreams and caught most of them," Reagan said. Just not that one.

The Roosevelts were in Hyde Park for the election returns on November 3. At midnight, a commotion arose outside. On the long driveway leading to the house, hundreds of neighbors and friends were marching, accompanied by red torchlights and a brass band. They gathered at the front of the house, singing and shouting. Strapping on his leg braces, FDR went out to the porch and greeted them. No matter how far he traveled, his Hudson Valley neighbors were always his people—and they thought of him that way, too.

The landslide gave Roosevelt new confidence in the path he'd chosen, even as others were urging him to be less strident in his approach. He refused. As he gave his second inaugural address, rain smearing the words on his reading copy, he proclaimed, "Hard-headedness will not so easily excuse hard-heartedness." Worried that he might transpose the two words—as he had done in a practice session—he had drawn a small head over "hard-headedness" and a small heart over "hard-heartedness" in his reading copy.

TWO WEEKS AFTER HIS inauguration, flush with victory and feeling his power, FDR fumbled and made one of the biggest mistakes of his presidency: he tried to remake the Supreme Court—and the lower courts along with it.

In the early years of his administration, there had been no need to grab power—it had been freely given. But later, as the Supreme Court began to bite back at the constitutionality of his programs and Congress began to waver in its support, FDR believed that desperate measures were needed to keep his New Deal rolling along.

On February 5, 1937, he unveiled a plan that had secretly been in the works for months: he asked Congress to give him the authority to appoint an additional justice for every Supreme Court and federal judge over the age of seventy. That could mean up to six additional Supreme Court judges and as many as forty-four judges in the lower federal courts. He explained his plan by citing the inefficiency of the courts, which, he said, was caused by the presence of too many older men with waning faculties. He didn't exactly call them doddering, but he might as well have. As he explained in a press conference:

A lowered mental or physical vigor leads men to avoid an examination of complicated and changed conditions. Little by little, new facts become blurred through old glasses fitted, as it were, for the needs of another generation. . . .

Life tenure of judges, assured by the Constitution, was designed to place the courts beyond temptations or influences which might impair their judgments. It was not intended to create a static judiciary. A constant and systematic addition of younger blood will vitalize the courts and better equip them to recognize and apply the essential concepts of justice in the light of the needs and facts of an ever-changing world.

FDR's proposal was widely panned by the press, led by chief Roosevelt critic Walter Lippmann, who called it a "bloodless coup d'etat." Congress was flooded with letters of outrage from the public. There was a growing consensus that Roosevelt had used a smoke screen in citing the overstressed judiciary. There was no evidence of the Supreme Court being behind in its cases. Most people understood the proposal for what it was: an effort to pack the Court before it dismantled more of the New Deal. Presumably, if such a scheme were adopted, Roosevelt would immediately appoint a slew of liberal judges who would favor his programs.

Even Eleanor weighed in. In a newspaper column she'd started in 1936, called "My Day," she abandoned her normally chatty style to defend her husband:

I read my Herald-Tribune this morning with considerable interest. One page was most amusing. Out of six headlines across the top of the page only one seemed to be without fear. This fear was all inspired by the fact that certain difficulties facing our courts today have been pointed out and tentative remedies suggested. One man felt that the suggested changes had precedents behind them and that we might not either be turning our liberties over to a dictator or weakening our courts but the others were filled with fore-bodings [*sic*]! . . .

One headline is particularly terrifying. It reads: "Plan to pack the court to favor power of a minority is seen." The meaning of this headline is explained below but at first reading you cannot help but link it up with the fact that the opposition to the changes comes largely from the same group which opposed so much of the social legislation of the present administration, and the views of the people on this legislation were rather clearly expressed in November last and they were not a minority group.

Despite Eleanor's attempt to characterize FDR's critics as the usual detractors, and to portray the president's proposal as being the will of the voters who reelected him, even his friends were concerned. FDR seemed to be reinventing the meaning of executive powers to his own liking. As he confided to Rosenman, "When the Chief Justice read me the oath and came to the words 'support the Constitution of the United States' I felt like saying, 'Yes, but it's the Constitution as *I* understand it, flexible enough to meet any new problem of democracy—not the kind of Constitution your Court has raised up as [a] barrier to progress and democracy.'"

FDR, encased in a bubble of his own making, did not appreciate the extent of the public disapproval of his actions. Shesol wrote, "He should have known . . . But it was clear right away that he had failed to anticipate the rage, hurt, humiliation, and betrayal that his Court-packing plan would unleash among his faithful—if often resentful—lieutenants.'"

FDR wasn't the only president ever to resent an uncooperative court or dream of choosing his own justices. But this time his party was against him. His court-packing scheme had crossed a line. "By 1937, FDR and the Democratic leadership were like an old, unhappily married couple, nursing innumerable grievances but unwilling, or unable, to separate," Shesol wrote. "They needed one another—and resented it fiercely."

Despite public disdain for his idea, FDR continued trying to sell it, saying at a dinner for Democrats celebrating the results of the election, "If three well-matched horses are put to the task of ploughing up a field where the going is heavy, and the team of three pull as one, the field will be ploughed. If one horse lies down in the traces or plunges off in another direction, the field will not be ploughed." He meant to say, of course, that the judiciary was letting down the other two branches of government, but it was not an apt analogy, given the separation of powers.

In fact, some of FDR's proposals for improving the efficiency and effectiveness of the judiciary at large were quite acceptable to Congress. But the Supreme Court proposal was so far off the mark that it got most of the attention and all of the negative blowback. In July, Congress defeated the measure soundly, and it never made a reappearance.

In the decades following FDR's presidency, there has been a continuing debate about whether his New Deal was responsible for ending the Depression. Some of Roosevelt's programs became codified in the US economy, and the country was better off, if only marginally, by the late 1930s. However, many experts believe it was World War II that was ultimately responsible for ending the Depression.

During Roosevelt's second term, the nation's attention was

increasingly drawn to the growing threat of war in Europe. FDR had been worried about the rise of Adolf Hitler for years, but he and the Congress maintained a policy of neutrality. During his 1936 presidential campaign, Roosevelt had promised that American boys would not be sent to fight in foreign wars. But the signs were clear that war was coming—if not yet for the United States, then for the world abroad.

Ironically, for the man who would rise to power on a platform of aggressive nationalism, Adolf Hitler was born not in Germany but in Austria-Hungary and did not become a German citizen until 1932. By then he had captured the imagination of the German people and would go on to annex his birthplace in 1936, making it part of the Fatherland.

Hitler's rise continues to baffle and intrigue people to this day. His innocuous roots—comfortably middle class—his lackluster education, and his early artistic temperament can seem contrary to his later rise to power. Although his father, a customs official, planned for Adolf to follow him into the civil service, his son had other ambitions. He dropped out of school at age sixteen to pursue his dream of becoming a great artist. In 1907, at eighteen, he applied to the pinnacle of art schools, the Academy of Fine Arts Vienna, and took the rigorous painting exam. He was bluntly informed that his paintings did not show the requisite talent for admission. Disbelieving, he tried a second time and was rejected again. He was devastated, his artistic identity shattered. Depressed, broke, and feeling purposeless, he moved to Munich, where he dressed like an artist and made a meager living drawing postcards of local sights. His rejection by the artistic community would in part fuel his anti-Semitism, as he believed that Jews controlled the arts.

Where Hitler failed in art, he found expression in politics. After serving in the Bavarian army in World War I, Hitler was adrift until 1919, when he found a home in the German Workers' Party, a small organization of rabble-rousers with only a scattered impact. In the political arena, Hitler discovered his gift: the ability to stir crowds with an unrestrained oratory that thrilled his audiences. That his rise occurred so swiftly is a testament to the extreme levels of despair and helplessness many Germans felt after their defeat in the First World War. Within a year, Hitler had seized control of the party, changing its name to the National Socialist German Workers' Party—Nazi for short.

The Nazis attacked the government for its failure to restore the economy, which was sinking due to the heavy burden of war reparations and the collapsing currency. The German government's impotence enraged Hitler and the Nazis. In 1923, he spearheaded a daring effort to overthrow the government, which landed him in jail for treason.

Sentenced to five years, Hitler would serve only nine months, but during his incarceration he would produce the first volume of *Mein Kampf*, or "My Struggle," which he dictated to his cell mate Rudolf Hess. It was a compilation of his grievances, which were encapsulated in a treatise on the supremacy of the Aryan—true German—race and a denigration of others, especially Jews. He described the struggle for world power as a war between the human Aryan and the subhuman Jew. He wrote that the Nazi Party was "obligated to promote the victory of the better and stronger, and demand the subordination of the inferior and weaker in accordance with the eternal will that dominates this universe." That premise would form the centerpiece of his justification for everything he did after that. Released from prison, a hero to many in his party, he fought off his rivals and continued to amass support. It was a slow process, but by the time the stock market crashed in 1929, the Nazis were poised to gain power.

It seemed an impossible dream. With only 100,000 members in a country of 60 million, the Nazi Party seemed destined to be nothing more than a loud and largely ineffective resistance party, but as the economy worsened, it steadily gained followers, and ultimately a place in the halls of influence.

In the national election on September 14, 1930, the Nazis received 6,371,000 votes, which earned them more than one hundred seats in the German Reichstag and a place as the second-largest political party in the nation. In 1932, the same year FDR won the presidency, Hitler ran against the elderly German president, Paul von Hindenburg. He failed to win but, with more than eleven million votes, robbed Hindenburg of the majority he needed to govern. The ensuing run-off failed to resolve matters, and the government was in chaos.

With Hitler demanding a new election and Nazis rioting in ever-growing hordes, Hindenburg chose to put an end to the upheaval by appointing Hitler chancellor. The appointment provided Hitler with more than a toehold. Within weeks, he systematically crushed the opposition and seized control of the levers of power. By March 1933, he had insinuated his allies into every aspect of government, forcing the increasingly befuddled Hindenburg to give him absolute "emergency" powers to stem the violence.

How to explain the complete sublimation of Germany's traditions and government? "In many ways Nazism was antithetical to what the great mass of Germans said they admired and certainly to what they paid homage," observed Hitler biographer Eugene Davidson. But, he noted, in Hitler the nation found a flourishing cult of personality that gave it a new reason for being. "It is a hard thing to describe, but the voice itself was mesmeric," the Jewish literary icon George Steiner told Hitler biographer Ron Rosenbaum, describing Hitler's radio addresses. "The physique is—the amazing thing is that the *body* comes through on the radio. I can't put it any other way. You feel you're following the gestures." He added that if Hitler had risen during the television era, he would have been "the ultimate master on TV."

Otto Strasser, an old associate who had broken with the party after Hitler's rise to power, succinctly captured Hitler's appeal in his memoir *Hitler and I*. He wrote, "Hitler responds to the vibration of the human heart with the delicacy of a seismograph, or perhaps of a wireless receiving set, enabling him . . . to act as a loudspeaker proclaiming the most secret desires, the least admissible instincts, the sufferings, and personal revolts of a whole nation." Those desires and instincts, no longer so secret, were found in the lingering bitter grievances of defeat in the war, the sense of being unappreciated, like a lonely child on the playground of Europe. Now Hitler was offering a vision of revenge by conquest and the rise of an Aryan identity into which they could instill a majestic destiny. That heady promise was on offer in Hitler's rhetoric, and it became even more seductive as the Great Depression crippled the German economy.

Soon after taking power, Hitler began pursuing a course to restore Germany's glory. Public discontent was the match that lit his ambition. Racial purity was the fever dream of his program. He immediately set about curtailing Jewish freedoms, organizing a brutal law enforcement body, the Gestapo, to carry out his will. With Hindenburg on his deathbed and powerless to stop him, Hitler increased his absolute control. When Hindenburg died, Hitler announced that he would assume power, not as president but as Führer—supreme leader.

His plan was a two-pronged attack on the system. The first prong was a policy of *Lebensraum*, meaning literally "living space"—which meant conquering other nations to increase German territory. The second was a philosophy of Aryan domination directed at the elimination of the Jewish people. He was deadly serious about both goals.

As the world watched with growing concern, there was little official resistance to Hitler. In England, the attitude was wait and see. Only one voice stood out—that of Winston Churchill, a conservative member of the House of Commons, who had been railing against Hitler since he had become chancellor. In 1935, Churchill scoped out the international situation pretty well, asking friends, "With Germany arming at breakneck speed, England lost in a pacifist dream, France corrupt and torn by dissension, America remote and indifferent . . . do you not tremble for your children?" But he was largely ignored.

On November 5, 1937, Hitler held a secret conference at the Reich Chancellery in Berlin, where he outlined his program, which he felt confident of executing with little resistance. By now the German people were in thrall to the gifted showman; he was unstoppable.

England and France were flummoxed, bowed into seeking appeasement by any means. British prime minister Neville Chamberlain approached Hitler with the proposition that they were two reasonable men, both seeking to avoid war, and proposed discussions to be held "in a spirit of collaboration and good will." He felt it his duty to prevent war, and he didn't believe that Hitler had the army or the aspirations of a conqueror. He thought that Nazism could be contained.

With that purpose in mind, Chamberlain convinced Hitler to hold a high-level meeting in Munich in September 1938 to bring together Germany, France, Great Britain, and Italy and carve out an agreement that would keep the peace. The issue on the table was Hitler's desire to annex the Sudetenland, a region of Czechoslovakia heavily populated by ethnic Germans—which Hitler felt rightfully belonged to Germany. Czechoslovakia had no representation at the conference, and with Italy's Benito Mussolini in Hitler's corner, Chamberlain and French prime minister Édouard Daladier gave in, thinking that a small appeasement would prevent all-out war. The Munich Pact allowed Hitler to annex the Sudetenland without resistance from their two countries.

In Great Britain, the news of the Munich Pact was met with relief. Churchill wasn't buying it, though. He was intent on raising an alarm to the world. The alarm would eventually reach the reluctant ears of the president in Washington. For the first five years of FDR's presidency, he was a lone wolf, content to behave as the sole director and in many respects administrator of his policies. Though most of his arrogance was masked by an easy humor, an enjoyment of people, and a clever intellect, there's no doubt that he viewed himself as the final arbiter of all disputes. But the war would change him, leading him to behave more collaboratively with leaders who could match him on the world stage. The times would demand it. And Winston Churchill would demand it.

CHAPTER 7

FRANKLIN AND WINSTON

October 16, 1938

His own countrymen thought of Winston Churchill as a has-been. At sixty-four, he was consigned to a seat in the House of Commons. He had little power as a parliamentarian, no government position, no stronghold but the one provided by his own defiance and sense of purpose. Yet he boldly decided to broadcast a rousing message to a US audience. His target: Great Britain's prime minister, Neville Chamberlain, and his policy of appeasement of Hitler, reflected in the newly signed Munich Pact. His audience: the American people, especially their leader in the White House. His tone: that of a preacher. His office called the style of his speech "psalm form"—phrases rising and falling in a melodic series of verses, each forceful and emotionally charged. Churchill always wrote his own speeches, as he did this one. He found power in words, both written and spoken.

After the Munich Pact was signed, Churchill knew that many of his countrymen were relieved that war had been avoided. He had watched Chamberlain's victorious return to London, with cheering crowds welcoming him home as he promised "peace for our time." But Churchill knew that appeasing Hitler was not the road to peace. Rather, it was a weakening of resolve that would in time exact an even higher price. Indeed, the following year, Hitler would break the pact, invading the whole of Czechoslovakia.

Churchill's initial response to the Munich Pact and Chamberlain's victory lap was a fiery speech in Parliament:

> Never will you have friendship with the present German Government. You must have diplomatic and correct relations, but there can never be friendship between the British democracy and the Nazi power, that power which spurns Christian ethics, which cheers its onward course by a barbarous paganism, which vaunts the spirit of aggression and conquest, which derives strength and perverted pleasure from persecution, and uses, as we have seen, with pitiless brutality the threat of murderous force. That power cannot ever be the trusted friend of the British democracy.

The speech produced carping from his colleagues, who rolled their eyes at the melodramatic Churchill spewing fire in his customary manner. Now he turned to the people of the United States, making clear, as he would do many times, that Hitler posed a global threat:

> Far away, happily protected by the Atlantic and Pacific Oceans, you, the people of the United States, to whom I now have the chance to speak, are the spectators, and I may add the increasingly involved spectators of these tragedies and crimes. We are left in no doubt where American conviction and sympathies lie; but will you wait until British freedom and independence

have succumbed, and then take up the cause when it is three-quarters ruined, yourselves alone? I hear that they are saying in the United States that because England and France have failed to do their duty therefore the American people can wash their hands of the whole business. This may be the passing mood of many people, but there is no sense in it. If things have got much worse, all the more must we try to cope with them. . . .

We must arm. Britain must arm. America must arm. . . .

But arms . . . are not sufficient by themselves. We must add to them the power of ideas. People say we ought not to allow ourselves to be drawn into a theoretical antagonism between Nazidom and democracy; but the antagonism is here now. It is the very conflict of spiritual and moral ideas which gives the free countries a great part of their strength.

That was Churchill throwing down the gauntlet, but it was an early volley when he was in his weakest position at home. That did not concern him. He would make his case as a citizen of the world and await his chance to do more. He would have that chance, but not yet.

Like FDR, Churchill was a man of notable flaws. He was stubborn and emotional, a reckless romantic with an explosive temper. He was high spirited but subject to dark moods, which could send aides scurrying for cover. He was quick to berate his long-suffering wife, Clementine, for her perceived failings, although she was his main source of stability and comfort. He was a heavy smoker and drinker who was often accused of giving speeches when he'd imbibed too much. His physical presence was like a battering ram—his bulky frame pressing forward restlessly, eyes slicing through his opponents, a fat cigar permanently affixed to the side of his mouth. He didn't walk, he stomped, spearing the ground with his walking stick. Also like FDR, he was the product of the aristocracy, somewhat pompous and entitled. Because his mother was American, he thought he had a window into the American soul. The consensus among his peers was that he should think about retirement. Churchill barreled on.

Churchill had a very high opinion of himself and didn't try to hide his self-importance. "We are all worms," he once said. "But I do believe that I am a glow worm." Indeed, he would shine a bright light on Hitler's true nature and intentions long before others could bring themselves to do so.

He set his sights on FDR, seeking to bring him and his nation to the fight he was determined to make against Hitler. Two men with such big personalities and great ambitions were not natural collaborators, but one thing Churchill understood, and FDR eventually came to realize, was that they would need each other.

Churchill was not naive about the scope of the challenge in engaging American hearts and minds. Throughout the 1930s, the forces of isolationism had gained an upper hand in the United States. Feeling burned by the losses suffered in the Great War and crushed by the economic calamities of the Great Depression, Americans were in no mood to give more of their lives and treasure to conflicts abroad. The United States was not yet fully out of the Depression, but the economy was starting to stabilize. An overseas fight was the last thing anyone wanted. Hitler was Europe's problem to deal with. Churchill believed that view was shortsighted. He could not know Roosevelt's heart, but he thought the president didn't fully appreciate the troubles ahead.

With the progress of the New Deal plateauing in Congress and his own party resisting his vision on the home front, FDR began turning his attention to the international crisis. Like Prime Minister Chamberlain, FDR still considered the threat posed by Hitler as something that could be managed and negotiated. He had "a tigerish devotion to his conviction that negotiations, however protracted, were preferable to warfare," Grace Tully wrote. In September, shortly before the Munich Pact was signed, FDR had sent a telegram to Hitler, urging him to find a way to negotiate peacefully with Czechoslovakia. His telegram arrived even as Chamberlain and Daladier were caving in to Hitler's demands.

Hitler's telegram in response essentially discounted FDR's position:

BERLIN, SEPTEMBER 27, 1938

TO HIS EXCELLENCY THE PRESIDENT OF THE UNITED
STATES OF AMERICA, MR. FRANKLIN ROOSEVELT,
WASHINGTON.

IN YOUR TELEGRAM RECEIVED BY ME ON SEPTEMBER
26 YOUR EXCELLENCY ADDRESSED AN APPEAL TO
ME IN THE NAME OF THE AMERICAN PEOPLE, IN THE
INTEREST OF THE MAINTENANCE OF PEACE, NOT TO
BREAK OFF NEGOTIATIONS IN THE DISPUTE WHICH HAS
ARISEN IN EUROPE, AND TO STRIVE FOR A PEACEFUL,
HONORABLE, AND CONSTRUCTIVE SETTLEMENT OF THIS
QUESTION. BE ASSURED THAT I CAN FULLY APPRECIATE
THE LOFTY INTENTION ON WHICH YOUR REMARKS
ARE BASED AND THAT I SHARE IN EVERY RESPECT
YOUR OPINION REGARDING THE UNFORESEEABLE

CONSEQUENCES OF A EUROPEAN WAR. PRECISELY FOR
THIS REASON, HOWEVER, I CAN AND MUST DECLINE
ALL RESPONSIBILITY OF THE GERMAN PEOPLE AND
THEIR LEADERS, IF THE FURTHER DEVELOPMENT,
CONTRARY TO ALL MY EFFORTS UP TO THE PRESENT,
SHOULD ACTUALLY LEAD TO THE OUTBREAK OF
HOSTILITIES.

IT IS MY CONVICTION THAT YOU, MR. PRESIDENT,
WHEN YOU REALIZE THE WHOLE DEVELOPMENT OF
THE SUDETEN GERMAN PROBLEM FROM ITS INCEPTION
TO THE PRESENT DAY, WILL RECOGNIZE THAT THE
GERMAN GOVERNMENT HAVE TRULY NOT BEEN
LACKING EITHER IN PATIENCE OR IN A SINCERE DESIRE
FOR A PEACEFUL UNDERSTANDING. IT IS NOT GERMANY
WHO IS TO BLAME FOR THE FACT THAT THERE IS A
SUDETEN GERMAN PROBLEM AT ALL AND THAT THE
PRESENT UNTENABLE CONDITIONS HAVE ARISEN FROM
IT. THE TERRIBLE FATE OF THE PEOPLE AFFECTED BY
THE PROBLEM NO LONGER ADMITS OF A FURTHER
POSTPONEMENT OF ITS SOLUTION. THE POSSIBILITIES
OF ARRIVING AT A JUST SETTLEMENT BY AGREEMENT
ARE THEREFORE EXHAUSTED WITH THE PROPOSALS
OF THE GERMAN MEMORANDUM. IT NOW RESTS, NOT
WITH THE GERMAN GOVERNMENT, BUT WITH THE
CZECHOSLOVAK GOVERNMENT ALONE, TO DECIDE IF
THEY WANT PEACE OR WAR.

Hitler was a master at characterizing aggression as righteousness and adept at adopting the victim's complaint that he had been forced into it by circumstances. He presented himself as a man of peace who was threatened by unreasonable foes.

That so many people bought the narrative is a testament to his oratorical skill. It's very possible that had the United States been present at the meeting in Munich, it would have joined the Munich Pact along with France and Great Britain. Churchill seemed to be the lone voice urging otherwise.

Unlike Churchill, FDR was tiptoeing into the discussion, cautiously testing the language. In a January speech, he posed the conflict as a tripart issue: religion, at the source, with its foundation of dignity and respect for others; democracy, a covenant among free people to respect the rights and liberties of their fellows; and international good faith, the will of civilized nations to respect the rights and liberties of others. Hitler's aggression failed each of those tests. FDR thought that Hitler, along with his ally Mussolini, could be pressured into compliance.

He spoke often of what the nation could do "short of war," but there was little clarity. One possibility was a repeal of the arms embargo, which prevented the United States from contributing any arms or materials to foreign belligerents, but isolationists in Congress had no interest in changing any elements of the neutrality laws that had been passed in the mid-1930s, which had directed the United States to stay on the sidelines in any future wars.

FDR was trying to find a path forward. In April, he teased an idea to Secretary of the Treasury Henry Morgenthau, who had become one of his closest advisers. "The President told me that he had an idea which he would like to do if the State Department would only let him," Morgenthau wrote, "namely, he'd like to write a letter to Hitler and Mussolini suggesting that they give sacred guarantees that they would not absorb any other countries in Europe and that if they were willing to give some guarantees that he in turn would be willing to meet with them at the Azores and sit around a table and discuss (1) disarmament and (2) world trade." FDR's thinking was that if they rejected that good-faith offer, it would strengthen his position.

On April 14, 1939, FDR went ahead with the plan, sending a seven-page telegram to Hitler and Mussolini. In part, it read:

YOU REALIZE I AM SURE THAT THROUGHOUT THE
WORLD HUNDREDS OF MILLIONS OF HUMAN BEINGS
ARE LIVING TODAY IN CONSTANT FEAR OF A NEW WAR
OR EVEN A SERIES OF WARS.

THE EXISTENCE OF THIS FEAR—AND THE POSSIBILITY
OF SUCH A CONFLICT—IS OF DEFINITE CONCERN
TO THE PEOPLE OF THE UNITED STATES FOR WHOM
I SPEAK, AS IT MUST ALSO BE TO THE PEOPLES OF
THE OTHER NATIONS OF THE ENTIRE WESTERN
HEMISPHERE. ALL OF THEM KNOW THAT ANY MAJOR
WAR, EVEN IF IT WERE TO BE CONFINED TO OTHER
CONTINENTS, MUST BEAR HEAVILY ON THEM DURING
ITS CONTINUANCE AND ALSO FOR GENERATIONS TO
COME. . . .

ARE YOU WILLING TO GIVE ASSURANCE THAT YOUR
ARMED FORCES WILL NOT ATTACK OR INVADE THE
TERRITORY OR POSSESSIONS OF THE FOLLOWING
INDEPENDENT NATIONS: FINLAND, ESTONIA, LATVIA,
LITHUANIA, SWEDEN, NORWAY, DENMARK, THE
NETHERLANDS, BELGIUM, GREAT BRITAIN AND
IRELAND, FRANCE, PORTUGAL, SPAIN, SWITZERLAND,
LIECHTENSTEIN, LUXEMBOURG, POLAND, HUNGARY,
RUMANIA, YUGOSLAVIA, RUSSIA, BULGARIA, GREECE,
TURKEY, IRAQ, THE ARABIAS, SYRIA, PALESTINE, EGYPT
AND IRAN. . . .

IF SUCH ASSURANCE IS GIVEN BY YOUR GOVERNMENT,
I SHALL IMMEDIATELY TRANSMIT IT TO THE
GOVERNMENTS OF THE NATIONS I HAVE NAMED
AND I SHALL SIMULTANEOUSLY INQUIRE WHETHER,
AS I AM REASONABLY SURE, EACH OF THE NATIONS
ENUMERATED WILL IN TURN GIVE LIKE ASSURANCE
FOR TRANSMISSION TO YOU.

RECIPROCAL ASSURANCES SUCH AS I HAVE OUTLINED
WILL BRING TO THE WORLD AN IMMEDIATE MEASURE
OF RELIEF.

I PROPOSE THAT IF IT IS GIVEN, TWO ESSENTIAL
PROBLEMS SHALL PROMPTLY BE DISCUSSED IN THE
RESULTING PEACEFUL SURROUNDINGS, AND IN THOSE
DISCUSSIONS THE GOVERNMENT OF THE UNITED
STATES WILL GLADLY TAKE PART.

This time there was no polite reply from Hitler. Instead, in an April 28 speech to the Reichstag, he gave a lengthy harangue, tearing into each of FDR's points, mocking the president's words. He addressed Roosevelt directly, as if he were speaking to him, blasting the United States' arrogance and wealth and essentially telling the president to stay on his own turf and not meddle in the affairs of foreign governments, which had their own priorities.

Hitler's aggression in the world was the major concern, but the total depravity of Nazism, especially its treatment of the Jews, was alarming. Jews had been suffering under the Nazis for years, but the world had mostly turned a blind eye until an event had occurred that made ignorance impossible. On November 9, 1938, the world had been shocked by the brutality against Jews in a tragedy known as Kristallnacht, the "Night of Broken Glass." In retaliation for the assassination of a German diplomat in Paris by a Jewish teenager of Polish descent, Nazis rioted across Germany, Austria, and the Sudetenland, destroying synagogues, smashing and burning Jewish stores, and assaulting Jews in the streets. The Gestapo instructed police and firefighters to stand by and do nothing. More than seven thousand Jewish businesses, homes, and schools were destroyed, and nearly one hundred Jews were murdered. Blaming the Jews for the riots, authorities arrested thirty thousand Jewish men and sent them to concentration camps. The terror ramped up calls for the United States and other friendly nations to increase efforts to help Jewish refugees find safe passage to other countries.

In June 1939, Morgenthau appealed to FDR to accept more Jewish refugees. Roosevelt seemed not to fully grasp the scope of the problem. He began to talk about raising funds and getting other countries to accept refugees, but he was talking in the low thousands.

"Mr. President," Morgenthau said, frustrated, "before you talk about money, you have to have a plan first." The plan was something Morgenthau was passionate about helping devise. FDR wasn't there yet—far from it—but Morgenthau hoped he could bring him around. In retrospect, FDR's record on helping the Jews would be mixed. Later, when the full scope of the Final Solution was revealed, FDR was harshly criticized for not doing enough early on when it might have made a difference.

He was making a calculated bet. He was convinced that Americans would not fight a war to save the Jews. So although he advanced projects to help resettle Jewish refugees, he didn't fight too hard for them, and his secretary of state, Cordell Hull, was mostly uninterested in the refugee problem. FDR failed to say much publicly about the plight of the Jews, fearing he would lose what support he had for any involvement in the war effort. As Richard Breitman and Allan Lichtman wrote in *FDR and the Jews*, "Like a triage physician, FDR gave urgent attention to some priorities at times in his presidency, while putting others aside." This was hardly an excuse, although the authors acknowledged that FDR "was a far better president for Jews than any of his political adversaries would have been." He was always calculating. Later, when the United States was in the war, he believed that the best way to save the Jews was to defeat Hitler.

It wasn't lost on FDR that among the appeasers were those who blamed the Jews for the conflict. One of them was Joseph Kennedy, the ambassador to Great Britain. Kennedy openly criticized the "Jew media" in the United States, which, he said, was conspiring to "set a match to the fuse of the world."

FDR didn't trust Joe Kennedy. "Joe always has been an appeaser and always will be an appeaser," he told Morgenthau. "If Germany or Italy made a good peace offer tomorrow, Joe would start working on the King, and his friend the Queen, and from there on down, to get everybody to accept it—and he's just a pain in the neck."

Kennedy could be an embarrassment to the administration, freelancing in efforts to make his own deal with Hitler, who he thought could be brought to the negotiating table with the promise of cash. Kennedy's reports home did their best to paint a picture of Churchill as a reckless drunk and elevate Chamberlain as a man of peace. Overall, Kennedy thought Great Britain didn't have a chance against Hitler, and he wasn't shy about making his feelings known.

But the appeaser who got the most attention was Charles Lindbergh. Lindbergh, whose solo flight across the Atlantic in 1927 had thrilled the masses, was a beloved American hero. People paid attention to him. A staunch isolationist with pro-Nazi sympathies, he said, "The British and the Jewish races, for reasons which are not American, wish to involve us in the war. Their greatest danger to this country lies in their large ownership and influence in *our* motion pictures, *our* press, *our* radio, and *our* government." In 1938, Lindbergh had accepted a medal from Hermann Göring, the commander of the German air force. Lindbergh insisted that Nazism was not a threat to the United States.

Radio correspondent William Shirer, who was stationed in Berlin, kept a low profile as he collected information about the Nazi state. He was dismissive of Lindbergh's claims. "The Lindberghs and their friends laugh at the idea of Germany ever being able to attack the United States," he wrote. "The Germans welcome their laughter and hope more Americans will laugh."

Increasingly, Harry Hopkins was becoming FDR's closest aide—the new Howe. Describing the similarities between Howe and Hopkins, Rosenman observed, "Each of these men could sift the good from the bad, the sound from the unsound, before any matter was submitted to the President. . . . Roosevelt, both as Governor and as President, liked to . . . have one man with whom he could exchange ideas at any time of day, whose judgment and loyalty he trusted, and whose disinterestedness he knew would make the advice impartial. In Louis and Harry he found such people."

When Howe died, he'd left a hole in FDR's life, and FDR missed having an aide for whom he had complete trust. Hopkins fit that role. He had something else in common with Howe, a chronic illness. Diagnosed with stomach cancer in 1939, Hopkins had most of his stomach removed, which severely compromised his ability to digest food. He was often ill, yet he managed to take on enormous responsibilities. Roosevelt came to rely on him as his most trusted adviser—and Churchill would as well, nicknaming him "Lord Root of the Matter." He became so indispensable that FDR would move him and his family into the White House in 1940.

Having Hopkins nearby not only was useful, it was a comfort. "He liked to keep people around him," White House stenographer Dorothy Jones Brady wrote of the president. "And he also was a very lonely man." The first lady operated mostly in her own orbit, and she was often away. Brady described how Missy LeHand used to go out of her way to organize dinner companions for the president so he wouldn't be alone.

A ROYAL CANADIAN PACIFIC train, painted royal blue and silver and carrying King George VI and Queen Elizabeth of the United Kingdom, pulled into Union Station in Washington, DC, on June 8 to the cheer of crowds. It had traveled down from Canada, passing Niagara Falls and heading south, arriving to a festive welcoming party. There to greet the special visitors were the president and first lady. Seeing the president, the king's face lit up. He offered his hand, and Roosevelt shook it vigorously. "Well, at last I greet you!" Roosevelt said, grinning broadly.

The idea of the visit, the first of its kind by British monarchs, had been in the works for months. FDR had extended the invitation after learning that the royal couple was planning a trip to Canada. In a letter to the king on September 17, 1938, he wrote, "I think it would be an excellent thing for Anglo-American relations if you could visit the United States. . . . It occurs to me that a Canadian trip would be crowded with formalities and that you both might like three or four days of very simple country life at Hyde Park, with no formal entertainments and an opportunity to get a bit of rest and relaxation." In his reply, accepting the offer, the king wrote, "I can assure you that the pleasure, which it would in any case give to us personally, would be greatly enhanced by the thought that it was contributing in any way to the cordiality of the relations between our two countries."

Chained by neutrality, Roosevelt was trying to reach out in a largely symbolic gesture—to publicize to the world his support of the king, whose nation seemed on the brink of war. He wanted to demonstrate the kinship of the two nations, even though he was legally prevented from going further.

Though many observers hailed the visit as the social event of the season, behind the scenes Roosevelt and the king were engaged in deep discussions. The president showed himself to be well aware of the dangers being faced by Great Britain, and he discussed naval strategy, doing his best to reassure the king of his support, even though he could make no promises.

The king was grateful for the frank discussion. He wrote in his diary, "Why don't my ministers talk to me as the president did tonight. I feel exactly as though a father were giving me his most careful and wise advice."

In a deeply human way, FDR also wanted to provide the royal couple with a taste of American pleasures, so he invited them to Hyde Park for an all-American picnic.

Sara's house was in a commotion of activity, and Sara demanded perfection. Lizzie McDuffie, on loan from the White House, was summoned by Sara right before the royals were due to arrive. "When everything was set and waiting for them Mrs. Delano Roosevelt called me and said that the carpet on the porch and steps was dusty. 'Can you get someone to sweep it again, Lizzie?' she asked. I took a broom and went over it myself . . . and in a little while King George and Queen Elizabeth were walking on my carpet!"

Soon Sara came upon FDR setting out cocktail glasses and a shaker of gin in the library. She was disapproving and told her son that surely the king and queen would prefer tea after their journey.

When the king entered the library, FDR told him, "My mother thinks you would prefer tea."

The king, whose mother, Queen Mary, was a force of nature as well, replied, "That's what my mother would say too," and he eagerly accepted a martini.

FDR was pleased with the friendly, relaxed mood of the Hyde Park visit, and so were the royals. "They are such a charming and united family," the queen wrote to her mother-in-law, "and living so like English people when they come to their country house."

The high point of the visit was the country picnic held outdoors at the cottage FDR had built on the property. Hot dogs and beer were on the menu, a plan that scandalized many people, including the proper Sara, who was nominally the hostess of the affair. The criticism provoked ribbing from Eleanor: "Oh dear, oh dear, so many people are worried that the dignity of our country will be imperiled by inviting royalty to a hot dog picnic!" Sitting on the porch, the king and queen were eager to try hot dogs ("these delicacies," the king called them) for the first time. According to *New York Times* reporter Felix Belair, Jr., who was on the scene, the king and queen were served their hot dogs on a silver tray but ate them off paper plates. They were a hit. The *Times* headline the following day read, "King Tries Hot Dog and Asks for More." The subhead read, "And He Drinks Beer with Them—Uses Own Camera to Snap Guests Photographing Him."

When it was time for them to leave on the train for Quebec, FDR felt gripped by emotion, knowing they would soon return home to much difficulty. "Good luck to you . . . all the luck in the world," he said sincerely, his eyes watering. The crowd spontaneously began to sing "Auld Lang Syne." Eleanor was moved. "There was something incredibly moving about the scene—the river in the evening light, the voices of many people singing this old song, and the train slowly pulling out with the young couple waving good-by. One thought of the clouds that hung over them and the worries they were going to face, and turned away and left the scene with a heavy heart."

The royal visit had a sobering impact on the Roosevelts. Now the king and queen were like friends. Until the visit, relations with the British had been chilly, since FDR and Chamberlain did not have a friendly relationship. FDR privately sided with Churchill's distaste for Chamberlain's soft touch with Hitler. Meeting the royals brought the fear felt in Great Britain home and made it real. Eleanor was struck by their courage and also by the fact that they had two small daughters at home, Elizabeth and Margaret, whose future was in jeopardy.

War was a looming threat but not yet a reality. Great Britain was desperate for allies, but none appeared. The United States was willing only to offer friendly, but distant support. Then, on August 23, 1939, Great Britain was dealt a severe blow when Germany and the Soviet Union signed a nonaggression pact, an agreement that further isolated Great Britain. Nonaggression was not the same as an alliance. It only meant that Stalin would not fight against Hitler, not that he would join Hitler's fight. His position, for the time being, was neutrality, but it was hard to imagine that the powerful dictator in the east would sit on the sidelines if war was declared. After the war, Stalin's minister of foreign affairs, Vyacheslav Molotov, who had orchestrated the pact, admitted that it was designed as a delaying tactic. Stalin was certain Hitler would eventually attack the Soviet Union. "We did everything to postpone the [inevitable] war," Molotov said. "And we succeeded—for a year and ten months."

Stalin, who had exercised absolute power over the Soviet Union since his rise after the end of Vladimir Lenin's life in 1924, was largely a mystery to the West. Whereas Roosevelt and Churchill had been born to privilege, Stalin was a child of poverty. He was born Iosif Vissarionovich Dzhugashvili on December 18, 1878 (although he would later order a different date, December 21, 1879, to be used in his official biography), in the small town of Gori, Georgia. His father, Besarion, was a cobbler, a tough man, given to drunken violence. Although Soso (as his mother, Ekaterine, nicknamed him) was their third child, he was raised as an only child—both his older brothers had died in infancy. His mother dreamed that he would become an Orthodox priest one day, an idea that infuriated his father, who expected his son to become a cobbler like himself. Stalin's childhood was difficult and often brutal; his father eventually abandoned the family, leaving Ekaterine to raise Iosif alone. She doted on her bright son and found a way to get him admitted to seminary. But Iosif was distracted and rebellious, in spite of his good grades, and became obsessed with the vision of Karl Marx for a revolution against the monarchy. When he was expelled from the seminary for bad behavior, he never looked back, disappointing his mother. Before her death in 1936, as Stalin began the Great Purge of his enemies, she wistfully said to him, "What a pity you never became a priest."

An acolyte of Lenin, Iosif rose quickly through the ranks, fending off rivals such as Leon Trotsky. He skillfully re-created his personal biography, destroying records of his early life so he could present himself in a stronger and more romantic light. He changed his name to Stalin, meaning "man of steel." Although Lenin himself grew disillusioned with Stalin at the end of his life, he was not able to stop Stalin's power grab.

Stalin's iron rule was puzzling to many, since the egalitarian vision of Marxism was of a people's revolution that would lead to a "withering away" of the state. Stalin justified his tight control by arguing that before the state could wither it must first prepare conditions, weed out objections, cull the herd of rebels and malingerers. Only then could it reach the Marxist ideal.

To this end, peasants were forced into collectives at the point of a gun. Farmers could no longer sell grain on the open market. All capitalist practices were forbidden. A deadly famine in 1932–1933 that killed an estimated five million people, most of them in Ukraine, was a direct outgrowth of collectivization. In *Red Famine: Stalin's War on Ukraine*, the journalist Anne Applebaum suggested that it was also a deliberate land grab and genocide of ethnic Ukrainians. Stalin was able to crush the resistance, thanks to a 1934 law allowing him to eliminate anyone he deemed to be an enemy of the state. That provision was as broad as he wanted it to be: If a plant did not meet production goals, it was due to saboteurs; if hungry farmers held back grain, they were robbing the people. Disloyalty to the state was punishable by death. Nearly one million people were murdered in the Great Purge between 1936 and 1938. Millions more were killed or sent to labor camps during his reign.

Stalin, whom his biographer Philip Boobbyer called "a kind of evil genius," survived, propped up by the grand fiction of his supremacy and the worshipful propaganda of his state. Numbed by the dangerous consequences of dissent, the masses were without avenues for rebellion. It was easier to just believe the myth.

As the French novelist and Communist Henri Barbusse wrote in his 1935 biography of Stalin:

> That man is the centre, the heart of everything that radiates from Moscow on the surrounding world. His portrait, either in the form of a sculpture or as a drawing, or as a photograph, is to be found everywhere throughout the Soviet continent, like Lenin and beside that of Lenin. There is hardly a corner of any factory, military barracks, office or shop window in which it does not appear on a red background, between a list of striking socialist statistics . . . and the emblem of the crossed hammer and sickle.

Stalin's daughter, Svetlana, who would defect to the United States after Stalin's death, wrote of her father's thirst for power:

> Human feelings in him were replaced by political considerations. He knew and sensed the political game, its shades, its nuances. He was completely absorbed by it. And since, for many years, his sole concern had been to seize hold and strengthen his power in the Party—and in the country—everything else in him had given away to this one aim.

Her admission was made with sadness. As a young girl, Svetlana had been an adoring daughter to a man who could be loving and playful. He was closer to her than to his two sons, Yakov, by his first marriage, and Vasily. But life in their home turned darker after Svetlana's mother, Stalin's second wife, Nadezhda Alliluyeva, shot herself in 1932 in a despairing act of suicide. "He had always considered my mother his closest and most faithful friend," Svetlana wrote. "He viewed her death as a betrayal and a stab in the back." Unable to comprehend any reality except through his own prism, Stalin grew even more embittered and remote. He never remarried.

Having safely consigned the Soviets to nonaggression, Hitler showed his hand. Deep in the night of September 1, Germany invaded Poland, with a million and a half troops fanning out along its borders. The invasion was the natural progression of Hitler's policy of *Lebensraum*—seizing more "living space" for the superior Germans. Having annexed Austria and Czechoslovakia with barely a response from other nations, perhaps he expected the conquest of Poland to be greeted with the same inertia. But this time he had over-reached. The day after the invasion, Great Britain and France informed Hitler that he must withdraw from Poland by September 3 or face grave consequences. Hitler did not respond. The evening of September 3, Great Britain and France declared war on Germany.

At 3:00 in the morning on September 3, 1939, FDR was woken from sleep with the news. The war was on. In a speech from the White House, he spoke to the American people, in a fireside chat:

> You must master at the outset a simple but unalterable fact in modern foreign relations. When peace has been broken anywhere, the peace of all countries everywhere is in danger.
>
> It is easy for you and me to shrug our shoulders and say that conflicts taking place thousands of miles from the continental United States, and, indeed, the whole American Hemisphere, do not seriously affect the Americas—and that all the United States has to do is to ignore them and go about our own business. Passionately though we may desire detachment, we are forced

to realize that every word that comes through the air, every ship that sails the sea, every battle that is fought, does affect the American future.

Later in the speech he added, "This nation will remain a neutral nation, but I cannot ask that every American remain neutral in thought as well. Even a neutral has a right to take account of facts. Even a neutral cannot be asked to close his mind or his conscience." That line was FDR's own insertion into the prepared draft. He was sending a message, perhaps urging Americans to think for themselves and not simply buy the line of isolationists wholesale.

Still warmed by the visit of King George and Queen Elizabeth, Americans felt a new stirring of sympathy for the Brits, which was echoed in the White House. Eleanor wrote to the queen:

Dear Queen Elizabeth

Ever since England was forced into the war I have wanted to write and tell you how constantly you and the King are in my thoughts.

Since meeting you, I think I can understand a little better what a weight of sorrow and anxiety must be yours.

We can but pray for a just peace and my warm sympathy is with you.

Sincerely yours,
Eleanor Roosevelt

After war was declared, Chamberlain finally brought Churchill into his cabinet as first lord of the Admiralty—Great Britain's version of secretary of the navy, and a position Churchill had held during the First World War. That delighted FDR, who felt he could relate better to a navy man. On September 11, he wrote Churchill:

My dear Churchill,

It's because you and I had similar jobs in World War 1 that I want you to know how glad I am that you're back again in charge of the navy, although I know there are new problems. I want you and the Prime Minister to know that I'd be happy for you to keep me informed of anything important that's happening. You can always send sealed letters directly to me.

I'm glad you finished writing the first parts of your history book before this war started—and I've much enjoyed reading them.

With my sincere regards,
Faithfully yours,
FRANKLIN D. ROOSEVELT

Churchill more than complied with the invitation to keep in touch. Over the course of their relationship, the two men would exchange some two thousand letters.

Feeling their position threatened, American isolationists heightened their rhetoric. On October 13, Lindbergh was on fire with a racially charged speech:

Our bond with Europe is a bond of race and not of political ideology. We had to fight a European army to establish democracy in this country. It is the European race we must preserve; political progress will follow. Racial strength is vital politics, a luxury. If the white race is ever seriously threatened, it may then be time for us to take our part in its protection, to fight side by side with the English, French, and Germans, but not with one against the other for our mutual destruction.

FDR would later tell Morgenthau, "If I should die tomorrow, I want you to know this. I am absolutely convinced that Lindbergh is a Nazi."

On September 21, FDR appeared before Congress to once again urge its members to repeal the arms embargo. He had called Rosenman to Washington to help him prepare the speech. When Rosenman arrived at the White House, he found an uproar. A large group of congressmen from both parties was huddled in the Oval Office with FDR, discussing potential legislation to lift the embargo, Rosenman recalled. "Reporters were swarming around the entrance hall in the executive offices waiting for the conference to break up."

LeHand gave Rosenman two speech drafts: one dictated by FDR and another prepared by aides. He sat down in the cabinet room and set out to create a cohesive whole. He worked late into the night, stopping only for dinner with the president, and after a few hours' sleep was up again early to continue his work. At 9:00 A.M., he took the speech into the president's bedroom, where they continued working on it together. The president was scheduled to deliver the speech at 2:00 P.M., and it was completed at 12:30.

His purpose was to reset the debate—to frame the issue as a return to American principles. He believed that the Neutrality Acts of the 1930s, which had been designed to limit the United States' involvement in foreign wars, damaged US interests by sidelining the nation in a time of true crisis. He presented his

proposal not as a step toward engagement in war but as a safe-
guard against the looming dangers:

> On July fourteenth of this year, I asked the Congress in
> the cause of peace and in the interest of real American
> neutrality and security to take action to change that Act.
>
> I now ask again that such action be taken in respect
> to that part of the Act which is wholly inconsistent with
> ancient precepts of the law of nations—the embargo
> provisions. I ask it because they are, in my opinion, most
> vitally dangerous to American neutrality, American se-
> curity and American peace. . . .
>
> I give to you my deep and unalterable conviction,
> based on years of experience as a worker in the field of
> international peace, that by the repeal of the embargo
> the United States will more probably remain at peace
> than if the law remains as it stands today. I say this be-
> cause with the repeal of the embargo this Government
> clearly and definitely will insist that American citizens
> and American ships keep away from the immediate per-
> ils of the actual zones of conflict. . . .
>
> Destiny first made us, with our sister nations on this
> Hemisphere, joint heirs of European culture. Fate seems
> now to compel us to assume the task of helping to main-
> tain in the Western world a citadel wherein that civili-
> zation may be kept alive. The peace, the integrity and
> the safety of the Americas—these must be kept firm and
> serene. In a period when it is sometimes said that free dis-
> cussion is no longer compatible with national safety, may
> you by your deeds show the world that we of the United
> States are one people, of one mind, one spirit, one clear
> resolution, walking before God in the light of the living.

That time it worked. Congress passed the Neutrality Act of 1939, which FDR signed on November 4. It lifted the embargo under a cash-and-carry system, allowing the sale of material to belligerents (e.g., Great Britain) if they paid in cash and arranged for transport with their own ships.

Critics charged that supplying material to Great Britain would compromise the United States' own military readiness. But Roosevelt saw the two needs as part of the same goal. He thought that by lending aid in this way, the United States would be able to stay out of the war. There might also have been a more strategic calculation. The US war machine was not fighting fit. For years during the Depression, military spending had been on the back burner, and it showed. The current military was only 100,000 strong, and the country was far behind on weaponry, air and sea vessels, and materials—especially when compared with the strength of the German army.

It was cause for alarm.

In September, FDR made three appointments designed to reverse that decline and prepare the US military apparatus for whatever threat might come its way. The first was General George C. Marshall as army chief of staff. Although he had never commanded troops on the ground, Marshall was a master strategist and one of the most revered generals in the United States, respected as well by his British counterparts. Roosevelt admired him for his temperament and for his problem-solving skills. Above all, the army needed a tactician more than a showman such as Douglas MacArthur, who was heroic but a loose cannon. Marshall was beloved by his subordinates because he treated them with dignity and respect. He was a listener, not a barker of orders.

A second appointment was the Republican Henry Stimson as secretary of war, replacing the isolationist Harry Woodring. Stimson, a military veteran of World War I and secretary of war under William Howard Taft, was a strong interventionist who was serious about the expansion of the military.

The third was the Republican William Franklin "Frank" Knox as secretary of the navy. Knox, a former newspaper publisher and vice presidential candidate with Alf Landon in 1936, was also an advocate of greater military readiness.

By FDR's side, as he had been since 1933, was Major General Edwin "Pa" Watson, his senior military aide. Watson, who had been a junior military aide to Woodrow Wilson while FDR was serving in the Department of the Navy, was FDR's most trusted liaison with the Department of War and a voice he often listened to.

Now Roosevelt had his bipartisan military coalition. The future was unpredictable, but the nation would be ready.

NO US PRESIDENT HAD ever served more than two terms in office. None had even tried, except for Ulysses S. Grant and Theodore Roosevelt, who had run his Independent Party campaign after he'd left office. Before February 27, 1951, when the Twenty-second Amendment was ratified, there was no term limit. But ever since President Washington had chosen to step down after two terms, a two-term maximum had been considered the unwritten rule. As the 1940 election year approached, many people were wondering if FDR was going to break it.

It didn't look like it. All signs pointed to Roosevelt's desire to retire. He often spoke longingly about his postpresidential life. He was deeply engaged in preparations for the Roosevelt Library at Hyde Park, and he was making plans to write his autobiography. He'd dangled the idea before Rosenman that Rosenman and his wife might move to the Hyde Park area so he could work with FDR on his papers. He'd invited Hopkins to do the same. He imagined a close cadre of the people he cared for most, living out a joint retirement in intellectual pursuits. It sounded idyllic after the heavy pressures of office.

Eleanor, as always, was circumspect in her opinion about whether her husband should retire or pursue a third term, but it was no secret that she didn't want him to run again. She felt that he had done his part and it was time to pass the torch and let the New Deal continue without him. She knew her husband well and had observed the diminishment of his passion for the job. Frankly, she thought he was bored, she confided to one of his advisers. And the strain on his physical well-being was obvious. The rest of the family agreed. Roosevelt told Morgenthau in January, "I do not want to run unless between now and the convention things get very, very much worse in Europe."

And things *were* getting worse.

In April, the Nazis invaded Denmark and Norway as a strategic positioning to establish a foothold in western Europe. Then, at 2:30 in the morning on May 10, in a "blitzkrieg"—a lightning attack—German forces flooded into Belgium and Holland, overwhelming their defenses and bombing airfields in Belgium, Holland, France, and Luxembourg.

FDR sat in his office late into the night, reviewing the reports from Europe, which were sketchy but increasingly grim. A report from London brought news that Prime Minister Chamberlain had resigned. Once lauded as a hero for preserving the peace, Chamberlain had faced a crumbling coalition in the days leading up to Germany's latest assault. Without support in the government, he had stepped down. Churchill was ready. His position as first lord of the Admiralty had restored his reputation. He was able to pull together a coalition, and the king invited him to establish a government. In a move that would have seemed fantastical a year earlier, Churchill became prime minister. (From then on, he would often sign his letters to Roosevelt, "Former Naval Person," acknowledging their naval ties.)

Still urging appeasement, Ambassador Kennedy wired FDR that perhaps the best option would be for Great Britain and France to negotiate a peace with Hitler. That, he felt, would be preferable to almost certain slaughter. In the coming weeks, German troops stormed into France. On June 14, Nazi troops marched into Paris, taking the city. William Shirer's poignant report stunned the world; it was a rebuke to those who thought negotiation with Hitler was still possible: "We hear the church bells ringing again today ringing the tidings of the entry of German troops into Paris. And tonight, the swastika flag with Adolf Hitler's Third Reich hovers from the Eiffel Tower there by the Seine in that Paris. . . . Now, Great Britain was alone against the Nazis."

Five days later, Churchill sent a message to FDR. "As you are no doubt aware, the scene has darkened swiftly." Laying his cards on the table, he wrote, "If necessary, we shall continue the war alone, and we are not afraid of that." But he warned Roosevelt that if the United States did not lend its voice and support, before too long it would be too late to have any impact.

The American people remained firm in their opposition to joining the war. But many thought the United States should help in some way. France was under devastating assault. The idea that Great Britain might fall to the Nazis was unthinkable.

Then, on June 10, Italy entered the war, aligned with Germany. The news coincided with a personal event for the Roosevelts. Their son Franklin, Jr., was graduating from the University of Virginia Law School, and FDR was scheduled to give the commencement speech. In the car on the way to the ceremony, he scribbled a new line in his prepared text, which he delivered to the graduates: "On this tenth day of June, 1940, the hand that held the dagger has struck it into the back of its neighbor." FDR's critics thought his words too inflammatory, and his supporters feared he might alienate Italian American voters in the upcoming election. But Roosevelt was furious at the Italians—and he vowed to stop any Italian money from leaving the country.

With Great Britain standing virtually alone against Germany and now Italy, FDR was growing increasingly gloomy about Great Britain's prospects, worrying that it was about to be "licked" by the Germans. He'd watched Churchill set hearts alight with his prose, and he admired Great Britain's resolve, but it felt futile.

At the same time, FDR was struggling with his own moment of truth. Time was running out for him to make a decision about whether or not he would run for a third term. In his private moments, he was beset by melancholy. He was at his best when a clear enemy could be sighted and defeated—such as the Great Depression. But now his hands were tied. The United States was not at war with Hitler. He could not be decisive when the decision was not his to make.

What should he do? What *could* he do? He was feeling a sense of obligation to continue in office and see the crisis through, but opponents of a third term were noisy, with their slogan. "I'm Against the Third Term . . . Washington wouldn't, Grant couldn't, Roosevelt shouldn't," read a campaign button. Even his own vice president, John Nance Garner, was openly opposing a third term and talking about running himself.

In a conversation with Nebraska senator George Norris, the senator joked that if he didn't run, where would all the liberals go? FDR gave a sober reply: "Did you ever stop to think that if I should run and be elected I would have much more trouble with Congress in my third term and much more bitterness to contend with as a result of my running for a third term than I have ever had before?"

When FDR described the conversation to Morgenthau, the

secretary nodded. "After all, Mr. President," he said, "you can make up your mind at the last moment, and make up your mind in a split second."

"Absolutely," the president agreed.

The Republican National Convention was held first, from June 24 to 28 in Philadelphia. The Republicans nominated a nonpolitician, Wendell Willkie, a successful business executive. Originally a Democrat and supporter of the New Deal, Willkie had changed his mind and his party over what he considered unfair burdens on business. In reality, his positions on the issues were not that far from FDR's. Republicans might have found Willkie a less-than-perfect loyalist, but they liked his style. Energetic, smart, a plainspoken midwestern breath of fresh air after nearly eight years of Roosevelt, they embraced him as their best hope against the president, if he should choose to run.

The Democrats were set to meet on July 15. Still, there was only silence from the White House. James Farley, the postmaster general and head of the Democratic National Committee, had largely fallen out with his mentor over the years, and now he was an open opponent of a third term. Farley was considering putting his own name into contention for the nomination. He was deeply frustrated by Roosevelt's failure to say one way or another whether he would run. Until he did, the delegates were on hold. No one wanted to buck the president.

In early July, Farley drove from New York City to Hyde Park, hoping to get a firm answer. Crossing the George Washington Bridge and driving up the Palisades, passing through his birthplace in Rockland County, Farley's thoughts were focused on the meeting ahead. "From time to time I turned my eyes to enjoy the grandeur of the Hudson," he wrote, "but for the most part my attention was on the impending meeting. I made up my mind that I would not take exception to anything that might be said, nor would I rake up irritations from the past." He was full of emotion but determined not to show it.

Arriving at Hyde Park to a warm welcome from Sara and Eleanor, he joined the family for a pleasant lunch. Hopkins and his secretary were there, as were Missy LeHand and Steve Early. Afterward, Farley and the president went to the study for a private conversation. To Farley's disappointment, FDR was cagey about his decision. He said he didn't want to run, but he stopped short of saying he wouldn't. Farley was looking for something more specific, more like William Tecumseh Sherman, the Civil War general who had said, "I will not accept if nominated and will not serve if elected."

FDR sat back in his chair and lit a cigarette. If Farley wanted Sherman, he would give him his own version. "Jim," he said, "if nominated and elected, I could not in these times refuse to take the inaugural oath, even if I knew I would be dead within five days."

Farley concluded that FDR was waiting to be drafted and he could expect no definitive statement. He felt his trip had been wasted. When he told FDR he was planning to put his own name into nomination, the president was noncommittal.

The president asked Hopkins to go to the convention and work the floor. He gave him instructions that made Hopkins uneasy. Roosevelt said he would not announce an intention to run. In fact, he would send a message saying he had no wish to be nominated and releasing his delegates. If the delegates wanted him, they would have to draft him.

It was a risky strategy, but Hopkins obliged. Once in Chicago, he appealed directly to Farley to withdraw his name and run FDR's campaign, a move that angered Farley. That was no way to run a convention!

When the delegates heard of Roosevelt's recusal, they were

stunned. But right after the announcement there was a cry in the hall: "We want Roosevelt!" The delegates took up the cheer: "We want Roosevelt! We want Roosevelt." No one stopped to wonder who had raised the cry. Later, it turned out that a Chicago official, Thomas Garry, superintendent of sewers, was in the basement with a microphone. The rally had been staged. The seemingly spontaneous chant had the effect of galvanizing the delegates for Roosevelt. The following day, most of them voted for him, with few breaking to cast votes for Garner, Farley, or a third candidate, Senator Millard Tydings of Maryland. The count was so lopsided that Farley, nearly in tears, took the stage and called for a suspension of the rules to nominate Roosevelt by acclamation—just what Roosevelt had wanted.

The real drama of the convention was the vice presidential nomination. Roosevelt let it be known that he wanted Henry Wallace, his secretary of agriculture. The delegates rebelled. They didn't consider Wallace, a former Republican, to be a true Democrat. The opposition was fierce. However, FDR wanted Wallace, believing he would be the most reliable caretaker of the New Deal if anything were to happen to Roosevelt.

Hopkins called the White House and reached Tully. He informed her that it was likely the nomination of Wallace would fail. When she told FDR, he blew up. "Well, damn it to hell," he cried, "they will go for Wallace or I won't run and you can jolly well tell them so."

After he calmed down, FDR realized that threats were not the answer. Instead, he sent Eleanor to Chicago. When the first lady arrived on the convention floor, it looked as if the delegates would go to war to defeat Wallace. She rose calmly to address them in her trilling voice, never mentioning Wallace's name but reminding them of the grave times in which they lived. "You will have to rise above considerations which are narrow and partisan," she chided them, and they responded. Wallace won the nomination. (Notably, Farley stepped down as postmaster general in September.)

FDR had always loved retail politics, getting out into the country to meet the people. But in 1940 he was barely on the trail, burdened by affairs in Washington. Meanwhile, Willkie was campaigning vigorously. Although he could be an electrifying speaker, Willkie was a disorganized campaigner, his inexperience constantly on display. Sometimes it seemed as though he forgot himself and supported policies the president was advocating, such as aid to Great Britain. The central issue of the election was not domestic policy but the international crisis. Republicans believed that a vote for Roosevelt was a vote for war and a vote for Willkie was a vote against war. Yet Willkie's primary appeal was that he was not Roosevelt, and there was always a chance it might be enough.

The news from Great Britain was demoralizing. In September, Germans launched bombing raids on London and other cities. It wasn't an invasion, in Germany's typical manner, but a campaign to terrorize the English and weaken their resolve. Night after night, bombs fell in a blitz that would continue well into 1941. Churchill was often on the streets, in his signature top hat and walking stick, surveying the damage and offering words of comfort. The king and queen sent their daughters away to safety at Windsor Castle while they remained behind, frequently visiting the bombed neighborhoods. While the king was touring the East End, which had endured much of the bombing, someone in the crowd cried, "Thank God for a good King!" The king replied, "Thank God for a good people." A few days later, when Buckingham Palace was also bombed, the queen remarked that now she could look East Enders in the face. They were all in it together.

A popular song captured the sense of solidarity:

The King is still in London
In London, in London,
Like Mr. Jones and Mr. Brown
The King is still in London Town.

As bombs fell on London, Ambassador Kennedy's star was
crashing to earth. He moved his family out of the city and asked
FDR to accept his resignation. He gave as his reason his sense
of being increasingly out of the loop on war discussions, but the
Brits thought he wanted to leave because he was a coward. They
called him "Jittery Joe."

FDR was relieved. He immediately appointed John Gilbert
Winant, a former governor of New Hampshire and avid New
Dealer, who won the affection of the British people as soon
as he landed in London. "There's no place I'd rather be at this
time," he said upon his arrival. After Kennedy, the British were
cheered to have an American ambassador who actually wanted
to be there.

Winant went about proving himself to be Kennedy's opposite. He walked the streets at night while bombs were falling,
helping the fire brigades pull people out of the rubble. London-
ers were stunned to see the tall, handsome American coming
toward them on their darkest nights, smiling warmly and asking what he could do to help.

Roosevelt realized that the bombings were aimed at undermining the public morale of the British. He speculated to Morgenthau that perhaps the way to destroy German morale was to
do the same. "I know south Germany, because I have bicycled
over every foot of it when I was a child and there is a town every
ten miles," he said. "I have suggested to the English again and

again if they sent a hundred planes over Germany for military objectives that ten of them should bomb some of these smaller towns that have never been bombed before. There must be some kind of a factory in every town. That is the only way to break the German morale."

At the end of September, Hitler strengthened his hand by formalizing a Tripartite Pact with Italy and Japan. The Axis Powers, as they became known, agreed to divvy up their efforts and their areas of action: Germany and Italy would lead the fight in Europe, with Japan concentrating on the Pacific. From FDR's point of view, Japan was the greatest threat to US interests. The country had been engaged in aggressive expansionism for nearly a decade, beginning with an invasion of Manchuria in 1931 and continuing with other clashes in China. The United States condemned the Japanese attacks on China, establishing economic sanctions and trade embargoes and providing aid to the Chinese. But Japan continued its aggressive movement into Southeast Asia, its eye on Pacific conquests as well. In 1939, FDR had moved the Pacific Fleet from California to Pearl Harbor, Hawaii, a US territory, as a means of halting Japan's path through the Pacific. The Axis Tripartite Pact specifically promised assistance from the others if one of the parties was attacked by a nation not involved in the war; were the United States to attack Japanese vessels, it would be tantamount to declaring war on Germany and Italy.

FDR was growing frustrated about being on the sidelines, and the campaign drove him farther away from engagement, as he was pressured to say time and again that Americans would not join the fight. Shortly before the election, James had a candid conversation with his father. He told him he thought he was being dishonest about his position on the war, especially his claim that Americans would not be sent to war. FDR admitted that war was almost certain but a delaying tactic was prudent. When Americans were on his side and the nation was better prepared, perhaps things would look different. For now he was determined to win the election. "I think I'm needed," he told James.

On election day, Roosevelt was ahead in the polls, but his margin had narrowed enough to cause him anxiety. The early returns showed Willkie doing better than Landon had in 1936, and a worried Roosevelt shut himself inside a room alone, contemplating the possibility of defeat. But the results soon turned around, and late in the evening it appeared that Roosevelt had won again—although Willkie would not concede until 11:00 the next morning. The final count was tighter than in his previous elections but still decisive—54.7 percent of the popular vote and 449 electoral votes for Roosevelt and 44.8 percent and 82 electoral votes for Willkie.

The traditional torchlight parade came up the driveway around midnight, and Roosevelt went out onto the porch to greet his neighbors. He seemed newly energized as he waved to them, but deep down he knew the hardest challenge was still to come.

A tightening inner circle was forming around the president, and that team would be responsible for speech writing until the end of FDR's presidency. It was a particularly significant time for a close collaboration that could create just the right message. FDR was not Churchill; he could not afford careless or overly emotional words. Each fireside chat, each speech to Congress, was like stepping onto a field littered with hidden mines. Reckless taunts might turn Americans away from the fight; inspiring prose could draw them closer.

The speech-writing team included Hopkins and Rosenman, as well as a newcomer, Robert Sherwood. Sherwood was an intriguing outsider, a two-time Pulitzer Prize–winning play-wright, who would help craft some of Roosevelt's most memorable speeches and fireside chats.

Two speeches would characterize FDR's defense of democracy as he prepared to begin his third term—the first, a fireside chat on December 29, known as the "arsenal of democracy" speech; and the second, on January 6, a State of the Union address, known as the "Four Freedoms" speech.

The day after Christmas, FDR asked Rosenman and Sherwood to come stay at the White House and work with him and Hopkins on a fireside chat he wanted to give on December 29. The president told them he was looking for simplicity and clarity—a way to convey what was at stake in language that would be as easy to grasp as his early New Deal appeals had been. They found that simplicity in the phrase "arsenal of democracy."

According to Rosenman, the phrase had first been used by Jean Monnet, a French diplomat, in a recent conversation with Supreme Court justice Felix Frankfurter, describing the United States' role in the fight against Hitler. Frankfurter had been so struck by the phrase that he had suggested that Monnet lend it to the president, who could give it more international weight. When Roosevelt saw the line in his speech, he brightened. "I *love* it!" he told the speechwriters.

In establishing the concept of that arsenal, Roosevelt went farther than he had gone before to describe the common path forward. And he took a direct jab at isolationists: "There are also American citizens, many of them in high places, who unwittingly in most cases are aiding and abetting the work of these [Nazi] agents." When the draft was sent for review by the State Department, "many of them in high places" was crossed out in red. FDR scoffed at that. "Leave it in," he told the speechwriters. "In fact, I'm very much tempted to say 'many of them in high places . . . including the State Department.'"

The State of the Union speech had been in the works for weeks. The State Department had submitted one draft, and FDR and his speechwriters worked on additional drafts. When Hopkins, Rosenman, and Sherwood gathered in the president's study one evening to review the third draft, FDR told them he had a new idea for an uplifting ending.

"We waited as he leaned far back in his swivel chair with his eyes on the ceiling," Rosenman recalled. "It was a long pause—so long that it began to become uncomfortable. Then he leaned forward again in his chair and said, 'Dorothy [stenographer Dorothy Brady], take a law.'" And he dictated the text of the Four Freedoms: "We must look forward to a world based on four essential human freedoms," he said, naming them as freedom of speech and expression, freedom to worship God, each in his own way, freedom from want, and freedom from fear.

The speech would become a standard of American values, repeated down through the decades. Forty-five years later, President Ronald Reagan would reprise it in a challenge to the Soviet Union. "You can see the real Roosevelt when he comes out with something like the Four Freedoms," Hopkins said approvingly. "And don't get the idea that those are any catch phrases. He believes them. He believes they can be practically obtained."

THE INAUGURATION ON JANUARY 20 felt somewhat understated. The nation was still adjusting to a third-term president. Republicans were demoralized, having also failed to win majorities in the House and Senate. It was easy to feel that they were stuck with a president for life and his legislative wing. At a White House dinner leading up to the inauguration, Supreme Court chief justice Charles Evans Hughes was discussing the oath of office with the president. "Mr. President," he joked, "after I have read the oath and you have repeated it, how would it do for me to lean forward and whisper, 'Don't you think this is getting just a little monotonous for both of us?'"

January 20, Inauguration Day, was cold and clear, and it was hard to miss the military theme. As the president took his seat on the reviewing stand after the ceremony, General George Marshall demonstrated the improving military forces, leading a large contingent from the army, navy, and air force down Pennsylvania Avenue, with tanks following, as fighters and bombers thundered across the sky above.

Roosevelt's address, which was broadcast throughout the world, reached back in history to recall the words of George Washington in his first inaugural address in 1789: "The preservation of the sacred fire of liberty and the destiny of the republican model of government are justly considered . . . deeply, . . . finally, staked on the experiment entrusted to the hands of the American people." He called on Americans to keep that sacred fire: "If we let it be smothered with doubt and fear—then we shall reject the destiny which Washington strove so valiantly and so triumphantly to establish."

Knowing he now had four years ahead of him, Roosevelt was becoming more decisive. Shortly after the New Year, he made a move to cement the United States' support of Great Britain: he sent Harry Hopkins to London as a personal envoy.

As Hopkins explained his role to the broadcaster Edward R. Murrow, "I have come here to try to find a way to be a catalytic between two prima donnas." Of course, his mission was far more profound. From then on, Hopkins was FDR's key emissary to Churchill, and he would later play a similar role with Stalin.

Soon after, Roosevelt appointed W. Averell Harriman as special envoy to Great Britain. (He gave him an invented title: Defense Expediter.) Harriman, a prominent banker, adviser, and old friend of the family, would become one of the most important diplomats of the era, later as ambassador to the Soviet Union. When FDR first approached him, Harriman found the mission to be vague. "The President talked to me as if it was mutually understood that it had been decided I should go for some time past," Harriman wrote in his notes of their meeting. "All in all, rambling on as he does on many subjects . . ." Although Harriman accepted the challenge, it was clear he would have to design the job on the ground.

With those two powerhouses on the scene, the president was telegraphing his intent to get an early start on his third term and grab the momentum to drive a clarifying message about America's proper role in the world.

CHAPTER 8

THE RISE OF THE ALLIES

On Inauguration Day, January 20, 1941, Roosevelt paused to pen a handwritten letter of support to Churchill, quoting a verse from Henry Wadsworth Longfellow's poem "The Building of the Ship":

> Sail on, O Ship of State!
> Sail on, O Union, strong and great.
> Humanity with all its fears,
> With all the hope of future years,
> Is hanging breathless on thy fate!

Churchill was so moved by the message that he quoted it in a February broadcast, directly addressing the United States: "Put your confidence in us. Give us your faith and your blessing, and under Providence all will be well. We shall not fail or falter; we shall not weaken or tire. Neither the sudden shock of battle nor the long-drawn trials of vigilance and exertion will wear us down. Give us the tools and we will finish the job."

Among the tools FDR was pushing was a program that came to be known as Lend-Lease. It was a simple idea: to provide military aid to allies with the agreement that materials would be returned at the end of the war. FDR used a neighborhood analogy to describe the idea in a press conference on December 17, 1940:

Suppose my neighbor's home catches fire, and I have a length of garden hose four or five hundred feet away. If he can take my garden hose and connect it up with his hydrant, I may help him to put out his fire. Now, what do I do? I don't say to him before that operation, "Neighbor, my garden hose cost me $15; you have to pay me $15 for it." What is the transaction that goes on? I don't want $15—I want my garden hose back after the fire is over. All right. If it goes through the fire all right, intact, without any damage to it, he gives it back to me and thanks me very much for the use of it. But suppose it gets smashed up—holes in it—during the fire; we don't have to have too much formality about it, but I say to him, "I was glad to lend you that hose; I see I can't use it any more, it's all smashed up." He says, "How many feet of it were there?" I tell him, "There were 150 feet of it." He says, "All right, I will replace it." Now, if I get a nice garden hose back, I am in pretty good shape.

The Lend-Lease Act was introduced in Congress in early January and was hotly debated for weeks. Resistance came from the usual suspects, such as Charles Lindbergh. In the Senate, the most fervent opponent was Robert Taft, a son of former president William Howard Taft, who had built his reputation largely on an isolationist platform. (He never changed. Years after World War II, in 1952, he would fight Dwight Eisenhower, an internationalist, for the Republican nomination and go down to defeat.) But during the debate over Lend-Lease it was becoming clear that both parties were beginning to grasp the hard realities. Even if the United States didn't enter the war directly, it could no longer refuse to help. The Lend-Lease Act was passed by a bipartisan coalition and signed into law on March 11. Now Harriman's role as expediter in Great Britain was clearer.

On June 22, Hitler made his boldest move yet, breaking the nonaggression pact with the Soviet Union with an overwhelming assault. He'd never taken the pact seriously, and he thought the Soviet Union was ripe for the picking, telling his generals, "We have only to kick in the door and the whole rotten structure will come crashing down." Furthermore, he was playing a long game. He believed the United States would eventually enter the war, and he wanted to dispose of the Soviet Union before a powerful tripartite alliance could form among England, the United States, and the Soviet Union. Furthermore, having conquered western Europe, an expansion into new territory would be the next step in his world domination strategy. He expected to be able to conquer the Soviet Union in a matter of months.

In the surprise attack, launched at 3:15 in the morning, more than three million soldiers and thousands of tanks and aircraft crossed into the Soviet Union in an area between the Baltic and Black seas. The Soviet army was overwhelmed and the air force virtually destroyed.

At first, the Soviets were ill equipped to fight back. In his memoirs, Nikita Khrushchev, who at the time was the head of the party in Ukraine, described a conversation he had had with Georgy Malenkov, the head of arms production. Khrushchev had asked for rifles, and Malenkov had told him that all the rifles had been shipped to Stalingrad.

"Then, what are we supposed to fight with?" Khrushchev asked.

"I don't know," Malenkov said. "Pikes, swords, homemade weapons, anything you can make in your own factories."

Khrushchev was stunned. "You mean we should fight tanks with spears?"

"You'll have to do the best you can," Malenkov told him. "You can make incendiary bombs of petrol or kerosene and throw them at the tanks."

For Churchill, it was unthinkable that the Soviet Union could fall to the Nazis. He recognized it would make winning the war nearly impossible. He went on the air to offer a rare hand of friendship. "No one has been a more consistent opponent of Communism than I have for the last twenty-five years," he said. "I will unsay no word that I have spoken about it. But all this fades away before the spectacle which is now unfolding." Churchill despised the Soviet regime, but Hitler's evils trumped all others. As he told his secretary, "If Hitler invaded hell I would make at least a favorable reference to the devil in the House of Commons."

What would the US administration say? Americans, too, preached the evils of communism under Stalin's totalitarian dictatorship. Roosevelt was more cautious than Churchill, weighing the implications of sending aid to Russia. He was also distracted by new dangers in the east. Japanese ships had moved into Indochina—a clear threat to the region, signaling a plan of aggression, despite Japan's insistence that its aims were peaceful. So, when Hopkins volunteered to go to Moscow and meet with Stalin, Roosevelt agreed. He sent a personal message: "Mr. Hopkins is in Moscow at my request for discussions with you personally . . . on the vitally important question of how we can most expeditiously and effectively make available the assistance which the United States can render your country in its magnificent resistance to the treacherous aggression by Hitlerite Germany."

Hopkins and Stalin met for two days, and Stalin was impressed with the envoy, who was obviously in poor health and had come so far to offer help. He admired that kind of steel. He was also impressed by Hopkins's sincere interest in learning everything he could about the Soviet Union's readiness and the challenges it faced. When it came to the matter of practical aid, Hopkins told Stalin he saw no reason why Lend-Lease would not apply to the Soviets, citing a clause in the bill extending aid to "any country whose defense the president deemed vital to the United States." Hopkins knew it was a hard sell for FDR; the nation might balk at sending military aid to the Red Army. But Hitler's attack had dramatically changed the calculation, making allies of old enemies. Hopkins once again proved his skill as an ally and negotiator. He had the ability to set aside preconceptions and look at the big picture.

Although Hopkins thought that meeting with Stalin was "like talking to a perfectly coordinated machine," he could not help but be struck by Stalin's personal strength as an old warrior and his courage in the face of what seemed a nearly insurmountable force. As Hopkins took his leave, he watched the dictator, standing alone, rugged and austere, "in boots that shone like mirrors," short and solid, with "huge hands, as hard as his mind."

Predictably, many Americans protested against giving aid to the Soviet Union, particularly Catholics, who couldn't square an alliance with godless communism to their faith. Roosevelt reached out to Pope Pius XII, with whom he had a friendly relationship, writing "In my opinion, the fact is that Russia is governed by a dictatorship, as rigid in its manner of being as is the dictatorship of Germany. I believe, however, that this Russian dictatorship is less dangerous to the safety of the nations than is the German form of dictatorship." He added that the Soviet Union was also less dangerous to religion, an arguable point. It was an uncomfortable accommodation, which Roosevelt would find himself making repeatedly in the coming years. The pope responded carefully, noting that the Russian people did not necessarily reflect the will of their leaders and should be helped. By the end of October, $100 billion in shipments was making its way to the Soviet Union.

ON THE THIRD OF August, FDR went fishing in Cape Cod. At least, that was what most people, including his wife, believed. He set off on his presidential yacht, the USS *Potomac*, heading north for what was supposed to be a week of rest and relaxation. But the fishing trip was a carefully staged subterfuge to hide a secret meeting with Churchill. On August 5, he transferred to a battleship, the USS *Augusta*, and headed for Placentia Bay in Newfoundland. The *Potomac* returned to Cape Cod and docked there. To keep the ruse going, Ed Starling, the chief of the Secret Service, sat on the deck, dressed in typical Roosevelt seagoing garb, smoking a cigarette in a long holder. From a distance, he could almost carry it off, though the press was suspicious and rumors of a meeting with Churchill circulated. However, regular dispatches kept the fiction alive: "Cruise uneventful and weather continues fair. President spent most of the day working on official papers."

Meanwhile, Churchill, accompanied by Hopkins, was departing England under cover of secrecy to make the dangerous journey. As they sped across the U-boat-infested Atlantic in the British battleship HMS *Prince of Wales*, Churchill and Hopkins played backgammon for a shilling a game. Hopkins took advantage of the prime minister's lack of skill, winning about $32 and change Canadian. It took their minds off the danger and calmed Churchill's nerves about the meeting with Roosevelt. "You'd have thought Winston was being carried up into the heavens to meet God," Hopkins joked, recalling that at one point Churchill nervously said, "I wonder if he will like me."

On August 9, as they neared the meeting area at Placentia Bay, the USS *Augusta* came into view, surrounded by the looming protection of destroyers. Churchill eagerly stomped on board and met FDR for the first time, save for the brief meeting they'd had in 1917, which Churchill, for one, did not remember. Now they greeted each other with the warmth of brothers.

For Churchill, that meeting meant everything. He was so full of relief and hope that he could barely contain himself. He had imagined Roosevelt as his partner in war for so long, he couldn't resist thinking this would be the turning point. It didn't happen that way, but it certainly commenced a promising courtship, if not a marriage.

On Sunday morning, FDR and his crew boarded the HMS *Prince of Wales* for Divine Service on the quarterdeck. British and US flags were draped side by side on the pulpit, and US and British chaplains took turns reading the prayers. Churchill himself had selected the hymns: "Eternal Father, Strong to Save," "Onward, Christian Soldiers," and "O God, Our Help in Ages Past."

The following day, Roosevelt wrote King George, "I wish you could have been with us at Divine Service yesterday on the quarterdeck of your latest battleship. I shall never forget it. Your officers and men were mingled with about three hundred of ours, spread over the turrets and superstructure—I hope you will see the movie of it."

The conversations of the coming days steered somewhat clear of the United States' commitment to the war—to Churchill's disappointment—focusing on articulating the two leaders' common principles. FDR and Churchill didn't always see eye to eye on what those would be. FDR spoke of the absolute sovereignty of nations, but Churchill disagreed. The British fight against totalitarianism had ignored the unsavory reality that the British had an empire, too, which practiced colonialism throughout the world. Colonialism was antithetical to American democracy (though the United States did have an array of territories), and FDR made that clear. In the end, Churchill chose not to insist on the point. So the statement of common principles, which would come to be known as the Atlantic Charter, was an ode to freedom and independence that would hardly have passed muster in Great Britain.

The principles were loosely stated, expressing the sovereign right of self-governance for all peoples, as well as equal rights to trade, open collaboration with all nations, peace on the seas, and a hope, after the defeat of Hitler, that all nations would abandon the use of force.

The Atlantic Charter was not a formal agreement and as such had no tangible impact. But at that first meeting of Roosevelt and Churchill, the symbolism was just as significant. When he was back in Washington, FDR would share the charter with Congress with little fanfare. His critics were unhappy with the entire episode and the language of the charter, which seemed presumptuous. Unbeknown to most people, it would be the starting framework of a postwar world.

On September 6, FDR was summoned to Hyde Park. Sara, just two weeks shy of her eighty-seventh birthday, was gravely ill. Roosevelt went to her room on the second floor and sat by her bed all day, talking softly to her. He remained in a vigil most of the night, sometimes joined by Eleanor. Sara Roosevelt died quietly just after noon the next day. She had lived to see her only son elected president three times and had presided over her own little empire. Shortly after her death, one of the property's most majestic oaks toppled to the ground.

The president did not break down in tears or show the depth of his emotion. He only wanted to be alone. He went out to his car, which he was able to drive by himself because it was equipped with special hand brakes, and prepared to take a solitary drive. He was stopped by a Secret Service agent, who gently informed him that he must be accompanied, with an agent seated beside him and a car following.

During the simple funeral held at Hyde Park, the president did not betray any outward sign of grief. He was stoic throughout, as his mother had been when his father died. It was a Roosevelt trait. But those around him knew the depths of his sorrow.

He returned to Washington with a heavy heart, and the world news added to his depression. "Mr. Roosevelt was not playing the part of a leading tragedian in a play on world history, nor did he consider himself a Messiah vested with the responsibility of leading the world along a path of his own choosing," Grace Tully would later write of FDR's mood. "He felt—and there was ample evidence that the American people shared his feeling—that the integrity and dignity of humanity were being devastated by the Axis program of conquest."

ON SEPTEMBER 22, 1941, the smiling, bespectacled face of Japanese ambassador to the United States Kichisaburo Nomura appeared on the cover of *Time* magazine with a story headlined "Japan: Honorable Fire Extinguisher." Nomura was generally viewed with favor among Americans, who believed his efforts for a peaceful resolution were sincere. For months, he had been in negotiations with Cordell Hull, often at night in Hull's apartment at the Wardman Park Hotel in Washington. Hull, a quiet, soft-spoken Tennessean, liked the personable Nomura, who had spent World War I in the United States as a naval attaché, but he was doubtful about his skills. "His outstanding characteristic was solemnity," Hull observed, "but he was much given to a mirthless chuckle and to bowing." He often wondered if Nomura was up to the task, and was constantly frustrated by his poor English; sometimes he wondered if Nomura understood what he was saying. Nevertheless, they were stuck with each other.

Essentially, Japan wanted the United States to stay out of its affairs in Indochina and to restore normal commercial relations. The United States sought Japan's assurances that it would cease aggression, withdraw from Indochina, and assume a non-aggressive stance in the Pacific. The United States also wanted to draw Japan away from the Tripartite Pact with Germany and Italy. As Hull put it bluntly to Nomura, "If we were to go into an agreement with Japan while Japan has an outstanding obligation to Germany that might call upon Japan to go to war with us, it would cause so much turmoil in the country that I might be lynched."

Hull, at the urging of the president, continued to try to find ways to stave off war, if only temporarily. That was made more difficult in October, when the government of Prime Minister Fumimaro Konoe collapsed and was replaced by a more militaristic regime under the leadership of Hideki Tojo. Hull didn't have much respect for Tojo, calling him "a typical Japanese officer, with a small-bore, straight-laced, one-track mind. He was stubborn and self-willed, rather stupid, hard-working, and possessed with a quantity of drive."

Although Nomura tried to convince Hull that they would proceed as before, Hull guessed that that wouldn't be the case. Very quickly Tojo had sent a message to Nomura, intercepted by US intelligence, that had set a firm deadline of November 25 for an agreement. The desperate Nomura met with the president and Hull on November 10, urging speed in the negotiations.

FDR, who knew about Tojo's deadline, regarded the ambassador thoughtfully. "Nations must think one hundred years ahead, especially during the age through which the world is passing," he said calmly. He essentially asked Nomura, why the rush? They'd been negotiating for only six months. Nomura kept pushing for a quick resolution, but his urgings sounded hollow.

FDR's strategy was to play for time. His military and defense advisers had suggested various worst-case scenarios of what could happen, including Japanese attacks in the Philippines or Indochina. He thought the US defenses in the Philippines were strong enough to discourage an attack there, but in either case he wanted to be ready. In spite of Tojo's private deadline, Nomura indicated that there would be a moratorium on "armed advancement" for three months as they negotiated.

On November 15, Hull presented Nomura with the outline of a proposal: if Japan would walk away from Indochina and agree to no further aggression, the United States would begin restoring its economic partnership. He hoped that could be a starting point, but the same day, he was jolted by the arrival of a special envoy from Japan, sent to work with Nomura and perhaps keep him on the straight and narrow. Hull felt an immediate dislike for the envoy, Saburo Kurusu, who struck him as the complete antithesis of Nomura. "I felt from the start that he was deceitful," he wrote, noting that Kurusu, in his previous position as Japanese ambassador to Berlin, had put his signature on the Tripartite Pact. Tully referred to Kurusu as that "sly-looking little man."

With Kurusu on the team, Japan presented its final offer, what Hull called a "take-it-or-take-the-consequences" proposal. Japan said it would withdraw its forces from southern Indochina if the United States would agree to end aid to China and Southeast Asia, lift the sanctions, and supply Japan with oil.

It was a nonstarter. The United States could not unilaterally take Japan at its word and withdraw aid to China, much less supply oil and other materials to a member of the Axis pact. Hull bristled. "It's a pity," he told Kurusu, "that Japan cannot do just a few small, peaceful things to help tide over this situation." In a message to the president, the war and defense secretaries, and General Marshall, he wrote, "There is practically no possibility of an agreement being achieved with Japan."

Although Hull realized that the situation was rapidly getting away from him, he tried one more effort; if nothing else, it might delay further action by Japan. He was well aware that Tojo's deadline was approaching. A second intercepted communication to Nomura and Kurusu read that the deadline had been moved to November 29, but "This time we mean it, that the deadline absolutely cannot be changed. After that things are going to happen."

Hull's response on November 26, the so-called Hull Note, was a hardball play. Rejecting Japan's latest offer, he outlined a ten-point plan that the United States would find acceptable. In Japan, the response was an immediate refusal, but this message wasn't sent right away. Instead, Nomura and Kurusu were instructed to continue to negotiate or at least give the appearance of doing so.

The evening of Saturday, December 6, the Roosevelts had dinner at the White House for thirty-four guests, followed by a musical performance by the Canadian violinist Arthur LeBlanc. As he sat listening to the music, FDR's thoughts were on Japan, calculating the next move. He believed that Japan might strike as early as the following week, as there were surveillance reports of movement by the Japanese fleet toward the Malaysian coast and Thailand. Late that afternoon he had dictated an urgent message for delivery to Japanese emperor Hirohito by Monday:

I address myself to Your Majesty at this moment in the fervent hope that Your Majesty may, as I am doing, give thought in this definite emergency to ways of dispelling the dark clouds. I am confident that both of us, for the sake of the peoples not only of our own great countries but for the sake of humanity in neighboring territories, have a sacred duty to restore traditional amity and prevent further death and destruction in the world.

He ended the letter, "May God have your Majesty in his safe and holy keeping. Your good friend, Franklin Delano Roosevelt."

The emperor had remained mostly silent as tensions mounted, as was the protocol, but earlier that fall, he had conveyed a rare expression of his desire for peace. FDR was hopeful that a final appeal from one peace-loving leader to another would strike a chord.

FDR sent the letter to Hull with the instruction: "Dear Cordell, Shoot this to [Ambassador] Grew—I think it can go in gray code [our least secret code]—saves time—I don't mind if it gets picked up. F.D.R."

But the message never reached Hirohito. Although Hull sent it Saturday evening, it didn't get to Grew in Tokyo in time to have any effect. It turned out that Hirohito was not so peace loving after all.

CHAPTER 9

THE COMMON CAUSE

December 7, 1941

Cordell Hull was in his office at noon on Sunday when he received a call from Nomura. Could he and Kurusu come by at 1:00 to discuss Japan's response to Hull's latest proposal? Hull said fine. When 1:00 came, Nomura called again. Could the meeting be postponed to 1:45? Hull agreed. The two men didn't arrive until 2:05 and were made to wait in a conference room.

Earlier, US intelligence had intercepted the Japanese response to the Hull Note, so Hull already knew it was a complete rejection of the US proposal. It was going to be a very tense and unproductive meeting, he thought gloomily. He felt that the Japanese were no longer negotiating in good faith, and short of an intervention by the emperor in response to Roosevelt's message—still to be delivered—there was no hope of a resolution.

Just as he was preparing to greet Nomura and Kurusu, Hull received a call from FDR. There was a report, not yet confirmed, of a Japanese attack on Pearl Harbor. The normally calm Hull felt a sense of outrage. If the report was true, what were Nomura and Kurusu doing in his office? FDR told him to go ahead with the meeting and make no mention of the attack.

Nomura and Kurusu entered Hull's office and handed him the documents.

He sat scanning them, trying to calm his emotions, but in the end his anger got the better of him. He stared down the two men in disgust. "I must say that in all my conversations with you during the last nine months I have never uttered one word of untruth," he said. "This is borne out absolutely by the record." He waved the papers at them. "In all my fifty years of public service, I have never seen a document that was more crowded with infamous falsehoods and distortions—infamous falsehoods and distortions on a scale so huge that I never imagined today that any government on this planet was capable of uttering them."

The men appeared stunned. Nomura began to speak, but Hull cut him off, motioning them to the door. (One version of the meeting had Hull cussing them out, but he denied it.)

Were Nomura and Kurusu in on the plot? Had they been pretending to negotiate while Japan prepared for the surprise attack? In his memoir, Kurusu tried to rebut the accusation that he and Nomura knew about the attack, writing that they only found out when they returned to the embassy after the aborted meeting. "It was then that we heard the news of the attack on Pearl Harbor," he wrote. The staff was in a state of shock— "We blankly stared at each other and could think of nothing to say." Some had tears in their eyes, and in Kurusu's description a sense of failure hung over the room.

But Hull was scathing in his account, issuing a statement: "At the very moment when representatives of the Japanese Government were discussing with representatives of this Government, at the request of the former, principles and courses of peace, the armed forces of Japan were preparing and assembling at various strategic points to launch new attacks and new aggressions upon nations and peoples with which Japan was professedly at peace, including the United States . . ."

News that Pearl Harbor had been bombed had come to FDR at 1:40 P.M., while he was lunching with Hopkins. Secretary of the Navy Frank Knox informed him of a radio message from Honolulu ending with the words "This is not a drill." After the attack was confirmed, FDR called for Early and gave him a statement for immediate release to the wire services, which he read to them in a conference call at 2:30: "This is Steve Early at the White House. At 7:55 A.M. Hawaiian time, the Japanese bombed Pearl Harbor. The attacks are continuing . . ." Reporters interrupted, wanting details of the dead and injured, but Early did not have them.

By the time of Early's announcement, the Pearl Harbor attack was nearly over and the worst of the destruction had already been suffered. It had been launched at 7:55 A.M. Hawaiian time (12:55 P.M. in Washington), but the signs had appeared earlier, seen only by two privates who had been manning a radar center north of Oahu. George Elliott and Joseph Lockard had been getting ready to go off duty at 7:00 when they had noticed what appeared to be the approach of incoming planes on their radar. They had decided to notify the Information Center and had gotten a switchboard operator on the line. He had told them he was the only one there and didn't know what to do. He'd said he'd find someone, and a couple of minutes later a lieutenant had called back. "The lieutenant said to forget it," Elliott recalled in his later testimony to Congress. They continued to follow the radar until the sightings disappeared in the blackout area about twenty miles offshore. Then they closed down the station and went to breakfast. Soon after, the planes were overhead.

Robert E. Thomas, Jr., the officer in charge of the antiaircraft battery on the USS *Nevada*, woke to loudspeakers blaring "General quarters! General quarters! All hands man your battle stations!" When he climbed to his station, he saw a stunning scene. "Overhead were flights of high-level bombers coming down battleship row," he remembered in an oral history of the attack. "As I watched, the USS *Arizona*, just three hundred feet ahead of us, erupted in an enormous flash and thunderous blast that knocked me twenty feet backwards and onto my back."

With no senior officers on board, Thomas and others quickly began to move the *Nevada* out of the harbor. Thomas said, "As we cleared the burning *Arizona*, the harbor became visible to us. Good God! The *West Virginia* was awash and burning, the *Oklahoma* had capsized, the *California* was listing and afire, and the *Pennsylvania*, in Dry Dock, was burning." Just as he was absorbing the scene, the *Nevada* was torpedoed. Fifty of the crew were killed and a hundred others injured, including Thomas.

As the ships burned, survivors plunged overboard, but that did not save them. Massive fuel spills had set the water on fire, and they burned alive in the water.

Marine Albert Berger was on guard duty at the main gate that sleepy Sunday morning when he saw planes flying overhead with foreign insignia he didn't recognize. "I could see the pilots. . . . They were looking right down on us. . . . They were dropping the bombs. They came in, waves of airplanes, and they were bombing everything they could—all the ships." Berger was stunned and traumatized. "I was a youngster," he said, remembering that day. "I was only eighteen years old. . . . I didn't know how to cope with it. And there was nobody there to tell me how to cope with it."

Hickam Field, the massive air base adjacent to Pearl Harbor, which was considered the jewel of Pacific defense, was demolished in a direct attack. "All but essential personnel were granted off-base pass requests" that weekend, recalled Master Sergeant John H. Koenig. "Thirty-nine hours and fifty-five minutes later, the United States was humiliated beyond belief. The billion-dollar fortress of the island of Oahu, the strongest fortification in the world, was in near-shambles. No U.S. military installation had suffered such mass destruction since the founding of the country in 1776."

Within two hours, the attack was over, leaving 2,335 dead: 2,008 navy personnel (1,177 from the *Arizona*), 218 army, 109 marines, and 68 civilians. There were 1,143 wounded. The Pacific Fleet in Hawaii was nearly obliterated.

FDR CALLED HIS CABINET together, and the press gathered outside as congressional leaders began arriving at the White House for meetings. Richard Strout, a correspondent with the *Christian Science Monitor*, was especially struck by the presence of California senator Hiram Johnson, a particularly avid isolationist. "What a sight. The great isolationist, Hiram Johnson, grim-faced, immaculately dressed, stalks across our little stone stage on the White House portico. All the ghosts of isolationism stalk with him, all the beliefs that the US could stay out of war if it made no attack."

In England, Ambassador Winant and Harriman were dining with Churchill at Chartwell, his country home, on December 7. Harriman observed, "The Prime Minister seemed tired and depressed. He didn't have much to say throughout the dinner and was immersed in his thoughts, with his head in his hands part of the time." As the dinner ended, Churchill's valet arrived with a radio, so they could listen to the BBC newscast. The report about Pearl Harbor came across the airwaves. Revived from his gloom, Churchill bounded from the table, shouting that he would declare war on Japan. Winant calmed him down, telling him that they must get a confirmation before taking such a drastic step.

Churchill called Roosevelt. "Mr. President, what's this about Japan?"

"It's quite true," the president said wearily. "They have attacked us at Pearl Harbor. We are all in the same boat now."

Churchill gave the phone to Winant, who listened with horror to the news.

When he hung up, Churchill told him of his intention to ask the House of Commons for a declaration of war against Japan the next day. (He would send a message to FDR, offering to delay his announcement so the United States could declare war first, but he received no reply, so he went ahead, making the United Kingdom the first nation to declare war on Japan.)

Churchill was relieved that the United States would now be forced into the war and said as much in his memoirs. However, a US war with Japan presented potential problems for his own fight with Hitler. He worried that Lend-Lease materials would no longer be available or would be substantially diminished and that he'd have less support, not more, from the United States.

At the White House, FDR continued his meetings throughout the day. At 5:00, he summoned Tully to his study for dictation. He sat calmly at his desk, grim and determined as he lit a cigarette and took a deep drag. "Sit down, Grace. I'm going before Congress tomorrow. I'd like to dictate my message. It will be short."

Tully sat, and the president took another drag from his cigarette and began to speak slowly and deliberately:

Yesterday comma December 7 comma 1941 dash a day which will live in infamy dash the United States of America was suddenly and deliberately attacked by naval and air forces of the Empire of Japan period paragraph.

He went on to dictate the entire message, which he wrote himself without speechwriters. The dictated version remained intact, except for edits he added in his own pen as events continued to unfold.

Throughout the evening, meetings with the cabinet and military leaders continued. FDR told them it was the gravest moment since Lincoln had announced a civil war in 1861. He said there was no choice but to declare war—indeed, with its attack, Japan had already declared war on the United States.

As night fell, crowds gathered in Lafayette Park across from the White House. UPI correspondent A. Merriman Smith described the scene: "They seemed to be waiting for someone to come out of the White House and tell them it was all a bad dream. Cars by the hundreds drove by as slowly as traffic officers would permit, the occupants hanging from the windows just to stare at the graceful old white structure which all of them had seen many, many times before."

James had been at the White House for most of the day, and he helped his father to bed late that night. He lingered to speak privately to Roosevelt. James, who was a captain in the Marine Corps Reserve, serving as a liaison between Marine Headquarters and the Office of the Coordinator of Information, which would become the Office of War Information, had been angling for an overseas assignment. James insisted that he must now be assigned to combat, even though he had health problems. FDR did not try to talk him out of it. He knew, with sadness and a degree of pride, that all his sons would want to fight. He recalled his own disappointment at having been denied the opportunity to fight during the First World War.

James would get his wish, serving in the Pacific theater. Elliott, whose poor eyesight made him officially unfit for combat, signed a waiver allowing him to serve despite his disability, and became a pilot. He'd fly more than three hundred combat missions, eyesight be damned. Franklin, Jr., would rise to become commander of a destroyer in the Pacific. And John, the youngest, who had joined the navy in early 1941, also served in the Pacific.

Their father would now be their commander in chief.

The following day, Roosevelt stood before Congress and delivered his response to the attack, five hundred words that pierced through the chamber with brevity and precision. Hull had urged him to give a longer speech, outlining the history of the negotiations and how they'd failed. Roosevelt ignored the advice, knowing that this was a moment to strike with a dagger, not explain like a professor.

> Yesterday, December 7, 1941—a date which will live in infamy—the United States of America was suddenly and deliberately attacked by naval and air forces of the Empire of Japan.
>
> The United States was at peace with that nation and, at the solicitation of Japan, was still in conversation with its Government and its Emperor looking toward the maintenance of peace in the Pacific. Indeed, one hour after Japanese air squadrons had commenced bombing in the American Island of Oahu, the Japanese Ambassador to the United States and his colleague delivered to our Secretary of State a formal reply to a recent American message. And while this reply stated that

"Did I ever think when he was little that Franklin might be president?" Sara Roosevelt wrote. "Never, oh never!" However, from the day of his birth, on January 30, 1882, Franklin was the only star in his mother's galaxy. *Franklin D. Roosevelt Presidential Library.*

James Roosevelt was fifty-four when his son Franklin was born, and he would only live long enough to see him reach his eighteenth birthday. But he instilled in his son a love of the outdoors, especially of sailing, and the importance of helping his neighbors. *Franklin D. Roosevelt Presidential Library.*

Franklin was ebullient and sociable by nature, and President Theodore Roosevelt's niece Eleanor was painfully shy and inexperienced with men. But Franklin appreciated her depth and her interest in the world. Their long marriage was hardly smooth sailing, but they were a powerful team. *Franklin D. Roosevelt Presidential Library.*

President Theodore Roosevelt was the family idol, and young Franklin did everything he could to emulate his cousin, including following him into politics and the presidency. He even took to wearing pince-nez instead of glasses and to mimicking the president's expressions, such as "de-e-e-lighted!" *Franklin D. Roosevelt Presidential Library.*

"I'm not Teddy," FDR told his audiences in his early campaigns, but he had gifts of his own, including a love for getting out among the crowds and shaking every hand possible. *Franklin D. Roosevelt Presidential Library.*

The Roosevelts. *Left to right:* (front row, seated) Anna, FDR, Sara, Eleanor; (back row) James, John, Franklin, Jr., Elliott. *Franklin D. Roosevelt Presidential Library.*

Until the age of thirty-nine, Franklin had led a charmed life, but then poliomyelitis struck him down. He would never walk again. For the rest of his life, he found solace at Warm Springs, the rehabilitation center in Georgia where he developed a deep kinship with his fellow "polios." *Franklin D. Roosevelt Presidential Library.*

Many believed FDR would never return to public life after he was struck with polio. But in 1924, he made a comeback. Gripping the podium to hold himself erect, he gave a fiery speech on behalf of Al Smith at the Democratic National Convention. He was back. *Franklin D. Roosevelt Presidential Library.*

In 1932, campaigning across the country by train, FDR perfected a whistle-stop routine, with his son James by his side to hold him steady so he could stand. *Franklin D. Roosevelt Presidential Library.*

As president, FDR was determined to shake things up. He instituted twice-weekly press conferences right in the Oval Office, with reporters crowding around his desk. *Franklin D. Roosevelt Presidential Library.*

With war approaching in Europe, King George VI became the first monarch to visit the United States. The Roosevelts treated the king and Queen Elizabeth to an all-American picnic at their cottage at Hyde Park. *Left to right:* Eleanor, King George VI, Sara, Queen Elizabeth, FDR. *Franklin D. Roosevelt Presidential Library.*

September 1939: Germany's Adolf Hitler looks on as his troops invade Poland, triggering the Second World War. Three years later, the Axis powers would control almost all of continental Europe. *Das Bundesarchiv.*

London in smoke during the German Blitz. St. Paul's Cathedral, which stands out here against the skyline, survived the bombing. *Library of Congress.*

"A date which will live in infamy"—the Japanese attack on Pearl Harbor, December 7, 1941, nearly obliterated the Pacific fleet. Pictured, the USS *West Virginia* being bombed. *Toland Collection / US Navy Photographs.*

DRAFT No. 1   December 7, 1941.

PROPOSED MESSAGE TO THE CONGRESS

Yesterday, December 7, 1941, a date which will live in ~~world history~~ *infamy*,

the United States of America was ~~simultaneously~~ *suddenly* and deliberately attacked

by naval and air forces of the Empire of Japan.

The United States was at the moment at peace with that nation and was

~~continuing the~~ *still in* conversation with its Government and its Emperor looking

toward the maintenance of peace in the Pacific. Indeed, one hour after,

Japanese air squadrons had commenced bombing in ~~Hawaii and the Philippines~~ *Oahu*

the Japanese Ambassador to the United States and his colleague delivered

to the Secretary of State a formal reply to a ~~former~~ *recent American* message ~~from the~~

~~Secretary.~~ *While* This reply ~~contained a statement~~ *stated it* that diplomatic negotiations

~~must be considered at an end, but~~ *it* contained no threat ~~and no~~ hint of ~~an~~ *or war or*

armed attack.

It will be recorded that the distance ~~of Manila, and especially~~ of

Hawaii from Japan make it obvious that the ~~this~~ attack ~~were~~ *was* deliberately

planned many days ago. *or join weeks* During the intervening time the Japanese Govern-

ment has deliberately sought to deceive the United States by false

statements and expressions of hope for continued peace.

The first draft of Roosevelt's speech to the nation after Pearl Harbor. In its opening line, he changed "a date which will live in world history" to "a date which will live in infamy." *National Archives.*

The price of war: six American graves in North Africa, the site of the first major Allied offensive. *Library of Congress.*

Guadalcanal, 1943: a battlefield sketch of four US servicemen transporting a wounded comrade. The early campaigns against the Japanese quickly proved how bloody the Pacific War would be. *Library of Congress.*

On November 29, 1943, Joseph Stalin, FDR, and Winston Churchill posed for photos before beginning the hard work of the Tehran Conference. *Franklin D. Roosevelt Presidential Library.*

In Tehran, FDR and Stalin hit it off, sometimes making jokes at Churchill's expense in order to cement their relationship. But the underlying debate over which strategy would win the war was deadly serious, and Churchill was often at odds with his counterparts. *Franklin D. Roosevelt Presidential Library.*

On the last night of the Tehran Conference, Churchill celebrated his sixty-ninth birthday with an elaborate party. Champagne and toasts flowed, and there were many expressions of goodwill. However, Churchill remained troubled by the decision to go ahead with Operation Overlord (D-Day) the following year. *Franklin D. Roosevelt Presidential Library.*

Key officials gather outside the Soviet Embassy in Tehran. On the left, US General George C. Marshall shakes hands with Sir Archibald Clark Kerr, the British Ambassador to the USSR. Ailing American diplomat Harry Hopkins stands hunched at the center, keeping a watchful eye on Joseph Stalin. Soviet foreign minister Vyacheslav Molotov and General Kliment Voroshilov are on the right. *Library of Congress.*

On the eve of D-Day, General Eisenhower visited the 101st Airborne Division as it prepared to take flight. He shook each man's hand, and they assured him he had no cause for worry. But he was fully aware that, for good or ill, the next day would bring a turning point in the war. *Franklin D. Roosevelt Presidential Library.*

On June 6, 1944, the Allies launched the invasion planned in Tehran. Operation Overlord was the decisive battle of World War II. Even now, we are moved by the raw courage of the men who stormed the beaches at Normandy. Many did not survive, but the course of the war was shifted toward victory. *AP Photo / Peter Carroll.*

With the war nearly at an end, FDR, Churchill, and Stalin met at Yalta to plan the postwar world order. FDR was thin and weak, and perhaps his guard was down. At Yalta, despite Churchill's protests, he gave in on some critical decisions, most notably regarding the future of Poland. It would later become devastatingly clear that Stalin was not an honest broker. *Franklin D. Roosevelt Presidential Library.*

On April 11, 1945, FDR was in Warm Springs to rest and recuperate after the long journey to and from Yalta. A portrait artist snapped this photograph, which was the last to be taken of the president before his death. The following day FDR suffered a stroke. He did not live to see victory over Germany, which came less than a month later. *Franklin D. Roosevelt Presidential Library.*

More than one thousand soldiers, sailors, and marines lined the route from the train station to Hyde Park as a horse-drawn caisson carried FDR to his final resting place. *Franklin D. Roosevelt Presidential Library.*

FDR loved figurines, and they crowded his desk in the Oval Office, including a set of Scottish terrier and West Highland terrier figurines mounted on magnets, an elephant, and a Missouri Mule constructed of nuts and pipe cleaners. *Photo by Karl Rabe.*

FDR's study is preserved in the FDR Museum, with a beautiful Persian rug given to him by the shah of Iran during the Tehran Conference. His armless wheelchair, which he preferred because it looked more like a regular chair, is small and utilitarian, with an ashtray attached. *Photo by Karl Rabe.*

it seemed useless to continue the existing diplomatic negotiations, it contained no threat or hint of war or of armed attack.

It will be recorded that the distance of Hawaii from Japan makes it obvious that the attack was deliberately planned many days or even weeks ago. During the intervening time the Japanese Government has deliberately sought to deceive the United States by false statements and expressions of hope for continued peace.

The attack yesterday on the Hawaiian Islands has caused severe damage to American naval and military forces. I regret to tell you that very many American lives have been lost. In addition American ships have been reported torpedoed on the high seas between San Francisco and Honolulu.

Yesterday the Japanese Government also launched an attack against Malaya.

Last night Japanese forces attacked Hong Kong.

Last night Japanese forces attacked Guam.

Last night Japanese forces attacked the Philippine Islands.

Last night the Japanese attacked Wake Island.

And this morning the Japanese attacked Midway Island.

Japan has, therefore, undertaken a surprise offensive extending throughout the Pacific area. The facts of yesterday and today speak for themselves. The people of the United States have already formed their opinions and well understand the implications to the very life and safety of our nation.

As Commander-in-Chief of the Army and Navy I have directed that all measures be taken for our defense.

But always will our whole nation remember the character of the onslaught against us.

No matter how long it may take us to overcome this premeditated invasion, the American people in their righteous might will win through to absolute victory.

I believe that I interpret the will of the Congress and of the people when I assert that we will not only defend ourselves to the uttermost but will make it very certain that this form of treachery shall never again endanger us.

Hostilities exist. There is no blinking at the fact that our people, our territory and our interests are in grave danger.

With confidence in our armed forces—with the unbounding determination of our people—we will gain the inevitable triumph—so help us God.

I ask that the Congress declare that since the unprovoked and dastardly attack by Japan on Sunday, December seventh, 1941, a state of war has existed between the United States and the Japanese Empire.

"There was none of Churchill's eloquent defiance in this speech," Sherwood observed. "There was certainly no trace of Hitler's hysterical bombast. And there was no doubt in the minds of the American people of Roosevelt's confidence. I do not think there was another occasion in his life when he was so completely representative of the whole nation."

The House of Representatives and the Senate quickly approved a declaration of war against Japan, with a near-unanimous vote. There was only one vote in opposition, from Montana Republican Jeannette Rankin, the first woman to serve in Congress. A lifelong pacifist, she had also opposed the United States' entry into World War I. This time was different, her colleagues argued—to no avail. At the last moment, fellow Republican Everett Dirksen begged her to at least vote "Present," to avoid standing in opposition. She refused, and her "No" echoed through the solemn chamber, a jarring note.

On December 11, Germany and Italy declared war on the United States, leading to a US declaration of war with Germany and Italy. This time the vote in Congress was unanimous. Rankin quietly voted "Present." She was so unpopular afterward that she chose not to run for reelection.

The war now upon the United States, Roosevelt didn't have time to second-guess his approach to the Japanese conflict leading up to December 7. But there were plenty of critics doing the job for him. Many openly suggested that Roosevelt had welcomed the attack on Pearl Harbor because it had given him an excuse to enter the war. There was no direct evidence of that. However, commanders in Hawaii later testified to Congress that they had deliberately left been in the dark about the Japanese intentions and had been provided only selective intelligence reports from Japan. "We had no information that an air attack on Pearl Harbor was imminent or probable," Rear Admiral Husband E. Kimmel testified, not hiding his anger and frustration. "Knowledge of the intercepted Japanese dispatches would have radically changed the estimate of the situation made by me and my staff." He offered a sobering thought of what might have been: "Even on the morning of December 7, four or five hours before the attack, had the Navy Department for the first time seen fit to send me all the significant information . . . my light forces could have moved out of Pearl Harbor, all the ships in the harbor would have been at general quarters, and all the resources of the fleet in instant readiness to repel an attack. . . . The Pacific Fleet deserved a fighting chance."

Perhaps FDR and the War Department were intent on playing out their bad hand and seeking resolution in the final hours. Perhaps they had accepted the inevitability of an attack but were convinced that it would not happen at Pearl Harbor. Perhaps FDR erred by trusting those who had repeatedly proven themselves to be untrustworthy. In *Roosevelt: From Munich to Pearl Harbor: A Study in the Creation of a Foreign Policy*, Basil Rauch speculated in 1950 that Roosevelt might have been the victim of his own political calculations, writing, "The Roosevelt administration failed to estimate the extreme daring and foolhardiness in aggression of the Japanese leaders. Roosevelt himself was accustomed to accusations that he exaggerated the scope of Axis designs; his error turned out to be that he underestimated the scope."

Now that the United States was in the war, Churchill was eager to iron out the issues of command and strategy with the president. On December 14, he set out for Washington on the British battleship HMS *Duke of York*, accompanied by Harriman. The *Prince of Wales*, the ship that had carried Churchill to his meeting in Newfoundland, was not available for duty. It had been sunk by Japanese torpedoes off the coast of Malaya on December 10. Churchill wondered aloud whether it had been bad judgment to send the *Prince of Wales*, such a valuable battleship, to the east but added that it was no time for regrets.

The trip to the United States was a battle in itself, against the stomach-wrenching forces of tumultuous seas. Most people on board were seasick, with Churchill popping seasickness pills the entire time. The ship finally arrived in Norfolk, Virginia, on December 22, and Churchill flew to Washington National Airport, where FDR was on hand to greet him and escort him to the White House. Amazingly, the president had failed to tell Eleanor of the visit until that very day. She buried her resentment with a gently chiding notation in her daily column: "It had not occurred to him that this [visit] might require certain moving of furniture to adapt rooms to the purposes for which the Prime Minister wished to use them."

That evening, they gathered in the president's study for drinks. Churchill despised mixed drinks, preferring whiskey or champagne. But FDR was so proud of his martinis that the prime minister couldn't bear to insult him. He accepted a martini and then found a way to excuse himself. He went into the bathroom, took the olive out, poured the drink down the sink, replaced it with water, and put the olive back in.

Near the end of dinner, FDR raised his glass of champagne. "I have a toast to offer—it has been in my head and on my heart for a long time. Now it is on the tip of my tongue: to the Common Cause!"

FDR admired many aspects of Churchill's character, but he found his rigidity hard to take. He confided to Eleanor that he didn't expect Churchill to have a long political career after the war because of his conservatism. "He likes the world he lived in too much." That amused Eleanor, who thought her husband was likewise inclined. Both men had trouble in their own countries. As the journalist Alistair Cooke observed, "It would be so much easier if Roosevelt would go to England and become Prime Minister and we'll have Churchill as President," because everybody in the United States loved Churchill and everybody in England loved Roosevelt.

The historian Jon Meacham noted that despite any difficulties, the two were perfectly matched for the times that called upon them to serve. "Churchill did something FDR couldn't do," he said. "Churchill stood alone, stared across the Channel, and said, 'Hitler has gone that far and would go no farther.' Roosevelt did something Churchill couldn't do. He shrewdly managed American public opinion to a moment when the greatest democracy was willing to . . . defend its values in a foreign land. They couldn't have done what they did without each other."

Churchill would remain at the White House until January 14, save for a side trip to Canada to address Parliament. The Roosevelts attempted to celebrate a somewhat normal Christmas with their high-level guest. As in most other American households, the ordinary rituals of the season seemed to take on a deeper significance for them. They, too, would be watching their children go off to war.

As night fell on Christmas Eve, they stood with Churchill on the South Portico of the White House for the lighting of the national Christmas tree:

"There are many men and women in America—sincere and faithful men and women—who asked themselves this Christmas: 'How can we light our trees?' " Roosevelt said. ". . . 'How can we meet and worship with love and with uplifted hearts in a world at war, a world of fighting and suffering and death?' " He had the answer: "Our strongest weapon in this war is that conviction of the dignity and brotherhood of man which Christmas Day signifies."

Christmas Day began with a church service, followed by a feast that to the British guests felt lavish. The table was laden with traditional fixings: roast turkey with chestnut dressing, sausage-and-giblet gravy, beans, cauliflower, a sweet-potato casserole, cranberry jelly, a grapefruit salad, and rolls. For dessert, there were plum pudding with hard sauce, ice cream, coffee, salted nuts, and assorted bonbons.

Churchill retired early to work on a speech he would give to a joint session of Congress the following day. It was only the third time in US history that a foreign leader had made such an address. Standing before a packed chamber, with observers crowding the ramparts, he began with a reminder of his American roots: "If my father had been an American and my mother British instead of the other way around, I might have got here on my own. In that case this would not have been the first time you would have heard my voice."

He spoke heatedly about the evil of Japan and that country's certain miscalculation: "What kind of a people do they think we are? Is it possible that they do not realize that we shall never cease to persevere against them until they have been taught a lesson which they and the world will never forget?"

His speech lasted thirty minutes, and at the end the chamber rose in thunderous applause as Churchill gestured with a "V" for victory. It was a thrilling day, but amid the excitement that evening Churchill suffered what might have been a heart attack, or close to one. Doctors ordered six weeks of bed rest. He ignored them and went on.

Day after day, FDR and Churchill met alone and with advisers, plotting a way forward. The conference was code-named Arcadia. Due to the extreme secrecy of the meetings, no official record was made, so it's hard to know exactly what was said. (Even Churchill was uncharacteristically circumspect in his memoirs.) No doubt high on the agenda was the extent of the United States' engagement in the war and in what arenas. Roosevelt and his military advisers had the task of organizing war efforts on two different fronts; it's doubtful that he made any firm promises.

Mostly the value of the meeting was the chance for the two men to take each other's measure and figure out how they would work together. Right away it became apparent that there was some friction in their schedules. Churchill was a night owl who did his best work late, often not going to bed until 1:00 or 2:00

and then remaining in bed until late into the morning. Eleanor worried that his schedule placed undue pressure on Roosevelt. "My husband . . . was so burdened with work that it was a terrible strain on him to sit up late at night with Mr. Churchill after working until 1 or 2 A.M. and then have to be at his desk early the next day while his guest stayed in his room until 11 A.M."

Long hours were spent discussing the shape of the world after war and how nations could be protected from future men like Hitler. The two men discussed what name they would give to an organization of nations allied against fascism. The morning following one such late-night discussion, FDR was inspired by an idea. Excited, he wheeled himself to Churchill's room and burst in, announcing "United Nations!" Churchill was just coming out of the bathroom, drying himself with a towel, and he was stark naked. Embarrassed, FDR apologized profusely.

Churchill harrumphed and said magnanimously, "The Prime Minister of Great Britain has absolutely nothing to hide from the President of the United States."

DWIGHT D. EISENHOWER DID not often show his temper, but the chaos of the War Department in Washington during the early days of the war set his nerves on edge. "There are lots of amateur strategists on the job, and prima donnas everywhere," he complained in his diary.

His mood was made worse by his personal frustration at once again being passed up for command duty at the front. When General Marshall had summoned him to Washington days after Pearl Harbor to assist him at the War Department, he had been disappointed. The man who could not have imagined he'd be president a decade later felt sidelined. All around him throngs of men were being drafted or rushing to enlist, forming a military force of nearly two million. They were leaving on ships for Europe and the Pacific, along with their hastily promoted commanders. Once again, he was left behind. He worried he'd grow old and gray in the army without ever having seen combat, hardly what he'd had in mind when he'd set off for West Point thirty-one years earlier. Every war needs its administrators as much as its warriors, and he knew that intellectually, but emotionally it was a blow. Nevertheless, he realized he had value in Washington as a strategic planner, and he swallowed his resentment to do his job under the command of Marshall, whom he admired more than any other general.

If Eisenhower was perturbed by the mess they were in, he was in good company. Marshall, who was responsible for overseeing a military apparatus that was mired in bureaucracy and clearly unprepared for a global war, didn't always hide his frustration. Eisenhower noted in his diary, "Anger cannot win, it cannot even think clearly. In this respect Marshall puzzles me a bit. I've never seen a man who apparently develops a higher pressure of anger when he encounters some piece of stupidity than does he. Yet the outburst is so fleeting, he returns so quickly to complete 'normalcy,' that I'm certain he does it for effect."

On Marshall's shoulders was the burden of structuring a massive force to defeat Hitler in the west and the Japanese in the Pacific and Far East. He didn't have even months of leeway to ease into the fight. During their evening walks, Marshall's wife, Katherine, would patiently listen to him describe his overwhelming problems, writing "I was listening to a man steeling himself to carry a burden so tremendous in magnitude and so diverse in its demands that it was difficult to imagine how one man could carry it alone." Marshall might have been frustrated and privately gloomy, but he tried to keep his doubts away from his staff, believing it his duty to appear decisive and confident even as he saw daily evidence that the United States' war machinery was in need of an extensive overhaul, with little time to accomplish the task.

With FDR in the White House angling to be his own director of war and Churchill posing as the forceful and outspoken expert on a battlefront he'd been engaged in virtually alone, Marshall had to avoid being sucked into a forced abdication of his independent views. In meetings, he was reserved and dignified; he tried to evade informal chatter, and he disliked personal dinners or other settings with the president that could lead to agreements he wasn't ready to make. With quiet reserve, he focused on cutting out the noise and deciding which course was best.

When necessary, Marshall had no trouble standing up to Roosevelt. He'd set the precedent back in their first meeting in 1939, after he had become army chief of staff. FDR had been in his usual mode, rallying the room for a strategy of military buildup that fell short of critical details. He had asked all present whether they thought it was the right plan, and everyone in the room had agreed until he reached Marshall.

"Don't you think so, George?" the president had asked.

"I am sorry, Mr. President, but I don't agree with you at all," Marshall had replied, leaving Roosevelt briefly speechless.

After the meeting Morgenthau had joked to Marshall, "Well, it's been nice knowing you."

FDR liked to have his way, as did Churchill, but both men reluctantly recognized how much they needed a man like Marshall.

While the War Department reorganized itself to meet the challenge, Americans were growing unnerved by what seemed a lack of action. They'd not expected a chess game of deliberate, strategic moves. They'd counted on the United States to hurl itself into the fight, applying brute force in the Pacific to beat back the Japanese. That wasn't happening. Meanwhile, Japan was continuing to expand its control of the Pacific. An attack on Manila had forced General MacArthur and his forces, US and Filipino, to flee to Bataan, leading Roosevelt to pull MacArthur from the Philippines and send him to Australia. The forces in Bataan, now under the command of General Jonathan Wainwright, would fight a losing battle, surrendering in April. Nearly eighty thousand American and Filipino prisoners of war were subjected to a grueling and inhumane sixty-six-mile march known as the Bataan Death March. Many died on the march; others condemned to near starvation and subhuman conditions in the POW camps would not survive the war.

Japan was casting a wide net. In February, Singapore, Great Britain's stronghold in the east, fell to the Japanese, and sixty-two thousand Allied troops were taken prisoner. It was an unexpected disaster for the British fighting forces, who had underestimated Japan's preparedness and the skill of its forces. It was a major defeat, one in a series of many.

Further rattling US citizens was the appearance in February of a submarine off the coast of California, which emerged to fire shells at the coast. The prospect of direct attacks on our shores was alarming to a nation still numb from Pearl Harbor. People were demanding protection, and in the heat of the moment, the prime target was the Japanese Americans living on the West Coast. Rumors and suspicions began to spread rapidly about the possibility of those Americans having a hidden loyalty to the Japanese cause. Were there spies in their midst who were working with the enemy? Suddenly everyone of Japanese ancestry looked suspicious, without regard to evidence of patriotism or lack thereof. The hysteria grew into an outcry in the west that spread to Washington. Congressmen from western states were demanding government action. Secretary of War Henry Stimson met with FDR and proposed a solution that would have been unthinkable in ordinary times: relocating Japanese Americans away from the coast for the duration of the war. FDR told him to do what he deemed necessary. Despite opposition by Attorney General Francis Biddle, Henry Morgenthau, and even FBI director J. Edgar Hoover, Roosevelt went forward with the plan; on February 19, 1942, he signed an executive order to remove Japanese Americans from "military exclusion zones" on the West Coast. More than 120,000 citizens were ordered from their homes and taken to inland internment camps, their civil rights suspended.

The internment of Japanese Americans would be a permanent stain on FDR's war record. It seems unlikely that he thought there was a real threat—and if so, why not intern German Americans or Italian Americans as well? More likely, with opinion polls showing 93 percent of Americans supporting internment, it was a political calculation. FDR needed Americans to get behind him in the war effort, and if that meant sacrificing a small segment of the population, so be it.

As an early test of FDR's war leadership, the decision was troubling. FDR, who prided himself on being a defender of the rights of people and the rule of law, who had been high minded at Arcadia about the democratic promise of the world to come, blundered into a grievous abandonment of human rights. It was Stalin's Communist regime that preached that the end justifies the means. Not the United States.

Decades after the war, two Republican presidents would try to make amends. In 1976, President Gerald Ford issued a formal apology to Japanese Americans, saying, "not only was the evacuation wrong, but Japanese-Americans were and are loyal

Americans." In 1988, President Ronald Reagan signed the Civil Liberties Act, giving reparations to families of the interned and stating that "here we admit a wrong; here we reaffirm our commitment as a nation to equal justice under the law."

However, in the winter of 1942, the public mood was bitter and scared. One blow after another was dispiriting. "Americans had become accustomed to thinking that they could lick any nation with one hand tied behind their backs," Rosenman observed. But it already looked as if they were losing. FDR decided he needed to give a fireside chat in the form of a tutorial on the war. Calling Hopkins, Rosenman, and Sherwood together, the president told them he wanted to ask newspapers to print maps of the world in preparation for his fireside chat on Washington's Birthday. "I am going to ask the American people to take out their maps," he said. "I'm going to speak about strange places that many of them have never heard of—places that are now the battleground for civilization. . . . I want to explain to the people something about geography—what our problem is and what the overall strategy of the war has to be." He thought that if he could explain it in layman's terms, "I am sure that they can take any kind of bad news right on the chin."

It was a challenge to the speechwriters to get the tone and the explanation just right. Americans must be helped to understand that the United States wasn't an isolated nation, needing only to protect its own shores. To win against the global Axis Powers, the nation needed a global strategy. The Nazis might seem far away on the other side of the world, but their progress across the globe endangered our shores.

On air, FDR told the American people to look at their maps and follow along. He explained that the Allies must act in concert for victory to be possible. Pulling resources from the British and the Russians would have a dire cascading effect, allowing Hitler to conquer Turkey, the Near East, and North Africa. That in turn would give the Nazis a clear route to South America, then on to the United States. At critical points in the journey, the Nazis and Japanese could actively join forces to overwhelm the Allies. He spoke of a "battlefield for civilization" and urged Americans to be patient and resolute.

So what *was* the plan? Under consideration was an invasion of northern France, code-named Operation Roundup, which would be a direct and dramatic attack at the heart of the Nazi front. A second possibility was Operation Sledgehammer, a cross-Channel assault. Stalin was in favor of either approach, as long as it could occur in 1942 and pull German resources away from the Soviet Union. Churchill was skeptical that either plan could be executed before 1943. Meanwhile, Marshall and Eisenhower were urging a Pacific-first strategy against the Japanese, and public opinion seemed to be in their favor. Roosevelt refused to consider it. He believed that the United States must make a dramatic assault against Hitler, so the world would see its determination and strength.

Behind the scenes, FDR had to face the true nature of the Allied collaboration. The Allies were not just one big happy, united family. Each nation had its own ambitions and larger purpose, and they were not always in alignment. In the Soviet Union, Stalin wasn't an entirely trustworthy ally; he was essentially operating on his own, with the aid but not the influence of the Allies. Success against the Nazis would undoubtedly allow the Soviet Union to extend its reach, causing potential problems down the road. And what if Stalin, with his back to the wall, gave in and formed an alliance with Germany to save what was left of his country?

The United States and Great Britain were constantly playing a game of "Which of these three is not like the other?" when it came to the Soviet Union. At best in the new world order they sought to create, the Soviet Union would have to be kept on a leash. The old proverb "The enemy of my enemy is my friend" surely applied. But the Western Allies were painfully aware that Stalin had complete control over his government and could essentially do as he pleased. The Western leaders had no such free rein.

Also troubling to FDR was the fact that Great Britain had its own empire to protect, fighting for freedom while protecting colonialism. For example, FDR's open support for India's independence didn't sit well with Churchill, and many Indians were so determined to end British rule that they supported Germany and Japan. FDR was advocating a postwar world in which every nation would be independent. But that future was a dream, maybe a distant one, and today's battles were being waged not in dreams but in an increasingly desperate reality.

WILLIAM STANDLEY HAD NEVER expected to find himself in the Soviet Union. A retired admiral in the US Navy and a longtime friend of FDR, he became a reluctant but loyal envoy when the president called him back into action as the new ambassador to the Soviet Union. His predecessor, Laurence Steinhardt, had not been a favorite of Stalin, who had complained to Harriman about Steinhardt's apparent disrespect for the Soviet government and his "defeatist" attitude about its potential to win against the Nazis. Hoping to mollify Stalin, FDR appointed Standley.

When Standley arrived at his new home at Spaso House, the residence of the US ambassador in Moscow, he would soon learn that being ambassador in that secretive country often meant cooling his heels out of the loop. From the start, he had problems learning critical plans, even from his own government. With Harriman and Hopkins conducting ad hoc diplomacy, Standley found he was often the last person to know what was going on.

He didn't even have the advantage of local immersion. There was virtually no contact with ordinary Russians. Not unexpectedly, conditions were harsh; the entire nation was under strict food rationing, and eggs and meat were rare commodities for most people. Even the embassy staff had to scrape for food—although they were in far better shape than the locals. Regular food shipments from the United States, stocked in a commissary, helped. The embassy staff also kept chickens on the grounds for eggs and occasional meat.

In contrast to the daily deprivations, official receptions were almost vulgar in their abundance—"We were handsomely wined (or vodka-ed) and dined," Standley wrote. He described a regular "battle of the vodkas," with eight or ten different kinds served, along with a variety of wines and sumptuous foodstuffs.

For Standley's first meeting with Stalin, twelve days after his arrival, he was shown into a conference room with a large, gleaming table. Stalin was seated at one end. Standley's first impression was that Stalin didn't take the meeting too seriously; his expressive eyes were showing a glint of humor and question, as if to demand, *What do you want?* Throughout the meeting, Standley noticed that Stalin was an inveterate doodler. As the ambassador gave a flowery prepared greeting from Roosevelt—"The president wishes me to express to you his admiration for the magnificent courage, fortitude and resourcefulness shown by the Red Army and the Russian people"—he watched Stalin, head bent, doodling what appeared to be "lopsided hearts of all sizes and positions." Only after the translator had conveyed Standley's message did Stalin stop doodling.

He raised his head and peppered Standley with his grievances, among them the persistent difficulty of receiving shipments of Lend-Lease supplies. There was no question that it was a problem. Traveling treacherous waters to the Soviet Union, the ships were often torpedoed and the shipments lost. But Stalin suggested that that was only a part of the problem. US suppliers didn't want to take orders from the Soviet Union, he complained. They'd rather take orders from Great Britain. Standley could do little but assure Stalin that he would do what he could to improve the situation.

As the meeting concluded, Stalin rose from his seat and shook hands with Standley. "If I can be of any help to remove obstacles to good American-Soviet relations, call upon me at any time," he said with a polite smile.

"Thank you, Mr. Stalin," Standley replied and added, somewhat flippantly, "If I can be of any help to you in killing Germans, please let me know."

Stalin frowned. "The Russians are killing many, many Germans at the front," he said gravely. "The poor Germans have orders that they must not retreat, must not give way to us a single inch. The result is that we are killing them like pigs. There is just nothing else to do with Germans but kill them."

Standley didn't react, but he might have noted the irony of Stalin's words. After all, Stalin himself had ordered a no-surrender policy for his troops, ruling that surrender was tantamount to treason against the Motherland and punishable by death. Nor was defeat acceptable. Early in the war he'd had commanders of failed missions executed and their families punished. Stalin believed that the chief cause of failure in battle was lack of nerve. An army determined to defeat Hitler *would* defeat Hitler.

In late May, Stalin sent foreign minister Vyacheslav Molotov to Washington. Molotov, full faced with a tight little mustache and hard eyes peering through rimless glasses, was an old Stalin ally from the early days of the Bolshevik Revolution, and he'd been a brutal henchman of the Great Purge, personally ordering the deaths of hundreds of citizens deemed disloyal. Now he was the second most powerful man in the Soviet Union. Like Stalin, he had abandoned his birth family name, Skryabin, choosing Molotov, which meant "hammer." Roosevelt privately called him "Stone Ass."

His arrival in Washington was shrouded in secrecy, under the name "Mr. Brown." He was housed in the Rose Suite at the White House, where Churchill had stayed after Pearl Harbor. Eleanor recalled that when a valet had unpacked his bags, he had found a sausage, a loaf of black bread, and a loaded pistol. "The Secret Service men did not like visitors with pistols," she wrote in a rare burst of humor, "but on this occasion nothing was said. Mr. Molotov evidently thought he might have to defend himself and also he might be hungry."

The situation in the Soviet Union was desperate, and Roosevelt and Churchill were concerned that the Soviet Union might drop out of the war. They could well imagine a scenario in which Stalin, facing the prospect of defeat, would turn around and become Hitler's ally. Standley didn't think that was likely. "Stalin had all the aces and the jokers in the pack in our games of diplomatic poker," he observed, "because he knew that we had to play the game with him on his terms. I don't think he ever had any intention of picking up his chips and quitting the game—although our State Department boys and the Boss and Harry Hopkins worried about that possibility."

Even so, it was FDR's instinct to be as accommodating as possible to Molotov, lest any crack form in the alliance. Apart from the continuing issue of the shipment of materials to the

Soviet Union, Molotov's main goal was to win Roosevelt's agreement on a second front in the war during 1942, which would pull Nazi troops and resources away from the Soviet Union. Roosevelt was also restless and wanting to make a big move. Marshall wasn't too sure. For one thing, the suggestion on the table, a cross-Channel assault on France, was a high-risk strategy and might be impossible to put together that year. For another thing, there was Churchill, who didn't support a cross-Channel invasion. But Roosevelt was so intent on accommodating Molotov that he urged Marshall to agree to a second front, staying vague about the exact details and timeline. Molotov left Washington with his promise. The plan was to begin a buildup in Great Britain to a location outside London, code-named Operation Bolero, for the cross-Channel assault, Sledgehammer; and, if conditions were right, Roundup—a full invasion of northern France.

Across the ocean, Churchill was fuming. A cross-Channel invasion in 1942, he felt, would be suicidal. His military advisers were warning him that they didn't have the landing craft to launch the full-on attack that would be needed. If they went ahead and then failed, it would be a potentially fatal blow to Allied interests and would make Hitler even stronger in Europe. Undoubtedly, it would also be the end of Churchill as prime minister. Although he had won a near-unanimous vote of confidence in the House of Commons in January, he couldn't count on that support if Great Britain appeared to be losing the war.

Churchill was pushing another idea, a mission code-named Operation Gymnast, a joint British-US invasion of French North Africa. On June 17, he left London for the United States to make his case in person. The trip, aboard the Boeing Bristol flying boat, took twenty-seven hours before landing on the Potomac River late in the evening of June 18. The following day,

Churchill flew to Hyde Park, where FDR greeted him at New Hackensack Field, the Hudson Valley regional airport, which had been commandeered by the military during the war. Driving his hand-controlled Ford convertible, FDR sped to Hyde Park over the high, winding roads above the Hudson River, devilishly delighting in the rattled nerves of his passenger.

Tucked into the luggage of one of Churchill's aides was a memo from the secretarial pool of the British War Rooms, typed on official paper and titled "Operation Desperate." Written in early May, it had been meant as a lighthearted gesture, but given the conditions in Great Britain, it was actually deadly serious. The memo read:

> In view of the recent changes in the Government policy of distribution of coupons, we have examined the situation, and the following conclusions have been reached:
>
> (a) The limitation of supplies in the U.K. has resulted in the following acute shortages—
> (i) silk stockings;
> (ii) chocolates;
> (iii) cosmetics.
> (b) The lack of those vital commodities is regarded as extremely serious, and may, in consequence, become a source of extreme embarrassment. This must be avoided at all costs.
> (c) It is felt that immediate steps should be taken to explore the possibilities of U.S. resources.
>
> 2. In the light of the above, it is considered that the most expedient method of implementing the proposal in (c) would be the early dispatch of a mission to the U.S.A.;

a Force Commander has already been appointed, in anticipation of instructions.

When Churchill's party returned to England, a cache of requested items was on board, and the secretaries were delighted to find Operation Desperate a complete success.

Roosevelt was in a good mood. The United States was finally on the offensive against Japan and had scored a major victory against the Japanese at Midway, an atoll of two critically positioned islands in the middle of the Pacific. Although the Americans had appeared to be outgunned, they had had the advantage of advance intelligence and had known about the attack beforehand. When Japanese warships had arrived, they had been ready. After a fierce two-day battle, the Japanese had been forced to retreat. Not only had the victory struck a military blow to Japan, destroying four of its carriers and more than three hundred aircraft and killing 3,500 Japanese, it had effectively halted Japan's march through the Pacific and would be considered one of the most decisive battles in the war. Although the war in the Pacific would continue for three more years, by holding on to that critical gateway, the Americans established a dominance and put Japan on the defensive for the remainder of the war.

Once settled at Hyde Park, Churchill aired his opposition to Sledgehammer and Roundup, at least in 1942, and pushed the North Africa strategy. Roosevelt and Churchill also made a critical decision, barely noted at the time, about whether to continue the development and testing of tube alloys—the eventual atom bomb.

After two days in Hyde Park, Roosevelt and Churchill returned to Washington by train to continue their discussions. While meeting with Churchill in the Oval Office, FDR received a note with devastating news for the British and the Allied cause: Tobruk had fallen. Tobruk was a vital port city in eastern Libya that had been the centerpiece of Middle East strategy since 1940, when British, Australian, and Indian forces had grabbed it from the Italians. Tobruk was a gateway to Egypt and the Suez Canal, and the Germans, under the command of General Erwin Rommel's Afrika Corps, had continued a drive to take it back. Rommel had finally succeeded. After he read the painful news, FDR gently broke it to Churchill. The prime minister slumped in his chair, so devastated he could barely speak. "Defeat is one thing, disgrace is another," he later wrote of that moment, describing it as "one of the heaviest blows" of the war.

"What can we do to help?" Roosevelt asked with genuine sympathy and concern. Churchill roused himself to ask FDR to send as many Sherman tanks as he could spare to the Middle East. There was no question about not responding. Although Roosevelt knew he'd take some flack at home for making such a large investment in the Middle East, he also realized he needed to do it for his friend and partner.

The defeat served to confirm Churchill's view that a North Africa invasion should be launched as soon as possible. Now the strategic sense of it was coming into focus. If Rommel were allowed to continue storming on to Egypt and Turkey, the whole region would be lost, cutting off access to the Allies. An Allied victory in North Africa would undermine Hitler's sweeping progress and give the Allies an opening to continue on to Italy and into Europe. Secondarily, Churchill argued, it would provide relief to the Soviet Union—although it was doubtful that Stalin would see it that way. Churchill began referring to the plan as "the true second front," hoping to make that case.

Sherwood noted that Churchill's push for a North Africa invasion might have been remarkably prescient, given the result.

But, he added, at the time the US joint chiefs thought the proposal was more of the same from Churchill, who had an "incurable predilection for 'eccentric operations,' which had guided him in the First as well as the Second World War; he preferred operations which depended on surprise, deception and speed, in terrain . . . where there was not sufficient room for huge ground forces to be deployed." North Africa fit the bill perfectly. By the end of the Roosevelt-Churchill conference, it had been decided to pursue the North Africa strategy, renamed Operation Torch.

Eisenhower had already been tasked with preparing a report, "Directive for the Commanding General European Theater of Operations," which would now include North Africa. It hadn't occurred to him that he'd be in charge. Earlier, Marshall had said as much. Speaking of promotions during the war, Marshall had bluntly told Eisenhower that although others were recommending him for command, he believed in promoting men from the field, not from staff positions. Marshall's words stung, and Eisenhower angrily replied, "General, I'm interested in what you say, but I don't give a damn about your promotion plans as far as I'm concerned. I came into this office from the field and I am trying to do my duty. . . . If that locks me to a desk for the rest of the war, so be it!"

Perhaps it had been a test. When Eisenhower handed his report to Marshall, he was shocked when Marshall told him, "You may be the man to execute it. If that's the case, when can you leave?" By June 24, Eisenhower was in London, preparing to lead the joint force in preparations for Operation Torch.

Once in Great Britain, Eisenhower was struck by two things: one was the "acute lack" of trained troops and equipment, a situation that needed to be remedied immediately. The second was the conviction that Torch must be so overwhelming in force that the surprise attack would completely neutralize the opposition.

With only months to plan and execute the operation, he had to act fast to get things into shape.

The problems were immeasurable, both large and small. When the first shipment of materials for the invasion arrived in England, Eisenhower was horrified to discover that none of the crates or boxes was labeled. That presented an enormous and immediate challenge. "Confronted by the awful headache of opening boxes, checking items, and re-crating them, our supply people undoubtedly wished that war had never advanced beyond the bow and arrow," he wrote.

A larger matter of command involved integrating the US and British troops under one banner. The British were battle hardened; the Americans were new to the fight. But Churchill and Roosevelt had agreed that an American, Eisenhower, would run the show, and he was determined to make sure that the troops would work seamlessly together. He told his men, "I will clamp down on anyone who tries to start any trouble between the Americans and British under my command. There will be neither praise nor blame for the British as British or the Americans as Americans. We will fight it shoulder to shoulder. Men will be praised or blamed for what they do, not for their nationality."

It was left to Churchill to travel to Moscow in August 1942 and explain to Stalin that there would be no second front in Europe in 1942, a mission he described as "like carrying a large lump of ice to the North Pole." It was his first meeting with the dictator for whom he had previously voiced such great contempt. His wife, Clementine, referred to it as a meeting "with the ogre in his den," and she wasn't far off the mark, in Churchill's opinion. As his plane approached Moscow, Churchill glumly reflected on what lay ahead. "I pondered on my mission to this sullen, sinister Bolshevik State I had once tried so hard to strangle at its birth, and which, until Hitler appeared, I had regarded as the mortal foe of civilised freedom," he wrote of his feelings. "What was it my duty to say to them now?" Seeking collaboration, he was nonetheless repelled by the Soviet state, even the conditions of his lodging, which "was prepared with totalitarian lavishness."

Meeting with Stalin at the Kremlin for the first time, Churchill understood the gravity of a moment that would bring him together with a man he had always despised. In the nearly four-hour meeting, with Harriman at his side, Churchill tried to explain the reasoning behind the decision to delay a direct assault on the continent.

Stalin, who, Harriman observed, looked older and grayer than during their first meeting, openly berated Churchill, repeating the dead-eyed standard he used with his own forces, blaming the Allied losses on a spinelessness and an unwillingness to take risks. "You must not be so afraid of the Germans," he lectured Churchill as the prime minister sat grim-faced before him. Later, Churchill complained to Molotov: "Stalin will make a great mistake to treat us roughly when we have come so far." Molotov placidly replied, "Stalin is a very wise man. You may be sure that, however he argues, he understands all. I will tell him what you say."

Stalin argued strongly but without emotion against the decision to delay a second front until Churchill stopped him cold, telling him the decision was final and it would do him no good to argue. Stalin's attacks on the courage of the British were hurtful, but Churchill kept his cool. "I repulsed all his contentions squarely, but without taunts of any kind," he wrote of their conversation. He even allowed that he forgave Stalin his harsh remarks about the courage of his army because he understood the bravery of the Russian army.

When the conversation switched to a discussion of Torch, Stalin became more interested, especially after Harriman assured him, "President Roosevelt, in spite of his serious preoccupations in the Pacific, looks upon the European theater of war as his principal concern. He will support it to the limit of the resources at his disposal."

Stalin, realizing that he would not succeed in getting his second front just yet, became a little less abrasive in his manner. The meeting ended cordially with an invitation to Churchill and Harriman to join him for dinner the following night.

Harriman, for one, understood Stalin's mood. "They were really desperate," he said of the Soviets. "Stalin's roughness was the expression of their need for help. It was his way of trying to put all the heat he possibly could on Churchill. So he pressed as hard as he could until he realized that no amount of additional pressure would produce a second front in 1942. He had the wisdom to know that he could not let Churchill go back to London feeling there had been a breakdown."

According to National Archives papers released for the first time in 2013, Churchill and Stalin did have a heavily lubricated meeting of the minds after dinner on the final evening. Late at night Churchill was invited to Stalin's private room to continue their discussion. Alexander Cadogan, Churchill's undersecretary of state for foreign affairs, went looking for the prime minister at 1:00 A.M. and entered Stalin's room. "There I found Winston and Stalin, and Molotov who has joined them, sitting with a heavily-laden board between them: food of all kinds crowned by a sucking [sic] pig and innumerable bottles. What Stalin made me drink seemed pretty savage. Winston, who by that time was complaining of a slight headache, seemed wisely to be confining himself to a comparatively innocuous effervescent Caucasian red wine. Everyone seemed to be as merry as a marriage bell."

They continued to talk until 3:00 in the morning, when Churchill had to leave to prepare for the flight back to England. He was in a positive frame of mind, Cadogan reported. "I think the two great men really made contact and got on terms. Certainly Winston was impressed and I think that feeling was reciprocated."

Colonel Ian Jacob, the military assistant secretary to the British war cabinet, who was also with Churchill, was less sanguine. He didn't believe a friendship with Stalin was possible. He wrote in his diary, "I should say that to make friends with Stalin would be equivalent to making friends with a python."

ROOSEVELT WAS A WAR president now, and his aides often chafed at his preternatural calm and viselike grip on power and decision making. Whereas Churchill wore his heart on his sleeve and paraded his views and emotions every chance he got and Stalin remained remote and inscrutable, constantly taking jabs at the Western Allies from afar, Roosevelt tried to project a steadier hand—at his desk in the Oval Office every morning and throughout the day, ushering advisers in and out, visiting the basement map room twice a week to get thorough briefings on the war. He thought of himself as his own secretary of state and often made unilateral decisions over the heads of his advisers.

At the same time, he acknowledged needing a primary adviser to coordinate the army, navy, and air force operations. In July, he appointed Fleet Admiral William Leahy as chief of staff to the commander in chief, US Army and Navy. Unlike modern presidential chiefs of staff, Leahy's job was related primarily to the military. The sixty-seven-year-old former chief of naval operations had also served as governor of Puerto Rico and ambassador to France after the Nazi takeover—a thankless job if ever there was one. FDR thought Leahy's experience and seasoning would make him an ideal power broker to the big egos of the military command. And he was comfortable with Leahy. Their relationship dated back to FDR's years as assistant secretary of the navy, when Leahy had commanded the secretary's dispatch boat and they'd become friends. "He said [at a press conference] that I would be a sort of 'leg man' who would help him digest, analyze, and summarize a mass of material with which he had been trying to cope singlehandedly," Leahy recalled.

Despite the best efforts of the staff, the White House was a glum place, with heavy blackout curtains draped on the windows and gas masks stashed under desks. A fallout shelter built in the basement was a constant reminder of how close the war could become. The battlefields of war might have seemed distant, but after Pearl Harbor, no one disputed that the fight could reach the United States.

Everything was shrouded in a veil of secrecy, especially the president's movements. Early sternly informed the press corps, "Nothing must be printed or broadcast about the movements of the president without authority. Think of him as a battleship and report his movements just as carefully as you would the position of one of our battleships."

The situation could get claustrophobic.

Roosevelt knew that a president needs opportunities to get away, if not from the workload, at least from the setting. Before the war, those excursions had occurred on his beloved *Potomac*, where he could be "at sea," catered to by his reliable crew of Filipino stewards. As often as he could, he took the yacht up to Hyde Park. But the war had changed all that. Security officials agreed that it was just too dangerous for FDR to be out on the water, where the threat of U-boat attacks was ever present. He was forced to abandon his seafaring retreats and look for a site on land. Sixty miles north of Washington in the Catoctin Mountains of Maryland were several recreation sites that had been part of a WPA project during the Depression. In April 1942, he'd taken a drive up to the mountain to look at the sites. Arriving at the topmost area, called Camp #3, FDR exclaimed, "This is my Shangri-La!"

There were already cabins scattered around the property, and the government set about doing renovations, including re-modeling the central cabin, which would be reserved for the president. Whenever he could get away, Roosevelt drove up to Shangri-La to oversee the work. The result was beautiful while still having a rustic flavor of the country. It had the added ad-vantage of being a secure site, manned by naval officers with marines patrolling the mountainous perimeters and staffed by Roosevelt's Filipino crew from the *Potomac*. Roosevelt chris-tened it a navy installation, the USS Shangri-La. (The rustic style and tight security remain to this day at the presidential retreat, which was renamed Camp David during Eisenhower's presidency.)

At Shangri-La, FDR was often accompanied by military aides, along with Tully and Suckley. Between scouring official papers, making calls, and consulting with advisers, he loved to sit on the screened-in back patio and work on his stamps. In the evenings, the stewards would serve fine meals, after which he and his guests and aides would sit and play cards (Grace Tully was a demon at poker) and tell stories. As a storyteller, FDR was unmatched. He took great delight in the oddities of life and relished the telling of tales, maybe true, maybe not, that sent his audience into spasms of laughter—sometimes at the expense of his wartime counterparts.

Always on hand to advise and console was Harry Hopkins. He was FDR's chief global representative, although he was frequently ill, often looking like a ghost, yet somehow managing to rise to every occasion. It was Hopkins who brought Churchill into line. It was Hopkins who eased tensions with Stalin. "I have been present at several great conferences where twenty or more of the most important executive personages were gathered together," Churchill wrote. "When the discussion flagged and all seemed baffled, it was on these occasions he would rap out the deadly question, 'Surely, Mr. President, here is the point we have got to settle. Are we going to face it or not?' Faced it always was, and, being faced, was conquered."

A widower living in the White House with his daughter, Diana, Hopkins was always by Roosevelt's side. But in 1942, their close personal connection would change somewhat when Hopkins fell in love with a vivacious fashion writer and editor, Louise Gill Macy. They were married at the White House in Roosevelt's Oval Study on July 30, 1942, and, in spite of Eleanor's trepidation, chose to live together in the White House, with Diana. Despite his continued physical proximity, Hopkins's new marriage left Roosevelt lonelier than ever.

Too often those days, his Scottish terrier, Fala, was the president's sole close companion. Eleanor was more absent than ever. She had purchased an apartment on Washington Square in Greenwich Village, New York, and she regularly spent two days a week there, doing business in the city. She secretly exulted in the independence and privacy it gave her. At the same time, she had increasingly become FDR's most valuable ambassador to the nation, not just with her daily columns but also with her frequent travels to meet the populace in person. The shy, retiring wife of old was a distant memory. She had truly come into her own. And although she often found herself in disagreement with her husband—over Japanese internment, for example—she practiced marital diplomacy and never publicly aired her contrary views.

In September, mindful of the upcoming midterm elections, FDR asked Eleanor to accompany him on a two-week train journey to visit defense plants and military facilities across the United States, and she reluctantly agreed to set aside her own jammed schedule to go with him at least as far as Chicago. The trip was top secret; Eleanor's daily columns made no mention of it, and the press was left behind to wonder where the president was.

In Detroit they witnessed the dramatic metamorphosis of the car industry—American commercial can-do applied to winning the war. General Motors, Ford, and Chrysler, the auto-making "Big Three," had turned over their production lines completely to war operations, literally embodying the "arsenal of democracy."

The tour carried FDR all the way west to Fort Lewis in Washington State and the Puget Sound Naval Shipyard in Seattle, ending at the Boeing plant, which would produce nearly 100,000 planes for the war effort.

At the naval hospital outside Seattle, the president asked that his car be parked outside the front entrance, so he could personally greet the war wounded, who came by foot and in wheelchairs to shake his hand.

AFTER MONTHS OF PREPARATION, Operation Torch was on for November 8. The plan was to simultaneously invade three ports: Casablanca on the Atlantic coast of Morocco, and Oran and Algiers, beyond the Strait of Gibraltar, with an advance on Tunis to follow. The command center where Eisenhower would direct the battle was deep inside the Rock of Gibraltar, which was a perfectly situated fortress between the Atlantic and the Mediterranean. British and US convoys would stage at Gibraltar, a British possession on the southern tip of Spain, then move out to their separate destinations. Major General George Patton would command an all-American force heading to Casablanca, judged to be the most difficult of the three landings. The Oran force, led by Major General Lloyd Fredendall, would also be American, with an escort by the British navy. Algiers would be a combined US-British force under the command of US major general Charles Ryder. The three landings would occur simultaneously in a surprise attack. "We were gambling for high stakes," Eisenhower recalled.

FDR would have liked to see Torch launched before the midterm elections, thinking it would boost Democrat wins, but it was not to be. November 3 came and went with substantial losses to Democrats in both Congress and the statehouses. However, the Democratic Party held its control of the House and Senate, albeit by narrower margins. Roosevelt told Tully that it was just as well the elections had come before Torch; otherwise he'd have been accused of playing politics with the war.

On November 5, Eisenhower flew from London to take his command post in Gibraltar, with the cover story that he was traveling to Washington. Deep inside the cavernous subterranean interior of the Rock, a makeshift operations center had been set up in the tunnels, and there Eisenhower began his final preparations. He would later call it "the most dismal setting" he had encountered during the war. He wrote:

> The eternal darkness of the tunnels was here and there partially pierced by feeble electric bulbs. Damp, cold air in block-long passages was heavy with a stagnation that did not noticeably respond to the clattering efforts of electric fans. Through the arched ceilings came a constant drip, drip, drip of surface water that faithfully but drearily ticked off the seconds of the interminable, almost unendurable wait that always occurs between the

completion of a military plan and the moment action begins.

Despite all that, he felt a certain sense of awe at finding himself at the historic fortress at a critical point in the war. "I simply must have a grandchild," he wrote in his diary, "or I'll never have the fun of telling this when I'm fishing, gray-bearded, on the banks of a quiet bayou in the deep South."

Worries about the poor weather forecast and a concern that the secrecy of the mission might be blown consumed him. But his greatest anxiety was the unknown factor of the Vichy French. After France had surrendered to Germany, two governments had been formed. The resistance government, the Free French, was under the direction of Charles de Gaulle, who was in London. The Vichy French, collaborating with the Nazis, were more influential in Europe and had a heavy presence in North Africa. In Algiers to visit his son, who had been stricken with polio, Vichy admiral Jean-François Darlan, a loyal Hitlerite, was on the scene and in control of the Vichy French troops, and Eisenhower knew that if Darlan called on his forces to fight the Allies, it could mean a long and bloody battle.

As it was, the French animosity toward the British was so intense that Torch was fronted as a largely US operation. According to Leahy, "There was some discussion in the Joint Chiefs meetings about dressing up British soldiers in American uniforms and painting United States insignia on British planes." The idea never came to fruition. "It simply isn't done by professional soldiers," he noted curtly.

At 1:00 on the morning of November 8, the Allies landed. Monitoring their progress from Gibraltar, Eisenhower was heartened to learn that there was less resistance than had been expected, although the fighting continued and was far from over.

Driving to Shangri-La with FDR the day before the landings, Tully had noticed that the president was nervous and on edge. She didn't know that Torch was imminent, but as she watched him throughout the day and into the next, she could see his anxiety growing. He would say only that he was awaiting an important message.

Finally the call came from Washington, and Tully noticed FDR's hand shaking as he took the phone.

He listened intently, said nothing as he heard the full message, then burst out:

"Thank God. Thank God. That sounds grand. Congratulations. Casualties are comparatively light—much below your predictions. Thank God."

He dropped the phone and turned to us.

"We have landed in North Africa. Casualties are below expectations. We are striking back."

With the fight ongoing, Eisenhower knew that Darlan still had the power to summon more forceful opposition. He hoped to do an end run around Darlan by elevating French military hero General Henri Giraud, who had escaped after two years in a German prison camp and joined Eisenhower at Gibraltar. Giraud was difficult. When offered a leadership position in the invasion in the hope that he could garner the support of French forces in North Africa, Giraud insisted that he would take no position lower than commander of the entire operation—Eisenhower's job. Eisenhower was forced to spend precious time wrangling with the general, and in any case, it made little difference. When Giraud finally broadcast an order to French forces to stop fighting against the Allies, the Vichy commanders dismissed him out of hand. Now Eisenhower was left with a terrible trade-off.

With Giraud's effort a failure and Vichy forces putting up

resistance, Eisenhower recalled Churchill telling him in colorful terms before he left England, "If I could meet Darlan, much as I hate him, I would cheerfully crawl on my hands and knees for a mile if by doing so I could get him to bring that fleet of his into the Allied forces." So with his deputy, Major General Mark Clark, Eisenhower worked out a deal with Darlan: if he called on his forces to stand down, the Allies would support his authority in North Africa. The "Darlan deal," as it was called, worked. Darlan was true to his word and ordered the French military to cease fighting; some even joined the Allies. Without Vichy resistance, the success of Torch was accomplished within days, allowing Eisenhower to strike out for Tunisia, the next target in North Africa. The Tunisian campaign would not go as smoothly as Torch. Large numbers of German forces were there to mount a defense. From his headquarters in Algiers, Eisenhower shuttled back and forth to the front. It was "a time when we worked harder, I think, than we ever had before," he recalled. He knew they could not afford to underestimate the challenge of fighting an entrenched German force—"Once the Nazis have taken a position, they organize it for defense within *two hours*," he warned his commanders. Tunisia was a critical pathway in the Mediterranean and the access point to Italy and southern Europe. The Nazis would not give in easily.

As Eisenhower battled on in Tunisia, back in the United States there was outrage over the Darlan deal. How could Eisenhower elevate a man who collaborated with the Nazis? If nothing else, it was a public relations nightmare, and Eisenhower was taking a lot of heat. Roosevelt was deeply concerned until he received a cable from Eisenhower, carefully outlining the necessity of making that temporary arrangement. Roosevelt cabled back that Eisenhower had his full support, based on the fact that he was on the ground and knew best. But he added that Darlan must be monitored very closely.

Despite Roosevelt's cautious support, the storm over the Darlan deal did not abate. Churchill was also upset, perhaps having forgotten his earlier comment to Eisenhower. In his view, making an arrangement with Darlan was tantamount to collaborating with the Nazis. Eisenhower might have felt some regret for stepping into that political minefield. But the ultimate result was as he'd hoped.

Darlan's role in governing ended up not being an issue; he was assassinated on Christmas Eve. Although a lone assassin was arrested and executed, people were left to wonder if the Americans, British, or de Gaulle had been behind his death. God knows it solved a big problem for all involved. Pragmatically, Churchill wrote, "Darlan's murder, however criminal, relieved the Allies of their embarrassment at working with him, and at the same time left them with all the advantages he had been able to bestow during the vital hours of the Allied landings."

Delighted with the progress of the North Africa campaign, Churchill nonetheless memorably warned, "Now this is not the end. It is not even the beginning of the end. But it is, perhaps, the end of the beginning."

A hoped-for meeting of the "Big Three" in early 1943 was not to be. Stalin had once again declined to join FDR and Churchill, citing pressing matters at home, where the Soviet Union was engaged in a cataclysmic battle with the Nazis in Stalingrad, which would exact more than a million Soviet military casualties. FDR and Churchill decided that it still made sense for them to meet, along with their combined chiefs of staff, to discuss the next steps in the war. To Hull's dismay, FDR chose to leave him at home, wanting to focus on military issues. The

setting was the Anfa Hotel outside Casablanca. It was a beautiful modern building, surrounded by palm trees, on a hill over-
looking the city. Well-appointed villas on the property would
house FDR and Churchill, while their staffs stayed at the hotel.

On January 9, Roosevelt and Hopkins left Washington on
a train bound for Miami, where they would take a flight south
to Brazil and then across the Atlantic. Secrecy was so great that
the usual civilian crew and attendants were replaced by Filipino
sailors from Shangri-La. Roosevelt was secured in a specially
built armored car designed for safety and comfort.

Taking copious notes on the trip, Hopkins described every
step along the way, beginning with the president's excitement at
flying once again. He hadn't been on a plane since his trip to the
convention in 1932, and he would become the first sitting president to fly. As they lifted off in the Boeing 314 flying boat, the
"Dixie Clipper," early on the morning of January 11, Hopkins
observed that FDR "acted like a sixteen-year-old."

Changing planes to a Douglas C-54 in West Africa, Roosevelt arrived in Casablanca on the afternoon of January 14.
Marshall and other staff were already in place, as was Churchill, who had suffered through a rough flight in a B-24 bomber.
He'd also left England in top secrecy, his flight booked in Harriman's name.

Dinner was a happy family affair. Two of Roosevelt's sons,
Elliott, now a lieutenant colonel, and Franklin, Jr., a lieutenant,
had been summoned to join their father, as had Churchill's son,
Randolph, a captain, and Hopkins's son Robert, a sergeant.
Despite whispers about special privileges in the midst of
war, it was a rare opportunity to be together with loved ones.

Eisenhower, annoyed to be called away from the Tunisian
campaign, flew in on a B-17. "The plane was rated 'battle-
fatigued,'" he would recall. "And it did look tired. The desig-

nation meant that the plane had been on bombing missions and had not had proper maintenance."

As the plane flew over the Atlas Mountains in Morocco, one engine began to fail, followed by a sputtering of the second engine. In fear that the flight was doomed, everyone on board was ordered to put on parachutes. At the last moment, the pilot was able to get one of the engines working, and it limped into Casablanca without the need to abandon the flight in midair. The relieved Eisenhower noted, "With an anxious thought for an old football injury, I was delighted that I did not have to adopt this method of disembarkation." Later Eisenhower was chagrined to receive a report that the plane had been scrapped. They'd come that close to disaster.

Wearily, Eisenhower joined the conference. Struggling in Tunisia, beset by political blowback from the Darlan episode, and suffering from a lingering bad cold, Eisenhower wasn't feeling his best. "Ike seems jittery," Roosevelt confided to Hopkins.

Eisenhower was frustrated by the distraction of French political problems. He hated politics and admitted to having little understanding of the ins and outs of the French power equation. But the problem had followed him to Casablanca, where the French situation was a main topic of discussion.

Invited to meet privately with Roosevelt, Eisenhower might have expected to be called on the carpet for subjecting the president to Darlan-related public relations problems. Instead, the president consoled and encouraged him and even joked that they'd simply had to convince people they weren't turning fascist. Eisenhower found the president's mood upbeat and credited his excitement to being out of the country for the first time in his presidency, save for Newfoundland. "Successful in shaking loose for a few days many of the burdens of state, he seemed to experience a tremendous uplift from the fact that he had secretly slipped away from Washington and was engaged in a historic meeting on territory that only two months before had been a battleground," Eisenhower wrote of their meeting. Later, sitting with Churchill, Eisenhower was cheered by his vote of confidence. It seemed that the British were fully on his side. Meanwhile, behind the scenes, Marshall was fighting for him, convincing Roosevelt to promote him to a four-star general.

Once back in the United States, Roosevelt would praise Eisenhower in a speech at the annual White House Correspondents' Association dinner. "I spent many hours in Casablanca with this young general, a descendent of Kansas pioneers," he said. "I know what a fine, tough job he has done and how carefully and skillfully he is directing the soldiers under him." Eisenhower might have laughed at the depiction of him as a "young general." He was fifty-two.

The strategy going forward was a matter of intense debate. Stalin was still demanding a second front in Europe in 1943, and Marshall, too, was pushing for a cross-Channel operation sooner rather than later. Churchill was equally certain that an invasion of France could not be ready until 1944. The plan favored by Roosevelt and Churchill was victory in Tunisia, allowing the Allies to press on to southern Europe via Sicily.

The key decisions made about 1943 priorities included: the invasion of Sicily (Operation Husky) under the command of Eisenhower, accelerated bomber strikes on Germany, continuation of food, supplies, and armaments to the Soviet Union, accelerated air attacks on Hitler's U-boats at sea, and a continuation of troop buildup in Great Britain for the eventual invasion of France.

Hopkins was worried that the plan seemed less ambitious than many had hoped. He visited Churchill in his villa and found the prime minister in a pink bathrobe drinking a bottle of wine for breakfast. Hopkins admitted to Churchill that he thought their plans "seemed to me like a pretty feeble effort for two great countries in 1943." Marshall certainly agreed. But Churchill was adamant about the wisdom of the strategy to delay a direct assault on western Europe until they had strengthened their position.

More time than anyone would have liked was taken up with the issue of French leadership in the aftermath of Darlan's assassination. Giraud and de Gaulle had been invited to join the conference, and FDR and Churchill hoped to enlist their agreement in forming a governing partnership. That was the best-case scenario in a situation with lousy choices. According to FDR's son Elliott, the president thought Giraud was "a dud of a leader." And he didn't trust de Gaulle, who was imperious and stubborn, more interested, he thought, in personal power than in the future of France. Churchill was even more vehement in his feelings about de Gaulle. The two men had a long history of mutual contempt, and Churchill suspected de Gaulle of having fascist leanings. It seemed like a long shot that de Gaulle would agree to a power-sharing arrangement with Giraud. FDR compared the two to an eager bridegroom (Giraud) and an unwilling bride (de Gaulle) who must be persuaded to consummate a marriage.

At first de Gaulle, who was deeply miffed that he'd deliberately been left out of intelligence on the Torch landings and enraged by the Darlan deal, declined the invitation to come to Casablanca. "De Gaulle is on his high horse," Churchill grumbled to Roosevelt. "Refuses to come down here."

Knowing that de Gaulle's operation was funded primarily by the British, Roosevelt snapped, "Who pays for de Gaulle's food?"

"Well, the British do," said Churchill.

"Why don't you stop his food and maybe he will come."

Something like that happened. Churchill was able to force de Gaulle's attendance by indicating that Great Britain might withhold funds for his Free French movement. He arrived in Casablanca near the end of the conference.

Giraud, who had been present for most of the conference, was equally unimpressed with the idea of sharing power with de Gaulle. Harriman noted that each man came with a plan designed to put himself at the top. "Each Frenchman offered the other the privilege of serving under him," he wrote. "De Gaulle said, 'You will be Foch, I Clemenceau' [a reference to Premier Georges Clemenceau and the insubordinate Marshal Ferdinand Foch after World War I—an odd and unflattering comparison]. Giraud offered a War Committee of three, himself as head."

To everyone's relief, on the last day of the conference, the two men set aside their conflicts in favor of the compelling need to defeat Hitler. Roosevelt quickly arranged a photo opportunity, with the four of them—Roosevelt, Churchill, de Gaulle, and Giraud—together in apparent unity. The stunned Frenchmen, feeling duped but having no choice, gamely shook hands for the cameras.

The press had finally been allowed inside, and about fifty newsmen sat cross-legged outside FDR's villa as the president and then Churchill described the conference and the Allies' military readiness in glowing terms. In his remarks, FDR made a statement that would become the keynote of the conference:

> Another point. I think we have all had it in our hearts and heads before, but I don't think that it has ever been put down on paper by the Prime Minister and myself, and that is the determination that peace can come to the world only by the total elimination of German and Japanese war power.
>
> Some of you Britishers know the old story—we had a

General called U. S. Grant. His name was Ulysses Simpson Grant, but in my, and the Prime Minister's, early days he was called "Unconditional Surrender" Grant. The elimination of German, Japanese, and Italian war power means the unconditional surrender by Germany, Italy, and Japan. That means a reasonable assurance of future world peace. It does not mean the destruction of the population of Germany, Italy, or Japan, but it does mean the destruction of the philosophies in those countries which are based on conquest and the subjugation of other people.

Churchill didn't necessarily agree with the concept of unconditional surrender—and was quick to say it hadn't been *his* idea. But he stood by FDR, based on his belief that negotiations with Hitler were and always would be impossible. FDR later admitted to Hopkins that the idea of unconditional surrender had come at the last minute. "We had so much trouble getting those two French generals together," he said, "that I thought to myself that this was as difficult as arranging the meeting of Grant and Lee—and then suddenly the press conference was on."

The hasty choice of words and the notion of unconditional surrender would inspire heated public debate. It had never before been US policy to obliterate the political systems of enemies, only to win the fight. Many experts worried that such a bold declaration of no negotiations for peace would lengthen the war. And if the purpose of unconditional surrender was the destruction of philosophies based on conquest and the subjugation of peoples, how, then, to view the Soviet Union under Stalin? Roosevelt was understandably reluctant to address this contradiction. In truth, if defeating the Axis Powers was the goal, he had little choice. But he had to worry about how Stalin would use the spoils of war to harden his hold on his region and beyond.

As the conference ended and Roosevelt prepared for the long journey home, Churchill, in his most persuasive voice, implored, "You cannot come all this way to North Africa without seeing Marrakesh. . . . I must be with you when you see the sunset on the snows of the Atlas Mountains." Roosevelt agreed, and he and Churchill made the 150-mile trip across the desert by car. In the evening of their arrival at a lavish privately owned American villa, Roosevelt was carried to the villa's tower, where he sat with Churchill and watched the sunset glowing on the snowy caps of Mount Atlas, just as Churchill had described it.

FDR arrived home to more heartening news. The Russians had triumphed at Stalingrad, after an epic battle. Apparently, one prediction of Churchill's seemed to have come true. Back in May, he'd reminded his citizenry that Hitler's apparent dominance in the Soviet Union was deceiving. "He forgot about winter," he had boomed in a radio broadcast. "There is a winter, you know, in Russia. For a good many months the temperature is apt to fall very low. There is snow, there is frost, and all that. Hitler forgot about this Russian winter." In the end, the cold, exhausted, dispirited German forces were defeated.

"Victory, however, made Stalin no more genial," Churchill noted. Newly emboldened by that significant victory, Stalin dug in his heels and demanded to be taken seriously. He'd run his end of the war much as he pleased, supported by aid from the Allies. But he didn't feel they were giving his needs full respect. The second front in Europe was a promise his counterparts had dangled in front of him time and again, only to pull it away with vague excuses. He wanted more, and he wanted it soon.

Indeed, as thrilling as the German defeat at Stalingrad was, it came at a heavy price, with casualties, both military and civilian, measuring in the millions. How much longer could Stalin hold off the Germans? And although the United States and Great Britain had scored significant victories in Italy and the Pacific, it was a critical moment in the war, when complacency and bad choices could turn into defeat. Most important, the Allies had yet to confront the Germans in western Europe, the setting where the war would be won or lost. As the Allied nations looked toward 1943, there was a grave awareness of being at the brink of the war's final, most decisive movement. They couldn't afford to get it wrong.

PART THREE

THREE DAYS
AT THE BRINK

CHAPTER 10

THE ROAD TO TEHRAN

Stalin was furious. Once again, his urgent request for an immediate second front in western Europe had been dismissed out of hand. He thought the Western Allies were cowards, afraid to make the bold choices that would dramatically shift the momentum of the war to their side. They were tiptoeing through the battlefields when they should be storming the Germans.

Stalin kept hammering at Churchill. How could the Western Allies say they weren't ready? First they'd promised a second front in 1942. Then they'd promised a second front in 1943. Now they were putting it off until 1944. His rage about the second front was a constant drumbeat.

After the war, Molotov would acknowledge that the second front clamor was mostly a ploy. The Russians knew as well as anyone that the Allies weren't ready. But by demanding it and being rebuffed, they had an opening to demand other forms of support, as if to say, "Well, if you can't help us in one way, help us in another, with arms, with aircraft." "We didn't believe in a second front, of course, but we had to try for it," Molotov said, seeming proud of the clever deception. "We took them in. 'You can't? But you promised' . . . that was the way." Perhaps Stalin could be forgiven for playing every last card, given the enormity of the German assault on his people.

Stalin enjoyed posturing as the beleaguered hero of the war who received little credit. In a message to his armed forces on February 22, 1943, he declared, "In view of the absence of a second front in Europe, the Red Army alone bears the whole burden of the war."

The remark angered Ambassador Standley, who held an ill-advised press conference, charging the Soviets with falsely downplaying the extensive aid they were receiving through Lend-Lease. Standley had grown increasing disillusioned with the Soviet system and was no longer even trying to hide his feelings. But Stalin mostly ignored him, sending frequent argumentative communications directly to FDR and Churchill.

On March 16, Stalin cabled Roosevelt, "I must give a most emphatic warning, in the interest of our common cause, of the grave danger with which further delay in opening a second front in France is fraught."

Was there an underlying threat? Those were dangerous times. Secret reports, not fully confirmed but alarming, had Stalin putting out feelers to Hitler regarding a separately negotiated peace, which would be made through Japan. If true, it gave a new dimension to Stalin's increasingly harsh warnings to the Allies.

With the Sicily operation delayed until July at the very least, the optics looked bad. As Churchill pointed out in a cable to Hopkins at the end of March, "I think it is an awful thing that in April, May and June, not a single American or British soldier will be killing a single German or Italian soldier while the Russians are chasing 185 divisions around."

Ever since the United States had entered the war, FDR had been asking Stalin for a personal meeting. Though a meeting of the Big Three was discussed, FDR thought it was important for him to first meet Stalin alone. And he didn't want Churchill to know about it yet, although Churchill might have guessed that it was on Roosevelt's mind to do it. He'd previously written to the prime minister, "I know you will not mind my being brutally frank when I tell you that I think I can personally handle Stalin better than either your Foreign Office or my State Department. Stalin hates the guts of all your top people. He thinks he likes me better and I hope he will continue to do so."

That's what FDR believed. "He had great confidence in his own ability to sway people if given an opportunity," Rosenman wrote, and Stalin was no different. In May, FDR enlisted his old friend Joseph Davies, who had served as US ambassador to the Soviet Union between 1936 and 1938, to travel to Moscow and see if such a meeting could be arranged. Davies carried a letter from FDR, telling Stalin "I want to get away from the difficulties of large staff conferences" to meet alone, just the two of them. He wrote that certain sites were off-limits as they would make it more difficult to exclude Churchill. "Therefore I suggest we meet either on your side or our side of the Bering Straits."

Stalin received Davies graciously and even gave a formal dinner at the Kremlin in his honor. Davies came away confident that Stalin had agreed to a meeting, and, indeed a cable from Stalin to Roosevelt confirmed Stalin's desire to convene as soon as possible. A plan was tentatively agreed to for a meeting in Fairbanks, Alaska.

Simultaneously, FDR was preparing for a conference with Churchill in Washington beginning May 12, code-named Trident, to discuss the Italian operation and future plans for the second front. Churchill journeyed aboard the *Queen Mary* after his doctors persuaded him that the flight would not be good for his health. As he traveled, Churchill filled the hours thinking about the terrible responsibility before him. He worried about how they could help Stalin see the bigger picture, reflecting that he and FDR could not be like Stalin, fully obsessed with one operation in a single territory. They had to consider the full map and make their decisions based on long-term strategies. But inevitably, when the two leaders met in Washington, discussion immediately turned to the second front. Roosevelt urged Churchill to consider moving up the date and wondered if the Italian operation would be the best use of their resources. Churchill repeated his by now familiar assertion that the cross-Channel operation could not occur before 1944—and Italy would be a cornerstone of the success of that mission.

At times they seemed to be reaching an impasse, but ultimately Churchill prevailed—this time. By the end of the meetings, they had reached a decision to launch a cross-Channel assault, code-named Operation Overlord, in May 1944. They also agreed that Eisenhower should proceed with the operation in Italy.

Later they would decide that Overlord should be a US-led operation, almost certainly commanded by General Marshall. Their discussion leaked out, and the press had a field day. In particular, an editorial in the *Army and Navy Register* presented the biting opinion in "some military circles" that command in Europe would represent a demotion for Marshall. To stir the pot even more, there were rumors that Hopkins wanted to get rid of Marshall as army chief and install a general he liked better.

In what today would be considered laughably naive, Hopkins wrote passionately about the horror of leaks: "I do not know who it was and it makes little difference on the final record but there was then and probably always will be the possibility of terrible dangers in the deliberate and irresponsible use of the malicious 'leak' as a political weapon."

As the rumors showed no signs of dying down, a Nazi broadcast in Paris even announced, "General George C. Marshall, the U.S. Chief of Staff, has been dismissed. President Roosevelt has taken over his command."

Marshall sent a sardonic note to Hopkins: "Dear Harry, are you responsible for pulling a fast one on me?"

When Hopkins showed the note to FDR, the president scribbled on it, "Dear George—only true in part—I am now Chief of Staff *but* you are President. F.D.R."

After the Washington conference, Churchill joined FDR for a trip to Shangri-La. Churchill enjoyed seeing slices of American life. When they drove through the town of Thurmont at the foot of Catoctin Mountain, he was impressed by the warm welcome of the townspeople who gathered on the road at the sight of the president's car. Hearing that there was a jukebox inside Cozy Restaurant, a popular local eatery, Churchill demanded that they stop so he could go inside and look. He'd never seen one before. The owners were stunned when the prime minister walked in, bought a beer, and produced coins to play the jukebox—while the president waited in the car.

Their time at Shangri-La was a rare chance to relax, and it did much to buoy Churchill's flagging spirits. He was a man who longed for intimacy, especially with the person he thought of as a brother in arms, and he cherished every opportunity to be with Roosevelt in private settings like this one. The two men spent an afternoon at a nearby stream, sitting in canvas chairs, fishing and talking about life and war. Apparently, few fish were caught that day, but Roosevelt's assistant naval aide, William Rigdon, noted, "The cigars created enough of a screen to protect both of them from mosquitoes."

When Stalin learned of the conference between Roosevelt and Churchill, he felt deceived. He bristled to learn that they were making plans behind his back, seemingly ignoring his sense of urgency. The worst part was the decision to further delay the second front. Once again, Stalin cited the Soviet Union's outsized sacrifice:

> One must not forget, that it is a question of preservation of millions of lives in occupied regions of Western Europe and Russia, and reduction of the tremendous sacrifices of the Soviet armies in comparison with which the sacrifices of the Anglo-American forces constitute a small quantity.

They were no closer to a date for the FDR-Stalin meeting. During Churchill's visit, FDR had neglected to mention the discussions he'd been having with Stalin. Instead, he took the coward's way out and had Harriman tell him when Churchill returned to London. It's impossible to overstate what a blow the idea was to Churchill. Was FDR replacing him with Stalin as his closest partner? He contacted FDR to register his complaint about his having a meeting with Stalin alone, and FDR lied to him and said it was all Stalin's idea.

But weeks went by without any further communication from Stalin. Davies reached out to Andrei Gromyko, the young Soviet Embassy attaché, and Gromyko said he didn't know how to reach Stalin. The meeting was still up in the air.

On June 13, Churchill sent Roosevelt a copy of a telegram he planned to send Stalin, whom he referred to as "Joe." It read, in part:

> I have received a copy of your telegram of about June 11 to the President. I quite understand your disappointment but I am sure we are doing not only the right thing but

the only thing that is physically possible in the circumstances. It would be no help to Russia if we throw away a hundred thousand men in a disastrous cross-channel attack. . . . You will remember that I have always made it clear in my telegrams to you that I would never authorize any cross-channel attack which I believed would lead only to useless massacre.

He went on to argue that the best way to help the Soviet Union would be to "knock Italy out of the war." Stalin, who had sacrificed millions of his countrymen to the war effort, found Churchill's caution galling.

Churchill would have argued that he was motivated by the best strategy. He believed that weakening Hitler's position in southern Europe, forcing him to fight for territory that had once been his, would make it harder for him to defend western Europe when the time came.

Although Stalin still insisted on a second front in western Europe, the Italian campaign, agreed upon at Casablanca, would be the next battleground for the United States and Great Britain. Sicily was strategically positioned across from North Africa and along the vital shipping lanes of the Mediterranean. And once Sicily was taken, US and British forces could move north into Italy. Operation Husky, planned for July 1943, involved some careful calculations by Eisenhower. He did not want to pull forces from Tunisia, yet an assault on the heavily defended enemy garrison in Sicily would require at least five or six divisions. Their commanders would have to be the most seasoned—for the Americans, General George Patton, and for the British, General Bernard Law Montgomery. Both had excelled fighting in North Africa.

Considering how he might buy some additional insurance,

Eisenhower decided to try a misinformation campaign. Calling together reporters, he described the plan of attack in detail, giving them the wrong disembarkation point of the attack. They were, of course, thrilled to be let in on the campaign and vowed silence. But not surprisingly, the details leaked out, and the Germans received a heads-up on the Sicily campaign, preparing for an assault on the opposite side of the island. Even with that diversion, US and British forces encountered heavy resistance when they arrived in combined air and sea landings before dawn on July 10. But within hours, some 150,000 Allied troops had gained a foothold on the island. Hitler's army, weakened by heavy losses in North Africa, was unable to hold off the Allies. Within thirty-eight days, Sicily was in the hands of the Allies. Patton's army, flanked by Montgomery and the British, kept surging forward across Italy, capturing Messina and moving deeper into the country.

Patton, whom Eisenhower had known since his early days in the army, was talented and fearless, but he was also arrogant and careless and often got himself into trouble with the brass. An incident in Sicily would follow him for the remainder of his career and stain his legacy. Visiting wounded troops in a hospital, he berated those suffering from battle fatigue for being cowards and even slapped one across the face. When Eisenhower heard about it, he was disgusted. He ordered Patton to apologize, which he did, but when the news got out, many people demanded his removal from the front. Eisenhower refused. He could not afford to lose Patton.

The Allied successes in Italy created a domino effect that threw the country into turmoil. Mussolini's regime was toppled, and he was jailed—though he was later rescued by Hitler's army. On September 3, Eisenhower would sign an armistice agreement between the new Italian government and the Allies.

Although fighting in Italy would continue for the rest of the war as Hitler's army counterattacked, the Axis would no longer have Italy officially on its side. It was a huge victory, which seemed to confirm Churchill's "soft underbelly" strategy.

Feeling the need for another conference to discuss the progress in Italy, FDR and Churchill accepted the invitation of Canadian prime minister Mackenzie King to hold a meeting in Quebec in August. Stalin once again declined. Clearly, King expected to join the conference, but FDR vetoed the idea. Although many Canadians were bravely fighting in the war, Canada was not an Allied power. That left King to play a largely ceremonial, irrelevant role. The theme of the Quebec discussions echoed those of the Washington conference. Had he been there, Stalin most surely would have sniped that the Westerners were all talk and little action.

In the Soviet Union, Stalin was busy trying to improve his position on the global stage and head off any fresh concerns by the Allies. He had begun to institute small changes that on careful examination would prove to be mere window dressing. He loosened restrictions on artists and writers and allowed poems to be broadcast on the radio—as long as they were "patriotic." He reversed the policy opposing religion. According to *The Allies: Roosevelt, Churchill, Stalin, and the Unlikely Alliance That Won World War II*, by Winston Groom, "By 1943 most everyone was feeling somewhat kindly toward Uncle Joe, whose heroic people, under his strong leadership, were defeating the Nazi scourge." But the underlying repression continued.

Ambassador Standley, for one, saw through Stalin's actions. Standley was feeling increasingly shut out of diplomatic efforts. He'd lost all hope of having a role of any consequence, and he'd grown increasingly despondent over what he saw as Soviet manipulation. In early May, he'd sent a letter of resignation to the president. Months went by, and there was no answer. Finally, in early September, he sent another resignation letter and received a cryptic reply from the State Department: "The Ambassador will be directed, early in October, to return home for consultation. He may plan in accordance with the expectation that he will not be required to return to the Soviet Union." In Washington, FDR had made his decision: Averell Harriman would take Standley's place as ambassador to the Soviet Union.

Standley returned home with a grim view of the Soviets, and he didn't think Harriman or the president was open to listening. Standley believed that Stalin was engaged in a competition, not a collaboration, while Roosevelt was convinced that Stalin "was gettable." As Standley later wrote of his growing discomfort with the association:

> We Westerners believed that the Soviets were in the War for the same reasons that we were—to defeat Hitler's conspiracy and to prevent the Nazis from dominating Europe and the world. Then we would all go home and have twenty to fifty years of peace. I am *now* convinced that the Soviet leadership regarded World War II as another "cataclysmic capitalist war" brought on by the inequities of the capitalist system, and planned to use it as another stepping stone toward their ultimate goal of world Communist revolution and the imposition of the "benefits" of Communism on all peoples everywhere.

Over dinner with Harriman in the ambassador's room at the Mayflower Hotel in Washington, Standley tried to give him a picture of the situation as he judged it. "I don't envy you, Averell," he said sympathetically when he'd finished. "It's a tough assignment."

Infected by his boss's overconfidence, Harriman brushed him off. "I know it will be difficult, but they're only human, those Russians. Stalin can be handled."

By the end of summer, it was clear that a personal meeting between Roosevelt and Stalin was not going to happen. On August 8, Stalin sent a handwritten letter to FDR that he would unfortunately need to break his promise to Davies—unless Roosevelt was willing to travel to him, perhaps to Astrakhan, in southern Russia, or Archangel, a port city in northern Russia. In his letter, he added, "I do not have any objections to the presence of Mr. Churchill at this meeting, hoping you will not have any objections to this." And just like that, the idea of a tripartite conference that would ultimately lead to Tehran was planted.

FDR immediately began an effort to set it up, now including Churchill in his messages to Stalin. Thus began a long exchange of correspondence on the matter of location. FDR suggested North Africa. Stalin replied no, it was too far. Stalin countered with Tehran. Roosevelt responded that Tehran was too remote—more than six thousand miles from Washington. He, too, had obligations. As he explained to Stalin, "new laws and resolutions must be acted on by me after their receipt and must be returned to Congress physically before ten days have elapsed. . . . The possibility of delay in getting over the mountain . . . is insurmountable."

Stalin responded, "Unfortunately, not one of the places proposed instead of Tehran by you for the meeting is suitable for me."

Roosevelt again insisted that Tehran was impossible, adding "It would be regarded as a tragedy by future generations if you and I and Mr. Churchill failed today because of a few hundred miles. . . . Please do not fail me in this crisis."

That message was personally delivered by Cordell Hull, who was in Moscow for a conference of foreign ministers. Harriman was in Moscow as well, now as ambassador. The Russians weren't yet sure about Harriman.

"We have found you a very tough man to deal with," Molotov told him.

"I have come as a friend," Harriman said.

"Oh, I know that," Molotov replied. "I intended my remarks to be complimentary."

When Hull and Harriman finally gained an audience with Stalin to press for a Big Three meeting time and date, Stalin suggested that maybe it should be put off until the spring—unless, of course, Roosevelt and Churchill agreed to go to Tehran. After the meeting, Harriman told FDR that it was so important that the meeting not be delayed that perhaps they should agree to Tehran. On November 8, Roosevelt sent a message to Stalin:

> You will be glad to know that I have worked out a method so that if I get word that a bill requiring my veto has been passed by Congress and forwarded to me, I will fly to Tunis to meet it and then return to the Conference. Therefore, I have decided to go to Tehran and this makes me especially happy. . . . The whole world is watching for this meeting of the three of us.

The conference, code-named Eureka, was on for Tehran, beginning November 28, 1943. But if a score had been posted on the board in that game of wits, it would have read "Stalin—1; FDR—0."

THE USS *IOWA*, "THAT great battlewagon," was one of the largest battleships in the American fleet—about nine and a half acres in size. In commission for less than a year, it was equipped with the most modern accommodations and impressive armaments. On November 11, FDR was rolled on board for a journey across the sea whose ultimate destination would be the most important conference of the war, a meeting of the Big Three in Tehran. Eleanor had asked to go, but her husband had been unwilling to take her. His excuse had been that there would be no other women present. More likely he didn't want the distraction of his wife's strident causes, or the prospect of her wandering the streets of Tehran, making headlines and giving the Secret Service heartburn.

The cares of recent months fell away with the pure pleasure of being at sea again, his massive ship accompanied by an escort of three mighty destroyers. But that show of might did not prevent a near catastrophe.

On the second day at sea, FDR was on the deck of the *Iowa* to observe an antiaircraft drill being conducted on one of the destroyers, the *William D. Porter*, or "Willie Dee," located only 6,000 yards away. He was enjoying the show when everyone started shouting. A torpedo had accidentally been released from the *Willie Dee*, heading directly for the president's ship. Panic stricken, the commander of the *Willie Dee* broke the enforced radio silence to contact the *Iowa* and report that a torpedo was coming: "Torpedo defense! This is not a drill!" The *Iowa* quickly changed course and raced in the opposite direction, avoiding a hit. Instead of taking cover, FDR ordered his valet, "Take me over to the starboard rail. I want to watch the torpedo." Had the torpedo struck, the president and most of the United States' top military leadership might have been doomed, the worst case of "friendly fire" imaginable. It exploded a thousand yards away.

A large-scale investigation would follow, but FDR gave the event a mere mention in his diary: "On Monday last at gun drill. Our escorting destroyer fired a torpedo at us by mistake. We saw it—missed it by less than 1,000 feet."

Hopkins was somewhat more riled, writing, "Can you imagine our own escort torpedoing an American battleship—the newest and biggest—with the President of the United States aboard—along with the Chief of Staff of the Army and the Chief of Naval Operations? In view of the fact that there were twenty Army officers aboard, I doubt if the Navy will ever hear the last of it."

Without further incident, the *Iowa* continued its nine-day journey, the president often out on the flag bridge deck, reading and enjoying the air. In the evenings, Roosevelt would host his regular cocktail hour, mixing martinis. That was a point of privilege, since strictly speaking liquor was not allowed aboard naval ships. "Who could stop him?" naval aide Rigdon asked. "Or, for that matter, who would want to?"

Toward the end of their journey, they passed through the Strait of Gibraltar, the site of the great Torch launch, and arrived at Oran, Algeria, on November 20, where the weather was clear and mild. The crew joked that it was special "Roosevelt weather," since the previous days had been intemperate.

They were met by a distinguished welcoming party, which included Eisenhower and two of FDR's sons, Elliott and Franklin, Jr., as well as Hopkins's son Robert. When he was informed that his father had requested him as an aide for the duration of his trip, Franklin was angry. He didn't want to be with his father at meetings; he wanted to be on his ship, the *Mayrant*, which was a destroyer escort docked in Gibraltar. Initially, FDR dismissed his son's request, but Franklin kept arguing, and finally his father gave in, saying "You're a pretty stubborn fellow—but if that's how you feel I guess you should go back to your ship."

The presidential party took off almost immediately in a

C-54 transport plane for Tunis. That night, FDR would stay in a lovely villa that only months before had been Rommel's and was now Eisenhower's home base when he was in Tunis. The president told Eisenhower he wanted to visit the battlefields the next day, despite misgivings by the Secret Service. They drove out and stopped for a picnic lunch by the road. "Ike," the president mused, "if, one year ago, you had offered to bet that on this day the President of the United States would be having lunch on a Tunisian roadside, what odds could you have demanded?" FDR seemed pleased by the idea, and he was having such a good time over lunch that he lingered there, ignoring the Secret Service's growing discomfort. Finally, a Secret Service man put it to him quite strongly that they should be on their way. FDR sighed and agreed, saying to Eisenhower, "You are lucky you don't have the number of bosses I have."

Later, in a private conversation, FDR idly speculated to Eisenhower about the future command of Overlord. He wondered if it would be the right decision to move Marshall to field command, asking if "it is dangerous to monkey with a winning team." Eisenhower, of course, had no answer to that, but he assured the president he'd do his best whatever his job. In his heart, though, he dreaded the prospect of returning to Washington.

On November 22, the president made the 1,800-mile flight to Cairo, where he would have a pre-Tehran meeting with Churchill. He stayed at the residence of Alexander Kirk, the US ambassador to Egypt, a beautiful setting with gardens overflowing with flowers in sight of the pyramids.

Agent Mike Reilly, who was supervising the Secret Service operation, was nervous about security in Cairo. "Cairo was filled with Axis spies and the price of a life was even cheaper than at Casablanca," he wrote. "A sixty-dollar fine was the general punishment meted out by the courts for killing a native . . . For ten dollars one could hire a professional agitator who would provide one thousand natives to create a frenzied demonstration for or against anything or anybody."

This was the setting that greeted Roosevelt and Churchill. To date, the Soviet Union had not declared war on Japan, and for that reason Stalin chose to have no representatives at the Cairo meeting, where Roosevelt and Churchill would sit down with Generalissimo Chiang Kai-shek, the leader of the Kuomintang, or Chinese Nationalist Party, to discuss the progress of the war with Japan. The Chinese leader's wife, Madame Chiang, who spoke perfect English, having been educated in the United States, was along as his interpreter.

Madame Chiang was very popular in the United States. Beautiful, passionate, and well spoken, she had a way of making the harsh realities about Chinese repression disappear behind the smoke screen of the noble endeavor to defeat the common foe in Japan. In February 1943, she had made a US tour, delighting the crowds with a "Free China" rally in Madison Square Garden and staying at the White House. FDR had been a bit dazzled, but Eleanor saw beyond her charm. Noting the reactions of the men who met her she observed, "They found her charming, intelligent, and fascinating, but they were all a little afraid of her, because she could be a coolheaded statesman when she was fighting for something she deemed necessary to China and to her husband's regime; the little velvet hand and the low, gentle voice disguised a determination that she could be as hard as steel."

However, their conversations, in the garden of the president's villa, had a feel of being perfunctory. Churchill called their story "lengthy, complicated and minor." The central issue, he said, must be defeating Hitler in Europe. Roosevelt, prone to agreeing despite the consequences and not always perfect on the follow-through, promised an operation in Burma. Once again Churchill was placed in the uncomfortable position of being the naysayer, emphasizing that the focus needed to be on Europe. But Roosevelt was constructing a concept of the postwar world in his mind, in which China would be one of four great powers. The others would be the United States, Great Britain, and the Soviet Union. It remained to be seen whether China would one day play such an equal role.

Roosevelt had planned for an elaborate traditional Thanksgiving dinner with all the trimmings: two large stuffed turkeys, which had been frozen and flown in from the United States, along with many side dishes. Toasting the prime minister, FDR spoke movingly of the Thanksgiving tradition, when close families are united; he spoke about the history and meaning of Thanksgiving, concluding, "And of course this leads me to the thought that I, personally, am delighted to be sharing this Thanksgiving dinner with Great Britain's Prime Minister—"

Churchill swiftly rose to his feet to deliver his own toast, but the president stopped him. He had more to say. "Large families are usually more closely united than small ones," he went on, "and so this year, with the people in the United Kingdom in our family, we are a large family, and more united than ever before. I propose a toast to this unity, and may it long continue!"

The entertainment was a GI orchestra from Camp Huckstep in Cairo, and people began shouting out requests. Churchill, dressed in a blue one-piece zippered suit, asked for "Ol' Man River" and "Carry Me Back to Old Virginny," while the president requested "The White Cliffs of Dover."

Brandy and liqueurs flowed after the meal, and, feeling no pain, Churchill rose and asked Pa Watson to dance. As they waltzed, FDR cheered and laughed. "For a couple of hours we cast care aside," Churchill wrote. It was a raucous, almost joyful, display, one last great celebration of Western friendship before they joined Stalin for the most important meeting of the war.

CHAPTER 11

YOUR HOUSE IS MY HOUSE

FDR approached the Big Three conference in Tehran caught between love and need. The intimacy he and Churchill had developed since the United States had entered the war was as strong as any that had ever existed between leaders of great powers. Roosevelt admired Churchill's passion and courage and recognized his moments of genius. He appreciated having a collaborator he could trust, and he never once doubted Churchill's devotion to their common cause. Furthermore, they shared a language, an Anglo point of view, and a commitment to core principles of freedom and common decency. They could argue fiercely but never break up, in the manner of an old married couple that knows its foundations are solid even when the windows rattle.

But as much as he loved Churchill, FDR needed Stalin. He needed him to hold his own against the Germans in Russia. He needed him to join the fight against Japan. Most of all, he needed him as a partner in a postwar world that would ensure a lasting peace. In that respect, necessity outweighed integrity, because clearly Stalin was not a man of similar principles. Left to his own devices, he might well exploit victory against Hitler to pursue his own power. However, Roosevelt thought that if the Allies kept Stalin close, gave him their respect, and brought him along, they could avoid a postwar calamity. So his goal at Tehran was to compartmentalize, to give Stalin as much room as he needed to become a full and willing member of the team.

FDR calculated that at that critical moment what meant most to Stalin was a show of respect and partnership. He believed he could pull it off, confident that Stalin would want that embrace from the president of the United States. There was a chauvinism in the United States' position that tended to give the Soviets an inferiority complex. After the war, Molotov would admit that "the Americans stood at a higher level than we. They had no need to take a great leap forward, but we did. And we were scarcely capable of this." Tehran was important to Stalin, too.

Although Iran was technically a favorable setting, since it had an alliance with the Allies, there was tumult in the country, given its recent history. When World War II had broken out, Reza Shah Pahlavi had declared his nation neutral, and he had continued that neutrality after Germany had invaded the Soviet Union. In calculating the odds, the shah thought they were with Germany, and he had expected the Soviet Union and Great Britain to be defeated. But as the war went on, the Allies began to exert more pressure, demanding that the shah expel all Germans from the country. He refused.

Iran was considered a strategic jewel, given its oil fields and the importance of the Persian corridor for supply lines. On August 25, 1941, in a joint Soviet-British operation, the British-led Indian army invaded Iran. Within a month, the Allies had taken control of the country—the Soviets in the north and the British in the south. Reza Shah abdicated, leaving control to his playboy son Prince Mohammad Reza. In January 1942, Iran signed a tripartite treaty with the Soviet Union and Great Britain and declared war on Germany. Now the country was playing host to the Big Three conference.

It was quite a challenge to keep such a big conference a secret, but the participants tried. Churchill's chief military adviser,
Alan Brooke, wrote of one cover story he heard explaining why
so many high-level people were in the city. The conference apparently coincided with a local election, and word got out that
the "Very Important Personages" were there to make sure of a
fair election.

However, there were still known to be German sympa-
thizers in the city, and that was a concern for the conference.
The original plan was for Roosevelt to stay at the US Legation,
which was a mile away from the Soviet and British compounds.
Since the meetings would be held there, Churchill and Stalin
would have to drive through Tehran's treacherous streets on
multiple occasions.

In Tehran to supervise Secret Service operations after his
duty in Cairo, Agent Reilly was aware even before FDR's arrival of reports that Nazi paratroopers had dropped into the
area and posed a direct danger to the conference. The NKVD,
Stalin's secret police, told Reilly that they numbered thirty-eight
and some had been captured.

"Are you sure it was thirty-eight?" Reilly asked.

"Very sure. We examined the men we caught most thoroughly" was the ominous reply.

Later, some intelligence would confirm the plot, code-named
Operation Long Jump. The plan was for German paratroopers
to drop into Iran, don Red Army uniforms, and pose as part of
Stalin's security team.

The evening of FDR's arrival, Molotov contacted Harriman
about the plot and urged the Americans to accept Stalin's invitation to relocate to the Soviet compound. Stalin, who had
endured a train journey and then a bumpy flight—his first flight
ever—to reach the conference before Roosevelt, was eager to

accommodate the president. FDR would be given the largest house in the compound, with Stalin taking a smaller one. Harriman was immediately suspicious about whether there had actually been a plot or whether it was a ploy to bring FDR under Stalin's roof. But he thought the danger was quite real.

In his daily diary, Roosevelt described the plot and his decision to move: "Yesterday morning the Russians discovered a plot to get him [Stalin] & W.S.C. [Churchill] & me as we drove to each other's legations so at Stalin's plea I moved down to the Russian compound where there is an extra house—and the danger of driving thro' the streets is eliminated as W.S.C. lives next door & there is a flock of guards."

Unquestionably, there were additional reasons for Stalin to want the president under his roof. The historian Keith Eubank pointed out that "Stalin was still suspicious of his capitalist allies. If the most powerful ally lived within the Soviet compound and the other stayed across a narrow street, then close check could be kept on their movements and discussions. Probably Soviet security technicians had installed listening devices in the building before Roosevelt moved in so that his private comments could be heard."

The ruse didn't fool the Americans one bit. As Reilly observed, "Everywhere you went you would see a brute of a man in a lackey's white coat busily polishing immaculate glass or dusting dustless furniture. As their arms swung to dust or polish, the clear, cold outline of a Luger automatic could be seen on every hip."

FDR didn't really mind the move and thought he could use it to his advantage in his goal of getting closer to Stalin. Had he instead stayed at Churchill's compound, it would have cemented the impression that the two were in cahoots against Stalin.

So the day after his arrival, plans were made to transfer the president, with all due care, to the Soviet compound. As the president was driven in an innocuous car along side streets, a full motorcade, with a Secret Service agent posing as the president, traveled along the crowded streets as throngs cheered.

"The Boss, as always, was vastly amused by the dummy cavalcade trick and the other cops-and-robbers stuff," Reilly said. "I was glad it amused him, because it did not amuse me much."

Almost as soon as Roosevelt was settled, Stalin arrived at his door, accompanied by an interpreter. "We could tell when Stalin was coming by observing the husky Russian guards who lined the passageway from the building he occupied to our quarters," William Rigdon observed.

Although Stalin usually dressed simply and informally, favoring a worn soldier's jacket, that day he was dressed in honor of the occasion in a sharply pressed formal military uniform, with red epaulettes on his jacket and red stripes on his pants. He greeted Roosevelt with a wide smile. Reilly observed that he had "a most engaging grin on his face" as he reached down and shook the president's hand. Rigdon noticed that in Roosevelt's presence, Stalin's pockmarked face "became actually kindly in expression, and often there was a twinkle in his eye." It was a side of Stalin the world seldom saw.

FDR grinned back. "Hello, Marshal Stalin. I am glad to see you. I have tried for a long time to bring this about."

Stalin sat down and offered Roosevelt a Russian cigarette—what Elliott described as "two or three puffs of strong, black tobacco at the end of a two-inch cardboard holder"—but Roosevelt declined, preferring his American brand. (Stalin was well known for smoking a pipe, but he often switched to cigarettes while on the road.)

Roosevelt observed Stalin with interest—and caution. It is

sometimes the case that great leaders have winning personalities and charisma, the better to persuade others. The charm can bowl people over and effectively mask the malevolence inside, causing a reaction of *He's not so bad after all*. Americans were particularly vulnerable to people who seemed forthright and openhearted. It was FDR's job to see behind the facade so he could make a judgment about Stalin's true intentions and trustworthiness.

Stalin asked Roosevelt whether he had any ideas for the topics they should discuss. Roosevelt suggested that they start with more general conversations and let the themes develop. That was his plan—to open things up and see where they went, although the British and US advisers had told him they preferred a more scripted approach. In his diary, Alan Brooke wrote of his worries about that freewheeling approach, lamenting, "It was evident that we were headed for chaos." Stalin, however, was in agreement with FDR's method. The two leaders proceeded to touch on a number of topics in their forty-minute conversation—the difficulty of supplying distant fronts, Roosevelt's meeting with Chiang Kai-shek (Stalin observed that the Chinese were poor fighters led by poor leaders), and the French. Stalin was incensed with the French government, which had caved in so completely to Hitler, and wanted to see it punished after the war. For starters, he believed that no Frenchman over forty years old and no Frenchman who had served in the Vichy government should be allowed to be in the government after the war. Roosevelt warned him that that was a sticking point with Churchill, who thought France should be allowed to once again become a great nation after the war. Stalin had harsh words for the French, and they extended to the matter of Indochina. He said he wasn't willing to spill the blood of allies so France could regain colonial rule of Indochina.

The topic of colonialism had been a sore point between Roosevelt and Churchill. Now Roosevelt seemed to throw Great Britain under the bus in his criticism of colonialism in India. He even said he thought the Soviets would do a better job of governing there, a peculiar statement considering the Soviets' thirst for control of nations beyond their borders. He also warned Stalin that India was a particularly touchy subject for Churchill and they should avoid discussing it at this conference.

In that way, Roosevelt was trying to send strong signals to Stalin about how they could get along and avoid conflict with Churchill. He was already playing the role of director, treating their conversation as something of a dress rehearsal. He was also saying, in effect, that he knew Churchill well, understood his trigger points, and could help steer the conference away from them. He was taking Stalin into his confidence, pressing them to be friendly collaborators in dealing with an unruly sibling.

"What'd you talk about?" Elliott asked his father when he arrived at the compound the following day. "Or was it state secrets?"

"Not a bit of it," Roosevelt said, not wanting to reveal the true substance of their conversation. "Mostly it was 'How did I like my quarters?' and 'Thank you very much for turning over the main house to me' and 'What is the news from the eastern front?'"

"Measuring each other, eh?"

Roosevelt didn't like that characterization. "I wouldn't say that . . . we were getting to know each other. We were finding out what kind of people we were."

"What kind of people is he?"

"Oh," the president replied, "he's got a kind of massive rumble, talks deliberately, seems very confident, very sure of himself, moves slowly—altogether quite impressive, I'd say."

At 4:30 P.M., the first plenary session came to order in a large meeting room with heavy tapestries on the walls. FDR was wheeled to the "head" of the large, round oak table built for the conference, with the flags of the three nations arranged in a centerpiece. The table was set for twelve delegates, four for each of the principals—though Stalin brought only two advisers, Molotov and Kliment Voroshilov, Stalin's longtime military and political adviser. According to Hugh Lunghi, Churchill's military aide and interpreter, who accompanied him to key conferences and was present in Tehran, Voroshilov was "once Stalin's companion in arms, baby-faced, murderous and cruel. Voroshilov had been in command of several army fronts when Hitler had invaded Russia. He had proved to be so hopeless that he had had to be sacked. Survivors of Stalin's inner circle tell us that often he shouted at him, 'Shut up, you imbecile!'" In Tehran, Stalin would often glower at Voroshilov, as if wondering why he'd brought him along.

Churchill brought Foreign Secretary Anthony Eden, Deputy Secretary to the British War Cabinet Hastings Ismay, and his interpreter, Major Arthur H. Birse. On the American side were Hopkins, Harriman, and Charles Bohlen, a US diplomat who served as interpreter. Notably absent at the table were General Marshall and air force commander Henry "Hap" Arnold. According to Marshall, FDR had told them that there would be no meetings that day, and they had gone sightseeing in Tehran. If true, it seems like a curious oversight. Perhaps it was deliberate. (In the official log of the trip, it was noted parenthetically that the first official meeting of the conference was held on very short notice, perhaps to explain what Roosevelt told Marshall. But that seems odd, too.)

The Big Three were men with starkly different styles and roles. As Sherwood put it, "Churchill employed all the debater's arts, the brilliant locutions, of which he was a master, and Stalin wielded his bludgeon with relentless indifference to all the dodges and feints of his practiced adversary; while Roosevelt sat in the middle, by common consent the moderator, arbitrator and final authority . . . it was he who spoke the last word."

Bohlen, whose close note taking was responsible for a more thorough record of the conference, was surprised to find how loosely organized the conference was. No one had even been assigned to take minutes, so he appointed himself chief note taker, then read his notes to an army stenographer. "It was my first experience with Roosevelt's informal method of operation," he wrote. "He did not like any rules or regulations to bind him. He preferred to act by improvisation rather than by plan."

Before the meetings, Bohlen had advised FDR to try to keep his comments brief and use short sentences to make it easier for the Russian interpreters to follow him. Roosevelt complied, making Bohlen's job easier. Churchill, on the other hand, "was much too carried away by his own eloquence to pay much attention to his pleasant and excellent interpreter," Major Birse. During the formal meetings, Churchill would occasionally lean over and ask Birse, "What's he saying?" as if afraid Stalin's words were being misrepresented. Birse would respectfully reply in a low voice.

FDR beamed at the men seated around him, called for the meeting to start, and welcomed the Russians as "new members of the family circle." He added expansively that he hoped that everyone would speak freely and expressed his high hope for the meeting. Birse thought he looked like "a rich uncle paying a visit to his poorer relations." Churchill, with typical hyperbole, added that their meeting was the greatest concentration of power the world had ever seen. Stalin added his greetings and spoke of the great opportunities ahead.

Roosevelt began with a brief account of the US perspective on the war, speaking of the Pacific theater. Acknowledging that the Pacific issues were of greater impact to the United States than to the others, he felt it important that all of them know the stakes, especially since one million men and most of the United States' naval power were in the Pacific. He described the strategy as a war of attrition—sinking more Japanese ships than could be replaced. One priority was to keep China in the war—"by opening the road to China and through increased use of transport planes to put ourselves in position to bomb Japan proper." He did not say at that point that he was seeking further Allied help, especially from Stalin. But that would come. Perhaps the unspoken message was that the United States was bearing a great burden against an Axis Power, virtually alone, even as its allies were making tremendous demands.

FDR then turned to the topic that was foremost on everyone's minds: Europe and Operation Overlord. The plan for a cross-Channel invasion of western Europe had been on everyone's minds for more than a year, but it had always been discussed as something they would do in the future when they were completely ready. Now the time had come to decide, ready or not.

Stalin spoke up, saying that in the opinion of Soviet military leaders, the best way to attack Hitler was to strike a blow in northern or northwestern France, where German forces were the weakest.

Churchill, who had a bad cold, launched into a refutation with a gravelly voice. He had expected Stalin to make this point, but now that it was his turn to speak, he wanted to lay out a fuller picture as he understood it. Churchill always assumed that he could persuade others, and he thought so now, even in such jaded company that had been subjected to the same treatise before. In his long-winded remarks, he kept expanding the map and questioning the timeline, suggesting other priorities that might delay Overlord. He spoke of finishing Italy first, then southern France, and added the Mediterranean, including Turkey along the way.

Stalin sat doodling drawings of wolves in red pencil while the prime minister spoke. When Churchill was finished, he scoffed at Churchill's concerns. Scattering the British and US forces was not a worthwhile plan, he said. They must focus on Overlord, and other operations would merely be diversionary. As for Turkey, he doubted that Turkey would get into the war. Roosevelt said he would do what he could to persuade Turkey to enter the war, but he feared that Turkey would exact too high a price for doing so. Stalin remarked that the Soviets did want Turkey in the war, but not taken in by "the scruff of the neck."

He believed, however, that another offensive in southern France could be valuable. Churchill countered that it was important to first take Rome, hopefully early in the year. He indicated that if Rome was not taken, his own political future would be in jeopardy, as he would lose the confidence of the House of Commons.

So, very quickly, Churchill and Stalin had defined their opposing visions—as Roosevelt sat silently and watched the back-and-forth. When FDR finally spoke, it was in support of Stalin. Overlord must be the focus—without further delay—and a companion operation in southern France must be considered.

Churchill left the meeting feeling sick with worry and depressed. He had not expected Roosevelt to take Stalin's side against him after all they had been through together. "Stalin has got the president in his pocket," Brooke observed.

Churchill's sense of isolation was very strong at that moment. He later reflected, "There I sat with the great Russian bear on one side of me, with paws outstretched, and on the other side the great American buffalo, and between the two sat the poor little English donkey, who was the only one who knew the right way home."

Brooke could not escape the fact that Stalin

had a military brain of the very highest caliber. Never once in any of his statements did he make any strategic error, nor did he fail to appreciate all the implications of a situation with a quick and unerring eye.

In this respect he stood out when compared with his two colleagues. Roosevelt never made any great pretense at being a strategist and left Marshall or Leahy to talk for him. Winston, on the other hand, was far more erratic, brilliant at times but far too impulsive and inclined to favor quite unsuitable plans without giving them the preliminary deep thought they required . . .

Chatting after the meeting, FDR's staff said they had been most surprised by Stalin. Leahy admitted that most of them had come to the conference thinking of Stalin as a "bandit leader." Instead, they had found him intelligent and well spoken. Leahy described the way he had maneuvered in the discussions: "The Marshal's approach to our mutual problems was direct, agreeable, and considerate of the viewpoints of his two colleagues—until one of them advanced some point that Stalin thought was detrimental to Soviet interests. Then he could be brutally blunt to the point of rudeness." He was impatient, too, a quality that appeared often during the conference. In one instance, he went to use the toilet, only to find the door locked. Since there was only one toilet available for everyone to use (except for a second in FDR's suite), it was in great demand. He pounded on the door loudly, pulling at the knob and almost yanking it off—until someone quietly told him that Churchill was inside.

Bohlen noticed Stalin's graciousness. When he returned to Washington and mentioned it to Boris Nicolaevsky, an old Russian revolutionary who had fallen out of favor with the government, Nicolaevsky asked him if Stalin had ever smiled. "When I told him, 'Yes, indeed,' he said this was an innovation, that with Russians he never smiled and was rough and abusive in his language." In Tehran, Bohlen noticed, Stalin used phrases such as "I could be wrong, but I think" and "in my opinion" in an effort to appear open minded.

Lunghi had a more skeptical view. "At close range, he looked like a humble, kindly uncle," he observed of Stalin. "But I was struck by the yellow whites to his greenish brown, cat-like eyes, which hardly ever met yours if you were a stranger, a foreigner. His own staff was often brought to order with a fearsome glare. You could see them freeze, almost literally tremble in their boots."

Roosevelt was hosting dinner the first night, a steak-and-baked-potato feast cooked by his Filipino crew in their makeshift kitchen. Before dinner, as he presided over cocktails, there was exuberant ribbing between army and navy men. In the annual Army-Navy Game, which had been held at West Point the previous day, Navy had defeated Army 13–0. Although the games had been canceled twice during World War I, the World War II military commanders encouraged the competition, thinking it was good preparation for combat—not to mention a huge morale booster for the troops and the nation. In the official log of the conference, it was noted that Pa Watson "spent the day today paying up many of his 'unfortunate' football bets."

Roosevelt was elated. When Elliott showed up on Monday,

he greeted his son with a hand out. "That'll be ten dollars, please," he said.

Elliott winced. "I wish you'd keep your mind on affairs of state."

During dinner, after the obligatory toasts, the contentious topics carried on as before. Stalin seemed determined to provoke Churchill, first repeating what he had told FDR earlier about France after the war. He also expressed his conviction that Germany, too, must be so hobbled in defeat that it could not recover any semblance of its prior strength.

At the same time, he raised a question about the policy of unconditional surrender. He thought the policy needed more clarity. What would the terms be? How would they avoid further uniting the Germans? Might not a demand for unconditional surrender force the Germans to dig in even more? Those were legitimate points that others had made, but the question would not be brought up again or resolved in Tehran.

Just as they began a potentially heated discussion on the fate of Poland, Roosevelt turned green and bent over in pain. He was quickly wheeled out of the room, and Dr. McIntyre was summoned. Stalin was stunned. Was this the poisoning he'd worried about, happening in his own compound? Someone else at the table speculated about whether Roosevelt had suffered a heart attack. Would the conference be canceled almost before it had begun? To everyone's relief, word came from Dr. McIntyre that the president was suffering from indigestion.

As the dinner broke up, Churchill took Stalin aside to a sofa in the corner of the room. He wanted to talk about life after the war.

"Let us first consider the worst that might happen," Stalin said soberly. He proposed a scenario where Germany lost the war but was not destroyed; it might reorganize itself and launch a new war. His point was legitimized by Germany's actions after World War I, when the fever of nationalism that had elevated Hitler to power had led to visions of world domination. Stalin thought the same thing could happen within fifteen to twenty years of Germany's defeat in the present war.

"Nothing is final," Churchill said. "The world rolls on. We have now learnt something. Our duty is to make the world safe for at least fifty years by German disarmament, by preventing rearmament, by supervision of German factories, by forbidding all aviation, and by territorial changes of a far-reaching character. It all comes back to the question whether Great Britain, the United States, and the U.S.S.R. can keep a close friendship and supervise Germany in their mutual interest."

"There were controls after the last war," Stalin reminded him, "but it failed."

"We were inexperienced then," Churchill argued. "It will be different this time."

Accustomed to totalitarian practices, Stalin thought the victors should step heavily on Germany and prevent its ability to achieve commercial success and military growth. On that point, Churchill was in full agreement, though it was less certain how it might be achieved. Stalin reminded him that the controls exerted on Germany after the First World War had been inadequate. But clearly Churchill imagined the Big Three allies taking the reins, working together as a cohesive force to prevent Germany from becoming a power center. Whether Stalin imagined a similar scenario is unclear. History shows that the Soviet Union took a very different path after the war.

Always one to say what was on his mind even when the topic was tricky, Churchill then dared to bring up the question of Poland. He pointed out that the invasion of Poland had been the trigger for Great Britain's entry into the war, and he wanted

to see the country thrive afterward as a strong and independent nation. The undercurrent of the issue was a fear that Stalin
would use victory in the war to carve into that independence,
establishing new borders out of concern for his own country's
security. Stalin sidestepped the question. It was late, and Poland
would not be resolved at that time.

As the two men ended their conversation and headed out of
the room, Reilly overheard a telling snippet. He caught Churchill's words, "But you won't let me get up to your front and
I want to get there." Stalin replied with a grin, "Maybe it can
be arranged sometime, Mr. Prime Minister. Perhaps when you
have a front that I can visit, too."

CHAPTER 12

CLASH OF TITANS

On Monday morning, Churchill woke desperate to speak privately with FDR. After the disastrous meeting the previous day, he wanted to be sure they were on the same side. He sent a message requesting that they have lunch together. He was rebuffed.

Roosevelt sent Harriman to explain to the prime minister why he did not want a private meeting that would make Stalin feel slighted. But knowing that Roosevelt had already had such a meeting with Stalin, it was Churchill who felt slighted. Harriman also expressed a concern over bugging. FDR didn't want the Russians to pick up a private conversation between him and the prime minister. (Sergo Beria, the son of Lavrentiy Beria, one of Stalin's chief enforcers, attended the conference and later confirmed that his job had been to translate the bugged conversations between Roosevelt and Churchill as well as the president's meetings with his advisers. Stalin was stunned when he reviewed the transcripts. Surely the president knew he was being bugged, yet he spoke so openly. "It's bizarre," Stalin told Sergo. "They say everything, in fullest detail!" However, FDR had cleverly avoided being overheard talking to Churchill, and it's likely that he deliberately said what he wanted Stalin to hear.)

Churchill said to Harriman, "I shall insist on one thing:

that I be host at dinner tomorrow eve. I think I have one or two claims to precedent. To begin with, I come first both in seniority and alphabetically. In the second place, I represent the longest established of the three governments. And in the third place, tomorrow happens to be my birthday."

To make matters worse, after lunch and before the second plenary session began, FDR sat down with Stalin and Molotov for a second meeting. Churchill might have felt ignored, but according to Molotov, Roosevelt quoted Churchill as saying, "I get up in the morning and pray that Stalin is alive and well. Only Stalin can save the peace." True or not, believable or not, FDR hoped this would mollify Stalin. He urged Stalin to join the war against Japan—one of FDR's primary goals for the meeting— and Stalin assured him he would—one day. Stalin believed that no promises could be made until Hitler was defeated.

Taking Stalin into his confidence, FDR said he wanted to discuss the future of the world after the war. He shared an idea for three governing bodies that would ensure the peace. One would be an assembly of United Nations members. A second would be a type of executive committee, composed of the United States, Great Britain, the Soviet Union, and China, plus representatives of two European nations, one South American, one Middle Eastern, and one British dominion. That body would address nonmilitary issues.

Finally, there would be a third body, what FDR called the "Four Policemen," composed of the United States, Great Britain, the Soviet Union, and China. It would be an enforcement body to deal with breaches of the peace anywhere in the world.

Stalin immediately balked at the notion of the Four Policemen. In addition to his contention that China had no place in such an august body, he said he thought that smaller nations would never support it. He suggested an alternative—dividing the authority between one Western (European) committee and one Far East committee. The Americans could be a part of the European committee. Roosevelt replied that Congress would never allow the United States to join a European organization.

FDR would continue to push for his plan. At one point, he drew by hand three circles in a row and labeled them: on the left, "40 U.N.," representing the general assembly; in the middle, "Exec Com," for the Executive Committee; on the right, "4 Police." Underneath the left-hand circle, he wrote "ILO—Health—Agric-Food." He then scribbled, "By FDR at Teheran, Nov. 30, 1943."

A special event was planned for 3:30 in the afternoon, before the second conference. Members of the three delegations gathered in a large conference room for a ceremony, where Churchill presented the "Sword of Stalingrad" to Stalin in the name of King George VI to honor the victory at Stalingrad. An honor guard was organized for the ceremony, with British and Soviet soldiers and a Soviet army band, which played both the Soviet and the British national anthems.

Presenting the sword to Stalin, Churchill read a prepared statement:

> I have been commanded by His Majesty King George VI to present to you for transmission to the City of Stalingrad, this sword of honor, the design of which His Majesty has chosen and approved. The sword of honor was made by English craftsmen whose ancestors have been employed in swordmaking for generations. The blade of the sword bears the inscription: "To the steel-hearted citizens of Stalingrad, a gift from King George VI as a token of the homage of the British people."

Stalin took the sword and kissed the scabbard before passing it to Voroshilov, who grabbed it nervously and, not expecting its heft, dropped it. Stalin glowered at him and clenched his fists as Voroshilov quickly recovered the sword. Then Stalin gave it to FDR for his inspection. Everyone agreed it was a very fine sword.

IF THE CEREMONY WAS intended to ease the tensions between Churchill and Stalin, it didn't have much effect. The second meeting was more contentious than the first.

At the start of the plenary session, the military staff presented a report from their morning meeting, which basically resolved nothing, as they essentially parroted their leaders' arguments from the first day. Leahy later wrote that he had been particularly frustrated by the Russian attitude that Overlord could be launched without further delay. He thought Voroshilov was just as inflexible as Stalin, noting:

> . . . like all the Russians that we met, he did not understand the difficulties of transporting an army and its supplies across a 3,000-mile ocean. Navies had never played a major role in Russian history, with the possible exception of the Russo-Japanese War in 1905, when such a navy as they had was sunk by the Japanese. In our conversations the Russians would insist that their armies could cross rivers, but they did not understand the difference between a river and an ocean. They sounded like Army or Air Force officers trying to understand naval operations.

The second plenary session was, in Brooke's view, "bad from beginning to end. Winston was not good and Roosevelt even worse." Stalin kept the pressure on for a cross-Channel invasion no later than May 1, 1944. At the meeting, he came right out with the big question: "Who will command Overlord?" He wouldn't trust that an operation was really being planned until a commander was named. FDR might have been tempted to say "Marshall" and put the matter to rest. All indications were that Marshall would be selected, and his wife had even started moving their possessions out of the chief of staff's residence in Washington. Still, FDR held back.

Harriman was frustrated by FDR's reluctance to name Marshall. In his view, Marshall was the only choice. He didn't think that Eisenhower could hold a candle to the great general, and "I felt we should put the first team in the field." But FDR wasn't yet sure, and he said so.

"In that case," Stalin countered, "nothing will come of Overlord. Who bears the moral and military responsibility for the preparation and execution of Operation Overlord? If that is unknown, then Operation Overlord is just so much talk."

FDR ignored the insult and replied calmly, "We know the men who will take part in carrying out Operation Overlord, with the exception of the commander-in-chief." He leaned over and whispered to Leahy, who was seated next to him, "That old Bolshevik is trying to force me to give him the name of our supreme commander. I just can't tell him because I have not yet made up my mind." Leahy, who believed the appointment would ultimately go to Marshall, thought FDR was right not to give in to Stalin's pressure. For although Stalin felt free to make whatever demands he wanted, he was less supportive when FDR was asking for Soviet help. Faced with specific requests for cooperation, he repeatedly demurred, saying he would have to wait until he returned to Moscow before agreeing. "Mr. President," he said slyly, "you tell me you frequently have to consult with your government before making decisions. You must remember that I also have a government and cannot always act without reference to Moscow."

Churchill then began a long-winded explanation of the broader strategy, which included winning in other territories in the Mediterranean and bringing Turkey into the war. Though the Mediterranean was certainly crucial, many in the US and Soviet delegations thought Churchill was simply opposed to any cross-Channel assault—ever. Churchill later wrote that he'd never been against Overlord. But that seemed to be his position.

Stalin quickly dismissed Churchill's wider concerns and demanded that the focus remain on Overlord. He emphasized the importance of avoiding diversions that would detract from the primary operation. Only the southern France operation had value because it would directly support Overlord.

FDR interjected that they should discuss the timing of Overlord. The date set in Quebec had been May 1, 1944, and he thought they should stick with that, at least within two weeks.

Churchill bluntly said that he could not agree to that date—although he'd been a participant in setting it. Once again, he insisted that they consider the Mediterranean operations before firmly committing to an Overlord date.

They're diversions, Stalin said again.

Churchill heatedly disagreed.

Finally, Stalin gave Churchill a hard look across the table. "I wish to pose a very direct question to the Prime Minister about Overlord. Do the Prime Minister and the British Staff really believe in Overlord?"

Silence fell over the room. Churchill narrowed his eyes at Stalin and bit down hard on his cigar. In his rumbling voice, he replied, "Provided the conditions previously stated for Overlord are established when the time comes, it will be our stern duty to hurl across the Channel against the Germans every sinew of our strength."

FDR, wanting to wrap things up, said they had a very good dinner—hosted by Stalin—awaiting them in an hour and people would be very hungry. He suggested that the military committee meet the following morning to work through the details. Stalin found the notion absurd. "Why do that?" he asked. "We are the chiefs of government. We know what we want to do. Why turn the matter over to some subordinates to advise us?" (That taunt would be echoed in 1988 by Mikhail Gorbachev, who was angered when President Reagan took the advice of his aides in a point of contention at the Moscow conference. "Quit listening to all your aides around you, Mr. President, and think for yourself," he shouted.) The Soviets never understood the Western concept of having informed advisers who didn't merely parrot the will of their leader.

It was high drama. Sherwood wrote, "The official records of these meetings were written with so much circumspection that the informal drama was largely obscured; but it was far too big to be totally disguised. One cannot read these deliberately dry and guarded accounts without the feeling that here were Titans determining the future course of the entire planet."

Brooke was so discouraged by the meeting that he wrote in his diary, "I have little hope of any form of agreement in discussions. After listening to the arguments put forward during the last 2 days I feel more like entering a lunatic asylum or a nursing home than continuing with my present job. . . . May God help us in the future prosecution of this war; we have every hope of making an unholy mess of it and of being defeated yet!"

When he returned to his suite before dinner, Roosevelt looked tired. Elliott suggested he lie down for a nap, but Roosevelt was too keyed up. Rubbing his eyes and lighting a cigarette, he said of Stalin, "He gets things done, that man. He really keeps his eye on the ball he's aiming for."

"Overlord?" asked Elliott.

"That's what he was talking about. And what *we* were talking about." He described Churchill's losing battle to fight the timeline: "Marshall has got to the point where he just looks at the P.M. as if he can't believe his ears."

FDR sighed wearily and asked Elliott to run him a bath and make him a weak old-fashioned. He sat drinking and ruminating for a while. "Elliott, our chiefs of staff are convinced of one thing. The way to kill the most Germans, with the least loss of American soldiers, is to mount one great big invasion and then slam 'em with everything we've got. It makes sense to me. It makes sense to Uncle Joe. It makes sense to all our generals . . . It's the quickest way to win the war." The problem was, Churchill disagreed. Roosevelt thought that Churchill's resistance and desire to expand into the Balkans were a way of calculating the Russian strength after the war more than a true strategic plan to win the war. "Trouble is, the P.M. is thinking too much of the postwar and where England will be. He's scared of letting the Russians get too strong."

If that was Churchill's concern, he had a point. None of the Westerners wanted to address the elephant in the room: Stalin's true ambitions. It was easier to see themselves as having a common cause and to leave it at that, as long as the true goal was winning the war more quickly.

At the lavish dinner hosted by Stalin, the toasts went on endlessly, in the Soviet manner. The toasting process itself was quite a workout, as everyone was required to rise (except Roosevelt, of course) with each toast. FDR would describe it in a press conference after his return home: "We had one banquet where we had dinner in the Russian style. Very good dinner, too. Russian style means a number of toasts, and I counted up to three hundred and sixty-five toasts. And we all went away sober. It's a remarkable thing what you can do if you try."

Noting the grand spread of many courses, Elliott had a theory: "The reason there are so many is that you don't have too much opportunity to get a bite of any one of them; you're on your feet too often . . ."

Stalin enjoyed Roosevelt's bonhomie, even though he recognized it as a form of manipulation. Roosevelt "was a wilier comrade [than Hitler] in earlier days or Churchill," Molotov said. "He drank with us, of course. Stalin nursed him along just right. He was very fond of Soviet champagne . . . Like Stalin."

According to Bohlen, "The most notable feature of the dinner was the attitude of Marshal Stalin toward the Prime Minister. Marshal Stalin lost no opportunity to get in a dig at Mr. Churchill. Almost every remark that he addressed to the Prime Minister contained some sharp edge, although the Marshal's manner was entirely friendly. He apparently desired to put and keep the Prime Minister on the defensive. At one occasion he told the Prime Minister that just because Russians are simple people, it was a mistake to believe that they were blind and could not see what was before their eyes."

At times Roosevelt's efforts to woo Stalin could go overboard and be downright embarrassing—especially when he joined Stalin in taunting Churchill. Referring to discussions they'd had that day in the plenary session, Stalin accused Churchill of wanting to go easy on Germany after the war, which was far from true but provoked a reliable explosion from Churchill. Then Stalin took the teasing a step further, presenting a proposal for how to handle the German General Staff in defeat. Rising from his seat he said, "I propose a salute to the swiftest possible justice for all Germany's war criminals—justice before a firing squad. I drink to our unity in dispatching them as fast as we capture them, all of them, and there must be at least fifty thousand of them." As Churchill turned red with rage, Roosevelt's eyes glimmered. He knew it was a joke, and it had produced the expected result. Churchill furiously cried that he would have no part in such barbarism. "Clearly there must be some sort of compromise," Roosevelt said, in on the joke. "Shall we say forty-nine thousand five hundred?"

Elliott, who was a little worse for wear having drunk many glasses of champagne, rose to enter the fray. "Isn't the whole thing pretty academic?" he asked. "Look: when our armies start rolling in from the west and your armies are still coming in from the east, we'll be solving the whole thing, won't we? Russian, American and British soldiers will settle the issue for most of those fifty thousand in battle, and I hope that not only those fifty thousand war criminals will be taken care of, but many hundreds of thousands more Nazis as well." Stalin rushed over to clap Elliott on the back, praising FDR's son.

But Churchill was enraged. "How can you dare say such a thing?" he shouted, jabbing a finger at Elliott. It was all too much for him. Churchill heaved himself up from the table and stormed out of the room. He was standing outside when he felt a firm grip on his shoulders. He turned to find Stalin, with Molotov behind him. Stalin was grinning. "It was only a joke," he insisted, and persuaded Churchill to rejoin them at the table.

Churchill reluctantly returned to dinner, but he clearly felt that the future of Germany was no joking matter. He stared mournfully at the president, the man who had been his closest partner, the one to whom he'd once written, "It's fun to be in the same decade with you." He had dreamed of the time after the war, when the United States and Great Britain would effectively be the Big Two in the world. Now he was faced with another vision that turned his stomach: the United States and the Soviet Union as the Big Two.

Feeling a need to soothe Churchill's wounded pride, Hopkins visited him at the British compound after midnight. He found Churchill looking worn out and utterly discouraged. Hopkins urged him to let it go, to accept the time frame for Overlord. After Hopkins left, Churchill, taking a sip of brandy, observed morosely, "Stupendous issues are unfolding before our eyes and we are only specks of dust that have settled in the night on the map of the world. . . . I fancy sometimes that I am nearly spent."

Gloomy thoughts for a man who had turned sixty-nine at the stroke of midnight.

CHAPTER 13

LIKE A RAINBOW

The weather brought events to a head. Earlier, FDR, Churchill, and Stalin had agreed that they would extend the conference if they needed more time to reach an agreement. But the mild, sunny days they'd enjoyed during their time in Tehran were threatened by an approaching cold front. Normally, that wouldn't have been an issue, but it had the potential of trapping the principals in the city. Dr. McIntyre was adamant that for health reasons, Roosevelt should not fly above eight thousand feet, and Churchill's doctor imposed a similar restriction. That meant they couldn't fly above the bad weather, if it were to come. They would need to get out of town by December 1, which left only one more full day for the conference.

On the morning of November 30, the US and British chiefs of staff had their work cut out for them. Would it be possible in so short a time to leap across the chasm of their differences? Somehow they broke through and reached an agreement on the priorities of the war, producing a document that was simple and straightforward:

Agreed:
a. That we should continue to advance in Italy to the Pisa-Rimini line. (This means that the 68 LST's [landing

craft] which are due to be sent from the Mediterranean to the United Kingdom for OVERLORD must be kept in the Mediterranean until 15 January.)

b. That an operation shall be mounted against the South of France on as big a scale as landing craft permit. For planning purposes D-day to be the same as OVERLORD D-day.

c. To recommend to the President and Prime Minister respectively that we should inform Marshal Stalin that we will launch OVERLORD during May, in conjunction with a supporting operation against the South of France on the largest scale that is permitted by the landing craft available at that time.

The exact date of Overlord within that window would depend on moon, tide, and weather conditions, an allowance that was prescient, as weather became the deciding factor in the final date.

And just like that, the debate that had consumed the first two days of the conference was resolved.

The British had caved in. "I never asked [them] what caused their change of heart," Leahy wrote, "but the American argument was so logical that I cannot but believe that as professional soldiers they knew Overlord was the most sensible move to bring an end to the war with Germany in the shortest possible time."

When the report was presented to Roosevelt and Churchill, they immediately agreed, and planned to discuss the arrangement with Stalin at lunch.

Before lunch Roosevelt received a visit from the shah of Iran. There had been a great deal of posturing leading up to the meeting. The Palace had first demanded that FDR must visit the shah out of respect; for the shah to travel to the Soviet Embassy might be seen as a humiliation. But Roosevelt held firm. He would not visit the palace. So the shah swallowed his pride and came to Roosevelt.

Despite his reputation for being a playboy, the young Mohammad Reza Shah was very serious and deferential. He brought a gift for the Roosevelts, a large Persian rug measuring eighteen by thirty feet, designed by a famous Iranian artist in a multicolored floral pattern. Roosevelt took it home and put it into his presidential study. (Today it can be viewed at Hyde Park in the replica of FDR's study at the Franklin D. Roosevelt Museum.)

The shah was concerned about Iran's independence after the war, including sovereignty over its oil. Roosevelt sought to reassure him that the Allies would reach such an agreement, which he fully favored. Indeed, the conference published a "Declaration of the Three Powers Regarding Iran," which established support for the process of rebuilding after the war and declared, "The Governments of the United States, the U. S. S. R., and the United Kingdom are at one with the Government of Iran in their desire for the maintenance of the independence, sovereignty and territorial integrity of Iran." Of course, future events would show that the promises made in Tehran were not always kept, and Great Britain's firm grip on the nation and its rich natural resources would be ended only after a revolution in 1979.

While FDR was meeting with the shah, Churchill was speaking privately with Stalin, hoping to put them on friendlier terms—and also to take a crack at the same underhanded game Roosevelt had been playing all week. He reminded Stalin that he was half American and had great affection for the American people. He didn't want to disparage them. However, he had a couple of matters on his mind.

Aware that Stalin had not yet been informed about the agreement of the chiefs that morning, Churchill took the opportunity to state his case once again that the argument was not about either keeping the Overlord date or continuing operations in the Mediterranean. The matter was more complex. He began one of his elaborate descriptions of the various issues, but Stalin cut him off. The Red Army was depending on the invasion of northern France in May of 1944, he said bluntly. If that didn't happen, they would lose confidence that there would be an operation at all. A sense of isolation and discouragement would come over his troops. He couldn't allow that to happen.

This was the same impasse they'd always been at, and one wonders why Churchill had decided to go into the meeting this way, knowing that shortly he, FDR, and Stalin would have lunch together and the Westerners would tell Stalin he was getting everything he wanted.

Lunch was a private affair among the three leaders and their interpreters. Roosevelt began by sharing the report of the chiefs with Stalin, who said he was very happy with the result, but asked again who the commander would be. FDR promised him an answer in three or four days. According to Bohlen, Eisenhower's name never came up at the conference as the potential commander, at least not in his hearing. Everyone expected Marshall's appointment, and at one point Stalin even offered his congratulations to the general.

At 4:30, the conference gathered for its final plenary session. Now that the decision about Overlord had been made, the discussion was more amiable than on the previous days.

The three talked about how to prevent the Germans from finding out about such a massive operation. Stalin described how the Soviets had built decoy tanks, airplanes, and airfields to trick German intelligence into thinking operations were planned in places where they weren't. He boasted that at times as many as five thousand false tanks and two thousand false airplanes had been used to draw German attention away from the real operations, which were being launched under cover of darkness. He added that the Red Army also used radio communications as a strategy to deliver false information to listening German ears.

Churchill said poetically that truth deserves a bodyguard of lies.

Stalin nodded. "This is what we call military cunning," he said.

Rather, it was military *diplomacy*, Churchill remarked, adding that the Three Powers should appoint a liaison to be in charge of deception and propaganda methods.

The plenary session that afternoon was much briefer than the others, meant primarily for the chiefs to put their stamp on the agreement they had made that morning. At lunch, the Big Three had decided that this short session would be the final one of the conference. However, before Roosevelt flew out the following evening, the three of them would meet, along with Eden, Molotov, and Hopkins, to talk about "political matters."

The main event on the third day was Churchill's gala birthday dinner at the British Embassy. Often feeling wounded in their meetings, Churchill hoped the dinner would be a dramatic crescendo to the conference.

FDR and Elliott arrived at the British Embassy to be met by turbaned Sikh guards. They greeted Churchill, whom Elliott described as being "wreathed in smiles and cigar smoke." Roosevelt had come to Tehran without a birthday gift for the prime minister, so he'd asked Harriman to find something suitable. Harriman had gone to a friend, Joseph Upton, a curator at the Metropolitan Museum of Art in New York, who was stationed in Tehran. Upton offered to sell Harriman at cost a twelfth-century Kashan bowl from his personal collection. FDR presented the gift to Churchill. "May we be together for many years," he said warmly.

Elegantly dressed Persian waiters swept through the room. The tables were so elaborately set that Stalin privately grumbled about not knowing which of the many forks to use. Turning to Birse, he said, "This is a fine collection of cutlery! It is a problem which to use. You will have to tell me, and also when I can begin to eat. I am unused to your customs."

Champagne and wine were liberally poured to accommodate the many toasts, and Churchill was in a position at last to be gracious, toasting the Soviet leader as "Stalin the great." The toasts and speeches went on, with Hopkins delivering a very funny "roast" of Churchill. At one point, he said in a deadpan manner that he had made a thorough study of the British system and had discovered that "the provisions of the British constitution and the powers of the war cabinet are just whatever Winston Churchill wants them to be at any given moment." Even Churchill laughed.

As Stalin was giving yet another toast, the lights dimmed and a waiter came walking toward them holding aloft a giant tower of ice cream set in ice and lit from within with a candle. When the waiter passed Stalin, the tower began to slant as the ice cream quickly melted from the heat of the candle. As Brooke would describe it:

> With the noise of an avalanche the whole wonderful construction slid over our heads and exploded in a clatter of plates between me and [Stalin's interpreter] Berezhkov. The unfortunate Berezhkov was at that moment standing up translating a speech for Stalin and he came in for

the full blast! He was splashed from his head to his feet, but I suppose it was more than his life was worth to stop interpreting! In any case he carried on manfully whilst I sent for towels and with the help of the Persian waiters proceeded to mop him down. To this day I can see large lumps of white ice cream sitting on his shoes, and melting over the edges and through the lace holes!

Despite the calamity, everyone was in high spirits fueled by alcohol and flattery. Summoning the Persian waiter who had served him to his side, Stalin poured a glass of champagne and handed it to him. The alarmed waiter looked questioningly at Birse. What should he do? "I told him to drink it on the spot," Birse wrote.

Churchill, eager to make a gesture toward Stalin, noted that their different views were all a matter of tints and that the British people's complexions were looking "a trifle pinker" these days. Stalin smiled, delighted. "That is a sign of good health!" he announced. Roosevelt picked up on the theme, describing the differences of those around the table as being like a rainbow, which in the United States was "a symbol of good fortune and of hope," adding, "We have proved here at Teheran that the varying ideals of our nations can come together in a harmonious whole, moving unitedly for the common good of ourselves and of the world. So as we leave this historic gathering, we can see in the sky, for the first time, that traditional symbol of hope, the rainbow."

After the party, which lasted until midnight, Churchill sent for Birse, who found the prime minister in his sitting room with Eden and other aides. Churchill wanted to know if Birse thought Stalin had enjoyed himself. Birse replied in the affirmative. Churchill was delighted. Forgotten were the moody regrets of the previous evening. The birthday dinner had been a conquest of sorts.

FDR WAS BROODING. THREE days had passed in Tehran, and now, on the morning of the day of his departure, he still didn't feel as if he'd broken through to Stalin. It wasn't that Stalin hadn't been courteous and even agreeable. He had. He'd been a thoughtful host, and his demeanor in the meetings had been decisive and serious. Best of all, he'd signed off on the joint plan. But to FDR, it didn't feel like enough. Perhaps it was his Americanism—the desire to achieve a relationship that felt more like friendship, the kind of understanding reflected in expressions of commonality, in unvarnished approval and laughter, in a spontaneity that nurtured trust, in a deeper understanding that happened when eyes met in mutual appreciation. FDR didn't want to leave Tehran without creating that moment.

Late in the day, when the Big Three met to discuss political matters informally, Roosevelt said to Churchill as they entered the room, "Winston, I hope you won't be sore at me for what I am going to do."

As Roosevelt later described the scene to Frances Perkins:

I began almost as soon as we got into the conference room. I said, lifting my hand to cover a whisper . . . "Winston is cranky this morning, he got up on the wrong side of the bed." A vague smile passed over Stalin's eyes, and I decided I was on the right track. . . . I began to tease Churchill about his Britishness, about John Bull [Britain's version of Uncle Sam], about his cigars, about his habits. It began to register with Stalin. Winston got red and scowled, and the more he did so, the more Stalin smiled. Finally Stalin broke out in a deep, hearty guffaw, and for the first time in three days I saw light. I kept it up until Stalin was laughing with me, and it was then that I called him Uncle Joe. He would have thought me fresh the day before, but that day he laughed and came over and shook my hand.

Perhaps that was the clearest manifestation of FDR's daring gamble in Tehran. For the sake of Overlord, for the sake of winning the war with Japan, he was willing to link arms with Stalin—who represented a clear future threat to American democracy—and dismiss Churchill, believing he could sort out the relationships at a later time.

Churchill obviously found the display insulting. Birse recognized what FDR was trying to do in his apparent seduction of Stalin, and it left him cold. "I came to the conclusion that if he knew how to deal with American problems and domestic politics, he knew little of Soviet mentality, or had been badly advised. It was not enough, as he evidently thought, to clap Russians on the back and say they were good fellows, in order to reach a mutually advantageous agreement with them. . . . Nor did I like his taking sides with Stalin, ostensibly as a joke, but nevertheless tactlessly, in allusion to British colonialism. . . . I felt he was too ready to play into Stalin's hands."

That was an easy conclusion to draw. But was FDR really so easily swayed by Stalin and so callous toward his old friend? Viewing the scenario more objectively, what were his choices? Roosevelt and Churchill had arrived at Tehran having already held five conferences between them. Churchill had been a guest at the White House, at Hyde Park, and at Shangri-La. They had become the most famous couple in the world. The Tehran Conference could easily have become an extension of that relationship, leaving Stalin to feel as if he were the odd man out. That could have been disastrous. FDR was a man who thrived on his ability to win hearts and minds by the force of his personality. He had come to Tehran with the ambition to accomplish that with Stalin, but it wasn't easy to break through Stalin's defensive shell. Provoking a spontaneous laugh from Stalin was a moment of success for FDR. Perhaps simplistically, he thought a man who laughed with you from the heart could be a true ally.

FDR's behavior might have seemed a betrayal to Churchill, but he thought the prime minister could take it in light of the greater purpose. (That calculation proved to be right.) In the end, Roosevelt figured, they'd achieved what they'd set out to do regarding the course of the war.

The main topic of their political discussion was the future of Poland. Earlier, FDR had privately told Stalin not to expect him to weigh in on that sensitive matter. There was a presidential election coming up in 1944, and although he didn't want to run again, the war might force him to do so. In that case, he had to consider the six million to seven million Americans of Polish extraction whose votes would be jeopardized if he made any declarations about its future or its borders. He had a chance at that moment to forcefully advocate for Poland's independence and place limitations on future Soviet expansion, but he allowed political considerations to mute his posture.

When the Big Three discussed Poland, Stalin had said he believed that Poland was primarily a Soviet concern, since it involved Soviet borders and security. A nasty complication was the matter of the Polish government in exile, which had been formed after the German-Soviet invasion in 1939, which had divided Poland between the two powers. Although technically aligned with the Allies, the government in exile had been a thorn in Stalin's side. It wasn't a simple matter to go along with Hitler's enemy. But the Soviets had their own atrocities to answer for. After the Soviet invasion of Poland, thousands of captured Polish officers and soldiers had been executed and buried in mass graves, most famously in the Katyn Forest. The government in exile was involved in bringing the mass graves to public attention, and the Nazis took advantage of the bad publicity to rail against the Soviets. (Decades later, the CIA would obtain documents showing that Stalin had signed off on the massacre.)

Now Stalin spoke out against what he termed the pro-Nazi propaganda of the government in exile, which was making the determination about Poland's future more difficult. With Roosevelt sitting back, unwilling to get into the discussion, Churchill suggested that maybe he could intervene with the government in exile. In the meantime, the Western Allies were prepared to concede control of Poland's eastern territory to the Soviet Union after the war. That concession would have devastating implications for the future of Poland.

The conversation then turned, once again, to Germany. FDR proposed a plan he'd been thinking about for some time: dividing Germany into five parts after the war. Referring to a map spread on the table, he showed the breakdown. The five parts would be self-governed and divided into two regions for the purpose of UN or international control. The five parts were: (1) a weakened Prussia; (2) Hanover and northwest Germany; (3) Saxony and the Leipzig area in eastern Germany; (4) Hesse-Darmstadt, Hesse-Kassel, and the area south of the Rhine; and (5) Bavaria, Baden, and Württemberg in the south.

Harriman recalled that FDR had told him about that idea long before Tehran. "Roosevelt had studied in Germany and felt that he was particularly knowledgeable on the subject. I did not think much of the idea that Germany ought to be split up. It was not really a plan and it seemed to me too drastic; I felt that German nationalism was so strong that it would bring the divided states together again. It was another case of Roosevelt dreaming aloud."

According to Harriman, "Churchill appeared dumbfounded by the audacity of Roosevelt's suggestion. It seemed to him, if he might borrow an American expression, that 'the President has said a mouthful.'" Churchill said that his own preference would be simpler. Yes, Prussia should be separated and weakened, he agreed, but he'd prefer that the south German regions be combined into a confederation.

Stalin disagreed. Germans were Germans, no matter how many parts you divided them into, he said—all Germans fought like devils. Overall, he preferred FDR's plan, as long as Germany was fully and completely dismembered.

Churchill hastened to add that he was not against breaking up Germany, but he believed FDR's scheme would only mean they'd eventually reunite.

A last worry nagged at Churchill: Was Stalin asking for Europe to be made up of little states, disjointed, separated, and weak?

Not at all, Stalin replied. He wanted a weak Germany, not a weak Europe. But was that actually true? Bohlen, for one, worried about what he thought was Stalin's view of postwar Europe. After the conference, he described his concerns in a memo to Harriman:

Germany is to be broken up and kept broken up. The states of eastern, southeastern and central Europe will not be permitted to group themselves into any federations or association. France is to be stripped of her colo-

nies and strategic bases beyond her borders and will not
be permitted to maintain an appreciable military establishment. Poland and Italy will remain approximately
their present territorial size, but it is doubtful if either
will be permitted to maintain any appreciable armed
force. The result would be that the Soviet Union would
be the only important military and political force on the
continent of Europe. The rest of Europe would be reduced to military and political impotence.

A compromised Poland, a weakened France and Italy, and
a dismembered Germany, along with greater Russian control
in the Baltic states, would give the Soviet Union free rein to
spread its influence. Stalin was always careful to say the right
thing about his desire for peace and his respect for the independence of others, but he wasn't particularly trustworthy. FDR
and Churchill gave him leeway because they didn't want to rock
the boat. "It must be remembered that we were in the midst
of a fearful struggle with the mighty Nazi power," Churchill
wrote defensively. "All the hazards of war lay around us, and
all its passions of comradeship among Allies . . . dominated our
minds."

Working with Harriman in the mostly deserted Russian
compound, Rigdon hurriedly typed up the final minutes, anxious to leave the place, which now had an "eerie feeling." Early
in the day, FDR had suggested giving each member of the
household staff a gift to show how much they appreciated their
services. Rigdon went to Vladimir Pavlov, Stalin's interpreter,
to get the staff's names, but they were never provided. After
two attempts, Rigdon gave up. Clearly, the idea of gifts didn't
fly with the Soviet brass—for good reason. Rigdon learned that
after their departure, some of the household servants had been
seen wearing the uniforms of Russian officers.

At a quick ceremony before leaving Tehran, FDR, Churchill, and Stalin signed the Declaration of the Three Powers, which would be circulated the following week. In part, it read:

> We express our determination that our nations shall work together in war and in the peace that will follow.
>
> As to war—our military staffs have joined in our round table discussions, and we have concerted our plans for the destruction of the German forces. We have reached complete agreement as to the scope and timing of the operations to be undertaken from the East, West and South.
>
> The common understanding which we have reached guarantees that victory will be ours.
>
> And as to peace—we are sure that our concord will win an enduring peace. We recognize fully the supreme responsibility resting upon us and all the United Nations to make a peace which will command the good will of the overwhelming mass of the peoples of the world, and banish the scourge and terror of war for many generations. . . .
>
> No power on earth can prevent our destroying the German armies by land, their U-boats by sea, and their war plants from the air.
>
> Our attack will be relentless and increasing.
>
> Emerging from these cordial conferences we look with confidence to the day when all peoples of the world may live free lives, untouched by tyranny, and according to their varying desires and their own consciences.
>
> We came here with hope and determination. We leave here, friends in fact, in spirit and in purpose.
>
> ROOSEVELT, CHURCHILL and STALIN
> Signed at Tehran, December 1, 1943

Harriman found himself astonished that Stalin would sign such a declaration. Maybe it was a turning point for the Soviet Union's role in the world—or maybe not. The fulfillment of the declaration relied on the good faith of its parties, and ultimately FDR and Churchill chose to suspend disbelief about Soviet compliance because the demands of the war were so pressing. "It would not have been right at Teheran for the Western democracies to found their plans upon suspicions of the Russian attitude in the hour of triumph and when all her dangers were removed," he wrote years later after relations with the Soviets had collapsed. In the moment, they cared most about ending the war, with faith that peace would sort itself out.

"WELL, IKE, YOU ARE going to command Overlord," Roosevelt said when he greeted Eisenhower in a stopover in Tunis after the conference. Eisenhower, who had expected orders to return to Washington, was shocked—along with almost everyone else. Churchill and Stalin had favored Marshall; so had Hopkins. But as FDR had told Marshall in breaking the news, "I feel I could not sleep at night with you out of the country."

Eisenhower fully grasped the nature of his charge. "Mr. President," he replied, "I realize that such an appointment involved difficult decisions. I hope you will not be disappointed." He would be leaving as soon as his replacement, British general Henry Maitland Wilson, arrived to take command of the Mediterranean.

Meanwhile, Eisenhower had a VIP staying with him in Tunis. When Churchill had stopped overnight on his way to Italy to visit the troops, Eisenhower had immediately seen that the prime minister looked very ill. He urged him to go to bed and rest, and Churchill's condition deteriorated overnight as his temperature rose. Brooke, who was with him, awoke to a commotion in the hallway—"A raucous voice re-echoing through the room with a series of mournful, 'Hullo, Hullo, Hullo!' When I had woken sufficiently I said, 'Who the hell is that?' and switched on my torch. To my dismay I found the PM in his dragon dressing gown with a brown bandage wrapped round his head, wandering about my room!" The prime minister was delirious with a 102-degree fever. The diagnosis was pneumonia.

Too sick to be moved, Churchill remained with Eisenhower for weeks as he recovered. He was an unruly patient, refusing to rest and full of agonies about the war. His long, bedridden days gave his mind room to roam through his many fears, replaying some of his largely ignored positions from Tehran. He was especially worried about Italy, but there would be no visit to the front now. Finally, Clementine, summoned by Brooke, arrived to nurse him. There was great relief among the beleaguered staff. FDR cabled, "I feel relieved that she is with you as your superior officer."

FDR made the long journey home, arriving in Washington on December 17. He had been away almost a month. His cabinet and staff gathered to greet him at the south entrance of the White House. He emerged looking tired but elated. "I do not remember the president looking more satisfied and pleased than he did that morning," Rosenman reported. "I never saw that same expression again."

PART FOUR

THE ENDGAME

CHAPTER 14

AT LAST, OVERLORD

The fruit of Tehran, a plan for Overlord, was the consuming matter of the early months of 1944. In London, Eisenhower found a seriousness of purpose and a collaboration between the British and Americans that was stronger than ever. They all knew what was at stake. This would be D-Day, the best shot at winning the war. All the hand-wringing in Tehran fell away before the mandate to conquer western Europe and put the Nazis on the run for good. Eisenhower wrote to the combined chiefs of staff, "Every obstacle must be overcome, every inconvenience suffered and every risk run to ensure that our blow is decisive. We cannot afford to fail."

At his headquarters in London, he was so busy entertaining dignitaries, including Churchill, that he decided to move to the outskirts of the city to Kingston, staying at the humble Telegraph Cottage. (An amateur artist, he would later paint a wistful portrait of Telegraph Cottage, where he had planned D-Day.)

"For the sort of attack before us we had no precedent in military history," he wrote. "Caesar and William the Conquerer had crossed the Channel to invade England successfully. But the England of that day was not guarded by an almost unbroken perimeter of guns and fighting men."

The invasion choreography was deceptively simple—at least on paper. The airborne divisions would launch first after midnight, dropping thousands of paratroopers inland to take the nearby towns and secure a beachhead for the advance of troops from the beaches. At dawn, the assault of five beaches would begin, with the infantry transferred from transport ships to landing craft about ten miles offshore, which would head in waves toward the beaches. The beaches were Sword and Gold to the east, led by the British, Juno, led by the Canadians, and to the west, Utah and Omaha, led by the Americans. They would be supported by amphibious tanks and gunfire from naval destroyers that would move into position as close as possible to the beaches. Constant aerial bombardments would clear a path for the invaders to progress into the countryside. The infantry would take the beaches and move inland. Well aware that the story of war is written on the battlefields, not in the war rooms, Eisenhower nonetheless felt growing confidence in the careful orchestration of his massive forces.

For the task, he needed the best commanders the war could deliver. He thought long and hard about who would be the commander of the ground forces on D-Day and ultimately settled on a British general, Bernard Law Montgomery, who would also lead the Twenty-first Army Group. Montgomery was a notoriously difficult character, arrogant and officious, a thorn in the side of the Americans. He also thought himself better than Eisenhower, once saying of him "Nice chap. No soldier." But Eisenhower was able to put any personal quibbles aside in light of Montgomery's excellence as a commander. "General Montgomery has no superior in the most important characteristics," he wrote graciously. "He quickly develops among British enlisted men an intense devotion and admiration—the greatest personal asset a commander can possess. Montgomery's other

outstanding characteristic is his tactical ability . . . he is careful, meticulous, and certain." The selection was an example of
Eisenhower's rare leadership skill of rising above the fray to
make a totally objective decision for the good of the mission.

He also chose another prickly but seasoned commander,
British marshal Sir Trafford Leigh-Mallory, as the commander
in chief of the Allied Expeditionary Air Force. That position
was vitally important because, in Eisenhower's view, air support would not be secondary in the conflict but essential, making it a "ground-air" operation.

On the ground, Eisenhower's old friend and West Point
classmate General Omar Bradley would command the American ground forces as they landed on Omaha and Utah beaches.
Eisenhower was always glad to have Bradley by his side. He
trusted him completely, and they were of a common mind.

Sir Bertram Home Ramsay, the Royal Navy admiral who
had been instrumental in Operation Torch, would come out of
near retirement to command the naval operations.

The fiery General George Patton, whom Eisenhower respected for his courage but who often got into trouble for being
a Lone Ranger, was sidelined for the day of the invasion but
would be instrumental in leading the US Third Army across
Europe to its final destination.

The invasion window was narrow due to the lunar calendar
and the tides. Perfect conditions were determined to be June 5
to 7, with the date of the invasion selected as June 5. The strategic plan, outlined by Eisenhower, was to land on the Normandy
coast and then fan out into the region, joining with forces attacking from the south to make an approach on Germany.

Despite the heavy burdens of command, Eisenhower took
time to visit the troops when he could. He viewed them not
as cogs in the war machine who would storm the beaches as a

powerful whole but as individuals of flesh and blood who were prepared to make the ultimate sacrifice. Before the invasion, he managed to meet many of them in person, shaking their hands. And they, heartened by the gesture, promised to win for him.

He met regularly with Churchill, who was in full-fledged worry about the invasion. "When I think of the beaches of Normandy choked with the flower of American and British youth, and when, in my mind's eye, I see the tides running red with their blood, I have my doubts . . . I have my doubts," he told Eisenhower. But then Churchill had always had his doubts about Overlord. Only as the date approached in the wake of the massive buildup did he begin to express hope.

"General," Churchill said to Eisenhower, "if by the coming winter you have established yourself with your thirty-six Allied divisions firmly on the Continent, and have the Cherbourg and Brittany peninsulas in your grasp, I will proclaim this operation to the world as one of the most successful of the war. And if, in addition to this, you have secured the port at Le Havre and freed beautiful Paris from the hands of the enemy, I will assert the victory to be the greatest of modern times."

Feeling bold, Eisenhower replied, "Mr. Prime Minister, we expect to be on the borders of Germany by Christmas, pounding away at her defenses. When that occurs, if Hitler has the slightest judgment or wisdom left, he will surrender unconditionally to avoid complete destruction of Germany."

At a final conference in London on May 15, with King George VI in attendance, Eisenhower and his generals described the plan for the mission, tracing its movements on a large map of the Normandy beaches and the surrounding countryside. Afterward, Churchill announced to Eisenhower his plan to observe the landings from a naval ship in the Channel. It was a last straw for Eisenhower, who imagined the personal stress of having to worry about the prime minister's safety while trying to coordinate the invasion. He argued against the idea, but Churchill was stubborn. He reminded Eisenhower that he had no authority over a ship's company in His Majesty's fleet. Resigned to having Churchill on the scene, Eisenhower was relieved when the king came to the rescue. Learning of the plan, the king told Churchill that if he was determined to go, the king must join him. That put an end to the idea.

But there were soul-racking matters that consumed Eisenhower's private thoughts. Only days before the operation, he received a plea from Air Chief Marshal Leigh-Mallory to abandon two of the easternmost airborne operations for fear of "futile slaughter." Leigh-Mallory told him that in his estimation the casualties in these divisions would be catastrophic and many thousands of men would perish in an effort that would not substantially impact the outcome of the operation.

"I went to my tent alone and sat down to think," Eisenhower recalled. "Over and over I reviewed each step. . . . I realized, of course, that if I deliberately disregarded the advice of my technical expert on the subject, and his predictions should prove accurate, then I would carry to my grave the unbearable burden of a conscience justly accusing me of the stupid, blind sacrifice of thousands of the flower of our youth."

Yet, as he examined the plan, he was gripped by the sobering recognition that if he canceled two of the airborne divisions, as well as the assault on Utah Beach, it would upset the careful orchestration of the entire mission. Utah Beach was crucial; it would put the Allies close to the port city of Cherbourg. He ultimately had to trust his own judgment, which was that Leigh-Mallory's pessimistic estimates were not consistent with what he believed to be the risk. He informed Leigh-Mallory that the full airborne operation would go forward as planned.

Then, on June 4, the day before the launch, the invasion was thrown into doubt by a weather report. "Some soldier once said, 'The weather is always neutral,'" Eisenhower wrote. "Nothing could be more untrue. . . . If really bad weather should endure permanently, the Nazi would need nothing else to defend the Normandy coast." And "really bad weather" seemed to be on the horizon. British group captain James M. Stagg, the operation's chief meteorologist, informed Eisenhower of a storm coming in across the Channel. He recommended that Overlord be delayed a day, to June 6. However, he could not guarantee that the weather would be clear on that day, either. With the next window of opportunity weeks away, Eisenhower had a terrible decision to make: go on June 6 and risk the lives of the troops in stormy waters or miss the chance altogether. It was the kind of decision no leader ever wants to have to make, and he decided to sleep on it for a few hours.

Arising at 3:30 A.M. on June 5, Eisenhower was heartened to hear from Captain Stagg that the weather outlook for June 6 had improved. "Okay, we'll go," he said.

Full of hope, anxiety, and the sobering awareness of the risk, that evening he traveled fifty miles to Newbury, the staging area for the 101st Airborne Division. Hundreds of paratroopers, their faces blackened, were ready for the jump of their lives. He spoke to as many of them as he could and remained there until the last man departed. He was humbled by their bravery, writing, "I found the men in fine fettle, many of them admonishing me that I had no cause for worry, since the 101st was on the job, and everything would be taken care of in fine shape."

Then it was back to base and waiting—the hard task of a commander, which he had learned at Gibraltar. Despite the aura of confidence he'd communicated to the troops, Eisenhower was plagued, as any man would be at the moment of decision, with the moody reflection that defeat was always a possibility. Earlier that day he had penned a note, which he folded into his wallet, accepting responsibility in the event of Overlord's failure:

> Our landings in the Cherbourg-Havre area have failed to gain a satisfactory foothold and I have withdrawn the troops. My decision to attack at this time and place was based upon the best information available. The troops, the air, and the navy did all that Bravery and devotion to duty could do. If any blame or fault attaches to the attempt it is mine alone.

Eisenhower did not know that German general Erwin Rommel, in spite of knowing that the Allies would attempt a landing somewhere in Europe, had become convinced that they would not risk a Channel crossing at that time. "There's not going to be an invasion," he told his troops with confidence. "And if there is, they won't even get off the beaches." Indeed, Rommel had left the theater, traveling to Berlin for a meeting with Hitler, and would miss the whole show. Later, his son, Manfred, would say in an oral history, "He was very surprised because he relied on the expert view of the German Kriegsmarine (Navy) that nobody could land under such weather conditions. It was a very courageous decision of General Eisenhower."

IN THE DARK OF night, the airborne divisions led the way by the hundreds, their formation so tight that the paratroopers risked running into one another as the fog banks grew heavier and as they began to be battered by German antiaircraft fire. Some of the planes exploded in flames. Paratrooper Robert Williams recalled that as he looked out the open door of his plane, preparing to jump, the plane to his left disintegrated in a ball of fire. The formation broke, sending many of the planes off course, and some planes came in lower than recommended for a jump. Williams jumped at six hundred feet and reported that many of his fellow paratroopers broke their legs or sprained their ankles upon landing in the flooded marshes behind the beaches. Some were tangled in trees, and one hapless para- trooper was caught on a church steeple and hung there for two hours before being captured by the Germans. The vision of an overwhelming landing force was dashed as paratroopers were strewn across Normandy. Throughout the night, in ones and twos and then in small groups, they found one another and began to steadily beat back the German resistance, capturing the town of Sainte-Mère-Église, one of their prime objectives. They had suffered heavy losses parachuting in but had mostly achieved their mission.

As dawn broke, the convoys began their surge toward the beaches. High winds and a choppy sea battered the seasick soldiers as they approached, wet and cold, the waves crashing around them. Many of the shuddering inhabitants of those craft were young men—nineteen, twenty, twenty-one years of age— who were seeing their first combat of the war in that desolate spot. Richard Fazzio, a US Navy coxswain, was in the first wave headed to Omaha Beach. As bullets began to fall around them, "I looked into the well of the boat and there was 35 soldiers in there and I don't think there was an atheist in there because every one of them was making the sign of the cross as we were going in."

The divisions headed to Utah Beach, the westernmost loca- tion, were faced with currents so strong they were pushed off course by more than a mile. Teddy Roosevelt's son Brigadier

General Theodore Roosevelt, Jr., at fifty-six the oldest man on the beach, was among the first to reach land. Seeing they were off course, he called out, "We'll start the war from here!" In fact, the mistake might have been a godsend, as there were few enemy forces at that end. By noon, they were off the beach and four miles inland.

On Gold Beach, there was heavy initial fire, although the aerial bombings had done their job of weakening resistance. An hour after landing, the British were headed inland. Canadian soldiers landing at Juno Beach were subjected to a devastating assault by Germans firing from behind bunkers, but they were quickly able to get off the beach and met little resistance as they moved into the countryside. British and Canadian soldiers landing at Sword Beach encountered little firepower but were heavily occupied in the countryside with a vigorous German assault.

The Americans who were headed to Omaha Beach encountered a more horrifying spectacle. Many who fought there have later said that the gripping, gut-wrenching, bloody opening scene of the movie *Saving Private Ryan* is entirely reflective of their experience. The beaches were heavily reinforced with stakes, barbed wire, mines, and hedgehogs—large steel contraptions that served as landing barriers—as well as concrete walls. Worse still, an unexpectedly well-armed and well-prepared German division, hunkered down on the bluff above the beach, easily picked off the first wave of infantrymen to reach the shore, cutting many of them down before they could alight from their craft. Others were swamped in the water, burdened by up to ninety pounds of arms and equipment. Guy C. Nicely, a kid seeing his first combat, later acknowledged, "We were scared to death. We figured every moment, when we went in on D-Day, that you'd be killed. . . . Twenty-six hundred men died there and a number of our boys drowned. When this tailgate went down on this LCI [landing craft], they went in over their head. I went in over my head about three times." Nicely, who was a small guy, was carrying forty-two pounds of ammunition in addition to his automatic rifle. Many others were carrying heavier loads still. Dunked in deep water, they lost their rifles and ammunition, and some lost their lives, drowned in the roiling waters.

With the front-facing troops being mowed down, "Somebody said, 'Go over the side,'" recalled Joseph L. Argenzio, "so I went over the side and I went right to the bottom. Goodbye helmet, goodbye carbine, goodbye ammunition cans." When he reached the beach, he just ran. "I zigzagged, slipping on these wet stones and tripping and falling. There were guys getting hit all around me and going down and screaming and yelling and yelling for medics. But, again, God was with me and I made it to this wall."

"It was a hot, hot, hot contest," remembered Arthur Schintzel. ". . . They [the Germans] had the advantage of height. They could look down at you. You would have trouble finding them when you looked up to search for them because the vegetation was giving them cover. It was a hot conflict. You could feel and sense the rounds going through your uniform. I took four bullet wounds that day."

Walter Halloran, a photographer who was assigned to film the landing, remembered that when they hit the beach and dropped the ramp, the German machine gun fire was "like a garden hose going back and forth"—cutting down men right to left. Many decades later, he was haunted by the order not to try to rescue anyone who fell but just to keep going so they wouldn't get jammed up. "I had to just step on, kick, push aside guys floating in the water. . . . I just ran." He shot his first film as he lay prone on the beach, filming soldiers marching toward him as one of them was killed by enemy fire.

The expected bombing support from the air did not materialize above them, due to command concerns that the bombs would take out the US troops. Furthermore, two companies of amphibious tanks, meant to support the beach landing, were prematurely launched 6,000 yards offshore and all but five of the thirty-two tanks were lost in the water, along with their men.

With the toll mounting and the survivors trapped on the beach, Omar Bradley briefly considered abandoning Omaha, which would almost certainly have meant the failure of Overlord. Only the supreme courage and tenacity of the infantrymen saved the situation. With many of their officers lying dead or wounded, they decided to move off the beach and press upward toward the German division, where they were able to overwhelm their opponents. By early afternoon, they had taken Omaha, but thousands of their brothers-in-arms lay dead on the beach and in the water.

The casualties from the Overlord launch were upward of ten thousand men, with many thousands more wounded. Victory came at a heavy price.

IN THE UNITED STATES and Great Britain, the populations were frozen in place in front of radios, listening to the breathless accounts of the invasion, some from brave reporters who had accompanied the mission. The radio reports had started in the early hours of June 6, with the BBC announcing, "D-Day has come." At 3:40 A.M., Edward R. Murrow read Eisenhower's Order of the Day, which had been delivered to the Overlord forces—his somber, resonant voice cutting through the static and filling the airwaves: "The tide has turned. The free men of the world are marching toward victory." That was followed soon after by Eisenhower's own voice, speaking to the Europeans: "People of western Europe . . . the hour of your liberation is approaching." His purpose was to instruct the French to stay safe and remain passive until told otherwise; ad hoc French uprisings would not be helpful to the grand strategy. He praised the courage of the French and told them to stay the course.

The details of the invasion were scarce in the early hours, and many of them came from the Germans themselves, who broadcast news of the invasion. Parents, wives, children, and siblings agonized, most not knowing if their loved ones were on those beaches and were even now stepping onto French soil for the fight of their lives.

Surely the most riveting report came just before 6:00 A.M., a live feed piped into the networks by George Hicks, a reporter aboard a US ship three miles from the coast. With the sound of bombs and firing in the background, he stood his ground and reported it all: "Very heavy firing now off our stern . . . fiery bursts . . . the whole seaside is covered with tracer fire . . ." until finally the sounds died down. "Well, it's quiet for a moment now," Hicks said with remarkable calm. "If you'll excuse me, I'll just take a deep breath for a moment and stop speaking." He paused until the firing started again.

In Washington, George Marshall had gone to bed early on June 5 because, as he said, "there was nothing I could do about it anymore. It was much better to get a good night's sleep and be ready for anything the morning might bring." Early the next morning, when a duty officer rushed to his home with Eisenhower's first positive report on the invasion, he was met by Katherine Marshall, who refused to wake her husband. Marshall went into the office at his usual time and didn't make any public statements.

But FDR was awake in the small hours of the night, and he

was heartened to receive Eisenhower's early report, with its premature but ultimately accurate conclusion that Overlord was a success. Throughout the day, he searched for words to convey to the American people the meaning of the moment. Rather than a speech, he chose to deliver his message over the radio in the form of a prayer. It is not an exaggeration to say that most Americans were tuned in to their radios to listen to the president's words on the evening of June 6:

> Almighty God: Our sons, pride of our nation, this day have set upon a mighty endeavor, a struggle to preserve our Republic, our religion, and our civilization, and to set free a suffering humanity.
>
> Lead them straight and true; give strength to their arms, stoutness to their hearts, steadfastness in their faith.
>
> They will need Thy blessings. Their road will be long and hard. For the enemy is strong. He may hurl back our forces. Success may not come with rushing speed, but we shall return again and again; and we know that by Thy grace, and by the righteousness of our cause, our sons will triumph.
>
> They will be sore tried, by night and by day, without rest—until the victory is won. The darkness will be rent by noise and flame. Men's souls will be shaken with the violences of war.
>
> These men are lately drawn from the ways of peace. They fight not for the lust of conquest. They fight to end conquest. They fight to liberate. They fight to let justice arise, and tolerance and good will among all Thy people. They yearn but for the end of battle, for their return to the haven of home.

Some will never return. Embrace these, Father, and receive them, Thy heroic servants, into Thy kingdom.

And for us at home—fathers, mothers, children, wives, sisters, and brothers of brave men overseas—whose thoughts and prayers are ever with them—help us, Almighty God, to rededicate ourselves in renewed faith in Thee in this hour of great sacrifice. . . .

In England, Eisenhower was single-minded on June 6, but he might have spared a thought for his son John, who was graduating from West Point that day. When John's name was called and he walked up to receive his diploma, wild cheering rose up from the cadets. Confused, his mother, Mamie, asked a reporter why they were cheering and was told about the invasion. "Why didn't someone tell me?" she asked.

In England, Churchill addressed the House of Commons with two pieces of good news. The first was the liberation of Rome, which had occurred on June 4. The second was the early success of Overlord. That afternoon he cabled Stalin:

Everything has started well. The mines, obstacles, and the land batteries have been largely overcome. The air landings were very successful, and on a large scale. Infantry landings are proceeding rapidly, and many tanks and self-propelled guns are already ashore. Weather outlook moderate to good.

He later amended that cheerful cable with a fuller account to acknowledge the "serious difficulty" encountered at Omaha Beach, although he said the losses had been fewer than expected: "We had expected to lose about ten thousand men." As it turned out, the early estimate was pretty accurate.

Stalin telegraphed a few days later, seeming exhilarated by the victory and more flowery in his prose than usual:

As is evident, the landing, conceived on a grandiose scale, has succeeded completely. My colleagues and I cannot but admit that the history of warfare knows no other like undertaking from the point of view of its scale, its vast conception, and its masterly execution. As is well known, Napoleon in his time failed ignominiously in his plan to force the Channel. The hysterical Hitler, who boasted for two years that he would effect a forcing of the Channel, was unable to make up his mind even to hint at attempting to carry out his threat. Only our Allies have succeeded in realizing with honour the grandiose plan of the forcing of the Channel. History will record this deed as an achievement of the highest order.

In light of events, the vaunted German propaganda machine seemed to miss its mark. On June 7, with the beaches held and the forces moving deeper inland, leaflets began floating to earth, designed to discourage the Allied soldiers:

ATTENTION! DANGER! WARNING! The Third Armored Division, ordered by stupid Allied High Command to break the iron ring enclosing your beachhead has been destroyed. Weary soldiers of the 115th Infantry! Your comrades lie dead in the foolish struggle against the might of the Wehrmacht! The Imperial English dream of conquering Europe is doomed.

The target audience of the fliers was not deceived. The lie was so preposterous, it was funny. At the same time, every rational man knew that there was a long fight ahead. "From the start of Overlord, we knew that we would win—but we knew it not factually but with faith," Eisenhower wrote. "When the Nazis' situation was hopeless, by any rational standard, they could still explode into fitful snatches of energy and deadliness. With the Russians on the east, and the Western Allies driving in from the other side, only in the frenzied mind of Hitler and those hypnotized by him could there have been the expectation of lightning strikes that would liberate Germany from our tightening, encircling armies." From then on, he never doubted that the Allies would be victorious. But the Germans would hold the Allies' feet to the fire every long step of the way.

Churchill, who had been itching to go to the battlefront since the planning days of Overlord, finally got his wish. On June 10, Montgomery let him know he was well enough situated that he could entertain a visit. So, accompanied by the British and US chiefs of staff, including Marshall, who had flown over, he crossed the Channel in a British destroyer and met Montgomery on the beach. After lunch at Montgomery's château, which was about five miles inland—and about three miles from the fighting—Churchill wandered around the area a bit before boarding the destroyer for home. Along the way, he witnessed British ships firing into shore at the German positions. Excited, Churchill said to Admiral Philip Vian, the ship's commander, "Since we are so near, why shouldn't we have a plug at them ourselves before we go home?"

"Certainly," Vian replied, and the ship fired its guns at the coast. Then it raced out of range, carrying the delighted and fulfilled prime minister back to the safety of England.

CHAPTER 15

FDR'S FINAL ACT

The burdens of the presidency weigh heavily on the occupant—more so in war. Every other president had served a maximum of two terms; those who had survived two terms had left the office with a stoop in their step. Now FDR was contemplating a fourth term, and he didn't look like a man who could survive it.

Even his most forgiving aides and friends could not escape the truth that at sixty-two he looked at least a decade older. He was unwell after Tehran, suffering a bronchial infection, but given his sallow face and rapid weight loss, some worried that the problem was much greater.

Grace Tully sadly recalled:

> I found the Boss occasionally nodding over his mail or dozing a moment during dictation. At first I was surprised but I considered it merely a fatigue of the moment. He would grin in slight embarrassment as he caught himself and there was no diminution of clarity or sparkle in his words or in his thoughts. But as it began to occur with increasing frequency I became seriously alarmed. It was evident that the grind was becoming too severe for him.

Steve Early was constantly fielding press questions about the president's health, but despite his own concerns he had nothing to tell them. Predictably, the press viewed Dr. McIntyre with suspicion and whispered about a cover-up—or at the very least incompetence. Perhaps Dr. McIntyre, who specialized in nose and throat medicine, was not up to the task of caring for a president whose ailments seemed well beyond sinus troubles and a propensity to colds and flu.

On March 27, FDR went quietly to Bethesda Naval Hospital. There he was examined by Dr. Howard Bruenn, a young navy cardiologist, who came away from the examination with a troubling list of ailments, including gallstones, an enlarged heart, high blood pressure, and hypertensive heart disease.

Bruenn proposed a rigorous protocol that would have had FDR laid up for months. McIntyre said there was little chance that the president would follow it. The word passed on to the nation was that he just had a bad cold, which was the truth but hardly the *whole* truth.

Bruenn would remain near FDR after that, assisting Dr. McIntyre in trying to rein in a very resistant patient and not often succeeding. In addition to his physical ills, FDR had a chronic case of denial about his condition.

FDR was also engaged in a deception of a different sort: his renewed relationship with Lucy Mercer. After Eleanor had discovered their affair in 1918, Lucy had left town and become governess to a wealthy New York widower, Winthrop Rutherfurd, who had six children. Although Rutherfurd was almost thirty years her senior, Lucy had married him in 1920, and they had one child of their own. By all accounts, the marriage was a good one, but Lucy and the president had kept up a correspondence. Lucy's first secret visit to the White House occurred in 1941 under the name "Mrs. Johnson."

After Rutherfurd died in 1944 following a long illness, Lucy's relationship with the president grew closer, abetted by

FDR's friends and his daughter, Anna, who had remained at the White House after the Tehran Conference. Anna agonized over keeping such an important secret from her mother, but she concluded that her father needed the easy companionship of Lucy, knowing that her mother was incapable of offering the same form of quiet, unfettered devotion. Eleanor, with her mind wrapped around the nation's problems and her own quest for independence, more often was a stressor than a stress reliever, peppering her husband with demands and passionate monologues about her favorite causes.

Daisy Suckley, who also thought of herself as an emotional gatekeeper for FDR, might have felt a bit sidelined by Lucy, but she recognized the greater good. "She & I have one very big thing in common: our unselfish devotion to F.," she wrote in her diary.

ONCE AGAIN, FDR HAD delayed announcing his decision about whether he would run for another term until the party elders were as good as banging their heads against the walls in frustration. Most people expected him to run, in spite of his health, because of the war. "Mr. Roosevelt did not want to run for a fourth term," UP's Merriman Smith accurately put it. "Age was beginning to tell on him. He had lost much of his vitality. The specter of illness was increasingly visible. But it was a thing he had to do. He was like a fire horse refusing to go to pasture." When he finally announced that he was running, no one was surprised.

In June, after another medical examination, McIntyre told the press that the president was in good condition for a man his age and termed his checkup "splendid." The press was not assuaged. Should they believe McIntyre or their own eyes?

At their convention in Chicago at the end of June, the Republicans nominated moderate New York governor Thomas Dewey, twenty years Roosevelt's junior, whose relative youth was thought to be a counterbalance to Roosevelt. The problem was that despite his age, he wasn't a particularly appealing candidate. "The man had one of the coldest personalities of anyone who had ever contemplated a run for the American presidency," his biographer David M. Jordan wrote. That they were both New Yorkers was about the only thing the two men had in common. Although he was thought to be a good governor, Dewey also had the significant challenge of running against a war president while the war was going well. It was an almost insurmountable feat to convince Americans that they should bring in a new team to lead the battle, led by a man with no foreign policy experience. If the nation had not been at war, Dewey's attacks on the New Deal might have been effective, but in talking about war policy he was hamstrung.

The Democratic National Convention opened in Chicago on July 19. With FDR confirmed to run for a fourth term, the only remaining question was who his vice president would be. FDR would have liked to keep Henry Wallace, but he was idealistically out of sync with the party—too liberal, too pro-Soviet, and generally ineffectual. Party leaders urged FDR to choose someone more in line with his priorities. Unspoken was the understanding that Roosevelt's fourth-term vice president might by default become president.

Facing the real danger of having Wallace's candidacy fail at the convention, Roosevelt began considering other options. Robert Hannegan, the chairman of the Democratic National Committee, suggested two names: Supreme Court justice William O. Douglas and Missouri senator Harry S. Truman. Roosevelt agreed to accept either of the two and wrote a note to

Hannegan to that effect. In his note, he put Douglas's name first and Truman's second, but at the last minute he asked Tully to retype the letter and switch the names: Truman first and Douglas second. However, he also said he had no objection to Wallace putting his name before the convention. In truth, FDR barely knew Truman, who later complained that the White House had not been very good about returning his calls when he was in the Senate.

Hearing that his name was in contention, Truman wanted nothing to do with it. "The Vice President simply presides over the Senate and sits around hoping for a funeral," he told a friend derisively. Even when people mentioned FDR's health and suggested that the vice presidency was a surer path to the highest office, Truman wasn't interested. He wrote to his daughter, Margaret, "1600 Pennsylvania is a nice address but I'd rather not move in through the back door—or any other door at sixty."

By the time of the convention, with seven other candidates of varying strengths throwing their hats in the ring, Truman didn't object to being nominated. It soon became clear that the real contest was between Wallace and Truman. On the first ballot, Wallace received over one hundred votes more than Truman. On the second ballot, Truman came out slightly ahead, and then, with fierce lobbying from Hannegan and others, most of the delegates fell into line behind him and he won the nomination with nearly unanimous support. Soon after the convention, he was invited to the White House for a lunch of sardines on toast with the president. They discussed nothing of consequence. They never would. Truman later said that he and FDR had only two meetings and never discussed the war plans or the existence of the atom bomb.

James Farley, having resigned his post as New York State Democratic Committee chairman, watched the campaign from the sidelines with dismay. He thought the party was being unfaithful to its principles by allowing Roosevelt to run for a fourth term. "Anyone with a grain of common sense would surely realize from the appearance of the President that he is not a well man and there is not a chance in the world for him to carry on four years more and face the problems that a President will have before him; he just can't survive another presidential term," he wrote. Farley thought that Democratic politicians were taking the easy way out, protecting their own hides at the expense of the national good. The elevation of one man to the level of savior was not new to the Republic, but neither was it a healthy impulse.

At the same time, if it was believed that FDR wouldn't survive another term and his vice president would become president during the next four years, Truman might not have been the best choice. He'd had very little to do with foreign policy in his career, except for one careless and damning statement he'd made after Germany had invaded the Soviet Union in 1941: "If we see that Germany is winning we ought to help Russia and if Russia is winning we ought to help Germany, and that way let them kill as many as possible, although I don't want to see Hitler victorious under any circumstances. Neither of them thinks anything of their pledged word."

As the war in Europe approached its endgame, FDR was anxious to arrange a second summit with Churchill and Stalin to discuss their vision for the postwar order. He wrote Stalin in July, "Things are moving so fast and so successfully that I feel there should be a meeting between you, Mr. Churchill and me in the reasonably near future." He suggested September, perhaps in northern Scotland. Throughout 1944, they engaged in the familiar dance of trying to convince Stalin to leave the Soviet Union for a conference. There would be no opportunity that year, although Churchill would travel to Moscow and

Churchill and Roosevelt would again meet in Quebec—neither meeting accomplishing much without all three in attendance.

As FDR engaged in the balancing act of being both a war president and a candidate, he seemed to be trying to defy his human condition and transcend the travails of war. "The politicians wanted me to conduct the coming campaign as commander-in-chief rather than as a Democratic candidate for president," he told Agent Mike Reilly. "I don't feel the same way about it." Although his war responsibilities didn't allow him to campaign as fully as he had in the past, he craved contact with the people. He longed to show them that he was up to the task ahead.

After a trip to Pearl Harbor in August aboard the USS *Baltimore*, where he met with General MacArthur about the progress of the Pacific War, he took a side trip to the Aleutians, lunching with enlisted men in a Quonset hut, where the menu was standard GI rations.

FDR planned to travel through Seattle after he left the Aleutians, and he asked Reilly if there was a baseball park where he could give a speech. There was, Reilly told him, but he discouraged it because it would have to be publicized while the president was traveling in seas hiding Japanese subs. The alternative location was the Bremerton Navy Yard.

By all accounts, his speech there was disastrous. For some reason, he decided to speak standing, wearing his leg braces, which he rarely did anymore. Propped behind a podium on the deck of a destroyer, his discomfort was apparent, and his shrunken form more noticeable to the cameras. He looked terrible, and the radio pickup was awful. Playing the speech back, Rigdon found that the president sounded "as if he was mumbling some words, dropping syllables from others, and talking as if his mouth was full of cotton." The physical weakness he had worked so hard to hide from the public was on full display.

On October 21, FDR and Eleanor spent a day driving through four of New York City's boroughs in an open car, despite a driving rain and high winds. Stopping at Ebbets Field, the home of the Brooklyn Dodgers, where he rode onto the field and then stood behind a lectern strapped into his leg braces, he said, "I have never been to Ebbets Field before, but I have rooted for the Dodgers. And I hope to come back some day and see them play."

At the end of the long day, FDR was drenched but grinning. In the Bronx, Reilly saw someone throw an object from a window, aiming directly at them. As it landed, he knocked it down. "It was a well-wrapped ham sandwich."

Roosevelt ended the tour chilled to the bone. "I was really worried about him that day," Eleanor wrote, "but instead of being completely exhausted he was exhilarated." She was in denial as well. When people have something to prove, they can get reckless, and a day in the rain seemed nothing to worry about. Were voters convinced that the president was in fighting form? Or had the maneuver felt desperate?

Visiting Washington before the election, Harriman stepped outside his role to broadcast an appeal on FDR's behalf: "If the people of this country fail to re-elect Roosevelt, doubt and suspicion of our intent cannot fail to be engendered," he said solemnly. He challenged Dewey's isolationist views, calling them alienating principles that would deal a blow to the postwar collaboration that was the basis of Roosevelt's hard work with Churchill and Stalin.

On election day Roosevelt prevailed, but not with the hoped-for landslide. Although he received 432 electoral votes to Dewey's 99, the popular vote margin was only a little over three and a half million. That night, knowing it would be his last election, he greeted neighbors and supporters on his front porch, sentimentally reminiscing about his childhood:

> I remember my first torchlight parade right here in 1892—Cleveland's election. And I was asleep, or supposedly asleep, right up in this window, a little room at the head of the stairs; and I was listening, and I didn't know what was the matter—a queer light outside the window, with people coming up on farm wagons— before the days of the automobile. . . .
>
> And I got up and appeared down here in an old-fashioned nightgown of some kind, on this porch, and I wrapped up in an old Buffalo robe that came out of a wagon. And I had a perfectly grand evening.

The inauguration was a modest affair, held on the South Portico of the White House. The previous inauguration had taken place before the United States had entered the war. Now FDR had neither the time nor the energy to devote himself to an elaborate event. "Dog catchers have taken office with more pomp and ceremony," Reilly observed. There was some concern that perhaps the president didn't have the strength for it. The previous day, when he had met with the press, telling them "The first twelve years were the hardest," he had looked tired. At the cabinet meeting that day, Frances Perkins thought "his face looked thin, his color was gray, and his eyes were dull. I think everyone in the room privately had a feeling that we must not tire him."

After standing outside in the bitter cold to take his oath, FDR stopped in the Green Room with James. He was thoroughly chilled and confessed that he was experiencing stabbing chest pains. He implored his son, "Jimmy, I can't take this unless you get me a stiff drink—you'd better make it straight." James poured him a tumbler of whiskey, which he drank right down as if it were medicine. "In all my life I had never seen Father take a drink in that manner," James recalled. But it restored him. Soon FDR joined the reception as if nothing were wrong.

Two days later, under cover of secrecy, he embarked upon an ambitious journey to the Crimea for a second conference with Churchill and Stalin, code-named Eureka II. There might have been some cause for alarm about the president's ability to withstand such a trip. He looked shrunken and wan, but his daughter, Anna, who accompanied him, and Dr. McIntyre insisted his condition was no more serious than a combined sinus infection and a cold.

BY THE FALL, THERE had been some visible cracks in the coalition. In a top secret message to Harry Hopkins, Harriman relayed news of a disturbing debate in the Soviet Union over relations with the Allies. "I have been conscious since early in the year of a division among Stalin's advisors on the question of cooperation with us," Harriman wrote. "It is now my feeling that those who oppose the kind of cooperation we expect have recently been getting their way and the policy appears to be crystallizing to force us and the British to accept all Soviet policies backed by the strength and prestige of the Red Army."

Without Stalin, the hastily arranged Quebec conference with Churchill in September had settled little, and to complicate matters, the impatient prime minister had arranged to visit Moscow alone, hoping to win concessions from Stalin about the future of eastern Europe. Hopkins was worried. Churchill could not speak for the United States, and he hoped he wouldn't try. FDR wasn't willing to make a stink about it, but he did write Stalin, "I am firmly convinced that the three of us, and only the three of us, can find the solution to the still unresolved questions."

Stalin replied that Roosevelt's message puzzled him. He'd assumed that Churchill's visit had been to discuss the agreements reached at Quebec. In that way, he was subtly trying to drive a wedge between Roosevelt and Churchill.

In Moscow, Churchill shared with Stalin his own plan— definitely not FDR approved—for the future of eastern Europe, which amounted to a division of spoils between Great Britain (and presumably the United States) and the Soviets:

Romania: 90 percent Soviet, 10 percent Great Britain
Bulgaria: 75 percent Soviet, 25 percent Great Britain
Yugoslavia: 50/50
Hungary: 50/50
Greece: 90 percent Great Britain, 10 percent Soviet

Edward Stettinius, a former undersecretary of state, who had replaced an ailing Cordell Hull as secretary in December 1944, was concerned about the Soviets and British tinkering with eastern Europe and felt it made the necessity of a tripartite conference all the more urgent. "We specifically desired a pledge by the Soviet Union and Great Britain that in liberated Europe free elections would be held and governments representative of the people would be established," he wrote.

Knowing that Stalin would not be willing to go far afield for their next meeting, Roosevelt proposed that they meet somewhere in the Crimea—an even longer journey than that to Tehran. Once again, the site would be under Soviet control. Stalin agreed, and FDR took the distant location in stride. "Well, you know," he told Elliott, "it's hard to refuse. He *is* in charge of the Red Army, and the Red Army *is* on the go."

By early 1945, the war on the eastern front was all but over, with Soviet forces moving west to join the Allies in Europe. Overlord had succeeded beyond all expectations, putting the Germans permanently on the defensive. France was liberated in August. Only one more major battle, a December conflict in the Ardennes region of Belgium, followed Overlord. Once the Germans were beaten back there, the path was open for a direct assault on Germany.

The Japanese had suffered a series of crushing defeats in late 1944, and US forces under the command of General MacArthur were poised to defeat them at Iwo Jima and Okinawa, before the US forces made their way into Japan. FDR hoped that the Soviets would soon join the Pacific War, hastening its end.

The Allied Powers were convinced that the war was effectively won, so, unlike at Tehran, the conference at Yalta would not focus as much on winning the war as on building the peace.

On January 22, FDR boarded the USS *Quincy* for the long journey, accompanied by Admiral Leahy and Stettinius. Hopkins, who was in Europe and London, would travel with Churchill. Once again Eleanor had wanted to go, but her husband told her that she would generate too much fuss and chose instead to take Anna. In addition to Anna, there would be other women present: Harriman's daughter Kathleen and Churchill's daughter Sarah.

Churchill had convinced FDR to stop in Malta first for a short meeting on military strategy before flying on to the Crimea. Elated to have a chance to make his case before meeting with Stalin, Churchill cabled FDR, "I shall be waiting on the quay. No more let us falter. From Malta to Yalta! Let nobody alter!"

Despite the rousing good cheer, they would, in a sense, limp into the conference. Churchill was running a fever, Hopkins was nearly on his back with severe colitis, and FDR looked so thin and ill that everyone who saw him was alarmed. They were a motley crew, yet they were in high spirits, their hopes for the conference and the future of the world serving as bracing medicine for their ills.

Once Yalta had been a glamorous place, the favored vacation spot of Tsar Nicholas II; it had then become a rest and recreation spot for the Russians until the Nazis had occupied it in 1941. The Russians had recaptured Yalta in 1944, but it was nearly in ruins. Churchill, for one, thought it was a grim location for the conference. On the *Quincy*, FDR received a radio message from the prime minister, stating "if we had spent ten years on research, we could not have found a worse place in the world than Yalta . . . good [only] for typhus and deadly lice which thrive in those parts."

It was also very inconvenient. Since the nearest airfield at Saki was ninety miles away, the original plan had been to take Roosevelt all the way to Yalta by ship across the Black Sea.

"You can't," the NKVD chief told Reilly.

"Why?"

"Mines," he replied.

"How many?"

"Who knows," he said. "The Germans put them there. They didn't leave a map."

So FDR flew from Malta into Saki and then drove to Yalta. Along the way, he was shocked by the destruction. As he would later describe it to Congress:

I saw the kind of reckless, senseless fury, the terrible destruction that comes out of German militarism. Yalta, on the Black Sea, had no military significance of any kind. It had no defenses.

Before the last war, it had been a resort for people like the Czars and princes and for the aristocracy of Russia—and the hangers-on. However, after the Red Revolution, and until the attack on the Soviet Union by Hitler, the palaces and the villas of Yalta had been used as a rest and recreation center by the Russian people.

The Nazi officers took these former palaces and villas—took them over for their own use . . . and when the Red Army forced the Nazis out of the Crimea—almost just a year ago—all of these villas were looted by the Nazis, and then nearly all of them were destroyed by bombs placed on the inside. And even the humblest of the homes of Yalta were not spared.

There was little left of it except blank walls, ruins, destruction and desolation.

The Livadia Palace, once the summer home of the tsar, where the Americans would be staying and the conference meetings were to be held, had likewise been ravaged and looted by the Germans as they had made their exit. When Roosevelt arrived there, he was impressed to see that the Russians had fixed the place up, and when he saw his Filipino stewards bustling about, he said with a twinkle in his eye, "I can't understand Winston's concern. This place has all the comforts of home." Even his bedroom, which used to be the tsar's, had been restored to its former elegance.

Stalin, traveling most of the journey by armored train, arrived a day later. Birse and Bohlen were on hand to continue their stewardship as translators, but as was true in Tehran, there was no official stenography of the conference. The minutes, written by Bohlen and the chiefs of staff, were mostly dry third-person accounts, giving no sense of the drama at the table. Fortunately, other observers, such as James Byrnes, the American director of the office of war mobilization, Harriman, and Stettinius produced their own accounts. As did Hopkins; although he'd spent much of the conference sick in bed, he managed to make his voice heard.

When Roosevelt and Stalin first met privately at Livadia Palace before the conference, Roosevelt described his dismay at the devastation he had witnessed while driving through the Crimea. As a result, he said, he was more bloodthirsty toward the Germans than he had been a year ago. Stalin agreed with the sentiment, saying that everyone was more bloodthirsty, because of the "honest blood shed" in fighting the Germans.

Dinner the first evening was hosted by FDR and included a hearty spread of American and Russian foods—fried chicken and caviar along with wine, vodka, and champagne. During dinner, a postwar conversation led to a spat about who should oversee the peace process. Roosevelt and Stalin thought that the peace should be written by the Three Powers represented at the table. Churchill thought the smaller nations should have a say. "The eagle should permit the small birds to sing and care not wherefor they sang," he recited. Despite his status as the head of a colonialist power, he would continue to argue on behalf of smaller nations.

Going in, the goals of the Big Three were less a common cause and more an advocacy mission—each wanting the others to make agreements that suited its own postwar needs. For Churchill, that meant maintaining the British Empire and preventing a strong nation from taking hold in continental Europe. For Stalin, it meant strengthening Soviet control in the east and having a presence in Europe that would ensure Germany's inability to reconstitute itself. For Roosevelt, it meant convincing Stalin to set a date for joining the war against Japan and solidifying plans for an international organization that would protect the peace in the future.

Once again, Stalin came out strongly for the complete dismemberment of Germany and argued that a high percentage of its resources (perhaps $10 billion) should go into reparations to the nations it had decimated—foremost among them the Soviet Union. He asked his deputy commissar for foreign affairs, Ivan Maisky, to give a report, with demands that Churchill thought were crippling. Neither Great Britain nor the United States wanted reparations.

"If I could see any benefit in reparations I would be glad to have them but I am very doubtful," Churchill said. "Other countries also have suffered great devastation—France, Belgium, Norway. We must also consider the phantom of a starving Germany and who is going to pay for that."

Churchill added, "If our treatment of Germany's internal economy is such as to leave eighty million people virtually starving, are we to sit still and say, 'it serves you right,' or will we be required to keep them alive . . . If you have a horse and you want him to pull the wagon you have to provide him with a certain amount of corn—or at least hay."

"But the horse must not kick you," Maisky replied.

"If you have a motorcar you must give it a certain amount of petrol," Churchill said, switching metaphors.

Roosevelt, always the arbitrator, tried to soothe Churchill, saying that of course the American people did not want the Germans to starve, but neither did they want them to have a higher standard of living than other states, such as the Soviet Republic. "All I can say is that we will do the best we can in an extremely bad situation."

Hopkins passed a note to Roosevelt: "The Russians have given in so much . . . that I don't think we should let them down. Let the British disagree if they want to and continue their disagreement in Moscow. Simply say it is all referred to the Reparations Commission with the minutes to show that the British disagree about any mention of the 10 billion." However, after the war, Stalin would take the $10 billion as a firm promise.

A discussion about which nations should be invited to participate in the postwar Security Council sparked a strong reaction from Stalin, who felt that only those nations who were allied with the cause should be invited. "I have a list of the states that declared war on Germany," he said. "It means that they become future members of the Assembly." But airing his sense of grievance, he added that ten of them (mostly from South America) had no diplomatic relations with the Soviet Union. "How is it possible to build up international security with states that have no diplomatic relations with us at all?"

FDR tried to ease his concerns. "I think most of them would like to establish diplomatic relations with the Soviet Union," he said. "They just have not got around to it yet." He added that the easiest way to establish diplomatic relations was to invite them. However, a condition of the invitation was that they had declared war.

"When should they act?" Marshall asked.

"Right away," FDR said. "Put a time limit on them."

"Say the first of March."

"All right," the president agreed. "The first of March."

In discussions about France, Churchill once again argued fiercely that France should be made a part of the postwar control machinery. Stalin balked. "I agree that the French should be great and strong but we cannot forget that in this war France opened the gates to the enemy. This is a fact. We would not have had so many losses and destruction in this war if the French had not opened the gates to the enemy. The control and administration of Germany must be only for those powers standing firmly against her from the beginning and so far France does not belong to this group."

Churchill defended France. (As Hopkins observed, "Winston and Eden fought like tigers for France" at Yalta.) He acknowledged that every nation had difficulties at the beginning of the war—not mentioning the burden his own nation had carried virtually alone—and France went down before the new tanks were used. But he pointed out that France was Germany's most important neighbor. He added that the British public would not understand if decisions vital to France were being made with regard to Germany over France's head.

Roosevelt leaned toward Stalin's position, but in the course of the conference he changed his mind and decided to side with Churchill. This time it was Stalin who gave in and agreed to put France onto the control council. But everyone realized that it would be difficult to deal with de Gaulle. The writing was already on the wall when de Gaulle canceled a previously scheduled meeting with FDR in Algiers on his way home, sending word that it wasn't convenient for him.

But it was the Polish question that consumed much of the conference. The existing temporary government in Lublin was essentially a pro-Soviet organization, while the Soviet Union had broken off relations with the government in exile in London and was openly attacking its loyal followers in the resistance movement. Stalin heaped praise on the Lublin government, which he said was embraced by most of Poland, although that was hardly the case. In his arguments, the outlines of future Soviet policy were becoming clear.

"Britain declared war on Germany in order that Poland should be free and sovereign," Churchill argued, reprising the discussion that had grown heated in Tehran. "Everyone knows what a terrible risk we took and how nearly it cost us our life in the world, not only as an empire but as a nation. Our interest in Poland is one of honor. Having drawn the sword on behalf of Poland against Hitler's brutal attack, we could never be content with any solution that did not leave Poland a free and independent sovereign state."

Stalin countered, "For the Russian people the question of Poland is not only a question of honor but also of security . . . of life and death for the Soviet state." But the border question was no longer front and center. "I am more interested in the question of Poland's sovereign independence and freedom than in particular frontier lines," Churchill said. "I want the Poles to have a home in Europe and to be free to live their own life there."

Perhaps, Churchill suggested, the Big Three should create the terms for a new Polish government. Stalin bristled. "They all say that I am a dictator but I have enough democratic feeling not to set up a Polish government without Poles." A noble sentiment, but it was plain that Stalin meant the Lublin government, not the government in exile. Roosevelt urged the organization of a provisional government, which would hold free elections as soon as possible.

"How long will it take you to hold free elections?" Roosevelt asked.

Molotov replied, "Within a month's time."

The election would actually take place twenty-three months later, and it could hardly be called free, as the Soviet Union was in full control. At the conference the American position was very strong that Poles should have self-determination. For his part, Churchill was suspicious about Stalin's declarations because the Western Allies didn't really know what was going on inside Poland, and couldn't judge Stalin's claims for themselves. As they battled over the terminology of the conference's declaration on Poland, Roosevelt interjected that he wanted the Polish election to be "beyond question, like Caesar's wife . . . They said she was pure."

Stalin replied, "They said that about her but she had her sins."

His thoughts on the six million Polish Americans back home, FDR restated his firm position that the elections must be beyond reproach, so that the Polish people would not question them. As they battled over the language, Leahy felt discouraged. "I had a distinct feeling that Poland was going to be treated very badly from our point of view, although Russia would be able to claim (and did) that the reorganized Polish regime was a self-formed republican government," he wrote later. He warned Roosevelt, "Mr. President, this is so elastic that the Russians can stretch it all the way from Yalta to Washington without ever technically breaking it."

"I know, Bill, I know it," Roosevelt replied. "But it's the best I can do for Poland at this time."

The question of votes in the General Assembly was also difficult to resolve. Great Britain had six votes, representing its territories, and in that spirit, the Soviet Union was asking for sixteen, which were ultimately whittled down to three, to include Soviet Ukraine and Soviet White Russia. That would put the United States at a disadvantage, though Stalin magnanimously offered to give the United States two extra seats, a blatantly unsupportable idea. Roosevelt knew that Congress would howl over the extra seats for the Soviets, and he deliberately left it out of his report when he returned home.

In a private meeting, Roosevelt finally had a chance to talk to Stalin about Japan. Stalin had always said he would join the war against Japan once the Allies had achieved victory in Europe. That now seemed imminent, but Stalin was hedging. He told FDR that his people would not understand why the Soviet Union should go to war with a nation with which they had no direct conflict. FDR dangled the opportunity for the Soviets to gain territory from Japanese conquests, and Stalin demurred, saying he only wanted to have returned to Russia what the Japanese had taken from them. However, he actually wanted much more. For one thing, he asked for the use of the Manchurian Railroad, which was owned by the Chinese, a condition FDR could not agree to until he spoke with Chiang Kai-shek. However, the Soviet final agreement to join the war was conditioned in part on this.

Afterward, when the Soviets did enter the war with Japan, they took control of several islands they had no right to. In the end, the Soviets reaped the benefits of victory over Japan, although it's arguable that they were really needed to win the war, given the atom bomb.

Stalin and Churchill both envisioned a world shaped largely in their own prewar image: Great Britain with its empire and the Soviet Union with its tight control of a constellation of nations. Free of the baggage of imperialism (be it benevolent or not), Roosevelt held a different vision: a world beyond colonial "ownership" in which independent states would be allowed to thrive, encouraged by a peacekeeping organization that would ensure harmony in the world.

Privately, he begrudged Churchill his desire to protect colonial rule. American boys were not dying for the sake of the British Empire! Nor were they dying so the Soviet Union could retain its grip on the east. They were dying for freedom, for the dismantlement of imperial rule, for the emergence of opportunity and prosperity in every corner of the world.

They agreed that the first meeting of the United Nations

would be held as soon as possible and debated back and forth about a location. Stettinius recommended San Francisco, the others agreed, and the date was set for April 25.

Stettinius recalled that the spirit of the meeting was cooperative. "Stalin impressed me as a man with a fine sense of humor," he wrote. "At the same time one received an impression of power and ruthlessness along with his humor . . . I noticed that the other members of the Soviet delegation would change their minds perfectly unashamedly whenever Marshal Stalin changed his."

At a dinner hosted by Stalin, everyone was in a good mood, and the toasts were more elaborate and flattering than ever, although now, in this lengthy second conference, the flowery words were beginning to sound hollow.

"History has recorded many meetings of statesmen following a war," Stalin said in one toast. "When the guns fall silent, the war seems to have made these leaders wise, and they tell each other they want to live in peace. But then, after a little while, despite all their mutual assurances, another war breaks out. Why is this? It is because some of them change their attitudes after they have achieved peace. We must try to see that doesn't happen to us in the future." Roosevelt added that he thought of the three nations as a family. Churchill might have remembered the times Roosevelt had said the same thing about the two of them, and thought that Uncle Joe wasn't exactly a reliably loyal family member.

During the many toasts, Leahy grew concerned as he watched FDR's daughter, Anna, down drink after drink—until she assured him that she was drinking ginger ale, not vodka. She was thoroughly enjoying her place at the center of the action. She saw the ways that beneath the surface, the true nature of the Russians was on display. On a walk one morning, accompanied by an English-speaking Russian secret service agent, Anna came upon a group of Russian children. She reached into her bag and handed them American chocolate bars. The agent quickly collected the chocolate and gave it back to Anna. "They have enough food," he said. "We do not want the American lady to think that they lack." The Russians always had something to prove.

Churchill hosted dinner at his villa at Voronstov on the final night of the conference. The mood among the Americans was exultant. "We really believed in our hearts that this was the dawn of the new day we had all been praying for and talking about for so many years," Hopkins told Sherwood. "We were absolutely certain that we had won the first great victory of the peace." Stettinius called the conference "a diplomatic triumph."

However, the British did not share the happy feelings. "It is the story of Teheran all over again," Churchill's close aide Lord Moran wrote bitterly. "Stalin fights for and gets what he wants. . . . Only a solid understanding between the democracies could have kept Stalin's appetite under control. The P.M. has seen that for some time, but the President's eyes are closed. What is more remarkable—for Roosevelt is a sick man—the Americans round him do not seem to realize how the President has split the democracies and handcuffed the P.M. in his fight to stem Communism."

As they left the conference, Hopkins, who had been in and out of bed for the last eight days, told the president he was too ill to make the trip back across the ocean and would be leaving the ship in Algiers so he could rest and recover. At first FDR didn't believe him—he'd always rallied before—and even sent Anna to beg him to stay aboard. He needed Hopkins to help him with the speech he planned to give to Congress on his return. But Hopkins told Anna, "I am too sick to work. I mean it. . . ." FDR let him go, but instead of feeling compassion and concern for his devoted old friend, he had no room in his heart. He resented Hopkins for leaving him and bade him a curt farewell. They would never see each other again.

Back in New York, Suckley was desperately worried about FDR's health. She thought he looked quite ill in photos. But when he wrote to her at the end of the conference, he was full of good cheer:

> We got away safely from the Crimea, flew to the Canal & saw King Farouk, then emperor Haile Selassie, & the next day, King Ibn Saud of Arabia with his whole court, slaves (black), taster, astrologer, & 8 live sheep. Whole party was a scream! Then, the way back I saw WSC to say goodbye. All goes well, but I still need sleep.

The trip across the ocean was far from relaxing. Along the way, FDR's close friend and military aide, Pa Watson, suffered a stroke and died on board. Hearing about Watson's death, Tully remembered a conversation she'd had with FDR some months earlier. "Grace," he'd said, "if anything should happen to me while I'm at sea, I want to be buried at sea. You know, it has always seemed like home to me."

CHAPTER 16

THE WORLD HE LEFT BEHIND

On March 1, Roosevelt rolled into Congress to report on the Yalta Conference. "I hope that you will pardon me for this unusual posture of sitting down during the presentation of what I want to say," he said in a rare reference to his infirmity, "but I know that you will realize that it makes it a lot easier for me not to have to carry about ten pounds of steel around on the bottom of my legs, and also because of the fact that I have just completed a fourteen-thousand-mile trip." Many in the audience were shocked to see Roosevelt's appearance—his face was like a death mask, the skin on his cheeks stretched and pale, and his body shrunken and bent. But Roosevelt didn't seem aware of his ailments. He joked that although he had not been ill a single day of the trip, he had returned to Washington to read press reports of his impending demise.

It was a grand speech and quite lengthy, his voice rising to the occasion his body could no longer manage. He spoke glowingly of the continued collaboration of the three nations:

> Of course, we know that it was Hitler's hope—and the German war lords'—that we would not agree, that some slight crack might appear in the solid wall of Allied unity, a crack that would give him and his fellow gang-

sters one last hope of escaping their just doom. That is the objective for which his propaganda machine has been working for many months. But Hitler has failed.

A rousing ovation greeted Roosevelt's words. For once Americans could feel victory in their grasp. Roosevelt was consumed with the next stage in the Big Three partnership: the time after the war. He had accepted an invitation from Churchill for him and Eleanor to visit the prime minister in London in May, and arrangements were under way for him to attend the first UN conference in San Francisco in late April.

He was full of plans, but he was worn out. When Suckley saw him during those weeks, he looked "so tired that every word seems to be an effort."

Needing a rest, he left for Warm Springs on March 29. Suckley and Tully accompanied him, along with his cousin Laura Delano and Dr. Bruenn. Lucy would join them later. Roosevelt was taking some of the burdens of office with him, as presidents always do, but he hoped that the mood of his retreat would put his mind at ease and help him recover. Eleanor remained behind in Washington, her instincts not calibrated to her husband's desperate state. In fact, one evening she called him and kept him on the phone for nearly an hour with entreaties on behalf of Yugoslavian partisans, for whom he could do little. Dr. Bruenn said the president's blood pressure had risen fifty points in the course of the call.

This time, Warm Springs did not offer him its usual solace. The aftermath of Yalta was complicated by unresolved tensions among the principals, especially now that the European war was drawing to an end. Things seemed to be unraveling. State Department officials speculated that Stalin had received heavy blowback from the Politburo for agreements made at the conference, and his mood of cooperation had changed. At Warm Springs, FDR received an irate message from Stalin claiming that Russian intelligence had picked up signs that the United States was trying to make a separate peace with Germans in Switzerland. It was outrageous, he raged, that Americans would betray the common agreement and allow one arm of Germany to make a deal for itself while others continued fighting.

FDR responded that it simply wasn't true. "I am certain that there were no negotiations in Bern at any time," he wrote, "and I feel that your information to that effect must have come from German sources which have made persistent efforts to create dissension between us to escape in some measure responsibility for their war crimes." He concluded the telegram emotionally: "Frankly I cannot avoid a feeling of bitter resentment toward your informers, whoever they are, for such vile misrepresentations of my actions or those of my trusted subordinates."

Stalin was partly mollified. "I have never doubted your integrity or trustworthiness," he wrote, although he had, and he did. And FDR had reason to doubt Stalin's. Even then, in the early days after Yalta, the Soviets were making a mockery of the agreement, brutally disbanding the Polish underground and setting the stage for rigged elections. Roosevelt could only hope those matters would be settled in San Francisco. At Warm Springs, he was drafting a Jefferson's Day speech, in which he would outline the new mission: "Let me assure you that my hand is the steadier for the work that is to be done, that I move more firmly into the task, knowing that you—millions and millions of you—are joined with me in the resolve to make this work endure."

Lucy arrived on April 9, and that eased FDR's mind. Lucy was attentive and sweet. She had nursed her own husband through his illness, and she knew just the right note to strike.

In the glow of her adoration, Roosevelt immediately felt better. She told him she thought he looked handsome and strong. Suckley may or may not have been glad to have Lucy there; she wrote in her diary, a bit sharply, "Lucy is such a lovely person, but she seems so very immature, like a character out of a book." By then Suckley had taken on the role of an overseeing matron, watching over Roosevelt's diet and pressing him regularly to drink cups of gruel, intended to help him put on weight.

Thursday, April 12, was a warm, sunny day. FDR woke with a headache and a stiff neck, which he eased with a hot-water bottle. Merriman Smith, who was camped with the press nearby, planned a barbecue for 4:00 that afternoon, and the president had accepted an invitation to attend.

Lucy had commissioned her friend the Russian American portrait artist Elizabeth Shoumatoff to paint a portrait of the president, and he was sitting for it that day. He emerged well dressed in a double-breasted gray suit and crimson tie, a cape arranged over his thin shoulders to give him the appearance of heft. He was smiling and seemed happy. In fact, for the first time in a long time he looked well. Shoumatoff was so struck by the difference from the previous day that she exclaimed, "Mr. President, you look so much better than yesterday, I am glad I did not start working before today."

At 1:00, as the valet began setting the table for lunch, Roosevelt told Shoumatoff they had only fifteen minutes remaining. Suddenly, at 1:15, Suckley, who was crocheting in the corner, looked up to see the president swipe at his forehead and bend over; she thought he'd dropped his cigarettes. He said, "I have a terrific pain in the back of my head." Then he slumped forward, unconscious.

Bruenn rushed in to examine the president, and together they lifted him onto a bed. "I was cold as ice in my heart, cold

& precise in my voice," Suckley remembered. "I opened his collar & tie & and held up the left side of his pillow, rather than move him to the middle of it . . . two or three times he rolled his head from side to side, opened his eyes. . . . I could see no signs of recognition in those eyes."

An hour followed, then another, and he never regained consciousness. Bruenn summoned Dr. James Paullin, a heart specialist from Atlanta, and just as he arrived, FDR's breathing grew heavy and then stopped. At 3:35, Roosevelt was pronounced dead. The cause was a cerebral hemorrhage. Immediately, Lucy and Shoumatoff packed their bags and left, before others—including Eleanor—started descending on Warm Springs.

When Roosevelt had not arrived at Smith's barbecue by 4:20, Smith called up to the house and received no answer. Finally, sensing that there was news—he thought perhaps Germany had surrendered—he drove up and was greeted by tear-stained faces and the terrible news. He put in a call to the UP office just as Early was making the official announcement in Washington.

"The night of April 12 was truly a nightmare," Smith wrote. "It was a horrible, discordant symphony of people shouting for telephones, automobiles racing along dusty clay roads, the clatter of telegraph instruments and typewriters."

Eleanor was at a benefit in Washington when she was called urgently to the White House. There, Early and McIntyre told her FDR had died. She stood stoically at Truman's side while he took the oath of office and then cabled her sons before leaving for Warm Springs:

DARLINGS: PA SLEPT AWAY THIS AFTERNOON. HE DID HIS JOB TO THE END AS HE WOULD WANT YOU TO DO. BLESS YOU. ALL OUR LOVE. MOTHER.

Hearing the news, Sherwood couldn't believe it—didn't want to believe it. "I listened and listened to the radio, waiting for the announcement—probably in his own gaily reassuring voice—that it had all been a big mistake, that the banking crisis and the war were over and everything was going to be 'fine—grand—perfectly bully,'" he recalled sadly. But Morgenthau, who had dined with FDR the evening of April 11, had noted his poor condition and was irritated when he heard McIntyre telling people that the president's death had been completely unexpected. He called the claim "sheer damned nonsense."

Arriving at Warm Springs, Eleanor was crushed to be told that Lucy had been with her husband in his final moments. The secret of their relationship had been successfully kept for years, and she felt betrayed, most of all by Anna. The purity of her grief was spoiled by the hard truth of her husband's infidelity, and as she accompanied his body back to Washington her mind was tormented. When she saw Anna, she did not console her daughter as a mother might but rather questioned her closely about Lucy, as if that were the most important issue in the midst of such overwhelming grief. Anna was shattered and on the defensive. She believed in her heart that she had done the right thing by her father, but her mother's searing judgment wounded her. Eleanor might have reserved her anger for her husband, but she had long since stopped viewing him in a romantic or intimate way. Instead she blamed her daughter for being a party to the deception. It would take time for their relationship to heal, but, feeling it was the right thing to do, Anna placed a call to Lucy several weeks later, acknowledging the fact that she was grieving, too.

It would always haunt James that his father had died without any family members around him. He thought that if the doctors had not been so dishonest about the dire state of Roosevelt's health, they would have been there. "I . . . hated the fact, and I could not make myself think otherwise, that Pa—our Pa, our early playmate, our sailing partner, our cruelly stricken father, so courageous in adversity, our sunny companion, our President, our Commander-in-Chief, but always our Pa—had died alone." By that he meant without his wife and children at his side. But FDR had not died alone. In a sense he had chosen a family, and they had been there.

FDR had not liked the practice of dignitaries lying in state with crowds walking by to gawk at their caskets. His coffin was placed in the East Room of the White House, where the gathering was by invitation only. Off to one side sat his empty wheelchair. At one point Eleanor requested a private moment, with the casket opened just for her. At another point Harry Truman, now president, entered the East Room. Nobody stood. After a simple Episcopal funeral service, the coffin was placed on a train for Hyde Park.

Struck by the beautiful simplicity of the service, Suckley wrote approvingly of the way it had been done—although it wasn't exactly what FDR would have wanted—"As he told several of us, he never even wanted to be embalmed. He wanted to be wrapped in a sheet and laid next to the ground. But that is hardly possible under the circumstances, & I am quite certain that he is not worrying about that at all where he is."

In his funeral plans, Roosevelt had stated his desire to be buried in the rose garden at Hyde Park. Preparations were made for a burial on Sunday, April 15.

A battalion from the Corps of Cadets at West Point was brought to Hyde Park, along with battalions from the army, navy, marine, and coast guard. The air force would fly in a formation above Hyde Park before the service.

Shoulder to shoulder, more than one thousand soldiers, sailors, and marines lined the route from the train station, saluting the flag-draped coffin as it passed on a caisson pulled by six horses from the army. A riderless horse draped in black followed the caisson. Bugles intoned "Hail to the Chief." As the processional approached the grave site, a twenty-one-gun salute boomed out, followed by the mournful chords of Chopin's funeral dirge.

Nearly two hundred close friends and relatives, along with assorted dignitaries, including President and Mrs. Truman and their daughter, Margaret, crowded into the area around the grave site. Several ministers were on hand, each reading a prayer. As the first prayer began, a single air force bomber that had circled back from the formation appeared overhead, dipping its wings in a salute. The requiescat was a recitation of lines from John Ellerton's hymn:

Now the laborer's task is o'er
Now the battle day is past . . .
Father, in Thy gracious keeping
Leave we now Thy servant sleeping.

Drums rolled as the casket was lowered into the ground, and cadets fired three volleys over the grave. Fala, held on a leash by Suckley, barked with each volley. The poignant notes of "Taps" were played as the commander in chief was sent to his final rest in the fragrant garden of the home he loved. A simple white stone marks the grave, with no inscription but Roosevelt's name and dates and Eleanor's name and dates. In the summer, it is surrounded by roses.

From across the Atlantic, Churchill paid tribute to his friend and partner with tears streaming down his face: "As the saying goes, he died in harness and we may well say in battle harness, like his soldiers, sailors, and airmen, who side by side with ours, are carrying on their task to the end all over the world. What an enviable death was his."

In Moscow, Stalin seemed bereft. "President Roosevelt has died but his cause must live on," he told Harriman in a rare moment of emotion. He couldn't possibly have meant it.

IN EUROPE, EISENHOWER WAS directing the endgame of the war, whose strategy now centered on Germany and the ultimate prize, Berlin. Churchill had wanted British troops to take Berlin, but Eisenhower made a different calculation. Given the strategic positioning of the Allied forces, it was more practical for the Russian army to be the first into Berlin—an expedient he believed would prevent some fifty thousand additional casualties. He got flak for it, of course, but he reminded Marshall that as commander he had authority in the field and believed his charge was to act in the most efficient and effective way possible to win the war. Perhaps, too, a part of him felt that the Russians, who had suffered such an intolerable blow at the hands of the Germans, deserved to deliver the coup de grâce.

As the Russians advanced on Berlin, they met little resistance from the Nazis, who were fleeing or surrendering to save their own lives even as their leader was preparing to end his. Hitler could not face the retribution of his enemies. He would not sit before tribunals. He chose the coward's way out. Isolated at the end, in an underground bunker with his longtime mistress, Eva Braun, whom he had married the day before his death, and their two dogs, he wrote his last will and testament. He then poisoned Braun and the dogs with cyanide before taking a cyanide capsule and shooting himself in the head. In his last will and testament, he wrote, "I myself and my wife—in

order to escape the disgrace of deposition and capitulation—
choose death." He instructed that their remains be immediately
cremated, and they were, unfortunately giving rise to endless
speculation about whether Hitler was really dead.

Within a week of Hitler's death, Germany unconditionally surrendered on May 7, and the following day Churchill
declared VE Day—Victory in Europe Day. Germany's unconditional surrender to the Soviet Union was signed on May 9.

Eisenhower remembered only how weary they all were after
the surrender documents were signed. "When the signing finally took place, a little before three in the morning of May 7, I
think no person in the entire headquarters gave much thought to
starting a public celebration or participating in a private one,"
he wrote. "My group went to bed to sleep the clock around."
But around the world, elated citizens swarmed into the streets
when they heard the news.

The May 7 issue of *Time* magazine featured a cover portrait of Hitler's face with a big red X crossing it out, accompanied by a victorious missive: "If they [his enemies] had been
as malign as he in their vengefulness, they might better have
hoped that he would live on yet a little while. For no death they
could devise for him could be as cruel as must have been Hitler's eleventh-hour thoughts on the completeness of his failure.
His total war against non-German mankind was ending in total
defeat. Around him, the Third Reich, which was to last 1,000
years, sank to embers as the flames fused over its gutted cities."

But the Japanese were still fighting, refusing to accept that
defeat was imminent. At a Big Three meeting in Potsdam, Germany, from July 17 to August 2, Truman, Churchill, and Stalin
signed a declaration calling for the unconditional surrender of
Japan. Privately, Truman informed Stalin that the United States
possessed "a new weapon of unusual destructive force" that

could be used against the Japanese if they refused to surrender. Stalin was pleased. Churchill already knew of FDR's atomic bomb program and agreed that using the bomb might be necessary. Truman was relieved at their response. He had learned of the atomic bomb program only after FDR's death—a pretty big secret to keep from the vice president—but he would not hesitate to use it if it would end the war.

Eisenhower was at Potsdam when he was told about the bomb, and he felt sickened. He urged Truman to reconsider—to offer the Japanese a way to save face. But Truman stood firm, and unfortunately the Japanese refused to budge. On August 6, the United States dropped the first atomic bomb on Hiroshima, followed by a second bomb on Nagasaki on August 9. The horror was unlike anything ever experienced. Tens of thousands of people were instantly carbonized or crushed in their homes, with many thousands more dying slowly of burns and a terrible radiation sickness. With the city centers in ruins, the homeless victims huddled in the streets, suffering, sick, and shell shocked by the destruction.

The Soviet Union declared war on Japan only on August 8, after the first bomb fell—late by any measure. However, with one million Soviet troops flooding into Manchuria to fight the Japanese, it might have been the extra pressure that made the difference.

On September 2, the unthinkable happened: Japan surrendered unconditionally. In an address to a stunned nation conditioned to *never* surrender, Emperor Hirohito explained that it had been the only choice. "The enemy has begun to employ a new and most cruel bomb, the power of which to do damage is, indeed, incalculable, taking the toll of many innocent lives," he said. "Should we continue to fight, it would not only result in an ultimate collapse and obliteration of the Japanese nation, but also it would lead to the total extinction of human civilization."

The rejoicing at the end of the war was blunted by the heartache of its price. A new form of warfare had been born, rising in the mushroom clouds over Japan's cities, replacing the bloody battlefields of World War II with a more frightening weapon that would stir nightmares and dominate foreign policy for generations to come.

FDR HAD ANTICIPATED HAVING years to build the peace, had dreamed of a postwar era when he could be a moderating influence on Stalin and when the ruins of war would sort themselves out. He imagined being able to resolve with money (aid) what had been difficult to manage at the conference table, buying time for the United Nations to assert itself formally. He expected the war-torn nations to be focused on rebuilding and weary of fighting, making them more malleable to compromise.

"Roosevelt believed in dollars," Molotov said cynically after the war. "Not that he believed in nothing else, but he considered America to be so rich, and we so poor and worn out, that we would surely come begging. 'Then we'll kick their ass, but for now we have to help keep them going.'" In that remark, he betrayed a fundamental grievance, undoubtedly shared by Stalin, that Roosevelt had never quite seen the Soviets as equals.

FDR had expected to be there to see it all through. With the San Francisco Conference only weeks away, he was focused on how to heal the rifts that had been developing after Yalta. In his heart, he remained a robust strategist, reliant on his old crew of advisers. He barely knew Harry Truman and had not taken him into his confidence about anything important, including the atom bomb. Perhaps he had expected the bomb to be the United States' final ace in the hole, not realizing that the Soviet Union was well on its way to developing its own nuclear technology.

In Tehran, FDR had executed a daring strategy to bring Stalin into alignment with the West and thus win the war. The central disagreement of the conference over Overlord had pitted him against Churchill and aligned him with Stalin, and he had seen a strategic purpose in the rift with his old ally. In the end, Tehran had produced the declaration that had paved the way for the war's end. It might be said that Tehran won the war but Yalta failed to secure the peace.

There has been much speculation in the past seventy-five years about whether Roosevelt had been too ill at Yalta to do justice to the finer points of the negotiations. Those who were with him there have disputed this characterization. More likely, he had pushed where he must and pulled back where he could, walking a fine line with Stalin to get what he wanted at the moment, figuring he could bring Stalin around more fully in future meetings. He had made the decision that the details could be ironed out later and it was more important to present a united front while Germany and Japan were still on the offensive. When questioned at a press conference after Tehran about the details of the agreement, he had replied, "We are still in the generality stage, not in the detail stage, because we are talking about principles." He thought there was time. (It is not surprising that the Soviets thought they were the ones who had made all the concessions at Yalta. Vladimir Pavlov, Stalin's interpreter, later said, "It was asserted in the United States after Roosevelt's death that he made too many concessions to Stalin at the conference. I believe that more concessions were made by the Soviet delegation than by the British or American delegations." He didn't elaborate.)

George Kennan, Harriman's deputy in Moscow and later briefly the US ambassador to Moscow under Truman, had been outspoken even during the war about the failure of the American government to fully appreciate the nature of Russia and Stalin. His analysis of Roosevelt's illusions about Stalin is brutal. Roosevelt, he wrote, relied on the conviction that he alone, by force of his personality, could change Stalin—"that the only reason why it had been difficult to get on with him in the past was because there was no one with the right personality, with enough imagination and trust to deal with him properly; that the arrogant conservatives in the Western capitals had always bluntly rejected him, and that his ideological prejudices would melt away and Russian cooperation with the West could easily be obtained, if only Stalin was exposed to the charm of a personality of FDR's caliber." Kennan was an outlier during the war, and his harsh judgment fails to recognize the realities Roosevelt faced. But there is just enough truth in his words to strike a recognizable chord.

Perhaps after the war Roosevelt would have been tougher. In the days before his death, he already saw that Stalin was reneging on his agreements. Perhaps if he had lived, he would have been the one to bring Stalin back into line. We'll never know.

When Stettinius first met with Truman, he told him about FDR's difficult dealings with Stalin after Yalta and his own opinion that relations had deteriorated since the conference. Truman reacted instantly by telling Stettinius that the United States must stand up to the Soviets and not go easy on them. Truman's subsequent hostility at the Potsdam Conference in July 1945, when he met Stalin, had a chilling effect on Soviet cooperation. "Roosevelt knew how to conceal his attitude toward us, but Truman—he didn't know how to do that at all," Molotov would say in 1975. "He had an openly hostile attitude."

At the same time, the Russians were boldly in retreat from conference niceties. Discussing the issue of free elections in eastern Europe during the Potsdam Conference, Stalin said what he had obviously believed all along: "A freely elected government in any of these countries would be anti-Soviet, and that we cannot allow."

Did FDR's concessions to Stalin at Tehran and Yalta set the stage for the Cold War? Though he was masterful as a war strategist, his choices have nonetheless been subject to debate. Did the United States fall on its sword in the final decisions of the war? Had Roosevelt lived, would relations with the Soviet Union have been better? Did Roosevelt know that the Soviets were developing nuclear technology? Could the Cold War have been avoided if FDR had played a different hand at Tehran and then Yalta? Or, considering that Stalin already had control of eastern Europe, was Roosevelt's only choice to edge toward agreement and buy time? Finally, was Eisenhower's decision to let the Russians take Berlin the act that gave them a stake in Germany that would lead to decades of hardship and separation?

It was in FDR's nature, for better or ill, to be a collaborator. "President Roosevelt was well aware of the nature of Soviet society," Stettinius observed. "Its dictatorial and authoritarian aspects were as repugnant to him as to any American. But he also had a strong sense of history. He knew that no society was static, and he believed that the United States could do much, through firmness, patience, and understanding, over a period of time in dealing with the Soviet Union to influence its evolution away from dictatorship and tyranny in the direction of a free, tolerant, and peaceful society." Those are nice words. The question is: Was Roosevelt on a productive path, cut short by his death, or was he blinded by his hopes for a different world?

It's easy to forget in the aftermath of the long Cold War the critical role the Soviets played in the fight against Hitler. It's easy to forget how desperate the Allies were for victory and how often that victory was in doubt. Roosevelt needed Stalin to be an *ally*, not an *enemy*. His strategy was to slowly reel him in, and it worked for his immediate purposes. Given Stalin's actions after the war and the Cold War–era abominations of the Soviet Union, one can doubt the wisdom of FDR's approach, but those three days in Tehran, which might have birthed the Cold War, were also the turning point in the hot war.

It was a grand deception on Stalin's part. The reasonable, friendly "Uncle Joe" of those conferences was a different person altogether in the Soviet Union. "The Western Allied leaders were unaware of conditions behind Soviet lines," R. C. Raack noted in *Stalin's Drive to the West 1938–1948: The Origins of the Cold War*, citing "In part censorship, in part preoccupations that distracted attention and desire to learn. The net effect: Stalin was effectively director of an institution, the 'Big Three,' where other members were self-blindfolded."

Entrapped by a desire to help Stalin help them win the war, the Western Allies missed or ignored his desire to move his power to the west, in what Raack called "conduct unbecoming an ally."

Germany became one focal point of that surge. In Tehran and then at Yalta, Stalin preached moralistically about the need to destroy Germany in order to prevent another Hitler, but in the process, he laid the groundwork for carving off the eastern part of the country and making it a subject of the Soviet Union. His true aim was offensive, not defensive. He wanted control, and weak nations were easier to conquer.

Hugh Lunghi, reflecting on FDR's and Churchill's accommodations with Stalin, wrote:

What amazed those of us, British and Americans, living and working in Moscow, experiencing the realities of life there, was the extraordinary ignorance, as it seemed displayed by our principals and their advisors. Most astounding and puzzling was why Roosevelt and Churchill, the State Department and the Foreign Office, could for a moment believe that Stalin would allow free elections, let alone the concomitant of a free press, in liberated Europe, when those very freedoms were denied to the peoples of the Soviet Union.

Roosevelt had convinced himself that he could handle Stalin after the war, without considering the transactional nature of Stalin's alliance with the West and his deeply rooted contempt for democracy. Roosevelt also believed that the Soviet Union would be so domestically shattered after the war that it would have neither the will nor the wherewithal to become an aggressor.

When the war ended, the change was instantaneous. Strong-arming the global organization that had been FDR's treasured vision, Stalin reveled in intransigence. Speaking out against Western values and institutions, he blamed capitalism for inspiring the rise of Hitler. After the war, he was now free to be more who he had truly been all along. When Roosevelt had spoken of self-determination, free elections, and a peaceful world, Stalin had nodded along and said he wanted those, too. His compliance was like a drug to Roosevelt. "The old Bolshevik," as Roosevelt jokingly referred to him, had not changed because of the war. He intended to do exactly as he pleased, regardless of anything he promised.

As General John R. Deane, a former chief of the US Military Mission in the US Embassy Moscow, wrote in 1947, "In my opinion there can no longer be any doubt that the Soviet leadership has always been motivated by the belief that communism and capitalism cannot coexist."

At the moment of victory, Stalin reverted to his default. In a speech in February 1946, he reveled in the triumph of the Soviet social structure, feeling he had free rein at last to do what he wanted. Roosevelt was dead; Churchill was out of office. Stalin had little respect for Truman as an adversary. And the Soviet Union was developing the bomb—the Cold War's centerpiece.

The harsh verdict of history may well be that faced with his moment of truth, FDR blinked. Every president since World War II has faced similar crises—standing up or standing down, recognizing that the negotiating table can be even more treacherous than the battlefield. There's a uniquely American perception that as long as we're talking, we're making progress. Roosevelt thought so, too. It takes faith and hubris to think you can talk your way out of a global jam, negotiate with someone who shares none of your values, and gain lasting consensus.

"If history teaches anything, it teaches self-delusion in the face of unpleasant facts is folly," Ronald Reagan said in a 1982 speech to the House of Commons, after the Cold War had stymied six presidents before him.

. . . During the dark days of the Second World War, when this island was incandescent with courage, Winston Churchill exclaimed about Britain's adversaries, "What kind of people do they think we are?" Well, Britain's adversaries found out what extraordinary people the British are. But all the democracies paid a terrible price for allowing the dictators to underestimate us. We dare not make that mistake again. So, let us ask our-selves, "What kind of people do we think we are?" And let us answer, "Free people, worthy of freedom and de-termined not only to remain so but to help others gain their freedom as well."

76 YEARS LATER: KEEP TALKING

June 2018

It was a long twenty-four-hour flight from Washington, DC, through Beijing to Singapore, and when we landed in the steamy Singapore summer, we were immediately swept into the task of preparing our reports on the first summit between President Donald Trump and North Korea's Supreme Leader Kim Jong Un. There was an almost carnival atmosphere on the streets, with performers and Trump-Kim impersonators entertaining the journalists and tourists from around the world who came to catch a glimpse at a piece of history—the first summit of its kind.

The two men met against a backdrop of deeply ingrained mutual hostility. For decades, North Korea has been a hidden land whose principal goal has seemed to be the destruction of the American way. Its children are indoctrinated to hate America. The fact that this brutal dictatorship with animosity toward the West was developing nuclear capabilities was a looming crisis, and each administration had tried to tackle it in different ways for almost two decades.

President Trump's courtship of Kim Jong Un seemed almost

unthinkable, especially after the president had threatened North Korea with "fire and fury" early in his presidency. But rhetoric can be distinguished from diplomacy. After all, Ronald Reagan called the Soviet Union "the evil empire," and then went on to sit at the table with Gorbachev and carve out substantial agreements on nuclear disarmament. Trump administration officials were using the Reagan framework—hoping that the formula would work with Kim as well.

So, President Trump decided to meet Kim face-to-face. Even the doubters were cautiously hopeful, just because the scene of an American president and a North Korean leader smiling broadly as they promised to explore cooperation was so unprecedented.

As President Trump prepared to leave Singapore, I had a rare opportunity to interview him aboard Air Force One while his impressions were still fresh from his meeting. A pleased and self-assured Trump told me, "I'm totally confident. And if we can't . . . we can't have a deal . . . we have to be—you know, it has to be verified. But one of the things that, really, I'm happy is that the soldiers that died in Korea, their remains are going to be coming back home. And we have thousands of people that have asked for that, thousands and thousands of people." Indeed, the return of soldiers' remains was a tremendous symbolic act of good will on the part of Kim. (Although even a year later, the process of getting the remains back to the United States has been slow and incomplete.)

Even so, many observers were still skeptical about trying to negotiate with a man whose regime—and those of his father and grandfather—was characterized by brutality.

Pointing out the human rights violations, I bluntly said to President Trump, "He's a killer. He's executing people."

The president's response was measured and conciliatory.

"He's a tough guy," he said of Kim. "Hey, when you take over a country, tough country, tough people and you take it over from your father, I don't care who you are, what you are, how much of an advantage you have. If you can do that at twenty-seven years old, I mean that's one in ten thousand that could do that. So, he's a very smart guy. He's a great negotiator, but I think we understand each other." Perhaps President Trump was relating as the son of an overbearing father, but his basic position was that it was better to talk to Kim than to shut him out. There was plenty of hand-wringing about President Trump's failure to repel this adversary, but in a larger sense it was the American way.

At the time of that interview, I was in the process of writing this book, so it's not surprising that my thoughts turned to FDR and Joseph Stalin. Researching the Tehran Conference of November 1943, I had been struck by how friendly FDR was toward Stalin, a dictator and known killer. At moments, he was almost obsequious. Winston Churchill, no admirer of Stalin, was affronted by FDR's charm offensive.

True, when FDR met Stalin our nations were in an alliance to defeat Hitler and the Axis Powers. It was also true that the Soviet Union had borne the brunt of casualties in the war, numbering in the millions. But beyond the discussions about ending the war, FDR also entered into a collaboration with Stalin in Tehran and later at Yalta that sought to reshape the postwar world. Still angling to convince Stalin to join the fight against Japan, FDR wanted more than anything else to get the Soviet dictator on his side.

FDR might have thought he had little choice but to play along with Stalin. He figured he could get away with it, but if he had a postwar strategy to rein in the Soviet Union, he didn't live to pursue it. And FDR's critics would later say that relationship and the leeway given to Stalin led to catastrophic consequences in Eastern Europe and for what would be a four-decade-long Cold War.

It's tempting to think of those long-ago summits as relics of the past. But decisions made more than seventy years ago have relevance to the way we pursue foreign policy today. President Trump's overtures to Vladimir Putin and Kim Jong Un have set many observers on edge. The bad faith of Russian and North Korean leaders is an old story for American negotiators. In 1943, Stalin said all the right things to FDR's face, preaching the value of freedom and independence for every nation. Then, once FDR was in the grave and the war was over, he proceeded to break every promise he had made. Knowing what we now know, we can only speculate about what would have happened had not FDR been so willing to allow Stalin to dominate eastern Europe after the war. For that matter, what would have happened had not the control of Germany been divided between east and west?

"Trust, but verify," Ronald Reagan said, and it's a mantra that gets repeated to this day. Can the United States ever trust Russia? Can it ever trust North Korea?

Donald Trump is not the first president to court America's enemies. Even in the darkest early years of the Cold War, Dwight Eisenhower tried to develop a working relationship with Nikita Khrushchev, and brought him to Camp David, where they watched westerns together. The two men were bitter adversaries, but they had one important issue in common: both agreed that a nuclear war was unthinkable. It would be mutually assured destruction (MAD). I've always thought Khrushchev described the nuclear standoff best when he said to Eisenhower: "We get your dust, you get our dust, the winds blow around the world and nobody's safe."

Camp David has witnessed many such outreaches over the

decades: Nixon gave Soviet general secretary Leonid Brezhnev the gift of a Cadillac and went for a heart-stopping drive with him on the property. Reagan never invited Gorbachev to Camp David, but George H. W. Bush did. There are photos of the president escorting Gorbachev in the camp golf cart—Golf Cart One. Later, Bush also invited Boris Yeltsin to Camp David. George W. Bush hosted Putin at Camp David when he was trying to establish a relationship with him, but when Barack Obama tried to get Putin to Camp David to attend the G8 summit in 2012, he was rebuffed.

The point is, American presidents have always tried to reach out to Russian leaders, even in the tensest times. The budding relationship between Eisenhower and Khrushchev was doomed when the Americans were caught spying with a downed U2 spy plane. In the same way, President Trump's outreach is dramatically complicated by Russia's interference in the 2016 election, which has soured most Americans to Russia's true intentions. Nevertheless, President Trump still tries to find a way in.

North Korea is a more complex overture. It's hard to overstate the level of antagonism that has existed between the United States and North Korea throughout its history. The 1945 division of Korea into two separated spheres was another outcome of World War II, which President Harry Truman signed off on. It led to war and then to a tense standoff that has survived to this day.

President Trump's 2018 summit with Kim Jong Un was a first. No previous sitting president had met with a North Korean leader, although Bill Clinton came close.

In Singapore, President Trump told me that he and Kim have "chemistry." And although he surely discovered that personal chemistry is not enough, he agreed to a second summit in Hanoi, Vietnam, in February 2019. It did not go so well, ending abruptly when the two sides could not agree on denuclearization. But President Trump held out hope—as he does to this day—that the talks are ongoing. A third summit is in the works.

I was in Hanoi. The anticipation that a deal would be struck between the United States and North Korea was high, but the framework was not set up. The North Koreans appeared to misjudge how far President Trump was willing to bend, and "denuclearization" had two different meanings for the two countries' negotiating teams. The setting seemed designed to send a message to Chairman Kim—a booming economy in Vietnam that continues to expand after Vietnam's Communist past. Statues of Vladimir Lenin are sprinkled throughout Hanoi, positioned across from coffee shops and cell phone stores—a dichotomy that President Trump is trying to sell North Korea as well.

The point seems to be to keep negotiating. It's easy to imagine Ronald Reagan throwing in the towel with the Soviet Union in 1986 after the disastrous summit in Reykjavik, Iceland, which ended with Reagan and Gorbachev walking away from the table. Yet a little over a year later, Gorbachev was in Washington, DC, where they signed a treaty to eliminate intermediate-range and shorter-range nuclear missiles. Months later, Reagan was in Moscow, with perhaps the most significant platform of his presidency, openly sharing American values with Soviet citizens—a speech that was unthinkable just months before.

Upheavals in the world order are a given, and it's fair to say that American presidents have made many mistakes in their efforts to balance our principles with undemocratic regimes. Critics will say FDR dropped the ball with Stalin. But, perhaps he had no choice. As Americans one thing seems certain—we've always been willing to keep the door open. To do otherwise is to make the world more dangerous.

When I first began this project to write about three American presidents at key moments in the Cold War era, I began with Eisenhower, who came to office at the most dangerous early period of the standoff. I focused on his warning to John F. Kennedy, his successor, about handling Khrushchev and the emerging crisis in Fidel Castro's Cuba—a lesson Kennedy ignored and which led to the Bay of Pigs catastrophe.

My second book focused on Ronald Reagan, a Cold War president who had been outspoken for most of his life about the evils of communism, but whose signature achievement was successfully negotiating with the Soviet Union for the reduction of nuclear arms. Although the Soviet Union's collapse happened during George H. W. Bush's presidency, Reagan usually gets credit for ending the Cold War.

FDR, my final book in the series, is an effort to go back to the beginning, before there was a Cold War, and examine the choices he made that, while ending World War II, set the stage for the world that came after.

Together, they form a compelling picture of who we have been as a nation during the last three quarters of a century. The takeaway is that all three presidents attempted to bridge what often seemed to be impossible divides. They taught us that we should not fear talk. We should fear the end of talks. We obviously don't know what the future holds, but looking back at our past and how leaders dealt with the major problems of the day can provide us a blueprint for what lies ahead.

ACKNOWLEDGMENTS

The third time is the charm. Like *Three Days in January* and *Three Days in Moscow, Three Days at the Brink* could never have been realized without the hard work, imagination, and dedication of my coauthor, Catherine Whitney. Catherine has the uncanny ability to throw herself into a project and absorb all of the details. In this case, we didn't have personal interviews like we did with major players in *Three Days in Moscow.* Catherine scoured thousands of pages of library documents, oral histories, biographies, and notes from the Tehran Conference, and in the same back-and-forth process we used for the other two books, the result was a very readable and dramatic telling of an important three days in history, and a look back at the life of one of our most consequential presidents.

The team was back together for this third effort, with our intrepid and industrious researcher, Sydney Soderberg, spending a lot of time at the FDR Library and Museum in Hyde Park, New York. The gems that Sydney was able to dig up provided the "crackle" in the detail and storytelling of that conference. A real-life drama told with the help of oral histories and notes from Tehran.

The professionals at presidential libraries provide a crucial role of preserving and protecting presidential history. And the treasures they hold inside can paint a picture of a moment or a presidency. The FDR Library and Museum opened its doors wide to me and the team. I would like to personally thank Paul Sparrow, the director of the library. Paul was enthusiastic about the project from the start and helped get everything we needed. The FDR archives staff—Kirsten Strigel Carter, Virginia Lewick, Patrick Fahy, Christian Belena, and audiovisual specialist Matthew Hanson—could not have been more helpful.

Clifford Laube, the public programs specialist, was a great help as well. And the tour from Scott Rector with the National Park Service really gave us an inside look at how FDR lived on the property growing up and until his death. We also returned to the Eisenhower Library for research into the relationship between FDR and General Eisenhower.

Special thanks to the team at William Morrow, led by our fabulous editor, Peter Hubbard. Peter has a keen eye for making something "sing" a little better and all of his edits have made the book that much stronger. Peter has a special love for World War II and said this book delivered. It's the "biggest" of the three in scope and completes the trilogy of books—the beginning, middle, and end of the Cold War. Peter and his team really boosted the book from the start.

As always, thank you to my manager, Larry Kramer, and book agent, Claudia Cross with Folio Literary Group, for their encouragement and guidance through all three books.

Thank you to my employer, Fox News, for allowing me the time to not only work on the book, but promote it during a busy news year (all years are busy now, it seems). And for putting together a one-hour documentary around this book as they did for the other two.

And a very special thank-you to my family—my beautiful wife, Amy, and my two sons, Paul and Daniel. Travel, late nights, and another book tour was not a great thing to look forward to for a family pulled in a lot of different directions . . . but Amy, my rock, held all together at home and supported me one hundred percent.

Finally, thank you to President Franklin Delano Roosevelt—FDR. His fight to bounce back after being stricken with polio likely made him the president he eventually became. The decisions he made and the relationships he cultivated changed the world, and it's my honor to be able to tell that story.

NOTES

PROLOGUE: THE "BIG THREE" DINNER PARTY

4   "was a hub of international intrigue": Bill Yenne, *Operation Long Jump: Stalin, Roosevelt, Churchill, and the Greatest Assassination Plot in History* (New York: Regnery History, 2015), p. 36.

4   "the greatest concentration": *The Hopkins Touch: Harry Hopkins and the Forging of the Alliance to Defeat Hitler* (Oxford, UK: Oxford University Press, 2013), p. 317.

4   "I am placing": Franklin D. Roosevelt and Joseph V. Stalin, *My Dear Mr. Stalin: The Complete Correspondence of Franklin D. Roosevelt and Joseph V. Stalin*, edited by Susan Butler (New Haven: Yale University Press, 2005), October 14, 1943.

5   "I am not": Ibid., October 21, 1943.

5   "I have decided": Ibid., November 8, 1943.

6   "a man hewn out of granite": Susan Butler, *Roosevelt and Stalin: Portrait of a Partnership* (New York: Alfred A. Knopf, 2016), p. 146.

7   "cold on the stomach": Jon Meacham, *Franklin and Winston* (New York: Random House, 2003), p. 253.

7   "No lover ever": Ibid., p. 245.

CHAPTER ONE: TO WHOM MUCH IS GIVEN

13   "Did I ever": Sara Delano Roosevelt, as told by Mrs. James Roosevelt to Isabel Leighton and Gabrielle Forbush, *My Boy Franklin* (New York: R. Long & R. R. Smith, 1933), p. 4.

14   "How this Hudson River": Jean Edward Smith, *FDR* (New York: Random House, 2007), p. x (preface).

14   "Franklin Roosevelt's ordeal": Doris Kearns Goodwin. *Leadership: In Turbulent Times* (New York: Simon & Schuster, 2018), p. 162.

14   "Just as the irons": George Will in Ken Burns, *The Roosevelts: An Intimate History*, PBS, 2014.

16   "At quarter to nine": Smith, *FDR*, p. 17.

17   "Oh, for freedom!": Sara Delano Roosevelt, *My Boy Franklin*, p. 5.

18   "I've always believed": Ibid., p. 14.

18   "I do not believe": Ibid., p. 14.

18   "never boring or bored": Grace Tully, *F.D.R., My Boss* (Chicago: Peoples Book Club, 1949), p. 2.

19   "Mummie," he replied: Sara Delano Roosevelt, *My Boy Franklin*, p. 26.

19   "As long as I live": Franklin D. Roosevelt, "Day by Day," January 1, 1935. A Project of the Pare Lorenz Center at the Franklin D. Roosevelt Presidential Library. http://www.fdrlibrary.marist.edu/dayby day/resource/january-1935-5/.

20   "It was no time": Sara Delano Roosevelt, *My Boy Franklin*, p. 40.

20   "The fact is": Letter from Charles R. Nutter, January 22, 1944, correspondence file, Franklin D. Roosevelt Presidential Library and Museum, Hyde Park, NY.

21   "Several times each day": Sara Delano Roosevelt, *My Boy Franklin*, p. 43.

22   "I am too distressed": Franklin D. Roosevelt, letter from Cambridge, "Dearest Mama & Papa," December 3, 1900, in Franklin D. Roosevelt, *F.D.R.: His Personal Letters, Early Years*, edited by Elliott Roosevelt (New York: Duell, Sloan and Pearce, 1947), p. 437.

24   "de-e-e-lighted!": Meredith Hindley, "The Roosevelt Bond," *Humanities* 35, no. 5 (September–October 2014), https://www.neh .gov/humanities/2014/septemberoctober/feature/politics-and-war -brought-teddy-roosevelt-and-franklin-delan.

24   She was also put off: Blanche Wiesen Cook, *Eleanor Roosevelt*, vol. 1: *The Early Years, 1884–1933* (New York: Penguin, 1933), p. 134.

26   When he saw: Eleanor Roosevelt, *The Autobiography of Eleanor Roosevelt* (New York: Harper & Brothers, 1961), p. 19. [This volume includes Mrs. Roosevelt's previous books, *This I Remember* and *On My Own*.]

27   "Her mouth and teeth": Jan Pottker, *Sara and Eleanor: The Story of Sara Delano Roosevelt and Her Daughter-in-Law Eleanor Roosevelt* (New York: St. Martin's Press, 2004), p. 71.

27   "As I try to sum up": Eleanor Roosevelt, *Autobiography*, p. 40.

28   "After lunch I have": Wiesen Cook, *Eleanor Roosevelt*, vol. 1, p. 140.

29   "It probably surprised": Sara Delano Roosevelt, *My Boy Franklin*, p. 63.

29   "Dearest Mama": Elliott Roosevelt, ed., *Personal Letters, Early Years*, p. 518.

29   "Dear Cousin Sally": Ibid., p. 517.

30   "We are greatly rejoiced": Wiesen Cook, *Eleanor Roosevelt*, p. 164.

31   "Much has been given us": Theodore Roosevelt, first inaugural address, March 4, 1905.

31   "I have no recollection": Eleanor Roosevelt, *Autobiography*, p. 48.

32   Eleanor looked luminous: "President Roosevelt Gives the Bride
       Away," *New York Times*, March 18, 1905.

32   "Well, Franklin": Wiesen Cook, *Eleanor Roosevelt*, p. 167.

32   "My father always has": Ken Burns, *The Roosevelts: An Intimate
       History*, PBS, 2014.

33   "On that occasion": Franklin D. Roosevelt, St. Patrick's Day Mes-
       sage to the Charitable Irish Society of Boston and the Hibernian
       Society of Savannah, March 17, 1937.

CHAPTER TWO: INTO THE ARENA

34   "The credit belongs": Theodore Roosevelt, "Citizenship in a Repub-
       lic," speech at the Sorbonne, Paris, France, April 23, 1910.

35   "I accept this nomination": Franklin D. Roosevelt, "Accepting Nom-
       ination for State Senator," October 6, 1910, Master Speech File,
       no. 2, Franklin D. Roosevelt Presidential Library and Museum,
       http://www.fdrlibrary.marist.edu/_resources/images/msf/msf00002.

36   "I'm not Teddy": Robert Dallek, *Franklin Roosevelt: A Political
       Life* (New York: Penguin Books, 2017), p. 43.

36   "I do not know who": Franklin D. Roosevelt, campaign speech,
       Hyde Park, NY, November 5, 1910, Master Speech File, no. 7,
       Franklin D. Roosevelt Presidential Library and Museum, http://
       www.fdrlibrary.marist.edu/_resources/images/msf/msf00007.

37   "What the voters": Ibid.

37   "You have known": Smith, *FDR*, p. 68.

38   "I felt . . . in some way": Eleanor Roosevelt, *The Autobiography of
       Eleanor Roosevelt* (New York: Harper & Brothers, 1961), p. 62.

38   "I wanted to be": Ibid., p. 65.

39   "There is nothing I love": Robert DiClerico. *The Contemporary
       American President* (Abington, UK: Routledge, 2016).

39   "I was so impressed": Lela Stiles, *The Man Behind Roosevelt: The
       Story of Louis McHenry Howe* (Cleveland: The World Publishing
       Co., 1954), p. 32.

40   "I realized that": Eleanor Roosevelt, *Autobiography*, p. 68.

41   "With unflinching hearts": Theodore Roosevelt, speech to support-
       ers at the Republican National Convention, Chicago, June 17, 1912.

41   "I'm as strong": Theodore Roosevelt, letter to Mark Hanna, 1900,
       believed to be TR's first use of "bull moose." Theodore Roosevelt
       Center. https://www.theodorerooseveltcenter.org/Learn-About-TR
       /TR-Quotes?page=3.

42   "Friends, I shall ask": "It Takes More Than That to Kill a Bull
       Moose." Address at Milwaukee, WI, October 14, 1912. Theodore
       Roosevelt Association. https://www.smithsonianmag.com/history
       /the-speech-that-saved-teddy-roosevelts-life-83479091/.

42   "It was in what": Julie M. Fenster, *FDR's Shadow: Louis Howe,
       The Force That Shaped Frank and Eleanor Roosevelt* (New York:
       Palgrave Macmillan, 2009), p. 95.

43   "I'd like it": James Tertius de Kay, *Roosevelt's Navy: The Educa-
       tion of a Warrior President, 1882–1920* (New York: Pegasus Books,
       2013), p. 86.

44   "I now find": Robert Dallek, *Franklin Roosevelt: A Political Life* (New York: Penguin Books, 2017), p. 54.

44   "I was very pleased": Meredith Hindley, "The Roosevelt Bond," *Humanities* 35, no. 5 (September–October 2014), https://www.neh .gov/humanities/2014/septemberoctober/feature/politics-and-war -brought-teddy-roosevelt-and-franklin-delan.

44   "I am baptized": James Roosevelt, ed., *Personal Letters*, 1905– 1928, p. 199.

44   "painful shyness weighed heavily": James Roosevelt, *Affectionately, F.D.R.: A Son's Story of a Lonely Man* (New York: Harcourt, Brace & Company, 1959), p. 66.

45   "In half an hour": Ibid., p. 83.

46   War was "structurally unavoidable": Jeremy Bender, "Henry Kissinger: World War I Was 'Structurally Unavoidable,'" *Business Insider*, July 28, 2014, https://www.businessinsider.com/kissinger -and-albright-world-war-i-2014-7.

47   "The United States must be neutral": Woodrow Wilson, message to Congress on neutrality, August 19, 1914.

48   "the lily-livered skunk": Erick Trickey, "Why Teddy Roosevelt Tried to Bully His Way onto the WWI Battlefield," *Smithsonian*, April 10, 2017, https://www.smithsonianmag.com/history/why -teddy-roosevelt-tried-bully-way-onto-wwi-battlefield-180962840/.

49   "My God, why doesn't": Hindley, "The Roosevelt Bond."

49   "Armed neutrality": Woodrow Wilson, message to Congress on joining the war, April 2, 1917.

50   "For ten years": Eleanor Roosevelt, *Autobiography*, p. 62.

51   "The good old ocean": Geoffrey C. Ward, *A First-Class Temperament: The Emergence of Franklin Roosevelt, 1905–1928* (New York: Harper & Row, 1989).

51   "Lieutenant Roosevelt": Eric Durr, "Presidential Son Quentin Roosevelt Was a Famous WWI Casualty," New York National Guard, July 2, 2018, https://www.nationalguard.mil/News/Article/1564930 /presidential-son-quentin-roosevelt-was-a-famous-wwi-casualty/.

52   "discarded overcoats": Ward, *A First-Class Temperament*.

52   "I have seen war": Franklin D. Roosevelt, "Address—Peace," Chautauqua, NY, August 14, 1936, Master Speech File, no. 889, Franklin D. Roosevelt Presidential Library and Museum, http://www.fdr library.marist.edu/_resources/images/msf/msf00913.

53   She would later: Hazel Rowley, *Franklin and Eleanor* (New York: Farrar, Straus and Giroux, 2010).

53   "So what *did* take place": Ibid.

53   "I long so to be with you": Letter July 10, 1916. Rowley, *Franklin and Eleanor*.

54   The *New York Times* reported: "Bury Roosevelt with Simple Rites as Nation Grieves," *New York Times*, January 7, 1919.

55   "the strenuous life": Theodore Roosevelt, "The Strenuous Life," speech at the Hamilton Club, Chicago, April 10, 1899.

55   "Oh! Dear": James Roosevelt, *Affectionately F.D.R.*, p. 133.

56   "His name is good": Ward, *A First-Class Temperament*.

56 "I always counted on": James Roosevelt, ed., *Personal Letters 1905–1928*, p. 490.

56 The slogans poured out: John A. Morello, *Selling the President 1920: Albert D. Lasker, Advertising, and the Election of Warren G. Harding* (Westport, CT: Praeger, 2001).

57 She described how the newsmen: Eleanor Roosevelt, *Autobiography*, p. 110.

CHAPTER THREE: THE CRUCIBLE

61 "the glow I'd expected": Smith, *FDR*, p. 188.

62 "It produces terror": Geoffrey Ward, in Ken Burns, *The Roosevelts: An Intimate History*, PBS, 2014.

62 "I am sure": Franklin D. Roosevelt, letter to Josephus Daniels, October 6, 1921, Franklin D. Roosevelt Presidential Library and Museum, Hyde Park, NY.

62 "Franklin has been quite ill": Hazel Rowley, *Franklin and Eleanor: An Extraordinary Marriage* (New York: Farrar, Straus and Giroux, 2010).

63 "His reaction": Ward, *A First-Class Temperament*, p. 591.

63 "Just the month before": James Roosevelt, *Affectionately F.D.R.*, p. 144.

64 "Pa read me": Ibid., p. 146.

65 "his own spirit": Bernard Asbell, *Mother and Daughter: The Letters of Eleanor and Anna Roosevelt* (New York: Penguin, 1982), p. 30.

65 "This is my job": James Roosevelt, *Affectionately, F.D.R.*, p. 144.

65 "Granny, with a good insight": Asbell, *Mother and Daughter*, p. 31.

66 "The day of the timid": James Roosevelt, *Affectionately, F.D.R.*, p. 149.

66 "I hoped he would devote": Sara Delano Roosevelt, *My Boy Franklin*, p. 101.

67 "My Dear Boss": Linda Lotridge Levin, *The Making of FDR: The Story of Stephen T. Early, America's First Modern Press Secretary* (New York: Prometheus Books, 2008).

67 "We found him": Ibid.

69 "He had always": Doris Kearns Goodwin, in Ken Burns, *The Roosevelts: An Intimate History*, PBS, 2014.

70 "He steadfastly refused": Sara Delano Roosevelt, *My Boy Franklin* (New York: R. Long & R. R. Smith, 1933), p. 102.

70 "Fellow Sufferer": Personal Letters File, Franklin D. Roosevelt Presidential Library and Museum, Hyde Park, NY.

72 "Jimmy," he said: James Roosevelt, *Affectionately, F.D.R.*, p. 204.

72 "His fingers dug": Ibid., p. 205.

73 "If you would know": Franklin D. Roosevelt, "Speech Nominating Smith," June 26, 1924, Master Speech File, no. 248, Franklin D. Roosevelt Presidential Library and Museum, http://www.fdrlibrary.marist.edu/_resources/images/msf/msf00252.

73 "Adversity has lifted him": H. W. Brands, *Traitor to His Class: The Privileged Life and Radical Presidency of Franklin Delano Roosevelt* (New York: Harper & Row, 1989).

74   "Do you really believe": Jean Edward Smith, *FDR* (New York: Random House, 2007), p. 195.

75   "When I began": Eleanor Roosevelt, *The Autobiography of Eleanor Roosevelt* (New York: Harper & Brothers, 1961), p. 135.

76   Their regular correspondence: Geoffrey C. Ward, *Closest Companion: The Unknown Story of the Intimate Friendship Between Franklin Roosevelt and Margaret Suckley* (New York: Houghton Mifflin, 1995).

77   "If the convention": Terry Golway, *Frank and Al: FDR, Al Smith, and the Unlikely Alliance That Created the Modern Democratic Party* (New York: St. Martin's Press, 2018).

78   "REGRET THAT YOU HAD TO": Rowley, *Franklin and Eleanor* (endnote).

78   "A governor does not": Christopher Clausen, "The President and the Wheelchair," *The Wilson Quarterly* 29, no. 3 (Summer 2005): 24–29.

79   "I had heard stories": Samuel Rosenman, *Working with Roosevelt* (New York: Harper & Brothers, 1952), p. 16.

79   "Sam," he said: Ibid., p. 18.

81   "a broken man": Golway, *Frank and Al*.

81   "Do you know": Ibid.

81   "Sam, I shall want": Rosenman, *Working with Roosevelt*, p. 30.

81   "Yes, I made up your mind": Ibid., p. 31.

82   "Tell me," he'd say: Ibid., p. 36.

82   "The first physical thing": Ibid., p. 37.

82   "I am very mindful": Ibid., p. 39.

83   "purely psychological": Herbert Hoover, "Message on the Economy," November 5, 1929, UVA Miller Center, https://millercenter.org/the-presidency/presidential-speeches/november-5-1929-message-economy.

84   "the country was sent": Hamilton Cravens and Peter C. Marshall, eds., *Great Depression: People and Perspectives*, Perspectives in American Social History (Santa Barbara, CA: ABC-Clio, 2009), p. 3.

85   "Our government is not": Franklin D. Roosevelt, address to a special session of the New York State Legislature, Albany, NY, August 28, 1931. Public Papers of the Presidents of the United States: F. D. Roosevelt, 1937, vol. 6 (Best Books, 1941).

86   "But how could a city": William Leuchtenburg, *The FDR Years: On Roosevelt and His Legacy* (New York: Columbia University Press, 1995), p. 213.

86   "No one is actually starving": Brian Farmer, *American Conservatism: History, Theory and Practice* (Newcastle upon Tyne: UK, 2008), p. 227.

86   "I want to step": Smith, *FDR*, p. 230.

CHAPTER FOUR: IN THE FOOTSTEPS OF COUSIN TEDDY

87   "My little man": Alonzo L. Hamby, *Man of Destiny: FDR and the Making of the American Century* (Basic Books, 2015), p. 10.

88   "The dictum of Macaulay": Samuel Rosenman, *Working with Roosevelt* (New York: Harper & Brothers, 1952), p. 55.

88   "grand opera never has had": James A. Farley, *Behind the Ballots: The Personal History of a Politician* (New York: Harcourt, Brace & Company, 1938), p. 68.

89   "It is said that Napoleon": Franklin D. Roosevelt, "Radio Address re a National Program of Restoration," April 7, 1932, Master Speech File, no. 469, Franklin D. Roosevelt Presidential Library and Museum, http://www.fdrlibrary.marist.edu/_resources/images/msf /msf00479.

90   "I will take off my coat": Terry Golway, *Frank and Al: FDR, Al Smith, and the Unlikely Alliance That Created the Modern Democratic Party* (New York: St. Martin's Press, 2018).

91   "Better bring a lot": Rosenman, *Working with Roosevelt*, p. 67.

91   "I am deeply grateful": Message Accepting the Republican Presidential Nomination, June 16, 1932. Public Papers of the Presidents of the United States—Herbert Hoover, January 1, 1932 to March 4, 1933 (US Government Printing Office, 1977), p. 260.

92   "dripping wet": Farley, *Jim Farley's Story*, p. 18.

93   "We presented a strange": Rosenman, *Working with Roosevelt*, p. 70.

94   "I pledge you": Ibid., p. 71.

95   "I'm a little older": James McGregor Burns, *Roosevelt: The Lion and the Fox 1882–1940.* (New York: Harcourt, Brace & Company, 1956), p. 138.

95   "California came here": Steve Neal, *Happy Days Are Here Again: The 1932 Democratic Convention, the Emergence of FDR—and How America Was Changed Forever* (New York: William Morrow, 2004), p. 290.

95   "Good old McAdoo": Ibid., p. 292.

96   "you know I can't deliver": Ibid., p. 76.

96   "Dammit, Louie": James Roosevelt, *Affectionately, F.D.R.*, p. 226.

96   "Out of every crisis": Franklin D. Roosevelt, "Acceptance Speech on Receiving Nomination," Chicago, IL, July 2, 1932, Master Speech File, no. 483. Franklin D. Roosevelt Presidential Library and Museum, http://www.fdrlibrary.marist.edu/_resources/images/msf /msf00493.

98   "You will use such force": Paul Dickson, *The Bonus Army: An American Epic* (New York: Walker Books, 2004), p. 173.

99   "Hello, Frank": Golway, *Frank and Al*, p. 251.

100   "There is nothing in politics": Farley, *Behind the Ballots,* p. 160.

100   "Campaigning for him": Raymond Moley, *After Seven Years* (New York: Harper & Brothers, 1939), p. 52.

101   "It won the Midwest": Ibid., p. 45.

101   "Now, before we get talking": Ibid., p. 46.

103   "would make up for": Eleanor Roosevelt, *The Autobiography of Eleanor Roosevelt* (New York: Harper & Brothers, 1961), p. 162.

103   "You know, Jimmy": James Roosevelt, *Affectionately, F.D.R.*, p. 232.

104   FDR viewed Hoover: Grace Tully, *F.D.R., My Boss* (Chicago: Peoples Book Club, 1949), p. 59.

105   "there was nothing ambiguous": Moley, *After Seven Years*, p. 70.

106   "it was clear": Ibid., p. 77.

107   "I have no Cabinet": Ibid., p. 81.

107   "I was no professional daredevil": Moley: *After Seven Years*, p. 115.

107   "Smoking, coughing": James Roosevelt, *My Parents, a Differing View* (Chicago: Playboy Press, 1976), p. 171.

108   "like sticking one's hand": Linda Lotridge Levin: *The Making of FDR: The Story of Stephen T. Early, America's First Modern Press Secretary* (New York: Prometheus Books, 2008).

109   "In many ways": Michael A. Butler, *Cautious Visionary: Cordell Hull and Trade Reform, 1933–1937* (Kent, Ohio: The Kent State University Press, 1998), p. 2.

110   "PREFER A WOODEN ROOF": Moley, *After Seven Years*, p. 122.

110   "I liked the cut": Ibid., p. 127.

110   he would title his memoir: Harold Ickes, *The Autobiography of a Curmudgeon* (Westport, CT: Praeger, 1985).

111   "the day the New Deal": Leah W. Sprague, "Her Life: The Woman Behind the New Deal" (Frances Perkins Center, June 1, 2014).

113   "There was nothing": Moley, *After Seven Years*, p. 139.

113   "By implication": Tully, *F.D.R., My Boss*, p. 63.

113   "Like hell I will": Jonathan Alter, *The Defining Moment: FDR's Hundred Days and the Triumph of Hope* (New York: Simon & Schuster, 2006), p. 200.

CHAPTER FIVE: THE MIGHTY PEN

117   "This is your speech now": Robert Schlesinger, *White House Ghosts: Presidents and Their Speechwriters* (New York: Simon & Schuster, 2008).

118   "Some historians accept": Moley, *The First New Deal* (New York: Harcourt, Brace & World, 1966), p. 96.

118   "Presidential speechwriters know": T. H. Baker, oral history with Malcolm Moos, November 2, 1972, Columbia University Oral History Project, Dwight D. Eisenhower Presidential Library.

118   "I am certain": Franklin D. Roosevelt, "Inaugural Address," March 4, 1933, Speech File, Franklin D. Roosevelt Presidential Library and Museum, http://www.fdrlibrary.marist.edu/_resources/images/msf/msf00628.

119   Rosenman investigated: Moley, *The First New Deal*, p. 118.

120   At least several evenings: Samuel Rosenman, *Working with Roosevelt* (New York: Harper & Brothers, 1952), p. 2.

121   "In preparing a speech": Tully, *F.D.R. My Boss* (endnote).

122   "I sat there fascinated": James Roosevelt, *Affectionately, F.D.R.*, p. 251.

122   "Mr. President": Ibid., p. 252.

124   "He had served": Eleanor Roosevelt, *The Autobiography of Eleanor Roosevelt* (New York: Harper & Brothers, 1961), p. 163.

124   "If I read the temper": Franklin D. Roosevelt, "Inaugural Address."

125   "Democracy is not": Herbert Hoover, *The Memoirs of Herbert Hoover: The Great Depression, 1929–1941* (New York: Macmillan, 1952), p. 344.

CHAPTER SIX: GOVERNING IN CRISIS

128   "I am told": Franklin D. Roosevelt, Presidential Press Conference, March 8, 1933.

128   "Mr. President," a reporter: Franklin D. Roosevelt, Presidential Press Conference, March 10, 1933.

129   "Mr. Roosevelt's features": John Gunther, *Roosevelt in Retrospect: A Profile in History* (New York: Harper & Brothers, 1950), p. 23.

130   Although they summoned up: Samuel Rosenman, *Working with Roosevelt* (New York: Harper & Brothers, 1952), p. 73.

130   "I want to talk": Franklin D. Roosevelt, "Fireside Chat #1—The Banking Crisis," March 12, 1933, Master Speech File, no. 616-1, Franklin D. Roosevelt Presidential Library and Museum, http://www.fdrlibrary.marist.edu/_resources/images/msf/msf00635.

133   "If he burned down": Arthur M. Schlesinger, Jr., *The Coming of the New Deal, 1933–1935* (New York: Houghton Mifflin, 1958), p. 13.

134   "was one expression": Blanche Wiesen Cook, *Eleanor Roosevelt*, vol. 3: *The War Years and After, 1939–1945* (New York: Viking, 2016).

134   "You are my life": Jan Pottker, *Sara and Eleanor: The Story of Sara Delano Roosevelt and Her Daughter-in-Law Eleanor Roosevelt* (New York: St. Martin's Press, 2004).

135   "I have never": Carl Sferrazza, *America's First Families: An Inside View of 200 Years of Private Life in the White House* (New York: Touchstone, 2000), p. 137.

135   "She's in prison": Eleanor Roosevelt, *The Autobiography of Eleanor Roosevelt* (New York: Harper & Brothers, 1961), p. 193.

135   "After the head": Ibid., p. 176.

136   "if inheritance has anything": Eleanor Roosevelt, "My Day," March 13, 1937.

136   "I hope Eleanor": H. W. Brands, *Traitor to His Class: The Privileged Life and Radical Presidency of Franklin Delano Roosevelt* (New York: Anchor Books, 2009), p. 307.

136   "Most of them sensed": Grace Tully, *F.D.R., My Boss* (Chicago: Peoples Book Club, 1949), p. 133.

137   "I and everyone else": Frances Perkins, *The Roosevelt I Knew* (New York: Viking, 1946), p. 369.

137   FDR was stunned: Jeff Shesol, *Supreme Power: Franklin Roosevelt and the Supreme Court* (New York: W. W. Norton, 2010), p. 137.

139   "In a hundred years": Joel Brinkley, "At a Party for 100th Birthday, Landon Receives a Kid of 76," *New York Times*, September 7, 1987, https://www.nytimes.com/1987/09/07/us/at-a-party-for-100th-birthday-landon-receives-a-kid-of-76.html.

140   "Hard-headedness will not": Franklin D. Roosevelt, "Inaugural Address," January 20, 1937, Master Speech File, no. 1030, Franklin D. Roosevelt Presidential Library and Museum, http://www.fdrlibrary.marist.edu/_resources/images/msf/msf01059.

141   "A lowered mental": Franklin D. Roosevelt, Presidential Press Conference, February 5, 1937.

141   "bloodless coup d'etat": Shesol, *Supreme Power*, p. 303.

141   "I read my Herald-Tribune": Eleanor Roosevelt, "My Day," February 10, 1937.

142   "When the Chief Justice": Rosenman, *Working with Roosevelt*, p. 144.

142   "He should have known": Shesol, *Supreme Power*, p. 307.

143   "By 1937, FDR": Ibid., p. 309.

143   "If three well-matched horses": Franklin D. Roosevelt, "Democratic Victory Dinner," March 4, 1937, Master Speech File, no. 1040-A, Franklin D. Roosevelt Presidential Library and Museum, http://www.fdrlibrary.marist.edu/_resources/images/msf/msf01069.

145   "obligated to promote": Adolf Hitler, *Mein Kampf* (Munich: Franz Eher Nachfolger, 1925).

146   "In many ways": Eugene Davidson, *The Making of Adolf Hitler: The Birth and Rise of Nazism* (Columbia: University of Missouri Press, 1997), p. 365.

146   "It's a hard thing": Ron Rosenbaum, *Explaining Hitler: The Search for the Origins of His Evil* (New York: HarperCollins, 1999).

147   "Hitler responds to the vibration": Otto Strasser, *Hitler and I* (Boston: Houghton Mifflin, 1940), p. 62.

148   "With Germany arming": Winston Churchill, *Churchill: The Power of Words*, edited by Martin Gilbert (New York: Hachette Books, 2012).

CHAPTER SEVEN: FRANKLIN AND WINSTON

151   "Never will you have": Winston Churchill, speech to the House of Commons, October 5, 1938.

151   "Far away": Winston Churchill, radio address, October 16, 1938.

153   "We are all worms": John Ramsden, "Churchill: A Man Who Believed," *Finest Hour* 129 (Winter 2005–06): 30.

154   "a tigerish devotion": Grace Tully, *F.D.R., My Boss* (Chicago: Peoples Book Club, 1949), p. 233.

154   "BERLIN, SEPTEMBER 27, 1938": "The German Chancellor (Hitler) to President Roosevelt," September 27, 1938—10:18 P.M. *Foreign Relations of the United States (FRUS)*: Diplomatic Papers, 1938, General, vol. 1. [There is a question mark on the date, as the telegram might have been received September 26.]

156   "The President told me": Henry Morgenthau, Jr., Diaries of Henry Morgenthau, Jr. (April 27, 1933–July 27, 1945), Franklin D. Roosevelt Presidential Library and Museum, diary entry April 11, 1939.

157   "YOU REALIZE I AM SURE": Franklin D. Roosevelt, "Day by Day," copy of the telegram sent from the White House, April 14, 1939.

159   "Mr. President": Henry Morgenthau, Jr., Diaries of Henry Morgenthau, Jr. (April 27, 1933–July 27, 1945), Franklin D. Roosevelt Presidential Library and Museum, diary entry June 19, 1939.

160   "Like a triage physician": Richard Breitman and Allan Lichtman, *FDR and the Jews* (Cambridge, MA: Belknap Press, 2013).

160   "set a match": Max Wallace, *The American Axis: Henry Ford, Charles Lindbergh, and the Rise of the Third Reich* (New York: St. Martin's Press, 2004).

160   "Joe always has been": Henry Morgenthau, Jr., Diaries of Henry

Morgenthau, Jr. (April 27, 1933–July 27, 1945), Franklin D. Roosevelt Presidential Library and Museum, diary entry October 3, 1939.

161 "The British and the Jewish": Susan Dunn, *1940: FDR, Willkie, Lindbergh, Hitler—Election amid the Storm* (New Haven, CT: Yale University Press, 2013).

161 "The Lindberghs and their friends": Ibid.

161 "Each of these men": Samuel Rosenman, *Working with Roosevelt* (New York: Harper & Brothers, 1952), p. 231.

162 "He liked to keep": Dorothy Jones Brady, Secretary to President Franklin D. Roosevelt, oral history interview, Franklin D. Roosevelt Presidential Library and Museum, Hyde Park, NY.

162 "I think it would be": Franklin D. Roosevelt, letter to King George VI, September 17, 1938. Rowley, *Franklin and Eleanor*.

163 "Why don't my ministers": Joseph P. Lash, "The Royal Visit of 1939," *Washington Post*, May 1, 1981, https://www.washingtonpost.com /archive/politics/1981/05/01/the-royal-visit-of-1939/9a2685c6 -cbe2-4768-ac3e-e3932d60d859/?utm_term=.8b61f74cae19.

163 "When everything was set": Recollections of Lizzie McDuffie, White House maid. Franklin D. Roosevelt Presidential Library and Museum, Hyde Park, NY.

164 "They are such a charming": The British Royal Visit, documents, Franklin D. Roosevelt Presidential Library and Museum, https:// www.fdrlibrary.org/royal-visit.

164 "Oh dear, oh dear": Eleanor Roosevelt, "My Day," May 26, 1939.

164 "King Tries Hot Dog": Felix Belair, Jr., "King Tries Hot Dog and Asks for More," *New York Times*, June 12, 1939, https://www .nytimes.com/1939/06/12/archives/king-tries-hot-dog-and-asks -for-more-and-he-drinks-beer-with-them.html.

165 "There was something incredibly": Eleanor Roosevelt, *The Autobiography of Eleanor Roosevelt* (New York: Harper & Brothers, 1961), p. 207.

166 "We did everything": V. M. Molotov and Felix Chuev, *Molotov Remembers: Inside Kremlin Politics* (trans.) (Chicago: Ivan R. Dee, 1993).

166 "What a pity": Svetlana Alliluyeva, *Twenty Letters to a Friend* (New York: Harper & Row, 1967), p. 124.

167 In *Red Famine*: Anne Applebaum, *Red Famine: Stalin's War on Ukraine* (New York: Anchor Books, 2017).

167 "a kind of evil genius": Philip Boobbyer, *The Stalin Era* (New York: Routledge, 2000), p. 100.

168 "That man is the centre": Henri Barbusse, *Stalin: A New World Order Seen Through One Man* (New York: Macmillan, 1935), p. vi.

168 "Human feelings in him": Svetlana Alliluyeva, *Only One Year: A Memoir* (New York: Harper & Row, 1969), p. 351.

168 "He had always considered": Alliluyeva, *Twenty Letters*, p. 110.

169 "You must master": Franklin D. Roosevelt, "Fireside Chat #14— War in Europe," September 3, 1939, Master Speech File, no. 1240,

Franklin D. Roosevelt Presidential Library and Museum, http://www.fdrlibrary.marist.edu/_resources/images/msf/msf01279.

170   "Dear Queen Elizabeth": Letter from Eleanor Roosevelt to Queen Elizabeth, May 1940, Franklin D. Roosevelt Presidential Library and Museum, https://www.fdrlibrary.org/royal-visit.

171   "My dear Churchill": Churchill to Roosevelt, September 11, 1939. Francis L. Loewenheim, Harold D. Langley, and Manfred Jonas, eds., *Roosevelt and Churchill: The Secret Wartime Correspondence* (New York: Saturday Review Press/E.P. Dutton & Co., 1975), p. 89.

171   "Our bond with Europe": Charles Lindbergh, speech, Mutual Radio Network, October 1939.

172   "If I should die": Henry Morgenthau, Jr., Diaries of Henry Morgenthau, Jr., April 27, 1933–July 27, 1945, Franklin D. Roosevelt Presidential Library and Museum, diary entry, May 20, 1940.

172   "Reporters were swarming": Rosenman, *Working with Roosevelt*, p. 189.

173   "On July fourteenth": Franklin D. Roosevelt, "Message to Congress at Extraordinary Session to Amend Neutrality," September 21, 1939, Master Speech File, no. 1243, Franklin D. Roosevelt Presidential Library and Museum, http://www.fdrlibrary.marist.edu/_resources/images/msf/msf01282.

175   He'd dangled the idea: Rosenman, *Working with Roosevelt*, p. 193.

176   "I do not want to run": Henry Morgenthau, Jr., Diaries of Henry Morgenthau, Jr. (April 27, 1933–July 27, 1945), Franklin D. Roosevelt Presidential Library and Museum, Hyde Park, NY, diary entry January 24, 1940.

177   "We hear the church bells": "Bringing Tales of WWII to American Radios and Bookshelves" (recording, NPR), https://www.npr.org/2015/05/30/410752402/bringing-tales-of-wwii-to-american-radios-and-bookshelves.

177   "As you are": Churchill to Roosevelt, May 15, 1940. Francis L. Loewenheim, Harold D. Langley, and Manfred Jonas, eds., *Roosevelt and Churchill: The Secret Wartime Correspondence* (New York: Saturday Review Press/E.P. Dutton & Co., 1975), p. 94.

177   "On this tenth day": Franklin D. Roosevelt, "Address of the President, University of Virginia," June 10, 1940, Master Speech File, No. 1285, Franklin D. Roosevelt Presidential Library and Museum, http://www.fdrlibrary.marist.edu/_resources/images/msf/msf01330.

178   "Washington wouldn't": John Jeffries, *A Third Term for FDR: The Election of 1940* (Lawrence: University Press of Kansas, 2017).

178   "Did you ever stop": Diaries of Henry Morgenthau, Jr. (April 27, 1933–July 27, 1945), Franklin D. Roosevelt Presidential Library and Museum, Hyde Park, NY, diary entry January 24, 1940.

179   "After all, Mr. President": Ibid.

179   "From time to time": James A. Farley, *Jim Farley's Story: The Roosevelt Years* (New York: Whittlesey House, 1948), p. 246.

180   "Jim," he said: Ibid., p. 251.

181   "We want Roosevelt!": Ibid., p. 280.

181   "Well, damn it to hell": Tully, *F.D.R., My Boss*, p. 239.

181 "You will have": The Eleanor Roosevelt Papers Project, July 18, 1940. https://www2.gwu.edu/~erpapers/myday/displaydoc.cfm?_y =1940&_f=md055635.

182 "Thank God for a good King!": Michael Paterson, *A Brief History of the House of Windsor: The Making of a Modern Monarchy* (London: Constable & Robinson, 2013).

183 "The King is still in London": Billy Cotton and His Band.

183 "There's no place": Robert Siegel, host, "Three Americans in London, Fighting for War," National Public Radio, February 3, 2010.

183 "I know south Germany": Diaries of Henry Morgenthau, Jr. (April 27, 1933–July 27, 1945), Franklin D. Roosevelt Presidential Library and Museum, Hyde Park, NY, diary entry August 4, 1941.

185 "I think I'm needed": James Roosevelt, *My Parents, a Differing View* (Chicago: Playboy Press, 1976), p. 163.

186 The day after Christmas: Rosenman, *Working with Roosevelt*, p. 258.

186 "I *love* it!": Ibid., p. 261.

186 "There are also American citizens": Ibid., p. 262.

187 "We waited as he leaned": Ibid., p. 263.

187 "You can see the real Roosevelt": James MacGregor Burns, "F.D.R.: The Last Journey Home," *American Heritage*, August 1970, vol. 21, no. 5, *1941–1946* (New York: Random House, 1975), p. 4.

188 "Mr. President," he joked: William D. Hassett, *Off the Record with FDR 1942–1945* (New York: Enigma Books, 2016).

188 "The preservation of the sacred": Franklin D. Roosevelt, "Inaugural Address," January 20, 1941 (reading copy), Master Speech File, no. 1335A, Franklin D. Roosevelt Presidential Library and Museum, http://www.fdrlibrary.marist.edu/_resources/images/msf/msf 01411.

189 "The President talked to me": W. Averell Harriman and Elie Abel, *Special Envoy to Churchill and Stalin, 1941–1946* (New York: Random House, 1975), p. 4.

CHAPTER EIGHT: THE RISE OF THE ALLIES

190 "Put your confidence": Winston Churchill, radio broadcast, February 9, 1941. "Give Us Your Tools," International Churchill Society.

191 "Suppose my neighbor's": Franklin D. Roosevelt, Presidential Press Conference, December 17, 1940.

192 "We have only": Drew Middleton, "Hitler's Russian Blunder," *New York Times*, June 21, 1981, https://www.nytimes.com/1981/06/21 /magazine/hitler-s-russian-blunder.html.

192 "Then, what are we": Nikita Khrushchev, *Memoirs of Nikita Khrushchev*, edited by Sergei Khrushchev, vol. 1: *Commissar, 1918–1945* (University Park: Pennsylvania State University Press, 2005).

193 "No one has been": Winston Churchill's broadcast on the Soviet-German War, 1941. National Churchill Museum.

193 "Mr. Hopkins is in Moscow": Butler, *My Dear Mr. Stalin*, July 26, 1941.

194 "in boots that shone": Christopher D. O'Sullivan, *Harry Hopkins:*

FDR's Envoy to Churchill and Stalin (Lanham, MD: Rowman & Littlefield, 2015).

194   "In my opinion": Franklin Delano Roosevelt and Pope Pius XII, *Wartime Correspondence Between President Roosevelt and Pope Pius XII*, edited by Myron C. Taylor (New York: Macmillan, 1947).

195   "Cruise uneventful": Synchrony of Atlantic Conference, August 1941, prepared by Les Dropkin, p. 11, synchrony_of_atlantic_con ference_august_1941.pdf.

195   "You'd have thought": Roll, *The Hopkins Touch*.

196   "I wish you could": Franklin D. Roosevelt, message to King George VI, USS *Augusta*, August 11th, 1941—handwritten letter, Franklin D. Roosevelt Library, www.fdrlibrary.marist.edu.

198   "Mr. Roosevelt was not": Grace Tully, *F.D.R., My Boss* (Chicago: Peoples Book Club, 1949), p. 253.

198   "Japan: Honorable Fire Extinguisher": *Time*, September 22, 1941.

198   "His outstanding characteristic": Cordell Hull, *The Memoirs of Cordell Hull*, vol. 2 (New York: Macmillan, 1948), p. 987.

199   "If we were to go": Ibid., p. 1062.

199   "a typical Japanese officer": Ibid., p. 1054.

200   "Nations must think": H. W. Brands, *Traitor to His Class: The Privileged Life and Radical Presidency of Franklin Delano Roosevelt* (New York: Anchor Books, 2009), p. 621.

200   "I felt from the start": Hull, *Memoirs*, p. 1061.

200   "sly-looking little man": Tully, *F.D.R., My Boss*, p. 249.

201   "It's a pity": Hull, *Memoirs*, p. 1075.

201   "This time we mean it": Smith, *FDR*, p. 526.

202   "I address myself": Roosevelt, message to Emperor Hirohito, December 6, 1941.

202   "Dear Cordell": Hull, *Memoirs*, p. 1094.

CHAPTER NINE: THE COMMON CAUSE

204   "I must say": "Hull accuses Japanese of outright lies." UPI, December 7, 1941, https://www.upi.com/Archives/1941/12/07/Hull-accus es-Japanese-of-outright-lies/6113254588380/.

204   "It was then": Saburo Kurusu, *The Desperate Diplomat: Saburo Kurusu's Memoir of the Weeks Before Pearl Harbor*, edited by J. Garry Clifford and Masako R. Okura (Columbia: University of Missouri Press, 2016), p. 123.

204   "At the very moment": Hull, *Memoirs*, p. 1098.

205   "This is Steve Early": Richard L. Strout, "War Comes to Washington on a Sunday Afternoon," *Christian Science Monitor*, December 8, 1941.

206   "Overhead were flights": K. D. Richardson, *Reflections of Pearl Harbor: An Oral History of December 7, 1941* (Westport, CT: Praeger, 2005), p. 2.

206   "As we cleared": Ibid., p. 3.

206   "I could see the pilots": Interview with Albert Berger, Veterans History Project, June 15, 2003, http://memory.loc.gov/diglib/vhp/story /loc.natlib.afc2001001.07573/transcript?ID=sr0001.

207   "All but essential": Interview with Sergeant John H. Koenig, Veterans

History Project, September 20, 2001, https://www.nj.gov/military /museum/summaries/korean_war/koenig.html.

207   "What a sight": Strout, "War Comes to Washington."

207   "The Prime Minister seemed": W. Averell Harriman and Elie Abel, *Special Envoy to Churchill and Stalin, 1941–1946* (New York: Random House, 1975), p. 111.

208   "Mr. President, what's this": Ibid., p. 112.

208   "Sit down, Grace": Grace Tully, *F.D.R., My Boss* (Chicago: Peoples Book Club, 1949), p. 256.

209   "They seemed to be": A. Merriman Smith, *Thank You, Mr. President: A White House Notebook* (New York: Harper & Brothers, 1946), p. 115.

210   "Yesterday, December 7": Franklin D. Roosevelt, "Address to Congress—Declaring War on Japan," December 8, 1941, Master Speech File, no. 1400, Franklin D. Roosevelt Presidential Library and Museum, Hyde Park, NY.

212   "There was none of": Robert E. Sherwood, *Roosevelt and Hopkins: An Intimate History* (New York: Harper & Brothers, 1948), p. 437.

213   "We had no information": Hans Louis Trefousse, ed., *What Happened at Pearl Harbor? Documents Pertaining to the Japanese Attack of December 7, 1941, and Its Background* (New York: Twayne Publishers, 1958), p. 36.

214   "The Roosevelt administration failed": Basil Rauch, *Roosevelt: From Munich to Pearl Harbor: A Study in the Creation of a Foreign Policy* (New York: Creative Age Press, 1950), p. 433.

215   "It had not occurred": Eleanor Roosevelt, "My Day," December 24, 1941.

215   "I have a toast": Ibid.

215   "He likes the world": Eleanor Roosevelt, interview, July 13, 1954, Franklin D. Roosevelt Presidential Library and Museum.

215   "It would be": Alistair Cooke, during oral history interview of Alistair Cooke by Curtis Roosevelt, October 20, 1993, New York City. Franklin D. Roosevelt Presidential Library.

215   "Churchill did something": Jon Meacham, in Ken Burns, *The Roosevelts: An Intimate History*, PBS, 2014.

216   "There are many": Franklin D. Roosevelt, "Christmas Tree Lighting Ceremonies," December 24, 1941, Master Speech File, no. 1406, Franklin D. Roosevelt Presidential Library and Museum, http://www.fdrlibrary.marist.edu/_resources/images/msf/msfb0011.

217   "If my father": Winston Churchill, "Address to Joint Session of U.S. Congress, 1941," December 26, 1941, National Churchill Museum, https://www.nationalchurchillmuseum.org/churchill-address-to-congress.html.

218   "My husband": Eleanor Roosevelt, *On My Own: The Years Since the White House* (New York: Harper & Brothers Publishers, 1958).

218   "The Prime Minister": Curtis Roosevelt, oral history interview of Alistair Cooke (undated), Franklin D. Roosevelt Presidential Library.

218   "There are lots": Dwight D. Eisenhower, *The Eisenhower Diaries*,

edited by Robert H. Ferrell (New York: W. W. Norton, 1981),
p. 40.

219   "Anger cannot win": Ibid., p. 52.

219   "I was listening": Ed Cray, *General of the Army: George C. Mar-
       shall, Soldier and Statesman* (New York: Norton, 1990).

220   "Don't you think": Jack Uldrich, *Soldier, Statesman, Peace-
       maker: Leadership Lessons from George C. Marshall* (New York:
       AMACOM, 2005), p. 100.

222   "not only was the evacuation": President Gerald R. Ford's Procla-
       mation, Confirming the Termination of the Executive Order Au-
       thorizing Japanese-American Internment During World War II,"
       February 19, 1976, Gerald R. Ford Presidential Library and Museum,
       https://www.fordlibrarymuseum.gov/library/speeches/760111p
       .htm.

223   "here we admit a wrong": Ronald Reagan, "Remarks on Sign-
       ing the Bill Providing Restitution for the Wartime Internment of
       Japanese-American Civilians," August 10, 1988, Ronald Reagan
       Presidential Library & Museum, https://www.reaganlibrary.gov
       /research/speeches/081088d.

223   "Americans had become": Rosenman, *Working with Roosevelt,*
       p. 329.

223   "I am going to ask": Ibid., p. 330.

225   his "defeatist" attitude: Harriman and Abel, *Special Envoy,* p. 93.

226   "We were handsomely wined": William Harrison Standley, *Admiral
       Ambassador to Russia* (New York: Regnery, 1955), p. 134.

226   "The president wishes": Ibid., p. 152.

227   "If I can be": Ibid., p. 158.

228   "The Secret Service men": Eleanor Roosevelt, *The Autobiogra-
       phy of Eleanor Roosevelt* (New York: Harper & Brothers, 1961),
       p. 235.

228   "Stalin had all the aces": Standley, *Admiral Ambassador to Russia,*
       p. 194.

230   "In view of": "Operation Desperate," Report by the J. P. Typing
       Pool, May 1942. Imperial War Museum, https://www.iwm.org.uk
       /collections/item/object/1030009701.

232   "Defeat is one thing": Churchill, *Second World War,* p. 584.

233   "incurable predilection": Sherwood, *Roosevelt and Hopkins,*
       p. 591.

233   "General, I'm interested": Dwight D. Eisenhower, *At Ease: Stories I
       Tell to Friends* (New York: Doubleday, 1967), p. 249.

234   "Confronted by the": Ibid., p. 253.

234   "I will clamp down": Dwight D. Eisenhower, *Crusade in Europe*
       (New York: Doubleday, 1948).

234   "like carrying a": Churchill, *Memoirs of the Second World War,*
       p. 619.

234   "with the ogre": Sonia Purnell, *Clementine: The Life of Mrs. Win-
       ston Churchill* (New York: Viking, 2015).

234   "I pondered": Churchill, *Memoirs of Second World War,* p. 618.

235   "was prepared with": Ibid., p. 619.

235 "You must not be": Harriman and Abel, *Special Envoy*, p. 152.

235 "Stalin will make": Churchill, *Memoirs of the Second World War*, p. 626.

235 "I repulsed": Ibid., p. 627.

236 "They were really desperate": Harriman and Abel, *Special Envoy*, p. 159.

236 "There I found": Tommy Norton, "Winston was . . . complaining of a slight headache," National Archives/ Blog, May 22, 2013.

237 "I think the two": Ibid.

237 "I should say": Papers of Sir Ian Jacob, Churchill Archives Centre, Cambridge University, Cambridge, UK.

238 "He said": William D. Leahy, *I Was There: The Personal Story of the Chief of Staff to Presidents Roosevelt and Truman Based on His Notes and Diaries Made at the Time* (New York: Whittlesey House, 1950), p. 97.

238 "Nothing must be printed": Linda Lotridge Levin, *The Making of FDR: The Story of Stephen T. Early, America's First Modern Press Secretary* (New York: Prometheus Books, 2008).

239 "This is my Shangri-La!": Michael Giorgione, *Inside Camp David: The Private World of the Presidential Retreat* (New York: Little, Brown, 2018), p. 26.

240 "I have been present": Churchill, *Memoirs of the Second World War*, p. 403.

242 "We were gambling": Eisenhower, *Crusade in Europe*.

242 playing politics with the war: Tully, *F.D.R., My Boss*, p. 264.

242 "the most dismal setting": Eisenhower, *Crusade in Europe*.

242 "The eternal darkness": Ibid.

243 "I simply must": Eisenhower, *Diaries*, p. 81.

243 "There was some discussion": Leahy, *I Was There*, p. 112.

244 "He listened intently": Tully, *F.D.R., My Boss*, p. 264.

245 "If I could meet": Eisenhower, *Crusade in Europe*.

245 "a time when": Eisenhower, *At Ease*, p. 258.

245 "Once the Nazis": Ibid., p. 262.

246 "Darlan's murder": Martin Gilbert, *Winston S. Churchill: Road to Victory* (Hillsdale, MI: Hillsdale College Press, 2013).

246 "Now this is not": Winston Churchill, speech at the Mansion House, London, November 10, 1942.

247 "acted like a": Sherwood, *Roosevelt and Hopkins*, p. 671.

247 "The plane was rated": Eisenhower, *At Ease*, p. 259.

248 "With an anxious thought": Eisenhower, *Crusade in Europe*.

248 "Ike seems jittery": Sherwood, *Roosevelt and Hopkins*, p. 676.

248 "Successful in shaking": Eisenhower, *Crusade in Europe*.

249 "I spent many hours": Franklin D. Roosevelt, speech "Address to White House Correspondents Association Dinner," February 13, 1943, Master Speech File, no. 1451, Franklin D. Roosevelt Presidential Library and Museum, http://www.fdrlibrary.marist.edu/_resources/images/msf/msfb0074.

250 "seemed to me": Sherwood, *Roosevelt and Hopkins*, p. 688.

250 "a dud": Elliott Roosevelt, *As He Saw It: The Story of the World*

Conferences of F.D.R. (New York: Duell, Sloan and Pearce, 1946), p. 91.

250   "De Gaulle is on": Ibid., p. 69.

251   "Each Frenchman": Harriman and Abel, *Special Envoy*, p. 186.

251   "Another point": Roosevelt-Churchill Press Conference, Casablanca, January 24, 1943, 12:15 P.M., *FRUS*: Diplomatic Papers, The Conferences at Washington, 1941–1942, 1943, https://history .state.gov/historicaldocuments/frus1941-43/ch9subsubch59.

252   "We had so much": Sherwood, *Roosevelt and Hopkins*, p. 671.

253   "You cannot come": Churchill, *Memoirs of the Second World War*, p. 674.

253   "He forgot about winter": Winston Churchill, radio broadcast, May 10, 1942.

253   "Victory, however": Churchill, *Memoirs of the Second World War*, p. 683.

CHAPTER TEN: THE ROAD TO TEHRAN

257   "We didn't believe": V. M. Molotov and Felix Chuev, *Molotov Remembers: Inside Kremlin Politics* (trans.) (Chicago: Ivan R. Dee, 1993).

258   "In view of the absence": Stalin, speech, February 22, 1943. J.V. Stalin Order of the Day, No. 95, https://www.marxists.org/reference /archive/stalin/works/1943/02/23.htm.

258   "I must give": Franklin D. Roosevelt and Joseph V. Stalin, *My Dear Mr. Stalin: The Complete Correspondence of Franklin D. Roosevelt and Joseph V. Stalin*, edited by Susan Butler (New Haven: Yale University Press, 2005), March 16, 1943.

258   "I think it is": David L. Roll, *The Hopkins Touch: Harry Hopkins and the Forging of the Alliance to Defeat Hitler* (Oxford, UK: Oxford University Press, 2013), p. 265.

259   "I know you will not": Churchill to Roosevelt, March 17, 1942. Francis L. Loewenheim, Harold D. Langley, and Manfred Jonas, eds., *Roosevelt and Churchill: The Secret Wartime Correspondence* (New York: Saturday Review Press/E.P. Dutton & Co., 1975), p. 196.

259   "He had great confidence": Samuel Rosenman, *Working with Roosevelt* (New York: Harper & Brothers, 1952), p. 403.

259   "I want to get away": Roosevelt and Stalin, *My Dear Mr. Stalin*, May 5, 1943.

260   In particular, an editorial: Robert E. Sherwood, *Roosevelt and Hopkins: An Intimate History* (New York: Harper & Brothers, 1948), p. 761.

260   "I do not know": Ibid., p. 761.

261   "Dear Harry": Ibid., p. 761.

261   Hearing that there was a jukebox: Michael Giorgione, *Inside Camp David: The Private World of the Presidential Retreat* (New York: Little, Brown, 2018), p. 33.

261   "The cigars created": William M. Rigdon, *White House Sailor* (New York: Doubleday, 1962), p. 219.

262   "One must not forget": Roosevelt and Stalin, *My Dear Mr. Stalin*, June 24, 1943.

262 "I have received": Churchill to Roosevelt, June 13, 1943. Francis L. Loewenheim, Harold D. Langley, and Manfred Jonas, eds., *Roosevelt and Churchill: The Secret Wartime Correspondence*. (New York: Saturday Review Press/E.P. Dutton & Co., 1975), p. 342.

265 "By 1943 most everyone": Winston Groom, *The Allies: Roosevelt, Churchill, Stalin, and the Unlikely Alliance That Won World War II* (Washington, DC: National Geographic Partners, 2018), p. 345.

266 "The Ambassador will be": William Harrison Standley, *Admiral Ambassador to Russia* (New York: Regnery, 1955), p. 475.

266 "We Westerners believed": Ibid., p. 474.

266 "I don't envy you": Ibid., p. 490.

267 "I do not have any": Butler, *My Dear Mr. Stalin*, October 14, 1943.

267 "new laws and resolutions": Roosevelt and Stalin, *My Dear Mr. Stalin*, August 8, 1943.

268 "We have found you": W. Averell Harriman and Elie Abel, *Special Envoy to Churchill and Stalin, 1941–1946* (New York: Random House, 1975), p. 239.

268 "You will be glad": Roosevelt and Stalin, *My Dear Mr. Stalin*, November 8, 1943.

269 "Torpedo defense!": "President's Daily Log," Sunday, November 14, *FRUS*: Diplomatic Papers, The Conferences at Cairo and Tehran, 1943, Log of the Trip.

269 "Take me over": Rigdon, *White House Sailor*, p. 64.

269 "On Monday last": FDR's private diary, given to him by Daisy Suckley. FDR Library and Museum.

270 "Can you imagine": Sherwood, *Roosevelt and Hopkins*, p. 768.

270 "Who could stop him?": Rigdon, *White House Sailor*, p. 62.

270 "You're a pretty stubborn": James Roosevelt, *Affectionately, F.D.R.: A Son's Story of a Lonely Man* (New York: Harcourt, Brace & Company, 1959), p. 345.

271 "Ike," the president mused: Dwight D. Eisenhower, *Crusade in Europe* (New York: Doubleday, 1948).

271 "it is dangerous": Ibid.

271 "Cairo was filled": Michael F. Reilly, *Reilly of the White House: Behind the Scenes with FDR* (New York: Simon & Schuster, 1947), p. 164.

272 "They found her charming": Eleanor Roosevelt, *The Autobiography of Eleanor Roosevelt* (New York: Harper & Brothers, 1961), p. 249.

272 "lengthy, complicated and minor": Winston S. Churchill, *Memoirs of the Second World War* (New York: Houghton Mifflin, 1959), p. 753.

273 "And of course this leads": Elliott Roosevelt, *As He Saw It*, p. 160.

274 "For a couple of hours": Dallek, *Franklin D. Roosevelt: A Political Life*, p. 535.

CHAPTER ELEVEN: YOUR HOUSE IS MY HOUSE

276 "the Americans stood": V. M. Molotov and Felix Chuev, *Molotov Remembers: Inside Kremlin Politics* (trans.) (Chicago: Ivan R. Dee, 1993).

277   "Very Important Personages": Lord Alanbrooke, *War Diaries 1939–1945* (London: Weidenfeld & Nicholson, 2001), p. 482.

277   "Are you sure": Michael F. Reilly, *Reilly of the White House: Behind the Scenes with FDR* (New York: Simon & Schuster, 1947), p. 177.

278   "Yesterday morning": FDR diary.

278   "Stalin was still suspicious": Keith Eubank, *Summit at Teheran* (New York: William Morrow, 1985), p. 196.

278   "Everywhere you went": Reilly, *Reilly of the White House*, p. 179.

279   "The Boss": Ibid., p. 178.

279   "We could tell": William M. Rigdon, *White House Sailor* (New York: Doubleday, 1962), p. 82.

279   "a most engaging": Reilly, *Reilly of the White House*, p. 179.

279   "became actually kindly": Rigdon, *White House Sailor*, p. 82.

279   "two or three puffs": Elliott Roosevelt, *As He Saw It: The Story of the World Conferences of F.D.R.* (New York: Duell, Sloan and Pearce, 1946), p. 179.

280   "It was evident": Alanbrooke, *War Diaries*, p. 482.

281   "What'd you talk about?": Elliott Roosevelt, *As He Saw It*, p. 175.

282   "once Stalin's companion": Hugh Lunghi, "Glimpses—Troubled Triumvirate: The Big Three at the Summit," *Finest Hour* 135 (Summer 2007), International Churchill Society, https://winston churchill.org/publications/finest-hour/finest-hour-135/glimpses -troubled-triumvirate-the-big-three-at-the-summit/.

282   In the official log: Log of the Trip, Sunday, November 28, 1943, *FRUS*: Diplomatic Papers, The Conferences at Cairo and Tehran, 1943.

282   "Churchill employed all": Sherwood, *Roosevelt and Hopkins*, p. 789.

283   "It was my first": Charles E. Bohlen, *Witness to History, 1929–1969* (New York: W. W. Norton, 1973), p. 136.

283   "What's he saying?": A. H. Birse, *Memoirs of an Interpreter* (New York: Coward-McCann, 1967), p. 154.

283   "a rich uncle": Ibid., p. 155.

283   was the greatest concentration: "First plenary meeting," November 28, 1943, 4 P.M., Bohlen Minutes, *FRUS*: Diplomatic Papers, The Conferences at Cairo and Tehran, 1943, Document 360, https:// history.state.gov/historicaldocuments/frus1943CairoTehran/d360.

284   "by opening": Ibid.

285   "the scruff of the neck": First Plenary Meeting, November 28, 1943, 4 P.M., Combined Chiefs of Staff Minutes. *FRUS*: Diplomatic Papers, The Conferences at Cairo and Tehran, 1943, Documents 360–361, https://history.state.gov/historicaldocuments/frus1943CairoTehran /d361.

285   "Stalin has got": Eubank, *Summit at Teheran*, p. 280.

286   "There I sat": Cray, *General of the Army*.

286   "had a military brain": Alanbrooke, *War Diaries*, p. 483.

286   "bandit leader": Leahy, *I Was There*, p. 205.

286   "The Marshal's approach": Ibid., p. 205.

287   "When I told him": Bohlen, *Witness to History*, p. 143.

287   "At close range": Lunghi, "Glimpses—Troubled Triumvirate."

287 "spent the day": Log of the Trip, Sunday, November 28, *FRUS*: Diplomatic Papers, The Conferences at Cairo and Tehran, 1943.

288 "That'll be ten dollars": Elliott Roosevelt, *As He Saw It*, p. 178.

288 "Let us first consider": Churchill, *Memoirs of the Second World War*, p. 758.

289 "Nothing is final": Ibid, p. 759.

290 "But you won't": Reilly, *Reilly of the White House*, p. 180.

CHAPTER TWELVE: CLASH OF TITANS

291 Sergo Beria, the son: Sergo Beria, *Beria, My Father: Inside Stalin's Kremlin* (London: Duckworth, 2001); also Gary Kern, "How Uncle Joe Bugged FDR." Central Intelligence Agency, April 14, 2007, https://www.cia.gov/library/center-for-the-study-of-intelligence /csi-publications/csi-studies/studies/vol47no1/article02.html.

291 "I shall insist": Sherwood, *Roosevelt and Hopkins*, p. 784.

292 "I get up": Molotov, *Molotov Remembers*.

292 He shared an idea: "Roosevelt-Stalin Meeting," November 29, 1943, 2:45 P.M., Bohlen Minutes, *FRUS*: Diplomatic Papers, The Conferences at Cairo and Tehran, 1943, Document 365.

293 At one point, he drew: "Sketch by Roosevelt to Illustrate His Concept of the United Nations Organization," November 29, 1943, *FRUS*: Diplomatic Papers, The Conferences at Cairo and Tehran, 1943, p. 622, https://history.state.gov/historicaldocuments/frus1943Cairo Tehran/pg_622.

293 "I have been commanded": "Log of the Trip," November 29, 1943, *FRUS*: Diplomatic Papers, The Conferences at Cairo and Tehran, 1943, Document 353, https://history.state.gov/historicaldocuments /frus1943CairoTehran/d353.

294 "like all the Russians": William D. Leahy, *I Was There: The Personal Story of the Chief of Staff to Presidents Roosevelt and Truman Based on His Notes and Diaries Made at the Time* (New York: Whittlesey House, 1950), p. 207.

294 "bad from beginning": Lord Alanbrooke, *War Diaries 1939–1945* (London: Weidenfeld & Nicholson, 2001), p. 485.

295 "Who will command Overlord?": "Second Plenary Meeting," November 29, 1943, 4 P.M., Bohlen Minutes, *FRUS*: Diplomatic Papers, The Conferences at Cairo and Tehran, 1943, Document 366, November 29, 1943, https://history.state.gov/historicaldocuments /frus1943CairoTehran/d366.

295 "I felt we should put": W. Averell Harriman and Elie Abel, *Special Envoy to Churchill and Stalin, 1941–1946* (New York: Random House, 1975), p. 272.

295 "In that case": Bohlen, *Witness to History*, p. 148.

295 "We know the men": Keith Eubank, *Summit at Teheran* (New York: William Morrow, 1985), p. 304.

295 "That old Bolshevik": Leahy, *I Was There*, p. 208.

295 "Mr. President": Bohlen, *Witness to History*, p. 146.

296 "I wish to pose": Kenneth W. Thompson, *Winston Churchill's World View, Statesmanship and Power* (Baton Rouge, LA: LSU Press, 1987), p. 160.

297   FDR, wanting: "Second Plenary Meeting," November 29, 1943, Joint Chiefs of Staff Minutes, 4 P.M., Bohlen Minutes, *FRUS: Diplomatic Papers, The Conferences at Cairo and Tehran, 1943,* Document 366, https://history.state.gov/historicaldocuments/frus 1943CairoTehran/d374.

297   "Why do that?": Leahy, *I Was There,* p. 207.

297   "Quit listening": Author interview: Bret Baier and Marlin Fitzwater, November 14, 2017.

297   "The official records": Robert E. Sherwood, *Roosevelt and Hopkins: An Intimate History* (New York: Harper & Brothers, 1948), p. 789.

297   "I have little hope": Alanbrooke, *War Diaries,* p. 485.

298   "He gets things done": Elliott Roosevelt, *As He Saw It: The Story of the World Conferences of F.D.R.* (New York: Duell, Sloan and Pearce, 1946), p. 183.

298   "Elliott, our chiefs of staff": Ibid., p. 185.

298   "We had one banquet": Franklin D. Roosevelt, Presidential Press Conference, December 17, 1943.

299   "The reason there are": Elliott Roosevelt, *As He Saw It,* p. 188.

299   "was a wilier comrade": V. M. Molotov and Felix Chuev, *Molotov Remembers: Inside Kremlin Politics* (trans.) (Chicago: Ivan R. Dee, 1993).

299   "The most notable": "Tripartite Dinner Meeting," November 29, 1943, 8:30 P.M., Bohlen Minutes, *FRUS:* Diplomatic Papers, The Conferences at Cairo and Tehran, 1943, Document 368, https:// history.state.gov/historicaldocuments/frus1943CairoTehran/d368.

299   "I propose a salute": Elliott Roosevelt, *As He Saw It,* p. 188.

300   "Clearly there must be": Ibid., p. 189.

300   "Isn't the whole thing": Ibid., p. 190.

300   "How can you dare": Ibid., p. 190.

300   "It was only a joke": Eubank, *Summit at Teheran,* p. 316.

300   "It's fun to be": "Visits by Winston Churchill," January 1942. Franklin D. Roosevelt Presidential Library and Museum, https:// fdrlibrary.tumblr.com/post/88377688254/day-19-visits-by-win ston-churchill-it-is-fun-to.

301   "Stupendous issues": Roll, *The Hopkins Touch,* p. 323.

CHAPTER THIRTEEN: LIKE A RAINBOW

302   "Agreed": "Combined Chiefs of Staff Minutes," November 30, 1943, 9:30 A.M., *FRUS:* Diplomatic Papers, The Conferences at Cairo and Tehran, 1943, Document 369, https://history.state.gov /historicaldocuments/frus1943CairoTehran/d369.

303   "I never asked": Leahy, *I Was There,* p. 209.

304   "The Governments": "The Declaration on Iran," December 1, 1943, *FRUS:* Diplomatic Papers, The Conferences at Cairo and Tehran, 1943, Document 419, https://history.state.gov/historicaldocu ments/frus1943CairoTehran/d419.

305   If that didn't happen: Churchill, *Memoirs of the Second World War,* p. 765.

305   Eisenhower's name: Bohlen, *Witness to History,* p. 149.

306   He boasted that: "Combined Chiefs of Staff Minutes," November 30, 1943, 4 P.M., *FRUS*: Diplomatic Papers, The Conferences at Cairo and Tehran, 1943, Document 374, https://history.state.gov /historicaldocuments/frus1943CairoTehran/d374.

306   Churchill said poetically: Ibid.

306   "That is what we call": Ibid.

306   "wreathed in smiles": Elliott Roosevelt, *As He Saw It: The Story of the World Conferences of F.D.R.* (New York: Duell, Sloan and Pearce, 1946), p. 195.

307   "May we be together": Ibid., p. 195.

307   "This is a fine collection": A. H. Birse, *Memoirs of an Interpreter* (New York: Coward-McCann, 1967), p. 160.

307   "the provisions of the British": Roll, *The Hopkins Touch*, p. 325.

307   "With the noise": Lord Alanbrooke, *War Diaries 1939–1945* (London: Weidenfeld & Nicholson, 2001), p. 488.

308   "I told him": Birse, *Memoirs of an Interpreter*, p. 160.

308   "a trifle pinker": "Tripartite Dinner Meeting," November 30, 1943, 8:30 P.M., Boettinger Minutes, *FRUS*: Diplomatic Papers, The Conferences at Cairo and Tehran, 1943, Document 375, https://history .state.gov/historicaldocuments/frus1943CairoTehran/d375.

308   "a symbol of good": Ibid.

308   Churchill wanted to know: Birse, *Memoirs of an Interpreter*, p. 161.

309   "Winston, I hope": "Teasing Churchill at Tehran," The Churchill Project, July 1, 2016, https://winstonchurchill.hillsdale.edu/teasing -churchill-teheran/.

309   "I began almost": Ibid.

310   "I came to the": Birse, *Memoirs,* p. 155.

312   FDR proposed a plan: "Tripartite Political Meeting," December 1, 1943, 6 P.M., Bohlen Minutes, *FRUS*: Diplomatic Papers, The Conferences at Cairo and Tehran, 1943, Document 379, https:// history.state.gov/historicaldocuments/frus1943CairoTehran/ch8 subsubch21.

312   "Roosevelt had studied": W. Averell Harriman and Elie Abel, *Special Envoy to Churchill and Stalin, 1941–1946* (New York: Random House, 1975), p. 281.

313   "Churchill appeared dumbfounded": Harriman and Abel, *Special Envoy*, p. 281.

313   A last worry: "Tripartite Political Meeting," December 1, 1943, 6 P.M., Bohlen Minutes, *FRUS*: Diplomatic Papers, The Conferences at Cairo and Tehran, 1943, Document 379, https://history.state .gov/historicaldocuments/frus1943CairoTehran/ch8subsubch21.

313   "Germany is to be": Charles E. Bohlen, *Witness to History, 1929–1969* (New York: W. W. Norton, 1973), p. 153.

314   "It must be remembered": Winston S. Churchill, *Memoirs of the Second World War* (New York: Houghton Mifflin, 1959), p. 746.

314   "eerie feeling": William M. Rigdon, *White House Sailor* (New York: Doubleday, 1962), p. 89.

314   FDR had suggested: Ibid., p. 89.

315   "We express our determination": "Communiqué: Third Draft,"

December 1, 1943, *FRUS*: Diplomatic Papers, The Conferences at Cairo and Tehran, 1943, Document 410, https://history.state.gov/historicaldocuments/frus1943CairoTehran/d410.

316   "It would not have been": Harriman and Abel, *Special Envoy*, p. 283.

316   "Well, Ike": Dwight D. Eisenhower, *Crusade in Europe* (New York: Doubleday, 1948).

316   "I feel I could not": "Marshall at the Tehran Conference." George C. Marshall Foundation, November 3, 2017, https://www.marshall foundation.org/blog/marshall-tehran-conference/.

316   "I realize that such": Eisenhower, *Crusade in Europe*.

317   "A raucous voice": Alanbrooke, *War Diaries*, p. 497.

317   "I feel relieved": Churchill, *Memoirs of the Second World War*, p. 781.

317   "I do not remember": Samuel Rosenman, *Working with Roosevelt* (New York: Harper & Brothers, 1952), p. 411.

CHAPTER FOURTEEN: AT LAST, OVERLORD

321   "Every obstacle must be": Dwight D. Eisenhower, *Crusade in Europe* (New York: Doubleday, 1948).

321   "For the sort of attack": Ibid.

322   "Nice chap": Nate Rawlings, "Top 10 Across-the-Pond Duos: Montgomery and Eisenhower," *Time*, June 20, 2010, http://content.time.com/time/specials/packages/article/0,28804,2005073_2005072_2005116,00.html.

322   "General Montgomery has": Eisenhower, *Crusade in Europe*.

324   "When I think of": Dwight D. Eisenhower, *At Ease: Stories I Tell to Friends* (New York: Doubleday, 1967), p. 273.

324   "General," Churchill said: Ibid., p. 274.

324   Afterward, Churchill announced: Eisenhower, *Crusade in Europe*.

325   "I went to my tent": Eisenhower, *Crusade in Europe*.

326   "Some soldier once said": Ibid.

326   Eisenhower had a terrible: Ibid.

326   "Okay, we'll go": There are different versions of Eisenhower's actual words. According to Timothy Rives, acting director of the Dwight D. Eisenhower Presidential Library: Ike's chief of staff, Lieutenant General Bedell Smith, recalled, "Well, we'll go"; intelligence officer Major General Kenneth Strong recalled, "Okay, boys, we will go"; Eisenhower himself recalled, "Okay, we'll go" in an interview with Walter Cronkite.

326   "I found the men": Eisenhower, *Crusade in Europe*.

327   "Our landings in": Ibid.

327   "There's not going to be": David Irving, *The Trail of the Fox* (New York: Dutton, 1977), p. 490.

327   "He was very surprised": "D-Day Oral Histories," World War II Foundation, https://www.wwiifoundation.org/students/d-day-oral-histories/.

328   "I looked into the well": Ibid.

329   "We'll start the war": Jesse Greenspan, "Landing at Normandy:

The 5 Beaches of D-Day," History, August 30, 2018, https://www
.history.com/news/landing-at-normandy-the-5-beaches-of-d-day.

329   "We were scared": Jason Simulcik, interview with Guy C. Nicely,
       John A. Adams Center for Military History and Strategic Analysis
       Military Oral History Project, Virginia Military Institute, Octo-
       ber 6, 2006, http://digitalcollections.vmi.edu/cdm/compoundobject
       /collection/p15821coll13/id/392/rec/52.

330   "Somebody said, 'Go over' ": Corey J. Bachman, interview with Jo-
       seph L. Argenzio, John A. Adams Center for Military History and
       Strategic Analysis Military Oral History Project, Virginia Military
       Institute, October 30, 2006, http://digitalcollections.vmi.edu/cdm
       /compoundobject/collection/p15821coll13/id/24/rec/3.

330   "It was a hot, hot, hot": William Doyle, interview with Arthur
       Schintzel, John A. Adams Center for Military History and Strategic
       Analysis Military Oral History Project, Virginia Military Institute,
       October 22, 2006, http://digitalcollections.vmi.edu/cdm/compound
       object/collection/p15821coll13/id/490/rec/66.

330   "like a garden hose": Walter Halloran oral history, The Digital Col-
       lections of The National WW II Museum, https://www.ww2online
       .org/view/walter-halloran.

332   "Very heavy firing": Robert Strunsky and Paul M. Hollister, *From
       D-Day through Victory in Europe: The Eyewitness Story as Told
       by War Correspondents on the Air* (New York: Columbia Broad-
       casting System, 1945), p. 79.

332   "there was nothing": Ed Cray, *General of the Army: George C.
       Marshall, Soldier and Statesman* (New York: Norton, 1990).

333   "Almighty God": Franklin D. Roosevelt, "D-Day Prayer," June 6,
       1944, Master Speech File, no. 1519, Franklin D. Roosevelt Pres-
       idential Library and Museum, http://www.fdrlibrary.marist.edu
       /_resources/images/msf/msfb0149.

334   When John's name was called: Strunsky and Hollister, *From D-Day
       through Victory in Europe*, p. 84.

334   "Everything has started well": Winston S. Churchill, *Memoirs
       of the Second World War* (New York: Houghton Mifflin, 1959),
       p. 813.

335   "As is evident": Ibid., p. 813.

335   "ATTENTION! DANGER! WARNING!": Marilyn Mayer Cul-
       pepper, *Never Will We Forget: Oral Histories of World War II*
       (New York: Praeger, 2008), p. 51.

336   "From the start": Eisenhower, *At Ease*, p. 290.

336   "Since we are so near": Churchill, *Memoirs of the Second World
       War*, p. 815.

CHAPTER FIFTEEN: FDR'S FINAL ACT

337   "I found the Boss": Grace Tully, *F.D.R., My Boss* (Chicago: Peoples
       Book Club, 1949), p. 274.

339   "She & I": Geoffrey C. Ward, *Closest Companion: The Unknown
       Story of the Intimate Friendship Between Franklin Roosevelt and
       Margaret Suckley* (New York: Houghton Mifflin, 1995), p. 380.

339   "Mr. Roosevelt did not want": A. Merriman Smith, *Thank You, Mr. President: A White House Notebook* (New York: Harper & Brothers, 1946), p. 145.

340   "The man had one": David M. Jordan, *FDR, Dewey, and the Election of 1944* (Bloomington: Indiana University Press, 2011), p. 27.

341   In his note: Tully, *F.D.R., My Boss*, p. 276.

341   "The Vice President": David McCullough, *Truman* (New York: Simon & Schuster, 1992).

341   "1600 Pennsylvania": Ibid.

342   "Anyone with a grain": James A. Farley, *Jim Farley's Story: The Roosevelt Years* (New York: Whittlesey House, 1948), p. 365.

342   "If we see that Germany": McCullough, *Truman*.

342   "Things are moving": Franklin D. Roosevelt and Joseph V. Stalin, *My Dear Mr. Stalin: The Complete Correspondence of Franklin D. Roosevelt and Joseph V. Stalin*, edited by Susan Butler (New Haven: Yale University Press, 2005), July 17, 1944.

343   "The politicians wanted": Michael F. Reilly, *Reilly of the White House: Behind the Scenes with FDR* (New York: Simon & Schuster, 1947), p. 191.

343   "as if he was mumbling": William M. Rigdon, *White House Sailor* (New York: Doubleday, 1962), p. 131.

344   "I have never been": Jordan, *FDR, Dewey, and the Election of 1944*, p. 273.

344   "It was a well-wrapped": Reilly, *Reilly of the White House*, p. 212.

344   "I was really worried": Eleanor Roosevelt, *The Autobiography of Eleanor Roosevelt* (New York: Harper & Brothers, 1961), p. 272.

344   "If the people": W. Averell Harriman and Elie Abel, *Special Envoy to Churchill and Stalin, 1941–1946* (New York: Random House, 1975), p. 367.

345   "I remember my first": Franklin D. Roosevelt, "Remarks to the Torchlight Paraders on Election Night, Hyde Park, New York," November 7, 1944, Franklin D. Roosevelt Presidential Library and Museum, http://docs.fdrlibrary.marist.edu/php11744.html.

345   "Dog catchers have taken": Reilly, *Reilly of the White House*, p. 200.

345   "The first twelve years": Franklin D. Roosevelt, Presidential Press Conference, January 19, 1945.

345   "his face looked thin": Frances Perkins, *The Roosevelt I Knew* (New York: Viking, 1946), p. 374.

346   "Jimmy, I can't take this": James Roosevelt, *Affectionately, F.D.R.: A Son's Story of a Lonely Man* (New York: Harcourt, Brace & Company, 1959), p. 355.

346   There might have been: James F. Byrnes, *Speaking Frankly* (New York: Harper & Brothers Publishers, 1947). p. 22.

346   "I have been": "The Ambassador in the Soviet Union (Harriman) to Mr. Harry L. Hopkins, Special Assistant to President Roosevelt," *FRUS*: Diplomatic Papers, 1944, Europe, vol. 4, Document 901, Moscow, September 10, 1944.

347   "I am firmly convinced": Roosevelt and Stalin, *My Dear Mr. Stalin*, October 4, 1944.

347 "We specifically desired": Edward R. Stettinius, *Roosevelt and the Russians: The Yalta Conference* (New York: Doubleday, 1950).

347 "Well, you know": Elliott Roosevelt, *As He Saw It: The Story of the World Conferences of F.D.R.* (New York: Duell, Sloan and Pearce, 1946), p. 222.

348 "I shall be waiting": "Arrangements for the Conference": Prime Minister Churchill to President Roosevelt, London, Roosevelt Papers, telegram, January 1, 1945, *FRUS*: Diplomatic Papers, Conferences at Malta and Yalta, 1945, https://history.state.gov/historicaldocuments/frus1945Malta/d38.

349 "if we had spent": "The President's Log at Malta," Log of the Trip, February 2, 1945, *FRUS*: Diplomatic Papers, Conferences at Malta and Yalta, 1945, https://history.state.gov/historicaldocuments/frus1945Malta/d290.

349 "You can't": Reilly, *Reilly of the White House*, p. 212.

349 "I saw the kind": Franklin D. Roosevelt, "Message to Congress re the Yalta Conference," March 1, 1945, Master Speech File, no. 1572-A, 1572-B, Franklin D. Roosevelt Presidential Library and Museum, http://www.fdrlibrary.marist.edu/_resources/images/msf/msfb0209.

350 "I can't understand": S. M. Plokhy, *Yalta: The Price of Peace* (New York: Penguin, 2010), p. 47.

351 more bloodthirsty: "Roosevelt-Stalin meeting," February 4, 1945, 4 P.M., Bohlen Minutes, *FRUS*: Diplomatic Papers, The Conferences at Malta and Yalta, Document 328, https://history.state.gov/historicaldocuments/frus1945Malta/d328.

351 "The eagle should permit": "Tripartite dinner meeting," February 4, 1945, 8:30 P.M., Bohlen Minutes, *FRUS*: Diplomatic Papers, Conferences at Malta and Yalta, 1945, Document 331, https://history.state.gov/historicaldocuments/frus1945Malta/d331.

352 "If I could see": Byrnes, *Speaking Frankly*, p. 26.

352 "If our treatment": Ibid., p. 27.

352 "All I can say": Ibid., p. 28.

352 "The Russians have given": Roll, *The Hopkins Touch*, p. 371.

353 "I have a list": *Speaking Frankly*, p. 38.

353 "When should they": Ibid., p. 39.

353 "I agree that": Byrnes, *Speaking Frankly*, p. 25.

354 "Winston and Eden fought": Sherwood, *Roosevelt and Hopkins*, p. 858.

354 He acknowledged that: "Second Plenary Meeting," February 5, 1945, 4 P.M., Bohlen Minutes, *FRUS*: Diplomatic Papers, Conferences at Malta and Yalta, 1945, Document 336–341, https://history.state.gov/historicaldocuments/frus1945Malta/d354.

354 "Britain declared war": Byrnes, *Speaking Frankly*, p. 31.

355 "For the Russian": Ibid., p. 31.

355 "They all say that": Ibid.

355 "How long will it take": Ibid., p. 32.

356 "beyond question": Dallek, *Franklin D. Roosevelt: A Political Life*, p. 611.

356   His thoughts on: Stettinius, *Roosevelt and the Russians*.

356   "I had a distinct feeling": Dallek, *Franklin D. Roosevelt: A Political Life*, p. 611.

358   "Stalin impressed me": Stettinius, *Roosevelt and the Russians*.

358   "History has recorded": Hiroaki Kuromiya, *Stalin* (New York: Routledge Publishing, 2013), p. 184.

359   "They have enough": Elliott Roosevelt, *As He Saw It*, pp. 242–43.

359   "We really believed": Robert E. Sherwood, *Roosevelt and Hopkins: An Intimate History* (New York: Harper & Brothers, 1948), p. 870.

359   "a diplomatic triumph": Stettinius, *Roosevelt and the Russians*.

359   "It is the story": Lord Moran, *Churchill at War* (New York: Carroll & Graf, 2002), p. 283.

359   "I am too sick": David L. Roll, *The Hopkins Touch: Harry Hopkins and the Forging of the Alliance to Defeat Hitler* (Oxford, UK: Oxford University Press, 2013), p. 377.

360   "We got away": Ward, *Closest Companion*, p. 396.

360   "Grace," he'd said: Tully, *F.D.R., My Boss*, p. 367.

CHAPTER SIXTEEN: THE WORLD HE LEFT BEHIND

361   "I hope that you": Franklin D. Roosevelt, "Message to Congress re the Yalta Conference," March 1, 1945, Master Speech File, no. 1572-A, 1572-B, Franklin D. Roosevelt Presidential Library and Museum, http://www.fdrlibrary.marist.edu/_resources/images/msf/msfb0209.

361   "Of course, we know": Ibid.

362   "so tired that": Geoffrey C. Ward, *Closest Companion: The Unknown Story of the Intimate Friendship Between Franklin Roosevelt and Margaret Suckley* (New York: Houghton Mifflin, 1995), p. 401.

362   one evening she called him: Michael Dobbs, *Six Months in 1945: FDR, Stalin, Churchill, and Truman from World War to Cold War* (New York: Alfred A. Knopf, 2012).

363   "I am certain": Franklin D. Roosevelt and Joseph V. Stalin, *My Dear Mr. Stalin: The Complete Correspondence of Franklin D. Roosevelt and Joseph V. Stalin*, edited by Susan Butler (New Haven: Yale University Press, 2005), April 4, 1945.

363   "I have never doubted": Ibid., April 7, 1945.

363   "Let me assure you": Franklin D. Roosevelt, "Day by Day," April 11, 1945.

364   "Lucy is such a": Ward, *Closest Companion*, p. 415.

364   "Mr. President, you look": Ibid., p. 417.

364   "I have a terrific pain": Ibid., p. 418.

364   "I was cold as ice": Ibid., p. 418.

365   "The night of April 12": A. Merriman Smith, *Thank You, Mr. President: A White House Notebook* (New York: Harper & Brothers, 1946), p. 189.

365   "DARLINGS: PA SLEPT": James Roosevelt, *Affectionately, F.D.R.*, p. 361.

366   "I listened and listened": Robert E. Sherwood, *Roosevelt and Hopkins: An Intimate History* (New York: Harper & Brothers, 1948), p. 880.

366   "sheer damned nonsense": John Morton Blum, *From the Morgenthau Diaries* (New York: Houghton Mifflin, 1959), diary entry April 16, 1945.

366   Anna placed a call: Bernard Asbell, *Mother and Daughter: The Letters of Eleanor and Anna Roosevelt* (New York: Penguin, 1982), p. 187.

367   "I . . . hated the fact": James Roosevelt, *Affectionately, F.D.R.: A Son's Story of a Lonely Man* (New York: Harcourt, Brace & Company, 1959), pp. 363–64.

367   "As he told several": Ward, *Closest Companion*, p. 422.

368   "As the saying goes": Winston Churchill, "Eulogy in the Commons for the Late President Roosevelt," April 17, 1945, http://www.ibiblio.org/pha/policy/1945/1945-04-17a.html.

369   "President Roosevelt has died": W. Averell Harriman and Elie Abel, *Special Envoy to Churchill and Stalin, 1941–1946* (New York: Random House, 1975), p. 442.

370   "When the signing": Dwight D. Eisenhower, *At Ease: Stories I Tell to Friends* (New York: Doubleday, 1967), p. 293.

370   "If they had been": Lily Rothman, "How the World Learned of Hitler's Death," *Time*, April 30, 2015, http://time.com/3829048/death-of-hitler-history/.

370   "a new weapon": McCullough, *Truman*.

371   "The enemy has begun": "Emperor Hirohito, Accepting the Potsdam Declaration," radio address, August 14, 1945, https://www.mtholyoke.edu/acad/intrel/hirohito.htm.

372   "Roosevelt believed in": V. M. Molotov and Felix Chuev, *Molotov Remembers: Inside Kremlin Politics* (trans.) (Chicago: Ivan R. Dee, 1993).

373   "We are still": Franklin D. Roosevelt, Presidential Press Conference, December 28, 1943.

373   "It was asserted": Bernard Gwertzman, "Stalin's Interpreter Recalls Roosevelt Was Conciliator," *New York Times*, February 8, 1970, https://www.nytimes.com/1970/02/08/archives/stalins-interpreter-recalls-roosevelt-was-conciliator.html.

374   "that the only reason": Arnold Beichman, "Roosevelt's Failure at Yalta," *Hoover Digest*, 2004, no. 4 (Hoover Institution, October 30, 2004).

374   When Stettinius first met: Edward R. Stettinius, Jr., *The Diaries of Edward R. Stettinius, Jr., 1943–1946*, edited by Thomas M. Campbell and George C. Herrings (New York: New Viewpoints, 1975), p. 118.

374   "Roosevelt knew how": Molotov, *Molotov Remembers*.

375   "A freely elected government": Robert C. Grogin, *Natural Enemies: The United States and the Soviet Union in the Cold War 1917–1991* (Lanham, MD: Lexington Books/Rowman & Littlefield, 2001), p. 80.

375   "President Roosevelt was": Edward R. Stettinius, *Roosevelt and the Russians: The Yalta Conference* (New York: Doubleday, 1950).

376   "The Western Allied leaders": R. C. Raack, *Stalin's Drive to the West, 1938–1948: The Origins of the Cold War* (Stanford, CA: Stanford University Press, 1995), p. 77.

376   "conduct unbecoming": Ibid., p. 103.

377   "What amazed those of us": Hugh Lunghi, "Glimpses—Troubled Triumvirate: The Big Three at the Summit," *Finest Hour* 135 (Summer 2007), International Churchill Society, https://winston churchill.org/publications/finest-hour/finest-hour-135/glimpses -troubled-triumvirate-the-big-three-at-the-summit/.

378   "In my opinion": John R. Deane, *The Strange Alliance: The Story of Our Efforts at Wartime Cooperation with Russia* (New York: Viking Press, 1947), p. 331.

378   "If history teaches": Ronald Reagan, speech to the House of Commons, June 8, 1982, https://teachingamericanhistory.org/library /document/speech-to-the-house-of-commons/.

INDEX